Antonio Gramsci
Selections from Political Writings
(1910–1920)

Antonio Gramsci
Selections from Political Writings
(1910–1920)
with additional texts by Bordiga and Tasca

Selected and edited by
Quintin Hoare

Translated by
John Mathews

ANTONIO GRAMSCI: SELECTIONS FROM POLITICAL WRITINGS
Selected and edited by Quintin Hoare

First Published in India 2014

ISBN 978-93-5002-257-3

Published in agreement with Lawrence and Wishart Limited, London for publication and sale only in the Indian Subcontinent (India, Pakistan, Bangladesh, Nepal, Maldives, Bhutan and Sri Lanka)

Published by
AAKAR BOOKS
28 E Pocket IV, Mayur Vihar Phase I, Delhi 110 091
Phone : 011 2279 5505 Telefax : 011 2279 5641
info@aakarbooks.com; www.aakarbooks.com

Printed in India at
D.K. Fine Art Press (P) Ltd.
Delhi - 110052

CONTENTS

INTRODUCTION

The earliest piece in this selection (the first of two volumes) from Antonio Gramsci's political writings prior to his imprisonment dates from 1910. The author wrote it at the age of twenty, in his final year at school in Sardinia, before he became a Socialist. The last piece was written just before the January 1921 Livorno Congress of the Italian Socialist Party (PSI), which was also the founding Congress of the Communist Party of Italy (PCd'I): Gramsci was then almost thirty and a major figure on the revolutionary left in his country. The decade which these texts span was perhaps the key watershed of our century. During those few years, the First World War left 10 million dead and twice as many wounded. The Second International was swamped by the upsurge of nationalist passions and pressures in 1914, and collapsed. In Russia, the February Revolution of 1917 overthrew the Tsarist régime. It was followed within a few months by the Bolshevik Revolution, which destroyed the fragile bourgeois order installed in February; took Russia out of the War; deprived capitalism at one stroke of the largest country on the globe; sent ripples of enthusiasm and fear throughout the world; successfully confronted foreign intervention and a terrible civil war (though at a price in internal repression which was destined to have heavy consequences); and embarked upon socialist construction. The Third International was founded in 1919, as a revolutionary wave swept through much of continental Europe.

In Italy itself, by the end of 1920 when this volume closes, that wave was already receding. But no one on the left believed – or allowed themselves to believe – that the tide itself had turned and was now on the ebb. The decade had seen a vertiginous expansion of the country's productive forces, above all during the war years (production of iron and steel multiplied five times during the course of the war, and firms like FIAT – whose work force rose from 4,000 to 20,000 in that period – increased their capital tenfold). At the same time, the war was followed by a severe economic crisis (the *lira* lost 80 per cent of its value between 1914 and 1920; the budgetary deficit rose from 214 millions in 1914–15 to 23,345 millions in 1918–19, with the main tax burden falling on the petty bourgeoisie; wheat production fell from 52 million quintals in 1911–13 to 38 million in 1920, and 40 per cent of the balance of payments deficit was accounted for by food imports; production dropped after the war by 40 per cent in the engineering industries, 20 per cent in chemicals, 15 per cent in mining, etc.; coal prices were over 16 times higher in 1920 than they had been in 1913; and so on) to which successive governments seemed to have no solution. The political crisis of the old order was manifest: incapable of creating any coherent political party with a stable structure, mass base or clear programme, the shifting cliques of 'notables' in parliament, with their personal followings, *clientele* and hired vote-gathering enforcers, appeared impotent either to control the worsening economic situation or to confront the inexorable growth of the socialist forces.

At the same time, the PSI had become the largest single party at the November 1919 elections, with 156 seats out of a total of 508. Membership of the Socialist trade-union federation (CGL) rose from 250,000 to two million between the end of the war and 1920. Moreover, in words at least, the Socialist Party stood for Revolution and Soviets, and the workers in the main industrial centres had shown in repeated actions that they were a formidably militant force. For the insurrectionary uprising in Turin in August 1917, the great general strike which created a situation of dual power throughout Piedmont for eleven days in April 1920 and the occupation of factories in all the main industrial centres of Northern Italy in August–September of the same year were fresh in the memories of all. These massive proletarian actions had failed, yet was that not essentially for want of firm, revolutionary leadership on a national scale: in short, a party? And if the PSI, despite its formal adherence to the Third International, was not prepared to become, or capable of becoming, that party, by applying the Comintern's twenty-one conditions, expelling the reformists and putting its own inflammatory rhetoric into practice, then a new Communist Party would take its place and lead the Italian proletariat to victory.

However, in reality, the revolutionary moment had passed. The occupation of the factories was itself essentially defensive in character. The refusal of the PSI to extend the April strike nationally marked a decisive turning-point. And the party's failure in the post-war period either to tap the revolutionary potential of the agricultural proletariat and peasantry or to channel the resentments of the urban petty bourgeoisie in a socialist direction had irreversible consequences for the balance of class forces. That autumn of 1920 saw the transformation of fascism from a marginal to a mass phenomenon. Fascist squads began to carry out raids on behalf of the landowners of North and Central Italy, against both the Socialist and Catholic peasant associations and against socialist-controlled municipalities such as that of Bologna or socialist papers such as the Trieste daily *Il Lavoratore*. Twenty years of reaction were just beginning. Gramsci had written presciently in April 1920 (see p. 191 below): "The present phase of the class struggle in Italy is the phase that precedes: either the conquest of political power on the part of the revolutionary proletariat and the transition to new modes of production and distribution that will set the stage for a recovery in productivity – or a tremendous reaction on the part of the propertied classes and governing caste. No violence will be spared in subjecting the industrial and agricultural proletariat to servile labour: there will be a bid to smash once and for all the working class's organs of political struggle (the Socialist Party) and to incorporate its organs of economic resistance (the trade unions and co-operatives) into the machinery of the bourgeois State." By the end of 1920, Gramsci's second alternative was coming to pass – though he and the first generation of Italian communists were to spend the next six years in a grim fight to the death premised on the assertion that the former was still on the agenda.

This momentous decade, then, was the period of Gramsci's basic political formation. When he arrived in Turin in 1911, on a scholarship for poor children from Sardinia, his political ideas (reflected in the *liceo* essay "Oppressed and Oppressors" printed here) were probably fairly typical of the "southernist" mélange of liberal and socialist themes which was so prevalent throughout the South and the Islands in the years preceding the War. Although Gramsci was quickly to shed any leanings in the direction of Sardinian nationalism when he came into contact with the proletarian reality of Italy's most advanced industrial city, he was never to lose his concern with the "Southern problem". The violent social upheaval that had swept Sardinia in 1906 – affecting peasant masses, urban workers and miners alike and brutally repressed by mainland troops – had been his first experience of class struggle; it had been the crucial stimulus impelling him towards revolutionary politics.

It was in Turin, however, that Gramsci became a socialist, joining the party towards the end of 1913. Soon after arriving in the city, he had struck up a friendship with Angelo Tasca, a fellow student, the son of a railway-worker, born in the same year as himself and active in the Socialist Party since 1909. Tasca was probably the decisive influence in introducing Gramsci to organized political activity. In fact, racked by ill health and desperately poor, Gramsci's main concerns until late in 1915 were cultural and academic. It was only in November 1915 that he abandoned his studies and joined the staff of the socialist paper *Il Grido del Popolo*. Prior to that date, he had (so far as is known) published just four articles: a 24-line piece on a local election campaign for a Sardinian paper in 1910; two cultural essays in a student paper in 1913 (one of them called for a serious critical analysis of Italian futurism, relating it to the cubism of Picasso); and most notably "Active and Operative Neutrality" (see pp. 6–9 below), in October 1914. This article, Gramsci's first real foray into political journalism, was a disastrous error of judgment, which may well have held him back from further writing for a whole period: it was certainly a mistake that was to be brought up against him for years to come.

When war broke out between the Entente and the Central Powers, the Italian Socialist Party adopted a policy firmly opposed to any intervention by Italy in the war. Soon afterwards Mussolini, the editor of *Avanti!* (the official PSI newspaper) and acknowledged leader of the party's left wing, began to shift away from the official line of neutrality. In response to an attack on Mussolini by Tasca, Gramsci wrote "Active and Operative Neutrality" in the former's defence. It was, however, not long before the real direction in which Mussolini was moving became clear; he was expelled from the party and Gramsci retreated into a silence of more than a year. What had in fact impelled Gramsci to make this blunder was not any capitulation to nationalist themes of the kind which motivated Mussolini, but rather a somewhat idealist voluntarism which was to remain an element of his politics for some years to come. There is an evident link between his rejection of the PSI's "passivity" in this early text and his saluting of the October revolution as the "Revolution against 'Capital'" (pp. 34–7 below). Moreover, it must be recognized that although Gramsci utterly misjudged Mussolini and advocated a wrong line for the PSI in 1914, he was not wrong in his estimate of the party's official policy, which was a far cry from the revolutionary internationalism of Lenin and was indeed thoroughly passive – with disastrous results in the post-war period.

At all events, it was not until November 1915 that Gramsci began to write regularly for the socialist press in Turin. In the ensuing five years, his printed articles totalled well over a thousand, if one counts only those which have already been positively identified. Although a scholarly edition of these articles is now announced, they have been published to date in a largely *ad hoc* fashion, partly grouped by subject matter, partly by journalistic form and partly by chronology. For the purposes of the present selection, Gramsci's 1916–20 theatre criticism (published as an appendix to the volume of Prison Notebooks entitled *Letteratura e vita nazionale*, Turin 1954) has been left on one side, as indeed have all his cultural writings. The volume *Sotto la mole* (Turin 1960), which contains almost four hundred short articles which appeared under that rubric between 1916 and 1920 in the Turin edition of *Avanti!*, commenting on every aspect of local intellectual, cultural, political and social life, has also been left unrepresented, with the exception of three pieces (pp. 14–18 below). Nor has anything been included from a recent volume of previously unidentified articles *Per la verità* (Rome 1974), although many are of undoubted interest. Just three articles have been included (pp. 326–9, 344–6 and 356–9 below) from an earlier collection of freshly identified articles *Scritti 1915–21* (Milan 1968), though again many of the pieces in that collection are of considerable value. The great majority of the texts translated here, therefore, have been taken from the collections entitled *Scritti giovanili 1914–18* (Turin 1958) and *L'Ordine Nuovo 1919–20* (Turin 1955). Moreover, whereas only eleven articles have been taken from the former volume, forty-nine have been included from the latter. The selection has been completed by five texts written by Amadeo Bordiga and two by Angelo Tasca.

Clearly, the criteria which have governed this selection require some explanation. What has been said should make it clear that no attempt has been made to offer a *representative* choice of Gramsci's writings prior to 1920. The first limitation is made explicit in the title of this volume. Despite the impressive variety of Gramsci's concerns, and the great intrinsic interest of what he wrote on a whole range of cultural, intellectual and social topics, the selection is focused on what was undoubtedly central for Gramsci himself: politics. Secondly, purely *biographical* considerations have not been determinant. For instance, it is undoubtedly interesting to note that Gramsci had no clear idea in September 1917 of who the Bolsheviks really were or what they represented (of course, this was not just a personal failing of his own, but reflected a general situation of ignorance or actual misinformation on the Italian left); nevertheless, such a consideration does not really seem to warrant inclusion of the article "Kerensky-Chernov" in which his confusion is expressed. Similarly, the selection does not have as a primary aim to demonstrate the *range* of Gramsci's political interests, notably in the international sphere, impressive as these were. Finally, the selection has not been motivated by strictly *historiographic* concerns, although Gramsci's writings do constitute an invaluable source for the historian of the period.

No, the guiding conviction which has governed the selection of Gramsci's political writings presented here is that, in confronting the great issues thrown up by the period through which he was living, Gramsci produced a profoundly original body of thought – in close relation with a concrete revolutionary practice – which remains centrally relevant to Marxists today, in its lacunae as in its strength. The selection seeks to present this body of thought in as powerful and concentrated a form as possible – without seeking to obscure any of its weaknesses or ambiguities. The articles translated show Gramsci discussing the impact of the World War upon the bourgeois order, internationally and in Italy; the significance of the Russian revolution; the potential of the revolutionary forces organized in the Communist International; the crisis of the Italian ruling class; the specific characteristics of the Italian petty bourgeoisie; the limitations and deficiencies of the mass organizations of the working class; the conditions for proletarian victory. Above all, these texts are the record of an attempt to hammer out, in intimate inter-relation with a mass proletarian practice in Turin, a theory of the specific organizational forms capable of harnessing the full revolutionary potential of the class and representing the embryos of a future soviet State in Italy.

Thus only a few articles have been translated from the period before the foundation of the weekly *L'Ordine Nuovo* in May 1919. In fact, until 1917, Gramsci was only in the most generic sense a Marxist. It was on the one hand the Russian revolutions, and on the other the August insurrection of that year in Turin (in whose wake he was elected to an important post in the local party organization – since almost all the established leaders had been arrested – and appointed editor of *Il Grido del Popolo*) which first seriously posed the problem of power for the young journalist. And it was only with the publication of "Workers' Democracy" (pp. 65–8 below) that his thought began to coalesce into a coherent and original political theory, which constitutes the main focus of this volume. Of course, it would be quite wrong to idealize that theory. As Gramsci was himself to acknowledge subsequently, in a letter to Alfonso Leonetti (written from Vienna in January 1924): "In 1919–20 we made extremely serious mistakes, which ultimately we are paying for today. For fear of being called upstarts and careerists, we did not form a faction and organize this throughout Italy. We were not ready to give the Turin factory councils an autonomous directive centre, which could have exercised an immense influence throughout the country, for fear of a split in the unions and of being expelled prematurely from the Socialist Party." Moreover, even this expresses inadequately the mistakes made. For what lay behind the failure to conduct a fight within the party, as Bordiga had from the end of 1918 (or even in a sense from 1912!), was a theoretical failure to grasp the essential role of the revolutionary party in centralizing the struggle against the existing order and organizing the insurrectionary seizure of power.

Consequently, some of the points made by Bordiga and by Tasca in the polemics against *L'Ordine Nuovo* included here are entirely correct, from their seemingly opposed but at times not dissimilar standpoints. These texts have been translated here, not simply to place in context the ideas developed by *L'Ordine Nuovo*, but also because of the importance the views expressed were to have throughout the early years of the Italian Communist Party. Yet for all that they were each in some ways formally right against Gramsci, their conventionality by contrast with his analyses is here manifest. Whereas what Gramsci wrote on the factory councils, for all its one-sidedness, is relevant to contemporary Marxist discussion on the forms of revolutionary mobilization, the character of dual power organs and the nature of the post-revolutionary State, Tasca's failure to grasp the fundamental nature and role of trade unions under capitalism and Bordiga's effective identification of the dictatorship of the proletariat with dictatorship of the communist party fatally flawed their respective positions in this debate.

This volume closes immediately prior to the founding congress of the PCd'I. In the latter two-thirds of 1920, Gramsci was increasingly isolated, as he came to recognize his fundamental mistake on the question of the party. Drawing closer to Bordiga and his abstentionist faction (though he did not share their abstentionism), he broke with Tasca in May and with most of the other members of the *L'Ordine Nuovo* group, including Terracini and Togliatti, in July. The question of the future Communist Party now, belatedly, came increasingly to dominate his thinking, but he entered it – for all the powerful working-class base that had been created in Turin – in a weak minority position. Moreover, despite his acceptance of the need to apply the Comintern's twenty-one conditions and break with the reformists, Gramsci had a very different appreciation from that of Bordiga – by now dominant –

as to the significance of the balance of forces within the PSI. He was to regard the Livorno split, in which the communist fraction took only a minority of the PSI with it into the new Party, as "the greatest triumph of reaction" – whereas for Bordiga, the question of trying to win a majority had never so much as been posed. Reading what Gramsci wrote in a text like "Predictions" (see pp. 356–9 below), it is hard not to conclude that he was at heart convinced that the revolutionary moment had passed, and that a period of reaction lay ahead. In the years that followed he was not always to be so lucid in his recognition of the realities of the situation. Or at least, not so explicit. But now, in contrast to the texts of the preceding years collected here, animated by the belief that a revolutionary situation existed and what was needed was a subjective effort of will, there is an unmistakable note of stoical resignation to the inevitable in "Predictions", despite the invocation of the Communist Party in the final paragraph.

So how should one judge these texts of the "Red Years"? In a sense, of course, texts written in the conviction that revolution is possible, is immediately on the agenda, inevitably take on a tragic aspect when the historical moment has passed; when the reader knows with hindsight that not revolution but black reaction was in store. When the author was himself destined to die a victim of that reaction, this tragic aspect is redoubled. Yet it would be quite wrong to read these texts simply as the record of a tragic *illusion*. For quite apart from the question – which can, of course, never finally be settled – of what was possible in Italy in 1919–20, the problems with which Gramsci sought to grapple are those which must arise in any pre-revolutionary situation. What kind of party is needed to organize the revolution? What role do the trade unions – quintessential expression of the class's corporative interest – play? What are the soviet bodies that can incorporate the whole working class? What allies can the proletariat win? What are the cultural and moral prerequisites for a successful revolution? What are the material prerequisites? To what extent, and in what conditions, can workers control production prior to the overthrow of capitalism? What is the potential significance of such control?

In any case, Gramsci was more free of illusions than most. His stark presentation of the alternative perspectives that faced the Italian working class in early 1920 has already been quoted. Neither during the April 1920 general strike nor during the August/September 1920 occupation of the factories did he succumb to facile optimism. In "Superstition and Reality", one of the many important texts which space did not allow to be included in this volume, written immediately after the April strike, he wrote: "The Turin working class was defeated and could not but be defeated. The Turin working class was dragged into the struggle; it had no freedom of choice, it could not postpone the day of the conflict because the initiative in the class war still belongs to the capitalists and to the power of the bourgeois State." And in "The Occupation" (pp. 326–9 below), written while the main factories of North Italy were in the hands of the workers, his entire concern was to warn against comfortable illusions. Not for nothing did *L'Ordine Nuovo* print Romain Rolland's watchword "Pessimism of the intelligence, optimism of the will" at the head of each issue.

* * *

I have not tried in this Introduction to duplicate the historical narrative background to this period provided in the General Introduction to *Selections from the Prison Notebooks*, particularly in view of the fact that – in addition to Giuseppe Fiori's admirable biography and John Cammett's *Gramsci and the Origins of Italian Communism* which were already available to English-language readers before the *Selections* appeared – the history of the period is now also covered in Gwyn Williams's well-documented *Proletarian Order* and Paolo Spriano's *The Occupation of the Factories*. There seemed little point in going over the same ground yet again, so I have simply tried – very briefly – to provide a framework for assessing the significance of the texts translated in this volume. I should like to take this opportunity of thanking Roger Simon for the assistance and encouragement he has given as the responsible editor at Lawrence & Wishart since the idea of a selection of Gramsci's political writings was first put forward.

A NOTE ON THE TRANSLATION

Translating the political writings selected in this volume has not posed the same conceptual problems involved in translating from the Prison Notebooks. After all, the articles were originally written for publication in newspapers or journals with a readership of active socialists, many if not most of them factory workers. Where problems have arisen, the rendering adopted aims to avoid the extremes of excessive anglicization or excessive fidelity to the Italian term. Thus *commissario* has been translated throughout as delegate, rather than the too specifically English "steward" or the un-English (in this sense) "commissar". *Riparto* has been translated as "workshop", since "shop" often gives rise to ambiguity in English, while John Reed's solution of "factory-shop" seems an unnecessary coining. *Sindacalismo* has posed a problem, as always, but hopefully its two senses of "syndicalism" and "trade-unionism" have been satisfactorily distinguished wherever the word occurs. The somewhat over-generic "leadership" has always been used for *direzione*, even though this sometimes really denotes the specific executive body of the PSI elected as a sub-committee of its National Council. It should be remembered that *controllo*, although it has been translated as "control" where it occurs, in fact has a different meaning in Italian: as Giovanni Giolitti once wrote, "In America and England 'control' virtually means command and statutory authority, whereas in Italy it means 'check'."

OUTLINE CHRONOLOGY, 1911–1920

1911	Libyan War
	Gramsci arrives in Turin
1912	Debate on socialism and culture between Bordiga and Tasca (see note 9 below)
1913	Gramsci joins PSI
	Socialists win 52 seats and over one million votes in general election
1914	
June	Red Week (see note 152 below)
August	World War breaks out
	Second International collapses
October	Mussolini begins to move towards interventionism (see note 5 below)
1915	
May	Italy enters War
September	Zimmerwald Conference
1916	
April	Kienthal Conference
1917	
March	"February" revolution in Russia
July	Florence meeting revives the "intransigent revolutionary" faction of the PSI, on Bordiga's initiative
August	Visit of Smirnov and Goldenberg, Menshevik delegates from the Petrograd Soviet, to Italy
	Insurrectionary rising in Turin crushed by military force, after eight days of fighting
	Gramsci appointed to the "provisional committee" of the Socialist section
November	Italian forces crushed at Caporetto
	Clandestine meeting of "intransigent revolution" faction in Florence, which Gramsci attends as delegate from Turin
	"October" revolution in Russia

1918	
August	War ends
September	Pact of Alliance between PSI and CGL (see note 84 below)
	Rome Congress of PSI proclaims maximum programme
December	Separate Turin edition of *Avanti!* and *Il Soviet* founded in Naples
1919	
February	*Il Soviet* calls for a new party
March	Third International founded
	PSI leadership votes adherence to Comintern
April	*Avanti!* offices in Milan burned down by nationalists and fascists
May	*L'Ordine Nuovo* founded
	Gramsci elected to executive of Turin Socialist section
July	International strike in support of the Russian and Hungarian Soviet Republics
October	PSI Congress at Bologna (see note 61 below)
November	PSI wins 156 seats and over 2 million votes in general election (see note 41 below)
December	General strike in protest at nationalist attack on PSI deputies (see note 42 below)
1920	
March	Lock-out in the engineering factories of Turin, as attempt to break the factory councils
April	Eleven-day general strike throughout Piedmont
May	Florence conference of abstentionist faction, which Gramsci attends as observer
June	Gramsci breaks with Tasca
	Giolitti comes to power
July	Second Congress of the Comintern
	Gramsci breaks with Togliatti and Terracini, forming a "Communist Education Group" in opposition to their "Electionist Communist Faction"
August/ September	Milan lock-out leads to factory occupations throughout Northern Italy (see note 129 below)
October	Meeting in Milan to prepare a Communist faction
	Fascist attacks begin on peasant organizations in the North

November	Imola convention of the Communist faction
December	Weekly *L'Ordine Nuovo* closes down; the Turin edition of *Avanti!* becomes the daily *L'Ordine Nuovo*, with Gramsci as editor

I

The Young Socialist

1. OPPRESSED AND OPPRESSORS

The struggle waged by humanity from time immemorial is truly amazing. It is an incessant struggle, one in which mankind strives to tear off and break the chains with which the lust for power on the part of a single man, or a single class, or even of a whole people, attempt to shackle it. This struggle is an epic that has had innumerable heroes and has been written down by historians all over the world. Men, when they come to feel their strength and to be conscious of their responsibility and their value, will no longer suffer another man to impose his will on them and claim the right to control their actions and thoughts. For it would seem to be a cruel fate for humans, this instinct that drives them to devour one another in place of bringing their united strength to bear on the struggle against Nature, the struggle to adapt it to men's needs. Indeed, once a people feel themselves to be strong and hardened, they think of nothing but of attacking their neighbours, of hunting and oppressing them. For it is clear that every victor desires to destroy the vanquished. But men, who by their very nature are hypocritical and false, do not say outright: "I wish to conquer in order to destroy", but say instead: "I wish to conquer in order to civilize". And the rest of mankind, who envy the victor, but await their turn to do the same, make a show of believing in it and offer their praises.

So it comes about that civilization has stopped in its tracks in place of further expanding and progressing; so it comes about that whole races of noble and intelligent people have been destroyed or are in the process of dying out. The liquor and opium that their civilizing masters distributed to them in such abundance have done their damaging work.

Then one day a rumour is sparked: a student has assassinated the English governor of the Indies; or the Italians have been defeated at Dogali; or the *boxers* have wiped out the European missionaries – and then horror-stricken old Europe inveighs against the barbarians, against the uncivilized hordes, and a new crusade against these unfortunate peoples is announced.

Yet it is a fact that the people of Europe have had their own oppressors and waged bloody battles to rid themselves of them. They now erect statues and monuments in marble to their liberators, their heroes, and raise to the level of a national religion the cult of those who died for the homeland. Just try to tell the Italians that the Austrians came to bring us civilization – the marble columns themselves would groan in protest. Yes, it is true that we have gone off to carry civilization overseas, and now you know those peoples have come to like us and thank heaven for their good fortune. But it is well known: *sic vos non nobis.*[1] The truth on the contrary consists in an insatiable greed shared by all men to fleece their fellows, to take from them what little they have been able to put aside through privations. Wars are waged for reasons of commerce, not civilization: the English bombarded who knows how many cities in China because the Chinese did not want to have anything to do with their opium. The very opposite of civilization! And Russians and Japanese slaughtered each other over the question of trade with Korea and Manchuria. The property of the wretched subjects is pillaged and they are deprived of any status whatsoever. Yet this is not enough for the highly civilized people of today. The Romans were content with binding their vanquished opponents to their triumphal chariots – then they made the defeated land into a province. But now the victors would like all the inhabitants of the colonies to disappear, to make room for the new arrivals.

But when the voice of an honest man is raised in protest at these outrages, these abuses, which a healthy social morality and civilization would try to prevent, people laugh in his face – for he is ingenuous, he is not acquainted with the machiavellian niceties that govern political life. We Italians adore Garibaldi; from the cradle we are taught to admire him, and Carducci has enthused us with his Garibaldian legends. If one were to ask Italian youngsters whom they would most like to be, the overwhelming majority would certainly opt for the blond hero. I remember a particular demonstration in commemoration of independence, when a friend said to me: "How come everyone is shouting 'Long live Garibaldi' and no one is shouting 'Long live the king'?" I was unable to give him an explanation. In short, everyone in Italy, from the reds to the greens to the yellows,[2] idolizes Garibaldi, but no one really understands his high ideals. When the Italian navy was sent to Crete to pull down the Greek flag which the insurgents had raised and hoist in its place the Turkish flag, no one raised a cry of protest. That's right: the fault lay with the people of Candia, who wanted to upset the European balance. And not one of the Italians who perhaps on that very day was acclaiming Sicily's heroic liberator paused to reflect that if Garibaldi were alive today, he would not have shrunk from taking on all the European powers in order to help a people gain their liberty. And then we Italians protest when someone comes along and accuses us of being a nation addicted to rhetoric!

And how long is this contrast to last? Carducci asked himself: "When will labour be joyful? When will love be secure?" But we are still awaiting a reply, and who will be able to give it? Many people say that men have now achieved all the liberty and civilization that is their lot, and now all they have to do is enjoy the fruits of their struggles. On the contrary, I believe that far more remains to be done. Men possess nothing more than a veneer of civilization – one only has to scratch them to lay bare the wolf-skin underneath. Instincts have been tamed, but not destroyed, and still the right of might is the only right that is recognized. The French revolution abolished many privileges, and raised up many of the oppressed; but all it did was replace one class in power by another. Yet it did teach us one great lesson: social privileges and differences, being products of society and not of nature, can be overcome. Humanity will need another bloodbath to abolish many of these injustices – and then it will be too late for the rulers to be sorry they left the hordes in that state of ignorance and savagery they enjoy today.

A school essay, hand-written probably in 1911, when Gramsci was in his final year at the Dettori secondary school in Cagliari.

2. ACTIVE AND OPERATIVE NEUTRALITY

Even in the midst of the extraordinary confusion which the present European crisis has triggered in individuals and in parties, there is one point on which all are agreed: the present historical juncture is a desperately serious one and its consequences could be extremely grave. Because so much blood has been spilt and so many efforts have come to nothing, let us arrange things so that the maximum number of questions left unsolved from the past may be resolved, and humanity may once more proceed without its way being blocked ever again by such a grim expanse of sorrow and of injustice, without its future being marred in a short time by another catastrophe demanding just as formidable an expenditure of life and activity as this present one.

As for us Italian socialists, the problem is this: "What role should the *Italian* Socialist Party (mark it well, not the *proletariat* or *socialism* in general) play at the present juncture of Italian history?"

For the Socialist Party in which we are active is also an *Italian* party, that is to say it represents that particular section of the Socialist International whose task it is to win the Italian nation to the International. This its *immediate*, its *present* task, gives it *peculiar*, *national* characteristics, compelling it to assume a specific function and responsibility of its own within Italian life. It is a potential state in the process of formation, one that is in opposition to the bourgeois state and that has sought, in the course of its long struggle with the latter and through the development of its own internal dialectic, to build up the organs it needs to overcome the bourgeois state and absorb it. Furthermore it is *autonomous* in its choice of the means needed to accomplish its task, being dependent on the International only for the supreme end to be attained and for the class nature of the struggle to be waged.

As for the *means* with which this struggle should be conducted, and for the *timing* of its revolutionary culmination, only the PSI is competent to judge: it alone experiences the struggle and is familiar with its various aspects.

This alone justifies the laughter and disdain with which we greeted the insults of G. Hervé and the tentative approaches of the German socialists, both speaking in the name of the International of which they claimed to be accredited representatives, when the PSI launched its slogan of "absolute neutrality".[3]

* * * * *

For we must make it clear that we are not questioning the concept of neutrality as such (neutrality of the proletariat, it goes without saying), but *how* this neutrality should be expressed.

The formula "absolute neutrality" was extremely useful in the initial phase of the crisis, when the events burst upon us and we were relatively unprepared for their enormity. It was only a dogmatically intransigent statement of this kind that could allow us to present a solid, impregnable bulkwark against the first rush of passions and particular interests. But now that the elements of confusion in the initial chaotic situation have settled somewhat and we all have to be responsible for our own actions, this slogan is of value only to the reformists, who say they have no wish to play *terni secchi*[4] (though they allow others to play and win). They would like to see the proletariat playing the role of impartial observer in these events and leaving them to create its hour for it; but all the while the proletariat's opponents are themselves creating their own hour and busily preparing their platform for the class struggle.

But revolutionaries who see history as the product of their own actions, made up of an uninterrupted series of wrenches executed upon the other active and passive forces in society, and prepare the most favourable conditions for the final *wrench* (the revolution), should not rest content with the provisional formula of "absolute neutrality", but should transform it into the alternative formulation "active and operative neutrality". Which means putting class struggle back at the centre of the nation's life – in so far as the working class, by forcing the class holding power to assume its responsibilities, by forcing it to push to their logical conclusion the premises from which it draws its raison d'être and to submit to a test of the preparation with which it has sought to attain the end it has proclaimed as its own, will force it (in our case, in Italy) to recognize that it has utterly failed to achieve its aims. For despite its claims to be the sole representative of the nation, it has led our country up a blind alley from which it can only escape by abandoning to their fate all those institutions which bear direct responsibility for its present parlous state.

Only in this way will class dualism be re-established, and the Socialist Party be able to free itself from all the bourgeois encrustations with which fear of war has encumbered it (never as in these last two months has socialism had so many more or less interested sympathizers). Then, having demonstrated to the country (which in the case of Italy is neither wholly proletarian nor wholly bourgeois, given the scant interest the broad mass of the people has always manifested in political struggle, and which can therefore be all the more easily won over by someone who knows how to display energy and a clear vision of where they are going) how its self-styled representatives have shown themselves incapable of any action whatsoever, the party will be able to prepare the proletariat to replace them: prepare it for that last supreme wrench which will signal the transition of civilization from an imperfect to an alternative, more perfect form.

For this reason its seems to me that A. T.[5] should have been more cautious in his article on the so-called Mussolini affair published in last week's *Grido*. He should have distinguished between what was due to Mussolini the man, the Romagnolo (even this was referred to), and what to Mussolini the *Italian* socialist. In short he should have concentrated on what was original in Mussolini's attitude and directed his criticism at this, whether to annihilate it or to locate within it a means of reconciling the doctrinaire formalism of the remaining party leadership and the *realistic concretism* of the editor of *Avanti!*.

But it is the central thesis of A. T.'s article that strikes me as wrong. When Mussolini declares to the Italian bourgeoisie "Proceed wherever *your* destiny summons you", in other words "If you see waging war on Austria as *your* duty, then the proletariat will not sabotage your actions", he is not at all renouncing his past attitude to the Libyan war – the war which gave rise to what A. T. calls "the negative myth of war".[6] When he speaks of "*your* destiny" he is referring to that destiny which, as a result of the bourgeoisie's historical function, leads to war; hence the war retains its character at an even more intense level, given the consciousness which the proletariat has gained, of irreducible antithesis to the destiny of the proletariat.

So it is not a general embrace that Mussolini is arguing for, not a general fusion of all parties in national unanimity – that would indeed be an anti-socialist position. He is arguing that the proletariat, now that it has acquired a clear consciousness of its class power and of its revolutionary potential, and recognizing for the moment its own unreadiness to take over the helm of state [. . .][7] an ideal discipline, and should allow the free operation in history of those forces which the proletariat considers strongest – and which it does not feel able to replace. Sabotaging a machine (and absolute neutrality comes down in the end to a real sabotage – one that is enthusiastically accepted, moreover, by the ruling class) certainly does not in itself imply that the machine is not perfect or that it cannot be used for something.

Nor does Mussolini's position exclude the possibility (on the contrary, it presupposes it) that the proletariat might renounce its antagonistic attitude and, after the ruling class has failed or shown itself to be impotent, eliminate it and take over public affairs itself – assuming that I have interpreted correctly Mussolini's somewhat disorganized declarations, and have developed them along the same lines as he would have done himself.

* * * * *

I cannot imagine a proletariat like a motor that is started by the switch of absolute neutrality in July and in October cannot be stopped without breaking.

On the contrary we are dealing with men who, especially over the past few years, have shown that they possess an intellectual agility and freshness of sensitivity which the amorphous and irresponsible bourgeois masses cannot begin to suspect. We are dealing with men who have shown that they are quite capable of assimilating and digesting the novel values that the resurrected Socialist Party has put into circulation. Or are we perhaps scared when we contemplate the work which must be done to make the proletariat undertake this new task, which could perhaps be the beginning of the end of its position as pupil of the bourgeoisie?

In any case, the convenient position of absolute neutrality must not allow us to forget the gravity of our situation, nor let us abandon ourselves for the slightest instant to an over-ingenuous contemplation and Buddhist renunciation of our obligations.

Signed A. Gramsci, *Il Grido del Popolo*, 31 October 1914, under the heading "The War and Socialist Opinion".

3. SOCIALISM AND CULTURE

A short time ago an article by Enrico Leone[8] came to our attention, where in that nebulous and convoluted style he all too often indulges in he repeated a few common-places on culture and intellectualism in relation to the proletariat, opposing to them *practice* and the *historical fact* that the working class is building its future with its own hands. We believe it would not be unproductive to return to this theme, one which has been aired before in *Il Grido* and which in the youth federation's *Avanguardia* received a more rigidly doctrinal treatment in the polemic between Bordiga from Naples and our own Tasca.[9]

Let us recall two passages. The first comes from a German romantic, Novalis (who lived from 1772 to 1801), and says: "The supreme problem of culture is that of gaining possession of one's transcendental self, of being at one and the same time the self of oneself. Thus it should not surprise us that there is an absence of feeling or complete understanding of others. Lacking a perfect comprehension of ourselves, we can never really hope to know others."

The other, which we summarize, is from G. B. Vico, who (in the "First Corollary concerning the speech in poetic characters of the first nations" in his *Scienza Nuova*) gives a political interpretation of the famous dictum of Solon which Socrates subsequently made his own in relation to philosophy: "Know thyself". Vico maintains that in this dictum Solon wished to admonish the plebeians, who believed themselves to be of *bestial origin* and the nobility to be of *divine origin*, to reflect on themselves and see that they had the *same human nature as the nobles* and hence should claim to be *their equals in civil law*. Vico then points to this consciousness of human equality between plebeians and nobles as the basis and historical reason for the rise of the democratic republics of antiquity.

We have not chosen these two fragments entirely at random. In them we believe the writers touch upon, though admittedly in a vaguely expressed and defined manner, the limits and principles governing the correct comprehension of the concept of culture even in relation to socialism.

We need to free ourselves from the habit of seeing culture as encyclopaedic knowledge, and men as mere receptacles to be stuffed full of empirical data and a mass of unconnected raw facts, which have to be filed in the brain as in the columns of a dictionary, enabling their owner to respond to the various stimuli from the outside world. This form of culture really is harmful, particularly for the proletariat. It serves only to create maladjusted people, people who believe they are superior to the rest of humanity because they have memorized a certain number of facts and dates and who rattle them off at every opportunity, so turning them almost into a barrier between themselves and others. It serves to create the kind of weak and colourless intellectualism that Romain Rolland has flayed so mercilessly, which has given birth to a mass of pretentious babblers who have a more damaging effect on social life than tuberculosis or syphilis germs have on the beauty and physical health of the body. The young student who knows a little Latin and history, the young lawyer who has been successful in wringing a scrap of paper called a degree out of the laziness and lackadaisical attitude of his professors – they end up seeing themselves as different from and superior to even the best skilled workman, who fulfils a precise and indispensable task in life and is a hundred times more valuable in his activity than they are in theirs. But this is not culture, but pedantry, not intelligence, but intellect, and it is absolutely right to react against it.

Culture is something quite different. It is organization, discipline of one's inner self, a coming to terms with one's own personality; it is the attainment of a higher awareness, with the aid of which one succeeds in understanding one's own historical value, one's own function in life, one's own rights and obligations. But none of this can come about through spontaneous evolution, through a series of actions and reactions which are independent of one's own will – as is the case in the animal and vegetable kingdoms where every unit is selected and specifies its own organs unconsciously, through a fatalistic law of things. Above all, man is mind, i.e. he is a product of history, not nature. Otherwise how could one explain the fact, given that there have always been exploiters and exploited, creators of wealth and its selfish consumers, that socialism has not yet come into being? The fact is that only by degrees, one stage at a time, has humanity acquired consciousness of its own value and won for itself the right to throw off the patterns of organization imposed on it by minorities at a previous period in history. And this consciousness was formed not under the brutal goad of physiological necessity, but as a result of intelligent reflection, at first by just a few people and later by a whole class, on why certain conditions exist and how best to convert the facts of vassalage into the signals of rebellion and social reconstruction. This means that every revolution has been preceded by an intense labour of criticism, by the diffusion of culture and the spread of ideas amongst masses of men who are at first resistant, and think only of solving their own immediate economic and political problems for themselves, who have no ties of solidarity with others in the same condition. The latest example, the closest to us and hence least foreign to our own time, is that of the French Revolution. The preceding cultural period, called the Enlightenment, which has been so misrepresented by the facile critics of theoretical reason, was not in any way or at least was not entirely a flutter of superficial encyclopaedic intellectuals discoursing on anything and everything with equal impertubability, believing themselves to be men of their time only if they had read the *Encyclopédie* of D'Alembert and Diderot; in short it was not solely a phenomenon of pedantic and arid intellectualism, the like of which we see before our eyes today, exhibited most fully in the popular Universities of the lowest order. The Englightenment was a magnificent revolution in itself and, as De Sanctis acutely notes in his *History of Italian Literature*, it gave all Europe a bourgeois spiritual International in the form of a unified consciousness, one which was sensitive to all the woes and misfortunes of the common people and which was the best possible preparation for the bloody revolt that followed in France.

In Italy, France and Germany, the same topics, the same institutions and same principles were being discussed. Each new comedy by Voltaire, each new pamphlet moved like a spark along the lines that were already stretched between state and state, between region and region, and found the same supporters and the same opponents everywhere and every time. The bayonets of Napoleon's armies found their road already smoothed by an invisible army of books and pamphlets that had swarmed out of Paris from the first half of the eighteenth century and had prepared both men and institutions for the necessary renewal. Later, after the French events had welded a unified consciousness, a demonstration in Paris was enough to provoke similar disturbances in Milan, Vienna and the smaller centres. All this seems natural and spontaneous to superficial observers, yet it would be incomprehensible if we were not aware of the cultural factors that helped to create a state of mental preparedness for those explosions in the name of what was seen as a common cause.

The same phenomenon is being repeated today in the case of

socialism. It was through a critique of capitalist civilization that the unified consciousness of the proletariat was or is still being formed, and a critique implies culture, not simply a spontaneous and naturalistic evolution. A critique implies precisely the self-consciousness that Novalis considered to be the end of culture. Consciousness of a self which is opposed to others, which is differentiated and, once having set itself a goal, can judge facts and events other than in themselves or for themselves but also in so far as they tend to drive history forward or backward. To know oneself means to be oneself, to be master of oneself, to distinguish oneself, to free oneself from a state of chaos, to exist as an element of order – but of one's own order and one's own discipline in striving for an ideal. And we cannot be successful in this unless we also know others, their history, the successive efforts they have made to be what they are, to create the civilization they have created and which we seek to replace with our own. In other words, we must form some idea of nature and its laws in order to come to know the laws governing the mind. And we must learn all this without losing sight of the ultimate aim: to know oneself better through others and to know others better through oneself.

If it is true that universal history is a chain made up of the efforts man has exerted to free himself from privilege, prejudice and idolatry, then it is hard to understand why the proletariat, which seeks to add another link to that chain, should not know how and why and by whom it was preceded, or what advantage it might derive from this knowledge.

Signed ALPHA GAMMA, *Il Grido del Popolo*, 29 January 1916.

4. JULY 14th

A prejudice. People say: "In pre-revolutionary Paris, in all France, there were no republicans." They should say: the French revolutionaries did not have the creation of a republic as their immediate aim. Their aim was more distant, more general; fundamentally it was an international aim. Their revolution was economic – like the one we are preparing – not political. They wanted the bourgeoisie to regulate production, they wanted the producers of that time to create their future and their life with their own hands. The land to the peasants who cultivated it, not to the feudal lords who used it only for coursing hares and pretty girls. Industry to the industrialists, and not to the clerics and nobility who burdened it with tallies, who wanted their cut – and what a cut! – and who obstructed the process of production with heavy taxes, a host of internal duties, etc. Then the monarchy decided to take charge of the situation, brought its power to bear to conserve the *status quo*, and was swept away. Everyone became a republican because everyone was already a potential republican, even if they were not members of the republican party and did not cry out to the four winds every day that what they wanted was a republic. So a republican Paris, a Paris bringing down the Bastille or massacring the hired Swiss guards, was no miracle. When we set ourselves a distant, general goal, one which has to arouse and capture the imagination of a whole class, it is no miracle if all manner of things and a whole range of organizational systems are brought down along the way, before we reach the ultimate goal – whereas to judge from what some people say, one would expect each of these results to demand a separate and specific action, as well as a daily polemic on the question.

So let us remember the 14th of July and Paris after the fall of the Bastille. It both strengthens us and teaches us.

(32 lines censored)

Unsigned, Turin edition of *Avanti!*, 15 July 1916, under the heading *Sotto la Mole*.

5. A VETERINARY SURGEON ON FILM

At 11.30 a.m. in the plant's medical consultation room, the workers are standing round in groups waiting for the visit of the veterinary surgeon who looks after them. Yes, he's a vet, say the patients, because all he gives you for examination is a single glance. True, the workers can speak, they know how to express what they feel, but by God, we all know that they fabricate their symptoms, they exaggerate them to get a holiday, to give themselves a good time. And so it's as though they can't speak, as though they were work-shy brutes – and so the doctor becomes a veterinary surgeon. The deduction is simple, but highly logical.

The delay makes the men waiting even more feeble; the minutes tick by, mid-day draws near. Meanwhile the foremen take note of their underlings' extended absence and tick off the 2 Lira fines. Ah, these workers, give them an inch of tolerance, and they take a mile; a nasty lot, don't we know it. Some shouting can be heard, and curses muttered between the teeth. The overseer looks on, and is far from inhibited in making reports against trouble-makers, against people who preach rebellion. Because it is well known that disorder is always in the ranks, and to protest against anyone not doing his duty is not promoting order, it is rebellion.

But the . . . veterinary surgeon arrives at last, and the forty workers line up before him. First is a very timid little old man who doubles himself up completely in front of the proud figure of his judge with his bristling, arrogant whiskers. Humbly the old man explains that he feels tired, that the thirteen hours of heavy work and the overtime wear him out; his kidneys ache, he frequently has attacks of nausea. . . . An all-inclusive glance: a purgative and an order to continue with the thirteen-hour day.

The second worker has a piece of grit in his eye; it is extracted in no time at all; the tweezers rummage in the wound . . . just as in those mountainous countries the blood-letters rummage with their rusty pincers in the throats of horses when they swallow leeches along with the water from the mountain streams. And there's little point in mentioning the all too comprehensible pain in the head: it's back to work at 2 o'clock. At the slightest hint of a protest, Dr. Bittersweet[10] takes name and surname, thus giving warning of a prompt visit from the royal *carabinieri* in case he is absent.

The siren announces the end of work. The number of visitors grows smaller. Many of the workers live far away, they have to be back in time, and they've got to eat as well. The doctor is quite satisfied – if they go away, then obviously there's nothing the matter with them. The doctor's delays, the fines for the others because they are held up, all lies. . . . The worker is a machine, by God, and he's got to go on producing. Illness, fatigue – all fabrications of undisciplined and maladjusted subversives. A third man: his kidneys hurt, he has a dry cough that shakes his whole body every other minute; he could be consumptive, and all he asks for is some rest, so that he can apply himself later with renewed vigour. A little sedlitz water, nod the two whiskers. A protest: 2 Lira fine, and order reigns once more. And so on: a fourth man, whose hand is half-crushed and was treated in haste and anger, without any examination of the wound, is put off to the next visit. Meanwhile he must not stay off work – the rhythm of the factory can't be allowed to slacken, and the industrialists can't be allowed to see their honest earnings reduced through the whim of a machine. And so the parody goes on until a car draws up, puffing smoke, to bear Aesculapius away to the dinner he deserves. He is still fresh, neat, and ruddy – no rolled up sleeves, no contact with dry, fevered skin, or bloody wounds, or soot-blackened wrists. . . . How these workers do go on: they would like a doctor, not a vet, they would like complicated cures. But Aesculapius doesn't allow himself to get worried by that – his duty is Gospel to him. And anyway, with all this preaching of materialism and peace-mongering,[11] it's little wonder that even underlings are now worrying about life and health and their physiological well-being. Were they the regiment horses, the vet would quickly become a doctor – the horses cost a packet, and there are only a few of them.

But of course: these are just rally phrases, good for stirring up the unaware. While the words: discipline, order, have a resonant tone and ensure victory.

Unsigned, Turin edition of *Avanti!*, 4 August 1916, under the heading *Sotto la Mole*.

6. INDIFFERENCE

Indifference is actually the mainspring of history. But in a negative sense. What comes to pass, either the evil that afflicts everyone, or the possible good brought about by an act of general valour, is due not so much to the initiative of the active few, as to the indifference, the absenteeism of the many. What comes to pass does so not so much because a few people want it to happen, as because the mass of citizens abdicate their responsibility and let things be. They allow the knots to form that in time only a sword will be able to cut through; they let men rise to power whom in time only a mutiny will overthrow. The fatality that seems to dominate history is precisely the illusory appearance of this indifference, of this absenteeism. Events are hatched off-stage in the shadows; unchecked hands weave the fabric of collective life – and the masses know nothing. The destinies of an epoch are manipulated in the interests of narrow horizons, of the immediate ends of small groups of activists – and the mass of citizens know nothing. But eventually the events that are hatched come out into the open; the fabric woven in the shadows is completed, and then it seems that fatality overwhelms everything and everybody. It seems that history is nothing but an immense natural phenomenon, an eruption, an earthquake, and that we are all its victims, both those who wanted it to happen as well as those who did not, those who knew it would happen and those who did not, those who were active and those who were indifferent. And then it is the indifferent ones who get angry, who wish to dissociate themselves from the consequences, who want it made known that they did not want it so and hence bear no responsibility. And while some whine piteously, and others howl obscenely, few people, if any, ask themselves this question: had I done my duty as a man, had I sought to make my voice heard, to impose my will, would what came to pass have ever happened? But few people, if any, see their indifference as a fault – their scepticism, their failure to give moral and material support to those political and economic groups that were struggling either to avoid a particular evil or to promote a particular good. Instead such people prefer to speak of the failure of ideas, of the definitive collapse of programmes, and other like niceties. They continue in their indifference and their scepticism.

Tomorrow they will begin anew their life of absenting themselves from any direct or indirect responsibility for things. This is not to say that they have no clear idea of the state of affairs, that they are not capable of dreaming up wonderful solutions to the most pressing of current problems, as well as to others which are just as pressing but need more time or preparation. Yet these solutions remain gloriously infertile; their contribution to collective existence is not motivated by any spark of moral feeling, but is the consequence purely of intellectual curiosity. Certainly they are not born of that sharp sense of historical responsibility that drives men to take an active part in life, that leaves them no room for agnosticism or indifference of any kind. Therefore this new sensibility must be drummed into us – we must have done with the inconclusive whinings of the eternally innocent. Every man must be asked to account for the manner in which he has fulfilled the task that life has set him and continues to set him day by day; he must be asked to account for what he has done, but especially for what he has not done. It is high time that the social chain should not weigh on just the few; it is time that events should be seen to be the intelligent work of men, and not the products of chance, of fatality. And so it is time to have done with the indifferent among us, the sceptics, the people who profit from the small good procured by the activity of a few, but who refuse to take responsibility for the great evil that is allowed to develop and come to pass because of their absence from the struggle.

Unsigned, Turin edition of *Avanti!*, 26 August 1916, under the heading *Sotto la Mole.*

7. REMEMBERING THE HISTORY OF THE COTTON-WORKERS' STRUGGLE

Mazzonis, Poma, Hofmann, Leumann, Wild, etc.[12] These names are brought to our attention once again. Ten years have passed. The workers' organizations have grown stronger, and class consciousness has transformed the proletariat. The workers are no longer helpless particles of dust in the chaos of capitalist society. They are soldiers fighting for an idea, a crusade advancing to the conquest of a promised land. They know what they want, they have tightened their ranks, they have forcibly demanded recognition of their value. Now they are currently moving on to the assault, well-disciplined, well-equipped, determined to overcome any resistance, determined to impose their will. In place of their pain and suffering they now have a lucid awareness of their rights, and their humility and resignation of just a short time ago has become a will to fight. The cotton-workers' strike is both a demonstration and confirmation of this fact. Ten years of work have produced these results. True, the names Mazzonis, Poma, Hofmann, Leumann, Wild are being brought once more to our attention, but how changed in their significance – even the bosses' consciousness has been transformed. The mediaeval castle has been largely pulled down by the assiduous blows of the workers' organization, the moat has been filled in, the feudal lord's throne has been left to rot on the garbage dump, and now it is two forces which stand facing one another: capital and labour. But now labour has just as much nobility as capital or even more so, it is no longer humiliated before it. Now labour is capital's equal and there is nothing servile in its gaze, for now it has the strength to outstare the vultures that gnaw at its vitals, that feed off its crimson blood, off its vital energy.

1906 was the year when the cotton workers' revolt began. On this occasion too it was blood that cemented the new edifice that was being built. The general strike was the concrete testimony that every section of the workforce was dependent on the solidarity of the whole of the working class for its victory. Let us recall the facts. Let us use these facts to strengthen our consciousness, let us immerse our spirit in the river of *our own* traditions, of *our own* history.

In 1906 the workers' organization was still at a critical stage in its development: it was not recognized by the bosses. These latter were seeking to kill it while it was still in the throes of birth, by refusing to grant it any status. They wanted to preserve intact the heritage of their privileges. They were aware of its fragile foundations; they were aware that the least fragment of masonry that became detached and fell into the abyss of oblivion would be followed by others, until the whole façade would come tumbling down. Hence they were tenacious in their resistance. In the first week of January 1906 a strike broke out in the weaving section of the Hofmann plant. A workers' committee led by Comrade Francesco Barberis presented itself to the directors. They refused to receive Barberis. They insisted the workers should return to their posts. What is more the directors reserved to themselves the right to readmit workers or not as they thought fit. The strike was strangled.

When a woman worker in the Druent cotton-mill asked for a reference (she was the wife of Comrade Pietro Vietti), the director replied: "You deserve the reference, but I won't give it to you; and if your socialist husband were to come here, and even if the police were to come, I would still refuse just the same. *You don't have the deference to the owner that a worker ought to have if she is to deserve a reference.*"

Early in March the women who operated the spinning machines in the Poma cotton-mill were told that from then on everyone would have to work 50 machines. The workers made their just remonstrances. Poma set an example by sacking all women who refused to work more than 25 machines.

Meanwhile the workers were trying to strengthen their organization so as to be able to reply with dignity to the bosses' provocations. Propaganda work, through newspapers and rallies, was stepped up. On 28 March the secretary of the Turin district office of the National Confederation of Textile Workers, Luigi Mainardi, gave a talk on the specific theme: "The textile industry must be organized."

The bosses reacted immediately. Over the first two weeks of April the textile industrialists of Turin and the surrounding district – Wild, Mazzonis, Leumann, Hofmann – sacked and booted out any worker who had been a member of the strike committees. The textile industry had been expanding at a tremendous rate: new factories mushroomed, while the existing ones doubled and tripled their output. And in the course of this flourishing growth the capitalists protected their interests behind thick barbed-wire entanglements. The living conditions of the wage-workers became truly hellish: their wages, their treatment, the shameful hours they worked, the directors and foremen like gaolers and their henchmen – every tiny lapse was punished by a fine. And woe to anyone who complained, who dared even grumble under her breath – she was sacked on the spot. The firm Mazzonis earned itself a reputation amongst the working women as the most tyrannical in its behaviour, the most savage in its reprisals. A strike by the wage-workers in 1904 had brought to light the exorbitant and infamous exploitation the women were subjected to in its workshops. The statistics published at the time make one shiver. Wages were rarely more than 1.20 a day, and even this wretched sum was continually clawed back by fines, withholdings and arbitrary dismissals. The statistical yearbook of the Ministry of Health provided the following figures for each thousand deaths as a result of pulmonary consumption.

Year	*Middle-class women*	*Milliners Seamstresses*	*Spinsters Weavers*
1899	52·27	390·95	342·07
1900	47·62	246·45	410·26
1901	35·09	266·36	250·72
1902	52·17	304·76	357·10
1903	50·91	253·97	484·85

In other words, in 1903, for every 1,000 women who died from pulmonary consumption, 484, or nearly half, were textile workers. The capitalist development of the textile industry had required a terrible holocaust of proletarian lives.

The firm Poma vied with Mazzonis. The "fabricôn" had become synonymous with penal servitude. In a socialist song in the local dialect, the "fabricôn" recurs again and again in the chorus;[13] it has been painfully hammered into the memory of the Turin proletariat.

Around 15 April the firm of Mazzonis sacked without any plausible reason 25 comrades, precisely the women whose activities had been most prominent, giving them 8 days' notice. The textile workers' union sent a communiqué to the socialist press that was both a cry of pain and an energetic protest. Agitation was stepped up. Besides, in that year 1906 the whole of the Turin proletariat was on the boil: there was an inflammable atmosphere as a result of a whole series of agitations. There had been the metal-workers' strike; there had been the administrative elections which the socialist minority won by 11,000 votes, preceded by furious polemics with the newspapers representing the bourgeoisie; there had been the trial of the anti-militarists; there had been the great funeral procession in honour of the victims of the Courrières mine disaster in France. As a result of these episodes, with feelings inflamed by such a succession of class actions, the consciousness of each worker had been welded into a unified whole, and the sense of solidarity was acute.

On 22 April a great meeting was held in the offices of the Borgo Vittori branch of the Socialist Party to discuss the victims of the sacking and how to organize. The representative from the textile workers' union declared that the meeting was called "to achieve an effective and solid organization of the 10,000 women textile workers that would enable them to stand up to the likely future battles against the grasping exorbitance of the all-powerful textile bosses".

In the first few days of May the agitation became threatening. In all the textile workshops the women, even those who were unorganized, were united in their demand for more humane treatment. Their principal demand was for a reduction in working hours from 11 to 10, without loss of wages. The industrialists prevaricated, and the authorities failed to cow them after successive interventions. The strike began: one by one the workshops emptied and production came to a halt. The masses thronged into the offices of the Chamber of Labour. A general textile strike was declared and immediately it began to spread: it was in fact a spontaneous outburst on the part of the women workers, most of whom were unorganized, that could not be contained. A manifesto issued by the Chamber finished with these words: "May these women workers bring to their struggle the tenacity and faith of people who know that they have right on their side, may they bring to it their utmost spiritual fervour, the throbbing of a mother's or a wife's heart, *determined to have done once and for all with this killing work*. Behind them the whole of the Turin proletariat stands alert, ready to rush to their aid."

On Sunday 6 May the strikers marched in a long procession up the Cavoretto hill from Corso Siccardi. Allasia, Castellano and Barberis spoke to the meeting. On Monday the strike spread to plants in other industries, particularly engineering shops. Demonstrators' banners crossed the city on their way to Corso Siccardi, and there the first incidents with the forces of law and order, who intervened to a considerable extent, occurred. The cavalry charged, trying to disperse the crowd that had gathered in the offices and in the streets around the Casa del Popolo in Corso Siccardi. The usual things happened. Around 6.30 in the evening when the lads and lasses were fleeing once again before the cavalry, there was a terrible crush just inside the main gateway.[14] A few stones began to fly. Policemen in plain clothes moved forward. One of them rushed forward with levelled revolver. The first shots were fired, and then the air was thick with them. The crowd sought refuge inside the building. Eight people were wounded. The most serious case was Giovanni Cravero, who had part of his skull blown off, his brains mangled and a terrible haemorrhage. The other seven were in better condition, suffering bullet wounds, sabre and dagger wounds. The front door was riddled with bullet holes. The Chamber of Labour was invaded, and 22 people arrested. Then the building was occupied by the army. In the evening representatives from the Central Office of the Chamber of Labour and many comrades from the political organization met in the Dora district office of the party and voted in favour of declaring a general strike, and at once proceeded to draw up a manifesto. On Tuesday, the day after, the strike was 100 per cent solid.

In this way the struggle for the 10 hour day had its baptism of blood. On the Monday after these tragic events the industrialists assembled together and voted in favour of this resolution: "In the light of the popular disturbances and for the sake of peace, the cotton industrialists hereby concede the 10 hour day. Plants will re-open from tomorrow, Tuesday, morning." But there was a general strike, and the textile workers did not return to work. Negotiations dragged on for the whole of Tuesday, until the industrialists had clarified their concessions in concrete terms. And it was only very late in the evening, at 11.30, that the industrialists released a declaration to the union, signed by Poma, Mazzonis, Wild, Abegg and Bass, confirming the reduction of the working day to 10 hours, with the assurance that this would not incur any loss of wages. On Wednesday at mid-day the general strike came to an end. In the morning an enormous procession 40,000 strong had marched through the streets, dispersing in Piazza Vittorio.

In this way the women workers succeeded in winning one of their rights. But the blood dried on the stones of the entrance hall to the Casa del Popolo. And those miserable speculators, those jackals of industrialists, were no longer afraid of its acrid smell. So they tried to exact revenge. The industrialist Poma lost no time in making himself an agent provocateur. He offered a novel interpretation of the declaration of 8 May in which it was guaranteed that there should be no reduction in textile workers' wages. *No reduction*, according to Poma, referred to the hourly, not the daily rate. In this way he sought to wrest back from the workers a part of their gains: he was trying to reduce their already meagre wages by a tenth. Poma's arrogance was unique. His cavilling, his arguments stand today as testimony to his shameless lack of moral rectitude. But his work-force had changed; the experience of the strike, at first a sectional one but culminating in a general stoppage, had produced its effects, and had consolidated a feeling of class solidarity. So his 200 workers stopped work again, and stayed out until they had won a decisive victory. The other industrialists had to keep in line to avoid getting troubles of their own. The strike was solid for 56 days, despite the intervention of the priests who organized scabbing and used their slimy propaganda to try to swing public opinion behind the poor industrialists. But the strikers were able to count on the total solidarity of their comrades: 40,000 Lire were distributed in subsidies, and the spectre of a general strike loomed up again. On 18 July the Right Hon. Anselmo Poma's wage-earners started work again after two months out, having had all their demands met in full.[15]

As a result of these struggles, which are rapidly summarized here through pressure of time, the textile workers created their solid class organization. Now they are confronting their bosses once again. And we are sure that once again it will be the bosses who bite the dust.

Signed A. G., *Il Grido del Popolo*, 9 December 1916.

8. MEN OR MACHINES?

The brief discussion which was held at the last council meeting between our comrades and some representatives of the majority, on the subject of vocational education programmes, deserves some comment, however brief and succinct.[16] Comrade Zini's observations ("There is still a conflict between the humanistic and vocational currents over the issue of popular education: we must endeavour to reconcile these currents, without forgetting that a worker is above all a man, who should not be denied the possibility of exploring the widest realms of the spirit, by being enslaved from his earliest youth to the machine.") and Councillor Sincero's attacks against philosophy (philosophy finds people opposed to it especially when it states truths that strike at vested interests) are not just isolated polemical episodes: they are necessary clashes between people representing fundamentally opposed interests.

1. Our party has still not settled on a concrete education programme that is in any way different from traditional ones. Until now we have been content to support the general principle of the need for culture, whether it be at an elementary, or secondary-technical or higher level, and we have campaigned in favour of this principle and propagated it with vigour and energy. We can state that the reduction in illiteracy in Italy is due not so much to the law on compulsory education, as to the intellectual awakening, the awareness of certain spiritual needs that socialist propaganda has succeeded in arousing amongst the ranks of the proletariat in Italy. But we have gone no further than that. Education in Italy is still a rigidly *bourgeois* affair, in the worst sense of the word. Grammar schools and higher education, which are State-run and hence financed from State revenues, i.e. by the direct taxes paid by the proletariat, can only be attended by the children of the bourgeoisie, who alone enjoy the economic independence needed for uninterrupted study. A proletarian, no matter how intelligent he may be, no matter how fit to become a man of culture, is forced either to squander his qualities on some other activity, or else to become a rebel and autodidact – i.e. (apart from some notable exceptions) a mediocrity, a man who cannot give all he could have given had he been completed and strengthened by the discipline of school. Culture is a privilege.

Education is a privilege. And we do not want it to be so. All young people should be equal before culture. Using the funds of all citizens, the State should not be financing the education of the children of wealthy parents no matter how mediocre or deficient they may be, while it excludes even the most intelligent and capable children of proletarians. Grammar-school and higher education should be open only to those who can demonstrate that they are worthy of it. And if it is in the public interest that such forms of education should exist, preferably supported and regulated by the State, then it is also in the public interest that they should be open to all intelligent children, regardless of their economic potential. Collective sacrifice is justified only when it benefits those who are most deserving. Therefore, this collective sacrifice should serve especially to give the most deserving children that economic independence they need if they are to devote their time to serious study.

2. Members of the proletariat, who are excluded from grammar schools and higher education as a result of the present social conditions – conditions which ensure that the division of labour between men is unnatural (not being based on different capacities) and so retards and is inimical to production – have to fall back upon the parallel educational system: the technical and vocational colleges. As a result of the anti-democratic restrictions imposed by the State budget, the technical colleges, which were set up along democratic lines by the Casati ministry, have undergone a transformation that has largely destroyed their nature. In most cases they have become mere superfetations of the classical schools, and an innocent outlet for the petty-bourgeois mania for finding a secure job. The continually rising entrance fees, and the particular prospects they open up in practical life, have turned these schools too into a privilege. Anyway, the overwhelming majority of the proletariat is automatically excluded from them on account of the uncertain and precarious life which the wage-earner is forced to lead – the sort of life which is certainly not the most propitious for fruitfully following a course of study.

3. What the proletariat needs is an educational system that is open to all. A system in which the child is allowed to develop and mature and acquire those general features that serve to develop character. In a word, a humanistic school, as conceived by the ancients, and more recently by the men of the Renaissance. A school which does not mortgage the child's future, a school that does not force the child's will, his intelligence and growing awareness to run along tracks to a predetermined station. A school of freedom and free initiative, not a school

of slavery and mechanical precision. The children of proletarians too should have all possibilities open to them; they should be able to develop their own individuality in the optimal way, and hence in the most productive way for both themselves and society. Technical schools should not be allowed to become incubators of little monsters aridly trained for a job, with no general ideas, no general culture, no intellectual stimulation, but only an infallible eye and a firm hand. Technical education too helps a child to blossom into a man – so long as it is educative and not simply informative, simply passing on manual techniques. Councillor Sincero, who is an industrialist, is being too meanly bourgeois when he protests against philosophy.

Of course, meanly bourgeois industrialists might prefer to have workers who were more machines than men. But the sacrifices which everyone in society willingly makes in order to foster improvements and nourish the best and most perfect men who will improve it still more – these sacrifices must bring benefits to the whole of society, not just to one category of people or one class.

It is a problem of right and of force. The proletariat must stay alert, to prevent another abuse being added to the many it has already suffered.

Unsigned, Piedmont edition of *Avanti!*, 24 December 1916, under the banner "Socialists and Education".

9. NOTES ON THE RUSSIAN REVOLUTION

Why is the Russian revolution a proletarian revolution?

Reading the papers, reading the confusing despatches that the censorship has passed for publication, one is hard put to it to know why. We know the revolution was carried out by proletarians (workers and soldiers) and we know of the existence of a committee of worker delegates overseeing the functioning of the administrative organs which have had to be maintained to see to everyday affairs. But is it enough that a revolution be carried out by proletarians for it to be a proletarian revolution? War too is made by proletarians, but it is not, for this reason alone, a proletarian event. For it to be so, other, spiritual, factors must be present. There must be more to the revolution than the question of power: there must be the question of morality, of a way of life. The bourgeois newspapers have emphasized the aspect of power. They have told us how the power of the autocracy came to be replaced by another power, which is not yet clearly defined but which they hope is a bourgeois power. And at once they have set up the parallel: Russian Revolution, French Revolution and found the events to be similar. But the events resemble each other only on the surface, just as one act of violence resembles another act of violence, and one destruction resembles another.

We, however, are convinced that the Russian revolution is more than simply a proletarian event, it is a proletarian act, which must naturally lead to a socialist régime. The small amount of really concrete, substantial news does not allow exhaustive proof of this. However, certain facts are available to support such a conclusion.

The Russian revolution has been innocent of Jacobinism. The revolution had to smash the autocracy – but it did not have to crush the majority of the people by the use of violence. Jacobinism is a purely bourgeois phenomenon: it characterizes the French bourgeois revolution. The bourgeoisie, after carrying out the revolution, had no universal programme. It carried it out to further its own, particularist class interests, and did so with the closed and mean mentality common to all people who pursue particularist ends. The violence of the bourgeois revolutions has a twofold character: it destroys the old order, and imposes the new. The bourgeoisie imposes its power and its ideas not only on the previously dominant caste, but also on the people it will in future dominate. It is one authoritarian régime replacing another authoritarian régime.

The Russian revolution has destroyed authoritarianism and replaced it by universal suffrage, extending the vote to women too. It has replaced authoritarianism by liberty, the Constitution by the free voice of universal consciousness. Why are the Russian revolutionaries not Jacobins – in other words, why have not they too replaced the dictatorship of one man by the dictatorship of an audacious minority ready to do anything that will ensure its programme's victory? It is because they are pursuing aims which are common to the vast majority of the population. They are certain that when the whole of the Russian proletariat is asked to make its choice, the reply cannot be in doubt. It is in everyone's mind, and will be transformed into an irrevocable decision just as soon as it can be expressed in an atmosphere of absolute spiritual freedom, without the voting being perverted by police interventions and by the threat of the gallows or exile. Even culturally the industrial proletariat is ready for the transition; and the agricultural proletariat too, which is familiar with the traditional forms of communal communism, is prepared for the change to a new form of society. Socialist revolutionaries cannot be Jacobins: in Russia at the moment all they have to do is ensure that the bourgeois organs (the *duma*, the *zemstvas*)[17] do not indulge in Jacobinism, in order to secure an ambiguous response from universal suffrage and turn violence to their own ends.

* * * * *

The bourgeois newspapers have attached no importance to another intriguing event. The Russian revolutionaries have not only freed political prisoners, but common criminals as well. When the common criminals in one prison were told they were free, they replied that they felt they did not have the right to accept liberty because they had to expiate their crimes. In Odessa they gathered in the prison courtyard and of their own volition swore to become honest men and resolved to live by their own labours. From the point of view of the socialist revolution, this news has more importance even than that of the dismissal of the Tsar and the grand-dukes. The Tsar would have been deposed by bourgeois revolutionaries as well. But in bourgeois eyes, these condemned men would still have been the enemies of their order, the stealthy appropriators of their wealth and their tranquillity. In our eyes their liberation has this significance: what the revolution has created in Russia is a new way of life. It has not only replaced one power by another, it has replaced one way of life by another. It has created a new moral order, and in addition to the physical liberty of the individual, has established liberty of the mind. The revolutionaries were not afraid to send back into circulation men whom bourgeois justice had stamped with the infamous brand "previous offender", men whom bourgeois justice had catalogued into various types of criminal delinquent. Only in an atmosphere of social turbulence could such an event occur, when the way of life and the prevailing mentality is changed. Liberty makes men free and widens their moral horizons; it turns the worst criminal under an authoritarian régime into a martyr for the cause of duty, a hero in the cause of honesty. It says in a report that in one prison these *criminals* rejected liberty and elected themselves wardens. Why had they never done such a thing before? Because their prison was ringed by massive walls and their windows were barred? The men who went to free them must have looked very different from the tribunal judges and the prison warders, and these *common criminals* must have heard words very different from the ones they were used to, for their consciousness to be transformed in this way, for them to become suddenly *so free* as to be able to prefer segregation to liberty and to voluntarily impose an expiation on themselves. They must have felt the world had changed, that they too, the dregs of society, now counted for something; that they too, the segregated, had the freedom to choose.

This is the most majestic phenomenon that human history has ever produced. As a result of the Russian revolution the man who was a *common criminal* has turned into the sort of man whom Immanuel Kant, the theoretician of absolute ethical conduct, had called for – the sort of man who says: the immensity of the heavens above me, the imperative of my conscience within me. What these brief news items reveal to us is a liberation of spirit, the establishment of a new moral awareness. It is the advent of a new order, one that coincides with everything our masters taught us. And once again it is from the East that light comes to illuminate the aged Western world, which is stupefied by the events and can oppose them with nothing but the banalities and stupidities of its hack-writers.

Initialled A. G., *Il Grido del Popolo*, 29 April 1917. This article was Gramsci's first comment on the events of the "February Revolution" that overthrew the Tsarist autocracy.

10. THE RUSSIAN MAXIMALISTS

The Russian maximalists are the Russian revolution itself.[18]

Kerensky, Tseretelli, Chernov – these men are the present expression of the revolution, they have brought about an initial social balance, a resultant of forces in which the moderates still have an important part to play. The maximalists are the continuity of the revolution – they are its rhythm, and hence they are the revolution itself.

The maximalists embody the idea of socialism taken to its limits: they want socialism *in its entirety*. And they have this task before them: they must prevent any final compromise being reached between the age-old past and this idea; they must be the living symbol of the goal to be achieved; they must prevent the immediate problem that has to be resolved today from growing to the point where it becomes the revolution's sole preoccupation, a spasmodic frenzy erecting insurmountable barriers to later possible achievements.

For this is the supreme danger in all revolutions: people become more and more convinced that a particular instant in the new life is definitive, and that they must halt to look behind them, to consolidate what has been achieved, to rejoice at last in their own success. To have a moment of rest. A revolutionary crisis rapidly wears men out. They tire rapidly. And one can understand their state of mind. Russia, however, has had this good fortune – it has been free of Jacobinism. Hence the lightning dissemination of all ideas has been possible, and numerous political groups have formed as a result, each one more audacious than the last, not wanting to call a halt, believing that the definitive stage to be reached is not yet at hand, is still far off. The maximalists, the extremists, are the last logical link in this revolutionary chain of development. Hence the struggle continues, advances are made; the whole society advances because there is always at least one group that wants to advance and is working among the masses, tapping new sources of proletarian energy and organizing new social forces, which threaten the weary and oversee them and show them that they can be replaced and eliminated if they do not renew themselves and pluck up the courage to go forward. Thus the revolution never pauses, and never completes the circle. It devours its men, it replaces one group by another more audacious group and, by virtue of this instability, this never-achieved perfection, is truly and solely revolution.

The maximalists in Russia are the enemies of the laggards. They spur on the lazy. Up to this point, they have frustrated all attempts to stem the revolutionary tide, and have prevented stagnant pools and backwaters from forming. This is why they are hated by the western bourgeoisies, and why the newspapers in Italy, France and England defame and seek to discredit them, to suffocate them under a mountain of calumnies. The Western bourgeoisies were hoping that the enormous effort of thought and action that the achievement of the new life demanded would be followed by a crisis of mental laziness, by a decline in the revolutionaries' dynamic activity, and that this would become the basis for a definitive stabilization of the new state of affairs.

But in Russia there are no Jacobins. The group of moderate socialists who have held power have not sought to destroy the vanguard elements, to suffocate them in blood. In the socialist revolution, Lenin has not met the fate of Babeuf. He has been able to convert his thought into a meaningful historical force. He has released energies that will never die. He and his Bolshevik comrades are convinced that socialism can be achieved at any time. They are nourished on Marxist thought. They are revolutionaries, not evolutionists. And revolutionary thought does not see time as a progressive factor. It denies that all intermediate stages between the conception of socialism and its achievement must have absolute and complete confirmation in time and place. It holds that it is enough that these stages be realized in thought for the revolution to be able to proceed beyond them. On the other hand, consciousness must be cured of its laziness, it must be conquered. And this is what Lenin and his comrades have been able to do. Their conviction has not remained audacious in thought alone. It has been embodied in individuals, in many individuals; it has borne fruit in activities. It has created the very group that was necessary to oppose any final compromises, any settlement which could have become definitive. And the revolution is continuing. Every aspect of life has become truly revolutionary: it is an ever-present activity, a continual exchange, a continuous excavation into the amorphous block of the people. New energies are released, new ideas which become historical forces are propagated. At last men – all men – are the makers of their own destinies. It would be impossible for a despotic minority to form. The people are ever alert to such tendencies. The revolution by this stage is a ferment ceaselessly dissolving and reforming social groupings and preventing crystallizations, preventing life from basking in momentary success.

Lenin and his most prominent comrades could be swept away by the onset of the storms they have themselves stirred up. But not all their followers would disappear. By now there are too many of them. And the revolutionary fire is spreading, scorching new hearts and minds, turning them into glowing torches of new light, new flames, devouring all laziness and fatigue. The revolution will move forward until its consolidation is total. The time is still far off when there can be a period of relative calm. And life is always revolution.

Initialled A. G., *Il Grido del Popolo*, 28 July 1917.

11. THE REVOLUTION AGAINST "CAPITAL"

The Bolshevik Revolution is now definitively part of the general revolution of the Russian people. The maximalists up until two months ago were the active agents needed to ensure that events should not stagnate, that the drive to the future should not come to a halt and allow a final settlement – a bourgeois settlement – to be reached. Now these maximalists have seized power and established their dictatorship, and are creating the socialist framework within which the revolution will have to settle down if it is to continue to develop harmoniously, without head-on confrontations, on the basis of the immense gains which have already been made.

The Bolshevik Revolution consists more of ideologies than of events. (And hence, at bottom, we do not really need to know more than we do.) This is the revolution against Karl Marx's *Capital.* In Russia, Marx's *Capital* was more the book of the bourgeoisie than of the proletariat. It stood as the critical demonstration of how events should follow a predetermined course: how in Russia a bourgeoisie had to develop, and a capitalist era had to open, with the setting-up of a Western-type civilization, before the proletariat could even think in terms of its own revolt, its own class demands, its own revolution. But events have overcome ideologies. Events have exploded the critical schemas determining how the history of Russia would unfold according to the canons of historical materialism. The Bolsheviks reject Karl Marx, and their explicit actions and conquests bear witness that the canons of historical materialism are not so rigid as one might have thought and has been believed.

And yet there is a fatality even in these events, and if the Bolsheviks reject some of the statements in *Capital*, they do not reject its invigorating, immanent thought. These people are not "Marxists", that is all; they have not used the works of the Master to compile a rigid doctrine of dogmatic utterances never to be questioned. They live Marxist thought – that thought which is eternal, which represents the continuation of German and Italian idealism, and which in the case of Marx was contaminated by positivist and naturalist encrustations. This thought sees as the dominant factor in history, not raw economic facts, but man, men in societies, men in relation to one another, reaching agreements with one another, developing through these contacts (civilization) a collective, social will; men coming to understand economic facts, judging them and adapting them to their will until this becomes the driving force of the economy and moulds objective reality, which lives and moves and comes to resemble a current of volcanic lava that can be channelled wherever and in whatever way men's will determines.

Marx foresaw the foreseeable. But he could not foresee the European war, or rather he could not foresee that the war would last as long as it has or have the effects it has had. He could not foresee that in the space of three years of unspeakable suffering and miseries, this war would have aroused in Russia the collective popular will that it has aroused. *In normal times* a lengthy process of gradual diffusion through society is needed for such a collective will to form; a wide range of class experience is needed. Men are lazy, they need to be organized, first externally into corporations and leagues, then internally, within their thought and their will [. . .][19] need a ceaseless continuity and multiplicity of external stimuli. This is why, *under normal conditions*, the canons of Marxist historical criticism grasp reality, capture and clarify it. *Under normal conditions* the two classes of the capitalist world create history through an ever more intensified class struggle. The proletariat is sharply aware of its poverty and its ever-present discomfort and puts pressure on the bourgeoisie to improve its living standards. It enters into struggle, and forces the bourgeoisie to improve the techniques of production and make it more adapted to meeting the urgent needs of the proletariat. The result is a headlong drive for improvement, an acceleration of the rhythm of production, and a continually increasing output of goods useful to society. And in this drive many fall by the wayside, so making the needs of those who are left more urgent; the masses are forever in a state of turmoil, and out of this chaos they develop some order in their thoughts, and become ever more conscious of their own potential, of their own capacity to shoulder social responsibility and become the arbiters of their own destiny.

This is what happens under normal conditions. When events are repeated with a certain regularity. When history develops through stages which, though ever more complex and richer in significance and value, are nevertheless similar. But in Russia the war galvanized the people's will. As a result of the sufferings accumulated over three years, their will became as one almost overnight. Famine was imminent, and hunger, death from hunger could claim anyone, could crush tens of millions of men at one stroke. Mechanically at first, then actively and consciously after the first revolution, the people's will became as one.

Socialist propaganda put the Russian people in contact with the experience of other proletariats. Socialist propaganda could bring the history of the proletariat dramatically to life in a moment: its struggles against capitalism, the lengthy series of efforts required to emancipate it completely from the chains of servility that made it so abject and to allow it to forge a new consciousness and become a testimony today to a world yet to come. It was socialist propaganda that forged the will of the Russian people. Why should they wait for the history of England to be repeated in Russia, for the bourgeoisie to arise, for the class struggle to begin, so that class consciousness may be formed and the final catastrophe of the capitalist world eventually hit them? The Russian people – or at least a minority of the Russian people – has already passed through these experiences in thought. It has gone beyond them. It will make use of them now to assert itself just as it will make use of Western capitalist experience to bring itself rapidly to the same level of production as the Western world. In capitalist terms, North America is more advanced than England, because the Anglo-Saxons in North America took off at once from the level England had reached only after long evolution. Now the Russian proletariat, socialistically educated, will begin its history at the highest level England has reached today. Since it has to start from scratch, it will start from what has been perfected elsewhere, and hence will be driven to achieve that level of economic maturity which Marx considered to be a necessary condition for collectivism. The revolutionaries themselves will create the conditions needed for the total achievement of their goal. And they will create them faster than capitalism could have done. The criticisms that socialists have made of the bourgeois system, to emphasize its imperfections and its squandering of wealth, can now be applied by the revolutionaries to do better, to avoid the squandering and not fall prey to the imperfections. It will at first be a collectivism of poverty and suffering. But a bourgeois régime would have inherited the same conditions of poverty and suffering. Capitalism could do no more *immediately* than collectivism in Russia. In fact today it would do a lot less, since it would be faced *immediately* by a discontented and turbulent proletariat, a proletariat no longer able to support on behalf of others the suffering and privation that economic dislocation would bring in its wake. So even in absolute, human terms, socialism *now* can be justified in Russia. The hardships that await them after the peace will be bearable only if the proletarians feel they have things under their own control and know that by their efforts they can reduce these hardships in the shortest possible time.

One has the impression that the maximalists at this moment are the spontaneous expression of a *biological* necessity – that they *had* to take power if the Russian people were not to fall prey to a horrible calamity; if the Russian people, throwing themselves into the colossal labours needed for their own regeneration, were to feel less sharply the fangs of the starving wolf; if Russia were not to become a vast shambles of savage beasts tearing each other to pieces.

Signed ANTONIO GRAMSCI, Milan edition of *Avanti!*, 24 December 1917. Republished by *Il Grido del Popolo*, 5 January 1918, with the following note: "The Turin censorship has once completely blanked out this article in *Il Grido*. We reproduce it here as it appeared in *Avanti!* after passing through the sieve of the Milan and Rome censorship."

12. CLASS INTRANSIGENCE AND ITALIAN HISTORY

La Stampa has just published a further two articles on the "socialist rift". *La Stampa* stresses the purely "cultural" and informative scope of these articles. What marvellous disinterest! What Franciscan good-will is evident in this desire to inform and educate the Italian nation! But let us not press the point. Let us concentrate on the issues of substance, on what real consequences there may be for political affairs and for Italian history in the attitudes represented by the intransigents and the relativists in this current dispute within our party.

To all intents and purposes, *La Stampa* has come out in support of the parliamentary group. The offensive against the intransigents is conducted cleverly, with all the cunning dexterity characteristic of Giolitti's followers. The articles in *La Stampa* are written by a "sympathizer", a useful status for lulling the critical sense of any proletarian reader of the newspaper. They are written by a man of talent, a man who is totally familiar with the critical terminology of Marxism, a man of high culture, a man who is a master of the subtle art of distinguishing between concepts in the light of the most recent advances in idealist philosophy. This "sympathizer", through the natural logic of things and of values, has become the theoretician of the collaborationists. He has provided, in the three articles published to date, a flood of polemical themes, thoughts and logical schemas which will be seized upon in articles and especially in private conversations to support the relativist thesis.

For this reason we believe it is necessary to expose the whole argument to line-by-line criticism. This we must do at length, unfortunately, but the readers of good-will who follow us through to the very end will no doubt be convinced it was worth it, and will see that the polemic between the editors of *Avanti!* and the collaborationists is far more than a skirmish over parliamentary tactics or party discipline, but is in fact the prelude to a formidable battle in which will be thrown into the balance . . . [one line censored] . . . for the next twenty years of Italian history.

The kernel of the dispute, in the words *La Stampa* places in the mouth of the relativists, is this: "The interventionist parties are gradually taking over all the powers and mechanisms of the State machine; they manipulate and control them both directly and indirectly. *Moreover*, they are capitalizing on this control over State powers, this gradual 'annexation' of State power by their parties to the point where they now identify the organization of the State with their own party organizations, in order to weaken, break up and finally reduce to impotence the political instrument of the working class, viz the Socialist Party."

This is the argument developed by the collaborationists, and *La Stampa* applauds it. Why? Because the first and only victims of the "annexationist" phenomenon are Giolitti and his party. Because for Italy this "annexationist" phenomenon represents the beginning of a new form of government, one which presupposes a class State, before which all bourgeois parties are equal, i.e. none has any position of privilege. It represents the beginning of a democratic era, which has emerged not as a result of the good offices of this or that party, but as a result of the inexorable logic of events. Giolitti's exclusive right to govern has received a setback; another party has succeeded in holding power for longer than expected, and is seeking to consolidate its position. The logic of history, in such cases, has led to the following optimal outcome (the history of political parties in England is a case in point): under the impact of lively competition between two equally powerful parties, each fearing the dominance of the other, the State is relieved of the burden of encumbering functions, the administration is decentralized, the tyranny of the bureaucracy is moderated and the seats of power become independent. The State loses its feudal, despotic and militaristic character, and is constituted in such a way that the dictatorship of a dominant party is made impossible, for there will always be the possibility of alternation in power: whoever represents the essence of the political and economic forces of the country succeeds to power. And the country, meanwhile, will see its natural and spontaneous energies arising from economic activity being encouraged, instead of being suffocated by the growth of the parasitic sectors – those sectors who manipulate politics for economic gain and who find in their super-privileges their only reason for existence.

Class, State, Parties

What does the State represent from the socialist point of view? The State is the economic-political organization of the bourgeois class. The

State is the bourgeois class in its modern, concrete expression. The bourgeois class is not a unified entity outside the State. As a result of the working of free competition, new groups of capitalist producers are constantly forming to fulfil the régime's economic capacity. Each one of these groups yearns to remove itself from the bloody struggle of competition through recourse to monopoly. The State's function is to find a juridical settlement to internal class disputes, to clashes between opposed interests; thereby it unifies different groupings and gives the class a solid and united external appearance. Competition between groupings is concentrated at the point of government, of State power. The government is the prize for the strongest bourgeois party or grouping; the latter's strength wins for it the right to regulate State power, to turn it in any particular direction and to manipulate it at any time in accordance with its economic and political programme.

The bourgeois parties and the Socialist Party have utterly different attitudes to the State.

The bourgeois parties are either the representatives of categories of producers, or they are simply a swarm of "coachman-flies" who make not the slightest impact on the framework of the State, but drone their speeches and suck the honey of favouritism.[20]

The Socialist Party is not a sectional, but a class organization: its morphology is quite different from that of any other party. It can only view the State, the network of bourgeois class power, as its antagonistic likeness. It cannot enter into direct or indirect competition for the conquest of the State without committing suicide, without losing its nature, without becoming a mere political faction that is estranged from the historical activity of the proletariat, without turning into a swarm of "coachman-flies" on the hunt for a bowl of blancmange in which to get stuck and perish ingloriously. The Socialist Party does not conquer the State, it replaces it; it replaces the régime, abolishes party government and replaces free competition by the organization of production and exchange.

Does Italy have a class State?

In discussions and polemics, words are too frequently superimposed on historical reality. When speaking of Italy we use words like capitalists, proletarians, States, parties, as if they represented social entities which had reached the peak of their historical development, or a level of maturity comparable to that achieved in the economically advanced countries. But in Italy capitalism is in its infancy, and the law is in no way adapted to the real situation. The law is a modern excrescence on an ancient edifice. It is not the product of economic evolution, but of international political mimicry, of the intellectual evolution of jurisprudence, not of the instruments of labour.

Giuseppe Prezzolini drew attention to this recently in connection with the polemic over "democracy". Behind a façade of democratic institutions, the Italian State has retained the substance and framework of a despotic State (the same can be said of France). There exists a bureaucratic, centralist régime, founded on the tyrannical Napoleonic system, with the express aim of crushing and containing any spontaneous drive or movement. Foreign affairs are conducted in the highest secrecy – not only are discussions not public, but even the terms of treaties are kept from those whom they nevertheless affect. The army (until the war made the antiquated system untenable) had a career structure; it was not the nation in arms. There is a State religion, supported financially and in other ways by the State; there is no separation of church and State nor equality of all religions. Schools are either non-existent, or the teachers, who come from a restricted number of needy folk, given the paltriness of the wages, are not equal to the demands of national education. The suffrage was restricted right up until the last elections, and even today is still far from giving the nation the capacity to express its will.[21]

Free competition, the essential principle of the capitalist bourgeoisie, has not yet touched the most important aspects of national affairs. So we have a position where political forms are mere arbitrary superstructures – they lack any effectiveness, and achieve nothing. The seats of power are still confused and interdependent; there are no large parties organized by the agrarian and industrial bourgeoisies. [8$\frac{1}{4}$ lines censored]

Hence there is no class State in which the principle of free competition ensures efficiency, with great parties representing the vast interests of Piedmont, who in order to keep the country united has dictatorship of one man,[22] the representative of the narrow political interests of Piedmont, who in order to keep the country united, has imposed on Italy a centralized and despotic system of colonial domination. The system is collapsing; new bourgeois forces have arisen and are growing stronger – ever more insistently they are demanding recognition of their interests. Interventionism is a contingent phenomenon, and so is pacifism – the war will not last forever. But what is in imminent danger is the despotic Giolittian State, the entire mass of parasitic interests encrusted upon this old State, and the old enfeebled bourgeoisie which sees its super-privileges threatened by the agitation of bourgeois youth wanting its place in the government, wanting to be part of the free play of political competition. Provided no new event cuts off its evolution, this new bourgeois generation will undoubtedly rejuvenate the State and throw out all the traditional dross. For a democratic State is not the product of a kind heart or a liberal education; it is a necessity of life for large-scale production, for busy exchange, for the concentration of the population in modern, capitalist cities.

*The Unspoken Promise**

These are the terms of the historical situation. In twenty years of unchecked dictatorship, the Giolittian grouping has made a show of formally recognizing freedoms, while in fact it has consolidated the despotic State dear to the memory of Emanuele Filiberto. The weapon of this grouping's dominance, its dictatorship, has now fallen into the hands of the opposition grouping (we cannot call either of them parties, since neither has a political or economic structure). This latter has held on to it for longer than expected and is making use of it, shaping it for its own ends and directing it against the former bosses. If this struggle between bourgeois groupings of sectional interests goes on, a new, liberal State will arise from the furious clash between the two sides. Minor discords will disappear as they are absorbed by higher interests, great parties will form and the era of party government will begin.

The Giolittians would like to avoid the clash. They have no wish to do battle over vast institutional programmes, which could make the nation's political climate uncomfortably hot. The bourgeoisie's god knows whether the nation can stand another overheating, and what

* In a fourth article published today (17 May) *La Stampa* explicitly discusses the possibility of collaboration for peace. *La Stampa* is of the opinion that this discussion must be deferred until the time is ripe. We on the other hand, given the democratic constitution of our party, believe it is necessary for the party federations and local sections to engage in immediate and exhaustive discussion on the question of peace as well, to provide the party with a precise and firm position of intransigent class struggle. We must not allow ourselves to be taken unawares by events, for that would allow the parliamentary group to sow confusion in the party and elevate itself into a pseudo-power. There would be the most colossal *marché de dupes* and the party would emerge from it destroyed for several decades; at the same time, the "realistic" parliamentary forces would triumph. . . . [Note added by Gramsci]

effect such disturbances could have on the proletariat. The Giolittians would like to avoid the clash; they would like to resolve the problems confronting them within the parliamentary arena. In other words, they are carrying on within the same old tradition of minimizing important problems, excluding the nation from political affairs, avoiding any check by public opinion. The Giolittians are in a minority. And behold the socialist deputies hunting butterflies; behold the sirens singing nostalgic arias of freedom, parliamentary control and the need for collaboration if the nation is to move, act and break with inertia.

And see how *La Stampa* comes to their aid with the "sympathizer"'s articles, placing at the service of the wrong cause the fresh culture that unfortunately the parliamentary representatives of the proletariat lack, lending them a "realism", a Marxist Hegelianism that is completely unknown to them. See how the intransigents are presented as mystical dreamers, vacuous abstractionists, even as stupid fools, since their ideas are based on nothing but the simplistic and gratuitous hypothesis that "the workers will return from the trenches with the conscious will and political capacity to achieve socialism". Intransigence is presented as mental and political inertia; the *improved situation* that the proletariat could win for itself is hinted at. An unspoken promise, at once imperious and seductive, underlies the whole approach, fascinating through the very fact of being unexpressed. The dry, nervous sentences seem to become pregnant with mysterious meaning as a result of it. What is insinuated is that the war can be resolved, the problem of peace resolved, through a parliamentary marriage. This is the dominant theme, though it is unspoken. The hope is that in this way, especially in this way, a state of intellectual disorientation will be produced in the proletariat, a blunting of its critical class sense, that may put pressure on the party leadership and so bring about, if not an enthusiastic or even a resigned consent to an alliance, at least a provisional loosening of the parliamentary group from their disciplinary obligations. What counts is parliamentary action, the vote that brings the Giolittians to power. A direct intervention of the proletariat in political affairs will thus be exorcized. The example of Russia and the pathetic end of the anti-Tsarist bourgeoisie, swept away by the rising tide of popular fury, terrifies the timid souls of these democratic troglodytes, these parasites, who are accustomed only to gnaw away in secret at the State finances and hand out regulations and favours in the way that monks hand out macaroni soup to hordes of scabby beggars.

Realism and Empiricism

The point of view that *La Stampa* attributes to the relativists is, even theoretically, fundamentally puerile. Collaboration cannot be justified either by contingent reasons, or by logical theorizing. It is both a historical error and a logical error.

Collaborationist realism is nothing but empiricism. It stands in the same relation to intransigence as a barber-surgeon does to Augusto Murri.[23]

> "History", according to *La Stampa*, "demonstrates how the contradiction between two social theses, i.e. the class antithesis, has always been resolved in a synthesis, as a result of which a part of *what was* is always alienated and *what will be* is increasingly incorporated, so that through these gradual transformations, utopia becomes reality and expresses in its design a correspondingly new social constitution."

History does demonstrate this, it is true, but it does not demonstrate that the "synthesis", "what will be", has been determined in advance by contract. To anticipate the historical synthesis is a puerile dream; to mortgage the future by making a contract between classes is empiricism, not a keen sense of history. In simpler terms we made the same point in last week's issue of *Il Grido*:

> "Day by day, a part of our maximum demands (utopia) is achieved (*what will be*); this part cannot be determined *a priori*, since history is not a mathematical calculation. The part that is achieved is the dialectical outcome of the continuous interplay between social activities and maximum goals. Only if these maximum goals are pursued intransigently can the dialectic be history and not puerile contingency, a solid achievement and not a mistake that has to be undone and corrected."

To put it in even simpler terms, both the intransigent and the relativist are saying: to get a spark, you have to strike the steel with the flint. But while the intransigent is on the point of striking it, the relativist says: hold on, I've got the spark in my pocket. He lights a match and says: here is the spark that would arise from the clash that now serves no purpose. And he lights his cigar. But who could take this miserable conjuring trick for the Hegelian meaning of history, or for Marxist thought?

The Function of the Proletariat

Just as the Socialist Party, the organization of the proletarian class, cannot enter into competition for conquest of the government without losing its intrinsic value and turning into a swarm of coachman-flies, so too it cannot collaborate with any organized bourgeois parliamentary grouping without causing harm, without creating pseudo-facts that will have to be undone and corrected. The political decadence which class collaboration brings is due to the spasmodic expansion of a bourgeois party which is not satisfied with merely clinging to the State, but also makes use of the party which is antagonistic to the State. It thus becomes a hircocervus,[24] a historical monster devoid of will or particular aims, concerned only with its possession of the State, to which it is encrusted like rust. State activity is reduced to mere legalities, to the formal settling of disputes, and never touches the substance; the State becomes a gypsy caravan held together by bit and pieces of wood – a mastodon on four tiny wheels.

If it wishes to maintain and secure its position as the executive organ of the proletariat, the Socialist Party must itself observe and make everyone else respect the method of the fiercest intransigence. And if the bourgeois parties wish to form a government from their own forces, they will have to evolve, put themselves in contact with the country, bring their sectional disputes to an end and acquire a distinctive political and economic structure. If they are unwilling to do so, then, since no party is capable of standing on its own, a permanent and dangerous crisis will arise: a crisis in which the proletariat, firm and tightly-knit, will accelerate its rise and evolution.

Intransigence is not inertia, since it forces others to move and act. It is not based on stupidities, as *La Stampa* so cleverly insinuates. It is a principled policy, the policy of a proletariat that is conscious of its revolutionary mission as accelerator of the capitalist evolution of society, as a reagent clarifying the chaos of bourgeois production and politics and forcing modern States to carry through their natural mission as dismantlers of the feudal institutions that still, after the collapse of the former societies, survive and hinder historical development.

Intransigence is the only way in which the class struggle can be expressed. It is the only evidence we have that history is developing and creating solid, substantial achievements, not "privileged", arbitrary "syntheses" cooked up by mutual agreement between a thesis and an antithesis who have thrown in their lots together, like the proverbial fire and water.

The supreme law of capitalist society is free competition between all social forces. Merchants compete for markets, bourgeois groupings compete for the government, the two classes compete for the State. Merchants seek to create monopolies behind protective legislation. Each bourgeois grouping would like to monopolize the government, and to be able to make exclusive use of the spell-bound energies of the class that is outside governmental competition. Intransigents are free-traders. They do not want barons – whether sugar and steel barons or barons in government. The law of freedom must be allowed unrestricted operation; it is intrinsic to bourgeois activity, the chemical reagent that is continually dissolving its cadres and forcing them to improve and perfect themselves. The powerful Anglo-Saxon bourgeois cadres acquired their modern productive capacity through the implacable play of free competition. The English State has evolved and been purged of its noxious elements through the free clash of bourgeois social forces that finally constituted themselves into the great historic parties, the Liberals and Conservatives. Indirectly from this clash the proletariat has gained cheap bread, and a substantial series of rights guaranteed by law and custom: the right to assemble, the right to strike, an individual security which in Italy remains a chimerical myth.

Class struggle is not a puerile dream – it is an act that is freely determined upon and an inner necessity of the social order. To obstruct its clear course, arbitrarily, by pre-established syntheses hatched by impenitent pipe-dreamers, is a puerile mistake, a historical waste of time. The non-Giolittian parties now in power (quite apart from the fact of the war, which is contingency – and already proving too much for the political capacity of the small nations' ruling classes) are unconsciously carrying out the task of dismantling the feudal, militarist despotic State that Giovanni Giolitti perpetuated in order to make it the instrument of his dictatorship. The Giolittians can feel the monopoly slipping from their grasp. Let them move, by God, let them struggle, let them call on the country to judge. But no, they would rather make the proletariat do their moving for them, or better still, they would like to make the socialist deputies vote.

So intransigence is inertia, is it? Movement, however, is never just a physical act; it is intellectual as well. Indeed, it is always intellectual before becoming physical – except for puppets on a string. Take away from the proletariat its class consciousness, and what have you? Puppets dancing on a string!

Unsigned, *Il Grido del Popolo*, 18 May 1918.

13. THE RUSSIAN UTOPIA

Political constitutions are necessarily dependent on economic structure, on forms of production and exchange. By simply enunciating this formula, many people believe they resolve every economic and political problem, believe they are in a position to impart lessons to right and to left and to judge events with certainty – coming to the conclusion, for example, that Lenin is a utopian, and the unfortunate Russian proletarians are prey to an utterly utopian illusion, so that a terrible awakening implacably awaits them.

The truth is that no two political constitutions are the same, just as no two economic structures are the same. The truth is that the formula is anything but the arid expression of a glaringly obvious natural law. Between the premise (economic structure) and the consequence (political constitution) the relations are anything but simple and direct; and the history of a people is not documented by economic facts alone. The unravelling of the causation is a complex and involved process. To disentangle it requires nothing short of a profound and wide-ranging study of every intellectual and practical activity. This sort of study is possible only after the events have settled into a definite continuity; i.e. long, long after the facts have occurred. The academic may be able to state with certainty that a particular political constitution will not emerge victorious (will not exist on a permanent basis) unless it is attached indissolubly and intrinsically to a particular economic structure – but his statement will have no value other than as a general indication. And while the facts are actually unfolding how could he possibly know what pattern of dependency would be established? The unknowns are more numerous than the facts which can be ascertained and verified, and every single one of these unknowns could upset the eventual conclusion. History is not a mathematical calculation; it does not possess a decimal system, a progressive enumeration of equal quantities amenable to the four basic operations, the solution of equations and the extraction of roots. Quantity (economic structure) turns into quality because it becomes an instrument for action in men's hands – men whose worth is to be seen not only in terms of their weight, their size and the mechanical energy they derive from their muscles and nerves, but in the fact that they have a mind, that they suffer, understand, rejoice, desire and reject. In a proletarian revolution, the unknown variable "humanity" is more mysterious than in any other event. The common mentality of the Russian proletariat, as of other proletariats in general, has never been studied, and perhaps it was impossible to study it. The successful or unsuccessful outcome of the revolution will give us reliable documentary evidence on its capacity to make history. For the moment we can do nothing but wait.

Those who do not wait, but seek to come at once to a definitive judgment, have other aims – current political aims, to be achieved among the people to whom their propaganda is directed. To assert that Lenin is a utopian is not a cultural fact, nor a historical judgment; it is a political act with immediate consequences. To state so bluntly that political constitutions, etc., etc., is not a statement of doctrine, but an attempt to arouse a particular mentality, to direct action one way rather than another.

In life no act remains without consequences, and to believe in one theory rather than another has its own particular impact on activity. Even an error leaves traces of itself, to the extent that its acceptance and promulgation can *delay* (but certainly not prevent) the attainment of an end.

This is a proof that it is not the economic structure which directly determines political activity, but rather the way in which that structure and the so-called laws which govern its development are interpreted. These laws have nothing in common with natural laws – even granting that natural laws too have no objective, factual existence, but are the constructs of our intelligence, designed to facilitate study and teaching.

Events do not depend on the will of a single individual, nor on that even of a numerous group. They depend on the wills of a great many people, revealed through their doing or not doing certain acts and through their corresponding intellectual attitudes. And they depend on the knowledge a minority possesses concerning those wills, and on the minority's capacity to channel them more or less towards a common aim, after having incorporated them within the powers of the State.

Is this because the actions of the majority of individuals are predetermined? No, it is because they have no social goal other than the preservation of their own physiological and moral well-being. So it comes about that they adapt to circumstances and mechanically repeat certain gestures which, through their own experience or through the education they have received (the outcome of others' experience), have proved themselves to be suitable for attaining the desired goal, viz. survival. This similarity in the activity of the majority induces a similarity in its effects, so giving a certain structure to economic activity: there arises the concept of law. Only the pursuit of a higher goal can destroy this adaptation to the environment. If the human goal is no longer mere survival, but a particular standard of survival, then greater efforts are expended and, depending on the dissemination of the higher human goal, the environment is successfully transformed and new hierarchic structures are established. These are different from those which currently exist to regulate the relations between individuals and the State, and gradually come to replace them on a permanent basis as the higher human goal is more and more generally attained.

* * * * *

Anyone who sees these pseudo-laws as absolutes lying outside individual will, rather than as a psychological adaptation to the environment due to the weakness of individuals (to their not being organized, and hence ultimately to the uncertainty of the future), is incapable of seeing that psychology can change, weakness can become strength. Yet such things do happen, and the law, or pseudo-law, is broken. Individuals abandon their solitary existence and associate together. But how does this association come about? It too is conceived only in terms of the absolute law, of normality – and if, through stupidity or prejudice, the law is not immediately obvious, then judgment is decreed and sentence passed: utopia, utopians.

Lenin is thus a utopian. From the time of the Bolshevik revolution to the present day, the Russian proletariat has been utterly utopian in its outlook, and a terrible awakening implacably awaits it.

If one were to apply to Russian history the abstract, general schemas constructed to follow the stages of the normal development of economic and political activity in the Western world, then one's conclusion could not be otherwise. But every historical phenomenon is "individual"; development is governed by a rhythm of "freedom"; research should not concentrate on generic necessity, but on the particular. The causal process must be studied strictly within the context of the Russian events, and not from an abstract and generic perspective.

In the Russian events, there undoubtedly exists a relationship of necessity, and it is a relationship of capitalist necessity. The war was the economic condition, the way of organizing practical daily life, that determined the development of the new State and made the dictatorship of the proletariat necessary: *the war that backward Russia had to fight along the same lines as the more advanced capitalist States.*

In patriarchal Russia those concentrations of individuals that occur in an industrialized society – and which are a necessary condition if proletarians are to recognize each other, to organize and acquire an awareness of their own class strength which could be used to attain a universal human goal – could not occur. A country of extensive agriculture isolates individuals and prevents any uniform and widespread awareness: it makes impossible proletarian social units and the concrete class consciousness that gives people an indication of their own strength and the will to establish a régime legitimized on a permanent basis by that strength.

The war represents the maximum concentration of economic activity in a few hands (the country's leaders); and to it there corresponds a maximum concentration of individuals in the barracks and trenches. Russia at war was truly a utopian country: with barbarian invaders, the State sought to wage a war demanding technology, organization, spiritual resistance – all of which could be achieved only by a people welded together intellectually and physically by factories and machines. The war was utopian, and patriarchal Tsarist Russia collapsed under the extreme strain of the effort which it had chosen to assume and that which was imposed upon it by a battle-hardened enemy. But the conditions created artificially by the all-embracing power of the despotic State brought about the necessary consequences: the broad masses of socially isolated individuals thrust together in a small geographical area developed new feelings and an unprecedented human solidarity. The weaker they had felt in their former state of isolation and the more they had bowed before despotism, the greater was the revelation of their existing collective strength and the more tenacious and adventurous was their will to preserve it, and to build upon it the new society.

Despotic discipline was liquidated; a period of chaos ensued. Individuals sought to organize themselves, but how? And how were they to preserve this human unity that had grown out of suffering?

Here the philistine comes forward and replies: the bourgeoisie had to restore order, because it has always happened in that way – a patriarchal and feudal economy has always been followed by a bourgeois economy and a bourgeois political constitution. The philistine does not see salvation outside the pre-established schemas; he conceives of history as simply a natural organism passing through fixed and predictable stages of growth. If you plant an acorn, you can be sure of getting an oak shoot, and of having to wait a certain number of years for the tree to grow and give fruit. But history is not an oak-tree, and men are not acorns.

Whereabouts in Russia was the bourgeoisie that was capable of fulfilling this task? And if it is a natural law that the bourgeoisie should prevail, how come the law has not operated in this instance?

This particular bourgeoisie has not been seen. A few bourgeois tried to take charge and were crushed. Did they have to win, did they have to take charge, even though they were few in numbers, incapable and weak? But with what holy chrism were these unfortunates anointed to have to triumph even in defeat? Is historical materialism then just a reincarnation of legitimism, of divine right?

Anyone who finds Lenin utopian, who states that the attempt to establish a proletarian dictatorship in Russia is a utopian attempt, cannot be a conscious socialist, and cannot have acquired his culture through study of the doctrine of historical materialism. He is a Catholic, he is bogged down in Holy Writ. It is he who is the real utopian.

* * * * *

Utopianism consists, in fact, in not being able to conceive of history as a free development, in seeing the future as a pre-fashioned commodity, in believing in pre-established plans. Utopianism is philistinism, of the kind Heinrich Heine mocked. The reformists are the philistines and utopians of socialism, just as the protectionists and nationalists are the philistines and utopians of the capitalist bourgeoisie. Heinrich von Treitschke is the foremost exponent of German philistinism (the German State-worshippers are his spiritual heirs), just as Auguste Comte and Hippolyte Taine represent French philistinism and Vincenzo Gioberti the Italian variety. These are the people who preach national historic missions, or believe in individual vocations; all of them are people who mortgage the future and seek to imprison it within their pre-established schemas, people who do not conceive of divine freedom, and are for ever groaning about the past because things have turned out so *badly*.

They do not conceive of history as free development – the birth and free integration of free energies – which is quite different from natural evolution, just as man and human associations are different from molecules and molecular aggregates. They have not learnt that freedom is the inner force in history, exploding every pre-established schema.

The philistines of socialism have degraded and soiled the socialist doctrine, and they become ridiculously angry with anyone who in their eyes does not respect it.

* * * * *

In Russia the free expression of individual and combined energies has swept aside the obstacles of pre-established words and plans. The bourgeoisie sought to impose its hegemony and failed. Accordingly the proletariat has taken over the direction of political and economic life and is establishing its own order. Its own order, not socialism, since socialism is not conjured up through a magical *fiat*. Socialism is a historical process, a development from one social stage to another that is richer in collective values. The proletariat is establishing its own order, it is constructing the political institutions which will ensure the autonomy of this development, which will place its power on a permanent footing.

Dictatorship is the fundamental institution guaranteeing freedom, through its prevention of *coups de main* by factious minorities. It is a guarantee of freedom, since it is not a method to be perpetuated, but a transitional stage allowing the creation and consolidation of the permanent organisms into which the dictatorship, having accomplished its mission, will be dissolved.

* * * * *

After the revolution Russia was not yet free, for there existed no guarantees of freedom, for freedom had not been organized.

The problem was one of creating a hierarchy, but one which was open, which could not harden into a class- and caste-order.

The hierarchy had to have the masses at its base and a single individual at its apex; but it had to form a social unity, whose authority was purely spiritual.

The living nuclei of this hierarchy are the Soviets and the popular parties. The Soviets are the basic organizations to be integrated and developed, and the Bolsheviks become the government party precisely because they maintain that State power should rest upon and be controlled by the Soviets.

Out of the Russian chaos these elements of order are crystallizing; the new order has begun. A hierarchy is being constituted, with the disorganized and suffering masses at the base, then the organized workers and peasants, then the Soviets, then the Bolshevik Party and finally one man: Lenin. It is a hierarchical gradation based on prestige and trust, which formed spontaneously and is maintained through free choice.

Where is the utopianism in this spontaneity? Utopianism is authoritarianism, not spontaneity; and it is utopian to the extent that it becomes careerism, a caste-system, and claims to be eternal. Freedom is not utopian, because it is a basic aspiration; the whole history of mankind consists of struggles and efforts to create social institutions capable of ensuring a maximum of freedom.

Once this hierarchy has been formed, it develops its own logic. The Soviets and the Bolshevik Party are not closed organisms; they are continually being integrated into the society. It is in this that freedom holds sway, that freedom is guaranteed. They are not castes, but organisms in a continuous state of devlopment. They keep in step with the development of consciousness, and represent the capacity of Russian society to become organized.

All workers can take part in the Soviets, and all workers can exert their influence in modifying the Soviets and bringing them closer into line with what is wanted and needed. The direction being taken by Russian political life at the moment is tending to coincide with that taken by the country's moral life, by the universal spirit of the Russian people. There is continual movement between the hierarchical levels: an uncultivated individual gets a chance to improve himself in the discussion over the election of his representative to the Soviet – he himself could be the representative. He controls these organs because he has them constantly under review and near to hand in the community. He acquires a sense of social responsibility, and becomes a citizen who is active in deciding the destiny of his country. Power and awareness are passed on, through the agency of this hierarchy, from one person to many: the society is such as has never before appeared in history.

This is the *élan vital* of the new Russian history. In what way is it utopian? Where is the pre-established plan that people want to bring into operation, even against the grain of economic and political conditions? The Russian revolution is the triumph of freedom; its organization is based on spontaneity, not on the dictates of a "hero" who imposes himself through violence. It is a continuous and systematic elevation of a people, following the lines of a hierarchy, and creating for itself one by one the organs that the new social life demands.

But is it then not socialism? . . . No, it is not socialism in the ridiculous sense that these philistines with their grandiose blue-prints give the word. It is a human society developing under the leadership of the proletariat. Once the majority of the proletariat is organized, social life will be richer in socialist content than it is at present and the process of socialization will be continually intensified and perfected. Socialism is not established on a particular day – it is a continuous process, a never-ending development towards a realm of freedom that is organized and controlled by the majority of the citizens – the proletariat.

Signed A. G., *Il Grido del Popolo*, 27 July 1918. The article was preceded by the following note: "The Turin censorship sabotaged this article in the last number of *Il Grido*, reducing it to just a few disconnected snippets. We reprint it here in its entirety from *Avanti!*, with the certificate of the Milanese and Roman censorships, so that readers may judge the criteria . . . [two lines censored] . . . which regulate journalistic activity in Turin, and because the article is closely related to others which have appeared in *Il Grido* on the Russian revolution."

14. OUR OBLIGATION TO BE STRONG

The Peace is already bearing fruit. Now that the Sacchi decree has been repealed, the relations between individuals and the State are coming to be regulated once again by ordinary statutory laws.[25] The political struggle is once again taking place in an atmosphere of relative freedom – an indispensable condition if citizens are to be able to know the truth; to assemble; to discuss economic and political problems and programmes; to join forces, once they have identified their own aims and consciousness with a social consciousness and set of aims organized into a party.

A huge task faces those workers and peasants in the Socialist Party and the Confederation of Labour who can recognize what organizational forms are necessary and sufficient if there is to be a disciplined and conscious development of the class struggle.

The Socialist Party and the Confederation must achieve their maximum potential in the shortest possible time, given the stage of economic growth that Italy has attained during the four years of war. Our most pressing obligation is to be strong; we must use the existing nuclei of economic and political organization to attract all the citizens who are with us, who accept our programme, who vote for our candidates in the elections, who come out into the street in response to our call. There must be millions of such citizens – and yet the party has at this time no more than 30,000 members. This is a derisory number. It is an index of laxity on our part, an index of our shortcomings in spreading and in hammering into people's consciousness the postulates of the socialist doctrine. This number is the most glaring evidence of our weakness *vis-à-vis* the bourgeois State – the State we seek to overthrow and replace by the dictatorship of the proletariat.

There is little point now in seeking out the reasons for this weakness of ours. We know that the major factor in the past was the backward state of the national economy: in a country where a patriarchal agricultural system, handicrafts and small workshops predominated, it was impossible for a tight-knit and consciously disciplined social democracy to be formed and assert itself with the permanent characteristics of any normal historical process. In Italy there was a tradition of instinctive rebellion that arose in response to the backward character of the despotic State which crushed all individual initiative, and in response to the heavy burden of economic life that drove individuals to emigrate in order to survive. There was no tradition of conscious and well-defined class struggle between capitalism and the proletariat. The Socialist Party enjoyed moments of enormous political prestige amongst the masses, but it did not succeed (and could not succeed) in promoting the formation of organs which could accommodate the masses on a permanent basis. The mass riots were individualistic rather than proletarian class phenomena; they were revolts against a State that was bleeding the nation white through excessive taxation, not against a State recognized as juridical expression of the property-owning class that imposes its privileges through violence.

Four years of war have rapidly changed the economic and intellectual climate. Vast work-forces have come into being, and a deeply-rooted violence in the relations between wage-earners and entrepreneurs has now appeared in such an overt form that it is obvious to even the dullest onlooker. No less spectacular is the open manner in which the bourgeois State, with all its powers and ranks, shows itself to be the instrument of this violence: from a government whose appendages are the mobilization committees,[26] the police force, the *carabinieri* and the prison officials to a judiciary which lends itself to statutory violations promoted by democratic ministers, and to an elective parliament which, through its supine indolence, allows the most basic liberties to be trampled on.

The miraculous growth in industrial output has necessitated a degree of class violence reaching saturation level. But the bourgeoisie has been unable to avoid giving the exploited people a terrible practical lesson in revolutionary socialism. A new class consciousness has emerged; and not only in the factories, but in the trenches as well, where the living conditions are so similar to those in the factory. This consciousness is at an elementary level – no doctrinal awareness has as yet touched it. It is raw material waiting to be moulded. And it must be our doctrines which do the moulding.

The proletarian movement must take these masses into its ranks; it must discipline them and help them to become aware of their own material and intellectual needs. It must educate individuals to forge permanent and organic links of solidarity with each other. It must give each individual a clear, precise, rationally acquired conviction that the only feasible road to individual and social well-being is via political and economic organization; that discipline and solidarity within the ranks of the Socialist Party and the Confederation are inescapable obligations, the obligations of anyone who declares himself a supporter of social democracy.

Today the Socialist Party should number at least 250,000 members, and the Confederation of Labour should represent at least two million workers; *Avanti!* should have a circulation of hundreds of thousands and a readership numbered in millions. Our obligation today has become power; the intellectual climate is no longer hostile to discipline and patient and persevering activity. It is up to us to transform this power into reality, to become the nation's most powerful party, not only in relative terms but absolutely, to become an Anti-state that is prepared to take over from the bourgeoisie all its social functions as ruling class. The workers and peasants, who are already struggling in unison, must step up their individual propaganda; the local branches and active groups of comrades must mount a systematic and tireless propaganda campaign (public talks, debates, meetings) to ensure that all wage-earners join the resistance organizations, and all socialists join the party.

Turin edition of *Avanti!*, 25 November 1918.

15. THE WAR IN THE COLONIES

In a resolution adopted by the Vth Congress of the Algerian Socialist Workers' Party, held at Constantine in 1902, these words were addressed to French capitalists: "If you declare yourselves to be incapable of carrying out this work (viz. educating the indigenous population, giving it a consciousness and moral awareness), thus revealing your impotence, we have the right to ask you just what your intentions in this country are, and whether you have come simply to substitute French for Turkish tax-collectors."

This attitude on the part of the indigenous peoples *vis-à-vis* the metropolitan countries was intensified considerably by the war. The war between capitalist imperialisms was quickly followed by the revolt of the colonies against the victorious imperialisms. During the war the colonies were exploited to an unprecedented degree, using inflexible and inhuman methods such as can be conceived only in periods of civilization as marvellous as that of capitalism. The indigenous peoples of the colonies were not even left their eyes for weeping; foodstuffs, raw materials, everything possible was combed from the colonies to sustain the resistance of the warring metropolitan peoples. This capitalist vice gripping the colonies worked wonderfully: millions and millions of Indians, Egyptians, Algerians, Tunisians and Tonkinese died from hunger or disease as a result of the devastation wrought on the wretched colonial economies by European capitalist competition. How could an Egyptian or Indian peasant make his prices competitive with the English or French or Italian State? Rice, wheat, cotton, wool – all this was secured for us Europeans, while the colonial peasant had to live on herbs and roots, had to subject himself to the harshest *corvée* labour in order to scrape a bare subsistence minimum, and had to suffer the raging of impetuous and untameable famines that rage in India like natural storms. For several years we Europeans have lived at the expense of the death of the coloured peoples: unconscious vampires that we are, we have fed off their innocent blood. As in Balzac's novel, the steaming plate of rice that was placed before our privileged mouths bore within its Hermetic numbers the death sentence of a distant human brother.[27]

But today flames of revolt are being fanned throughout the colonial world. This is the class struggle of the coloured peoples against their white exploiters and murderers. It is the vast irresistible drive towards autonomy and independence of a whole world, with all its spiritual riches. Connective tissues are being recreated to weld together once again peoples whom European domination seemed to have sundered once and for all. Out of its defeat, Turkey itself is regaining prestige, and seems to be setting an example to the world. For millions upon millions of human beings, the Anatolian shepherd is worth more than the Manchester cotton manufacturer; the Sultan is a beacon that beams brighter than any Liverpool ship-owner. Armoured cars, tanks and machine-guns perform wonders on the dark skins of the Arab and Hindu peasants. But the extortions of capitalism are far more deadly than modern weapons: they kill women, children and old people through starvation and despair, by degrees, implacably. And those drowsy coloured peoples are now defying aeroplanes, machine-guns and tanks to win independence; to crush the monstrous vampire that feeds off their flesh and blood.

Signed A. G., *L'Ordine Nuovo*, 7 June 1919, Vol. I, No. 5; under the heading "International Political Affairs".

16. THE REVOLUTIONARY TIDE

International reaction is on the march against the Russian Commune. In the streets and squares of countries all over the world, the revolution is kindling its camp-fires.

The British Imperial government, already incapable of holding back its domestic workers' movement, whose advance is slow but sure and irresistible, with all the massive bulk of a heavy war-tortoise, is now faced with the spectre of innumerable forces right across the vast Empire rising in revolt. In Ireland the military occupation has to be maintained. In Canada the industrial strikes have taken on the overt character of a bid to instal a soviet regime. The Trans-Caspian Bolshevik Red Army has reached the Persian and Afghanistani frontiers, and now controls the highways to India, Turkestan and Asia Minor; it is stirring up, much more effectively than the Germans, the revolt of the Moslem peoples against the exploitative merchants of Christianity. The Afghan Army is threatening to invade India, thereby rekindling the insurrection in the Punjab and Ganges region.

In France the class struggle is spilling out of the putrid reservoirs of the sacred union: the major industrial corporations are wracked by strikes, while the Army is shot through by threatening spasms of rebellion.

In Germany, now that the promises of majoritarianism with its trafficking and petty politics remain unfulfilled, communism stands revealed as the only historical force that can victoriously stand up to Entente imperialism on the level of class struggle, thereby saving the German people from ruin and slavery.

All over the world, in Europe, Asia, America and Africa, the people are intensifying their revolt against the mercantilism and imperialism of capital, which continues to generate antagonisms, conflicts, destruction of life and goods, unsated by the blood and disasters of five years of war. The struggle is now on a world scale. The revolution can no longer be exorcized by democratic swindlers, nor crushed by mercenaries without a conscience.

Unsigned, *L'Ordine Nuovo*, 14 June 1919, Vol. I, No. 6; under the heading "The Week in Politics".

II

L'Ordine Nuovo *and the Factory Councils*

17. WORKERS' DEMOCRACY

An urgent problem today faces every socialist with a keen sense of the historical responsibility that rests on the working class and on the Party representing the critical and active consciousness of the mission of this class.

How are the immense social forces unleashed by the war to be harnessed? How are they to be disciplined and given a political form which has the potential to develop normally and continuously into the skeleton of the socialist State in which the dictatorship of the proletariat will be embodied? How can the present be welded to the future, so that while satisfying the urgent necessities of the one we may work effectively to create and "anticipate" the other?

The aim of this article is to stimulate thought and action. It is an invitation to the best and most conscious workers to reflect on the problem and collaborate – each in the sphere of his own competence and activity – towards its solution, focusing the attention of their comrades and associations on it. Only common solidarity in a work of clarification, persuasion and mutual education will produce concrete constructive action.

* * * * *

The socialist State already exists potentially in the institutions of social life characteristic of the exploited working class. To link these institutions, co-ordinating and ordering them into a highly centralized hierarchy of competences and powers, while respecting the necessary autonomy and articulation of each, is to create a genuine workers' democracy here and now – a workers' democracy in effective and active opposition to the bourgeois State, and prepared to replace it here and now in all its essential functions of administering and controlling the national heritage.

The workers' movement today is led by the Socialist Party and the Confederation of Labour. But for the great mass of workers, the exercise of the social power of the Party and Confederation is achieved indirectly, by prestige and enthusiasm, authoritarian pressure and even inertia. The Party's influence grows daily, spreading to previously unexplored popular strata; it wins consent and a desire to work effectively for the advent of communism among groups and individuals hitherto absent from the political struggle. These disorderly and chaotic energies must be given a permanent form and discipline. They must be absorbed, organized and strengthened. The proletarian and semi-proletarian class must be transformed into an organized society that can educate itself, gain experience and acquire a responsible consciousness of the obligations that fall to classes achieving State power.

It will take the Socialist Party and the trade unions years, even decades of effort to absorb the whole of the working class. These two institutions will not be identified immediately with the proletarian State. In fact, in the Communist Republics, they have continued to exist independently of the State, with the party functioning as a driving force, and the unions as instruments for supervision and the achievement of limited reforms. The Party must carry on its role as the organ of communist education, as the furnace of faith, the depository of doctrine, the supreme power harmonizing the organized and disciplined forces of the working class and peasantry and leading them towards the ultimate goal. It is just because it must strictly carry out this task that the Party cannot throw open its doors to an invasion of new members who are not accustomed to the exercise of responsibility and discipline.

But the social life of the working class is rich in the very institutions and activities which need to be developed, fully organized and co-ordinated into a broad and flexible system that is capable of absorbing and disciplining the entire working class.

* * * * *

The workshop with its internal commissions, the socialist clubs, the peasant communities – these are the centres of proletarian life we should be working in directly.

The internal commissions are organs of workers' democracy which must be freed from the limitations imposed on them by the entrepreneurs, and infused with new life and energy. Today the internal commissions limit the power of the capitalist in the factory and perform functions of arbitration and discipline. Tomorrow, developed and enriched, they must be the organs of proletarian power, replacing the capitalist in all his useful functions of management and administration.

The workers should proceed at once to the election of vast assemblies of delegates, chosen from their best and most conscious comrades, under the slogan: "All power in the workshop to the workshop committees" together with its complement: "All State power to the Workers' and Peasants' Councils".

The communists organized in the Party and the ward clubs would thus be presented with a vast field for concrete, revolutionary propaganda. The clubs, in agreement with the urban party sections, should carry out a survey of the working-class forces in their area, and become the seat of the ward council of workshop delegates, the ganglion co-ordinating and centralizing all the proletarian energies in the ward. The electoral system could vary according to the size of the workshops: the aim, however, should be to elect one delegate for every fifteen workers, divided into categories (as is done in English factories) and ending up, through a series of elections, with a committee of factory delegates representing every aspect of work (manual workers, clerical workers, technicians). The ward committee should also seek to incorporate delegates from other categories of workers living in the ward: waiters, cab-drivers, tramwaymen, railwaymen, road-sweepers, private employees, clerks and others.

The ward committee should be an expression of *the whole of the working class* living in the ward, an expression that is legitimate and authoritative, that can enforce a spontaneously delegated discipline that is backed with powers, and can order the immediate and complete cessation of all work throughout the ward.

The ward committees would grow into urban commissariats, controlled and disciplined by the Socialist Party and the craft federations.

* * * * *

Such a system of workers' democracy (integrated with corresponding peasants' organizations) would give the masses a permanent structure and discipline. It would be a magnificent school of political and administrative experience and would involve the masses down to the last man, accustoming them to tenacity and perseverance, and to thinking of themselves as an army in the field which needs a strict cohesion if it is not to be destroyed and reduced to slavery.

Each factory would make up one or more of the regiments of this army, which would have to have its own N.C.O.'s, its own liaison services, officer corps and general staff, with all powers being delegated by free election and not imposed in an authoritarian manner. Meetings held inside the factory, together with ceaseless propaganda and persuasion by the most conscious elements, should effect a radical transformation of the worker's mentality, should make the masses better equipped to exercise power, and finally should diffuse a consciousness of the rights and obligations of comrade and worker that is both concrete and effective, because spontaneously generated from living historical experience.

* * * * *

As we said above, these brief proposals are put forward only to stimulate thought and action. Every aspect of the problem deserves special study, detailed elucidation, coherent extension and integration. But the concrete and complete solution to the problems of socialist living can only arise from communist practice: collective discussion, which sympathetically alters men's consciousness, unifies them and inspires them to industrious enthusiasm. To tell the truth, to arrive together at the truth, is a communist and revolutionary act. The formula "dictatorship of the proletariat" must cease to be a mere formula, a flourish of revolutionary rhetoric. Whoever wills the end, must will the means. The dictatorship of the proletariat represents the establishment of a new, proletarian State, which channels the institutional experiences of the oppressed class and transforms the social activity of the working class and peasantry into a widespread and powerfully organized system. This State cannot be improvised: the Russian Bolshevik communists laboured for eight months to broadcast and concretize their slogan: "All power to the Soviets" – and the Russian workers had been familiar with Soviets since 1905. Italian communists must treasure this Russian experience and economize on time and effort: the work of reconstruction itself will demand so much time and effort that every day and every act should be dedicated to it.

Unsigned, written by Antonio Gramsci in collaboration with Palmiro Togliatti, *L'Ordine Nuovo*, 21 June 1919, Vol. 1, No. 7.

18. THE RETURN TO FREEDOM...

With the installation of the Nitti–Tittoni ministry, the mythical post-war era, the period of reconstruction, the restoration of peace, has its "official" beginning.[28] Freedom returns. Political parties and social currents are re-established on an equal competitive footing. Competition returns on the economic and political levels.

In our eyes, the arrival of the Nitti ministry represents the first in a series of historical experiences that will mark the process of dissolution of the bourgeois-democratic State. These experiences, in fact, will serve only to demonstrate in practice how insufficient are the national capitalist methods and forms.

* * * * *

The economic and political crisis into which Italian society is plunging can only be understood and resolved within a world context. The essential conditions for its resolution lie beyond the reach and power of the Italian State, and hence of all the ministries that may succeed each other in government.

When we say that the capitalist régime, even in Italy, has reached deadlock in its development, Marxist "pedants" call our statement "anti-scientific" and superficial; apparently it is not based upon the impartial study of the structure of the Italian economy. But capitalism is a world historical phenomenon, and its uneven development means that individual nations cannot be at the same level of economic development at the same time. In the international sphere, competition, the struggle to acquire private and national property, creates the same hierarchies and system of slavery as in the national sphere; and further, competition is eliminated in favour of monopoly far more efficiently in the international than in the national sphere.

Once competitive conditions and struggle have been eliminated from the world, the capitalist régime has reached deadlock. It loses all reason for its existence and progress; its institutions become rigid, parasitical encrustations, without any useful role or prestige. A revolution becomes necessary to restore a dialectical rhythm to world affairs; to reveal a new social class and invest it with the power of controlling history.

Capitalism has not developed to the full in Italy, in the sense that the production of material goods is not industrialized, not intensely industrialized. But the fact that the world has now been subjected to a monopoly of economic exploitation, as well as to an unparalleled political and military supremacy, has had the effect of creating in Italy too the same conditions of a rigidified life lacking all freedom of initiative. Italy today can be compared with Russia under Kerensky: in order to fight the war, which England and Germany stamped with an uncompromisingly capitalist character, Italy had to destroy more than its economic apparatus can reproduce in time to avoid a lingering death. The world situation created by England's victory robs Italy even of the opportunity to work. International economic competition has been eliminated by monopoly. The primary-commodity and consumer-good markets have been cornered. One nation alone can trade, buy and sell as it chooses. All other economic entities have to defer to this single privileged one. The post-war problem can be seen as the need to arrange the totality of means of production in accordance with the requirements of marginal competition; the need to integrate world affairs after English capitalism has exploited all their best and richest opportunities. Hence the problem can be seen to be enormously complicated and difficult, and a solution will be reached only at the cost of new and very grave crises, new and yet vaster destruction.

In a word, Italian capitalism has lost its autonomy; it has lost its freedom and cannot regain it. Any attempt to re-establish competitive conditions by armed force, through a new world war, is doomed from the start; for there is a political and military monopoly that corresponds to the economic monopoly. With the ridiculous petulance of the weak, Italian nationalists are claiming that they have created "rights" for themselves with their victories and sacrifices: they are answered by the very arguments of force which the right they had recognized as being supreme in history engenders. On the capitalist plane it is power today that counts – not the merits, the strengths and victories of the past. If Italian capitalism is to regain any freedom of movement, its national State will have to be capable of producing another Vittorio Veneto[29] – and this time not just against a State that is falling apart like Austria, but against a system of victorious powers like England and France.

* * * * *

The current disorder in Italian economic and political life arises from these conditions of economic and political oppression and slavery systematized on a world scale.

This disorder, which is a function of seemingly perpetual conditions, is complicated by certain residues of the war: the existence of irresponsible groups of armed men, no longer bound by any State discipline or controlled by any responsible central authority, who are striving to establish local Praetorian powers and possibly a national military dictatorship; coalitions of pseudo-political forces, who have no vital and long-term interests to defend or aims to propagate, but only their own individual and contingent interests and goals. Hence they are forever dissatisfied and eager for novelty, and keep the ruling class under constant pressure and in a state of uncertainty about the future. Under such conditions, no ministry could pursue a patient and persevering policy or set itself an overall general programme. For to accomplish such ends would cost great efforts, partial renunciations, and a dense network of individually minor but co-ordinated actions which, when added together, could effect the great transformation of the whole economic and political set-up that is demanded by the international circumstances in which Italy is forced to exist.

* * * * *

Italy would need to dispose of a certain amount of economic and political freedom to be able to make good its destroyed wealth. Neither can be provided by the ministries that may succeed each other in government.

Internal economic freedom would subject the Italian people to starvation. Political freedom would give them the opportunity to organize on a broad basis, to arm themselves, to strengthen themselves and overthrow the State. The bourgeois class is caught on the horns of this dilemma and does not know which way to turn.

This is the hour of the charlatans, of the confidence tricksters, of the grand promises that will never be fulfilled. We are passing through a period of social panic. This dependence of national affairs on external laws, that come into play suddenly and in an unpredictable and uncontrollable fashion, places Italian society in the same position as a collection of animals cowering before an earthquake.

One force alone can arrest this process of dissolution: communism. On the bourgeois plane, international competition has been abolished by monopoly. But a different dialectical rhythm can be substituted for the one that has been smashed: class competition and class struggle. The victory of the Entente has destroyed the balance of powers that underwrote world freedom. With the conclusion of the England–

Germany struggle, the England–Russia clash opened. As a people, the Italian nation can save itself only by taking an active part in the system of proletarian power that is expressed in the Soviet republic; by actively intervening in the international class struggle, where it will find allies in the ranks of the enemy coalition that is oppressing it and reducing it to starvation. But within Italian society, only the proletarian class is equipped to undertake this national and international mission; it must undertake it against the other part of society, by eliminating class struggle and private property within the national sphere. Revolution is the only road to salvation for the whole of Italian society. Only when the proletariat takes State power will the Italian crisis start to be resolved, both nationally and internationally.

Until that day, Italian society and the State will continue to decompose and dissolve, without any hope of reprieve or stabilization. The Nitti ministry is a stage in this process of decomposition; it is the "official" beginning of the State's progress towards dissolution.

Signed A. G., Piedmont edition of *Avanti!*, 26 June 1919, Vol. XXIII, No. 176.

19. THE CONQUEST OF THE STATE

Capitalist concentration, determined by the mode of production, produces a corresponding concentration of working human masses. This is the fact that underlies all the revolutionary theses of Marxism, that underlies the conditions of the new proletarian way of life, the new communist order destined to replace the bourgeois way of life and the disorder of capitalism arising from free competition and class struggle.

In the sphere of general capitalist activity, the worker too operates on the level of free competition; he is an individual and a citizen. But the starting conditions in the struggle are not the same for everyone, at the same time. The existence of private property places the social minority in a privileged position and makes the struggle uneven. The worker is continuously exposed to the most deadly hazards: the bare necessities of his life, his culture, the life and future of his family, are all exposed to the sudden consequences of a shift in the labour market. So the worker attempts to free himself from the sphere of competition and individualism. The principles of combination and solidarity become paramount for the working class; they transform the mentality and way of life of the workers and peasants. Organs and institutions embodying these principles arise; they are the basis upon which the process of historical development that leads to communism in the means of production and exchange begins.

The principle of combination can and must be seen as the central feature of the proletarian revolution. The emergence and development of the Socialist Party and the trade unions in the period preceding this present one (what we might call the period of the Ist and IInd Internationals, or the period of recruitment) was dependent upon this historical tendency.

The development of these proletarian institutions and of the whole proletarian movement in general was not, however, autonomous. It was not constrained wholly by laws inherent in the living conditions and historical experience of the exploited working class. In fact, the laws of historical development were laid down by the property-owning class organized in the State. The State has always been the protagonist of history. In its organs the power of the propertied class is centralized.

Within the state, the propertied class forges its own discipline and unity, over and above the disputes and clashes of competition, in order to keep intact its privileged position in the supreme phase of competition itself: the class struggle for power, for pre-eminence in the leadership and ordering of society.

In this period the proletarian movement was merely a function of capitalist free competition. Proletarian institutions developed in the way they did not through inner necessity, but through external influences: under the formidable pressure of events and compulsions dependent upon capitalist competition. In this lies the origin of the inner conflicts, the deviations, the hesitations, the compromises that characterized the whole of the proletarian movement's existence prior to the current period, and which have now culminated in the bankruptcy of the IInd International.

Some of the currents in the socialist and proletarian movement had emphasized trade-union organization as the essential feature of the revolution, and directed their propaganda and activity accordingly. At one stage, the syndicalist movement appeared in the light of the true interpreter of Marxism, the true interpreter of reality.

The error of syndicalism consists in this: it assumes that the present form and functions of the trade unions are permanent and represent the perennial form of the principle of combination, when in fact they have been imposed on the unions and not proposed by them,[30] and so cannot have a constant and predictable line of development. Syndicalism, while presenting itself as the initiator of a "spontaneist", libertarian tradition, was in fact one of the many disguises of the Jacobin and abstract spirit.

This was the origin of the errors of the syndicalist current, which did not succeed in replacing the Socialist Party in the task of educating the working class for the revolution. The workers and peasants felt that, so long as the propertied class and the democratic-parliamentary State are dictating the laws of history, any attempt to remove oneself from the sphere of operation of these laws is inane and ridiculous. There is no denying the fact that within the general configuration of an industrial society, each man can actively participate in affairs and modify his surroundings only to the extent that he operates as an individual and citizen, as a member of the democratic-parliamentary State. The liberal experience is not worthless and can only be transcended after it has been experienced. The apoliticism of the apoliticals was merely a degeneration of politics: to reject the State and fight against it is just as much a political act as to take part in the general historical activity that is channelled into Parliament and the municipal councils, the popular institutions of the State. The quality of the political act varies. The syndicalists worked outside of reality, and hence their politics were fundamentally mistaken. On the other hand, the parliamentary socialists worked in close contact with events, and while they could make mistakes (and indeed they committed many mistakes, and grievous ones too), they made no mistake in the direction their activity took and so they triumphed in the "competition"; the broad masses, the people who objectively modify social relations through their intervention, favoured the Socialist Party. Notwithstanding all its mistakes and shortcomings, the Party did succeed, in the final analysis, in accomplishing its mission: namely, to transform the proletariat into something whereas before it had been nothing, to give it an awareness, to point the liberation movement firmly and enthusiastically in the direction corresponding in its general lines to the process of historical development of human society.

The gravest error of the socialist movement was akin to that of the syndicalists. Participating in the general activity of human society within the State, the socialists forgot that their role had to be essentially one of criticism, of antithesis. Instead of mastering reality, they allowed themselves to be absorbed by it.

Marxist communists should be characterized by what may be called a "maieutic" mentality. Their activity does not consist in throwing themselves into the course of events determined by bourgeois competition, but in a critical biding of their time. History is a continuous process of development, and hence is essentially unpredictable. But this does not mean that "everything" is unpredictable in the process of development of history; that history, in other words, is the domain of arbitrariness and irresponsible caprice. History is at once freedom and necessity. The institutions in whose development and activity history is embodied emerged and continue to exist because they have a task and a mission to accomplish. There emerged and developed particular objective conditions for the production of material wealth and for men's intellectual awareness. If these objective conditions, which by virtue of their mechanical nature are almost mathematically commensurable, change, then there is a corresponding change in the totality of relations that regulate and inform human society and a change in the degree of men's awareness. The social configuration is transformed; traditional institutions are impoverished and become inadequate to their task, obstructive and lethal. If man's intelligence were incapable of discerning rhythm or establishing a process in the course of history, then civilized life would be impossible. Political genius can be recognized precisely by this capacity to master the greatest possible number of concrete conditions necessary and sufficient to determine a process of development; by the capacity, therefore, to anticipate both the immediate and distant future and on the basis of this intuition to prescribe a State's activity and hazard the fortunes of a people. In this sense Karl Marx was by far the greatest of contemporary political geniuses.

The socialists have simply accepted, and frequently in a supine fashion, the historical reality produced by capitalist initiative. They have acquired the same mistaken mentality as the liberal economists: they believe in the perpetuity and fundamental perfection of the institutions of the democratic State. In their view, the form of these democratic institutions can be corrected, touched up here and there, but in fundamentals must be respected. An example of this narrow-minded conceit is evident in Filippo Turati's Minoan judgment that Parliament stands in relation to the Soviet like the city to the barbarian horde.[31]

Now the modern formula of the "conquest of the State" arises precisely from this mistaken conception of historical development, from the old game of compromise and from the "cretinous" tactics of parliamentarism.

We, on the other hand, remain convinced, in the light of the revolutionary experiences of Russia, Hungary and Germany, that the socialist State cannot be embodied in the institutions of the capitalist State. We remain convinced that with respect to these institutions, if not with respect to those of the proletariat, the socialist State must be a fundamentally new creation. The institutions of the capitalist State are organized in such a way as to facilitate free competition: merely to change the personnel in these institutions is hardly going to change the direction of their activity. The socialist State is not yet communism, i.e. the establishment of a practice and an economic way of life that are communal; but it is the transitional State whose mission is to suppress competition via the suppression of private property, classes and national economies. This mission cannot be accomplished by parliamentary democracy. So the formula "conquest of the State" should be understood in the following sense: replacement of the democratic-parliamentary State by a new type of State, one that is generated by the associative experience of the proletarian class.

And here we come back to our starting-point. We said that the institutions of the socialist and proletarian movement in the period prior to this present one did not develop autonomously, but in response to the general configuration of human society under the sway of the sovereign laws of capitalism. The war turned the strategic conditions of the class struggle upside down. The capitalists have lost their pre-eminence; their freedom is limited; their power is reduced to a minimum. Capitalist concentration has reached its maximum possible level, with the achievement of a global monopoly of production and exchange. The corresponding concentration of the working masses has given the revolutionary proletarian class an unprecedented power.

The traditional institutions of the movement have become incapable of containing such a flowering of revolutionary activity. Their very structure is inadequate to the task of disciplining the forces which have become part of the conscious historical process. These institutions are not dead. Born in response to free competition, they must continue to exist until the last remnant of competition has been wiped out, until classes and parties have been completely suppressed and national proletarian dictatorships have been fused in the Communist International. But beside these institutions, new, State-oriented institutions must arise and develop – the very institutions which will replace the private and public institutions of the parliamentary-democratic State. The very institutions which will replace the person of the capitalist in his administrative functions and his industrial power, and so achieve the autonomy of the producer in the factory. Institutions capable of taking over the management of all the functions inherent in the complex system of relations of production and exchange that link the various workshops of a factory together to form a basic economic unit, link together the various activities of the agricultural industry, and through horizontal and vertical planning have to construct the harmonious edifice of the national and international economy, liberated from the obstructive and parasitical tyranny of the private property-owners.

Never has the drive and revolutionary enthusiasm of the Western European proletariat been more vigorous. It seems to us, however, that a lucid and precise awareness of the end is not accompanied by a comparably lucid and precise awareness of the means that are needed at the present moment to achieve that end. The conviction has already taken root in the masses that the proletarian State is embodied in a system of workers', peasants' and soldiers' Councils. But the tactical conception which will objectively ensure that this State comes into being is not yet evident. So a network of proletarian institutions must be set up without delay, a network rooted in the consciousness of the broad masses, one that can depend on their discipline and permanent support, a network in which the class of workers and peasants, in their totality, can adopt a form that is rich in dynamism and in future growth possibilities. It is certain that if a mass movement with a revolutionary character were to develop today, in the present conditions of proletarian organization, all it would achieve would be a purely formal correction of the democratic State. The outcome would simply be increased powers for the Chamber of Deputies (via a constituent assembly) and the arrival in power of the bungling, anti-communist socialists. The forces of the democratic State and of the capitalist class are still immense: we must not blind ourselves to the fact that capitalism survives mainly through the activity of its sycophants and lackeys, and this scurvy race is certainly far from extinct.

To sum up, the creation of the proletarian State is not a thaumaturgical act: it is itself a process of development. It presupposes a preparatory period involving organization and propaganda. Greater emphasis and powers must be given to the proletarian factory institutions that already exist, comparable ones must be set up in the villages, they must be composed of communists conscious of the revolutionary mission these institutions must accomplish. Otherwise all our enthusiasm, all the faith of the working masses, will not succeed in preventing the revolution from degenerating pathetically into a new parliament of schemers, talkers and irresponsibles, nor in avoiding the necessity to make further and more dreadful sacrifices to bring about a proletarian State.

Unsigned, *L'Ordine Nuovo*, 12 July 1919, Vol. 1, No. 9.

20. TOWARDS THE COMMUNIST INTERNATIONAL

At the last minute, the men who lead the French General Confederation of Labour and the men who led the Italian railwaymen's union refused to support the proletarian demonstration of 20–21 July in solidarity with the Russian and Hungarian Soviet Republics.[32] Here we have a problem which we must face squarely and resolve: how was it possible for the leaders of the organized French proletariat and of the Italian railwaymen, men carrying a freely-contracted responsibility towards the masses, to commit such a grave act of treachery and disloyalty? Was it a human failing? Can it be expected that, if certain individuals are removed from leading positions, similar cases will not occur again? Or was this treachery and disloyalty favoured and made possible by real objective conditions which could be repeated in the future?

Posed in these terms, this problem becomes the fundamental problem of the proletarian revolution.

* * * * *

In Russia the Soviet State was slowly formed (over the period from March to November 1917) as the reaction of the industrial workers, the poor peasants and the troops against the social hierarchies generated by universal suffrage and bureaucratic careerism. The proletariat became aware of this intrinsic need during the war, and created some rudimentary, experimental organs of self-government. Kerensky's democratic régime allowed the Bolshevik communists to mount a systematic and concentrated propaganda campaign, as a result of which the workers and peasants gradually acquired a precise and lucid awareness of the importance of the new institutions. These institutions grew, they encompassed more and more administrative functions, until finally, upon becoming the constituent organs of the proletarian State, they expressed the sovereign autonomy of labour in the production and distribution of material goods and in all the internal and external relations of the State.

Coming back to the countries of Western Europe, a similar process of development of the socialist and proletarian movement has not even started in France, has barely begun in Italy, already appears promising in England. In these countries, however, the proletariat is still organized essentially along parliamentary and bureaucratic lines and not on the Soviet model. There is a potent revolutionary ferment in these countries, but its thrust is not being channelled into the sort of structures needed to accomplish its ends. Good-will on the part of individuals can be instrumental in producing revolutionary demonstrations, like the strike on 20–21 July of Italian workers and peasants belonging to the Socialist Party and the General Confederation of Labour. But by the same token, ill-will can brake enthusiasm and sabotage the revolution. If such a state of affairs is allowed to continue, it will inevitably result in the most painful struggles and disorder.

* * * * *

To belong to the Communist International means something quite different from belonging to the First or Second Internationals. To opt for the Communist International is to opt for the Soviet conception of the State and to repudiate any residue of democratic ideology, even within the existing organization of the socialist and proletarian movement. The Communist International already has a practical reality in the Russian and Hungarian Republics. The existence of these two proletarian states means that the actions of the workers and peasants of western Europe should be directed towards a particular end: that of preventing the bourgeois governments from strangling the Soviet republics. Hence we must work inside the productive process of capitalism, to control it and immobilize it in so far as its activity is directed against Russia and Hungary.

An action of this sort cannot be carried out by the Socialist Party and craft federations: only the workers and peasants themselves can carry it out on a sustained basis, in the factories, the railway stations, the mines, the ports, on the steamships and the farms. And if it is to be carried out successfully, the proletarian organs that emerged during the war must be further developed and systematized on a national and international basis: the anti-State must be organized.

To belong to the Communist International, therefore, is to link one's own institutions organically to the Russian and Hungarian proletarian States. The Communist International is not a bureaucratic headquarters of "leaders" of the masses; it is a mass historical consciousness, objectified in a vast and complex general movement of the international proletariat. Hence, it must consist of a network of proletarian institutions which themselves give birth to a complex and well-articulated hierarchy, capable of waging all aspects of the class struggle such as it takes place today both nationally and internationally. These institutions must form a homogeneous continuity within Western Europe and with the State organs of the Russian and Hungarian Communist Republics.

* * * * *

During the war, to meet the demands of the struggle against Imperial Germany, the states making up the Entente formed a reactionary coalition with its economic functions powerfully centralized in London and its demagogy choreographed in Paris. The enormous administrative and political apparatus that was set up at that time is still in existence: it has been further strengthened and perfected, and is now effectively the instrument of Anglo-Saxon world hegemony. With Imperial Germany prostrated, and the Social-Democratic *Reich* incorporated into the global politico-economic system controlled by Anglo-Saxon capitalism, capitalism has now forged its own unity and turned all its forces to the destruction of the Communist Republics.

This complex and massive formation of capitalism must be opposed by an equally massive organization of the international proletariat, whose interests lie in preventing Russia and Hungary from being crushed. The most powerful weapon that the capitalist coalition is directing against the two proletarian States is the economic blockade, the lock-out that reduces its victims to starvation. The peoples of Russia and Hungary are now in the same position as a mass of workers who have gone on strike and subsequently been locked-out by the employer to force them into unconditional surrender. But in this case the usual forms of solidarity with workers who are locked-out will not suffice. What is needed is revolutionary solidarity, expressed by the permanent exercise of control over production and exchange. Its aim must be to limit – and eventually to destroy – the power of the capitalist over the instruments of production and exchange. It must aim to ban the manufacture of certain products, to ban the export of certain products, to ban the export of arms and munitions stock-piled after the armistice and force the resumption of trade with Russia and Hungary. A systematic and concentrated campaign has to be mounted by the workers and peasants of the Entente, through organs which are adequate to the task – and these can be neither the socialist parties nor the craft federations.

These institutions will carry on fulfilling their mission of educating and co-ordinating the various aspects of proletarian activity, but at this point they can no longer cope with the task of disciplining and leading the whole movement. Their adhesion to the Communist International will be devoid of any historical sense if it does not signify the adhesion of the totality of the proletarian masses, conscious of their mission and organized in such a way as to be able to accomplish it. This must be the immediate task of the communist fraction of the Italian Socialist Party: to promote the development of proletarian factory institutions wherever they exist and to set them up where they have not yet emerged. To co-ordinate them locally and nationally. To make contact with similar institutions in France and England. And finally – from the base upwards, from the inner reality of the industrial process, from the capillary sources of capitalist profit (for whose protection and expansion all the various functions of the democratic-parliamentary State are organized) – to generate teeming communist forces who, quite independently of the good or ill will of "leaders", will defend the Republics in the first instance and, in subsequent stages of the general process of development of revolutionary consciousness and power, will bring into being the International of Communist Republics.

Unsigned, *L'Ordine Nuovo*, 26 July 1919, Vol. 1, No. 11.

21. WORKERS AND PEASANTS

During the war and as a result of the necessities of the war, the Italian State took over regulation of the production and distribution of material wealth as one of its functions. A sort of industrial and commercial trust has been set up, a sort of concentration of the means of production and exchange, an equalization of the conditions of exploitation of the proletarian and semi-proletarian masses – which have had their revolutionary effects. One cannot hope to understand the essential character of the current period if one fails to take account of these phenomena and their psychological consequences.

* * * * *

In the countries which are still backward in capitalist terms, like Russia, Italy, France and Spain, there is a clear separation between town and country, between workers and peasants. In agriculture, more or less feudal economic patterns have survived, together with a corresponding mentality. The idea of the modern liberal-capitalist State is still unknown. Economic and political institutions are not seen as historical categories, i.e. as categories having a beginning, then undergoing a process of development, and finally dissolving, after having created the conditions for a higher form of social system. Instead, they are seen as natural, perpetual, irreducible categories. In reality big landed property has remained impervious to free competition – and the modern State has respected its feudal essence, devising juridical formulae such as *fidei commissum*, which effectively perpetuate the investitures and privileges of the feudal régime.[33] Hence the peasant still has the mentality of a glebe serf: he erupts in violent revolt against the "gentry" every now and then, but he is incapable of seeing himself as a member of a collectivity (the nation for the landholders, the class for the proletarians), nor can he wage a systematic and permanent campaign designed to alter the economic and political relations of society.

Under such conditions, the psychology of the peasants was inscrutable: their real feelings remained occult, entangled and confused in a system of defence against exploitation that was merely individualist, devoid of logical continuity, inspired largely by guile and feigned servility. Class struggle was confused with brigandage, with blackmail, with burning down woods, with the hamstringing of cattle, with the abduction of women and children, with assaults on the town hall – it was a form of elementary terrorism, without long-term or effective consequences. Objectively, therefore, the peasant's psychology was restricted to a tiny number of elemental feelings dependent upon the social conditions created by the democratic-parliamentary State. The peasant was left completely at the mercy of the landowners and their hangers-on and corrupt public officials; his principal concern was to defend himself physically from the assaults of the elements, and from the abuses and cruel barbarities of the landowners and public functionaries. The peasant has always lived outside the rule of law – he has never had a juridical personality, nor a moral individuality. He lives on as an anarchic element, an independent atom in a chaotic tumult, constrained only by his fear of the police and the devil. He had no understanding of organization, of the State, of discipline. Though patient and tenacious in his individual efforts to wrest a lean harvest from nature and capable of making unheard of sacrifices in his family life, he was impatient and savagely violent in class struggle, incapable of setting himself a general goal for action and pursuing it with perseverance and systematic struggle.

Four years of the trenches and exploitation of his blood have radically changed the peasant psychology. This change occurred especially in Russia, and was one of the essential factors in the revolution. What industrialism had not brought about in its normal process of development was produced by the war. The war forced those nations which were less advanced in capitalist terms, and hence less endowed with technological equipment, to enrol all available men and to oppose wave after wave of living flesh to the war instruments of the Central Powers. For Russia, the war meant that individuals who had previously been scattered over a vast territory came into contact with each other. It meant that humans were concentrated together uninterruptedly for years on end under conditions of sacrifice, with the ever present danger of death, and under a uniform and uniformly ferocious discipline. The lengthy duration of such conditions of collective living had profound psychological effects and was rich in unforeseen consequences.

Selfish, individual instincts were blunted; a common, united spirit was fashioned; feelings were universalized; the habit of social discipline was formed. The peasants came to see the State in all its complex grandeur, its measureless power, its intricate construction. They came to see the world no longer as something infinitely vast like the universe and as circumscribed and small as the village bell-tower, but as a concrete reality consisting of States and peoples, social strengths and weaknesses, armies and machines, wealth and poverty. Links of solidarity were forged which would have taken decades of historical experience and intermittent struggles to form. Within four years, in the mud and blood of the trenches, a spiritual world emerged that was avid to form itself into permanent and dynamic social structures and institutions.

In this way there emerged the Councils of military delegates on the Russian front, and the peasant soldiers were able to play an active part in the Soviets of Petrograd, Moscow and the other industrial centres and so acquired a consciousness of the unity of the working class. In this way too, as fast as the Russian army was demobilized and the soldiers returned to their jobs, the entire territory of the Empire, from the Vistula to the Pacific, became covered in a tight-knit network of local Councils, basic organs of the Russian people's reconstruction of their State. It was on this new psychology that the communist propaganda which radiated out from the industrial cities was based, and the same was true of the new social hierarchies freely advocated and accepted as a result of the experience of collective revolutionary living.

Historical conditions in Italy were not and are not very different from those in Russia. The problem of the class unification of the workers and peasants is expressed in identical terms: it will be achieved through the practice of the socialist State and will be based on the new psychology created by communal life in the trenches.

Italian agriculture must radically transform its procedures if it is to emerge from the crisis caused by the war. So much livestock was destroyed that machinery will have to be introduced: there will have to be a rapid transition to centralized industrial farming, with generously equipped technical institutions available. But a transformation of this order could not occur under a régime of private property without provoking a disaster: it will have to be effected by a socialist State, and in the interests of the peasants and workers combined in communist labour units. In the past, the introduction of machinery into the process of production has always provoked profound unemployment crises, only gradually overcome through the elasticity of the labour market. Today, labour conditions have been radically altered, and agrarian unemployment has already become an insoluble problem as a result of the virtual impossiblity of emigrating. The industrial transformation of agriculture can only be achieved with the agreement of the poor peasants, via a dictatorship of the proletariat that is embodied in Councils of industrial workers and poor peasants.

Factory workers and poor peasants are the two driving forces of the proletarian revolution. For them, especially, communism is a vital necessity: its advent signifies life and liberty, while the continued existence of private property signifies the imminent danger of being crushed, of losing everything, including life itself. They are the revolution's irreducible element; they sustain revolutionary enthusiasm; they represent the iron will not to accept compromises, but to carry on implacably until everything has been accomplished, without either being demoralized by temporary and partial set-backs or manufacturing too many illusions as a result of easy victories.

They represent the backbone of the revolution, the iron battalions of the advancing proletarian army, which overturns obstacles by its sheer weight or lays siege to them with its human tides that demolish and corrode, through patient work and tireless sacrifice. For them, communism represents civilization: it stands for the system of historical conditions in which they will acquire a personality, a dignity, a culture, and through which they will become a spirit creating progress and beauty.

Any revolutionary work has a chance of succeeding only to the degree that it is based on the necessities of their life and on the needs of their culture. It is essential that the "leaders" of the socialist and proletarian movement understand this. And it is essential that they see the urgency of the problem of giving this irrepressible revolutionary force the structure best adapted to its diffuse mentality.

In the backward conditions of the pre-war capitalist economy, there was no scope for the emergence and development of mass peasant organizations on a wide scale, in which the agricultural workers could acquire an organic conception of class struggle as well as the discipline needed to reconstruct the State after the capitalist catastrophe.

The spiritual advances made during the war, the communistic experiences accumulated over four years of bloody exploitation, undergone collectively, standing elbow to elbow in the muddy, bloody trenches – all this will be frittered away unless every individual is involved in organs of a new collective life. In the functioning and practice of these, the advances can be consolidated, the experiences developed and linked and directed consciously towards the accomplishment of a concrete historical goal. Organized in this way, the peasants will become an element of order and of progress; left to themselves, incapable as they are of waging any systematic and disciplined action, they will become a disordered rabble, a tumultuous horde driven to the cruellest barbarities by the unprecedented sufferings which are becoming ever more frighteningly evident.

* * * * *

The communist revolution is essentially a problem of organization and discipline. Given the actual objective conditions of Italian society, the protagonists of the revolution will be the industrial cities, with their tightly packed and homogeneous masses of factory workers. Hence we must devote maximum attention to the new life that the new form of class struggle is evoking within the factory and in the process of industrial production. But with the forces of the factory workers alone, the revolution will not be able to establish itself on a stable and widespread basis. The cities must be welded to the countryside; institutions of poor peasants must be set up in the countryside, on which the Socialist State can be established and developed, and through which the Socialist State will be able to foster the introduction of machinery and direct the immense process of transformation of the agrarian economy. In Italy this undertaking is not so difficult as it might seem. During the war, vast numbers of the rural population entered the urban factories; communist propaganda rapidly took root among them. They can now act as a bond between the town and countryside. They must be used to mount an intense propaganda campaign in the countryside, to destroy suspicion and resentment. Taking advantage of their profound understanding of the rural psychology and the confidence they inspire, they must be used precisely to begin the activity necessary to bring about the emergence and development of the new institutions that will draw the vast forces of the agricultural workers into the communist movement.

Unsigned, *L'Ordine Nuovo*, 2 August 1919, Vol. 1, No. 12.

22. ELECTORALISM

In expounding the grounds for his abstentionism, Comrade Cerri confuses the contingent fact of participating in elections with a "faith" in Parliament.[34] Like other comrades in the Turin section of the Socialist Party, he starts from a mistaken interpretation of the programme agreed upon at the Moscow Congress of the IIIrd International.[35] This programme polemicizes against those self-styled revolutionary tendencies that have not yet grasped the true character of the proletarian dictatorship and see Soviets and Parliament – i.e. the proletarian and bourgeois dictatorships, socialism and "democracy" – as being able to exist alongside each other. In other words, the Moscow programme is referring to those countries (Germany and Austria) where a Soviet system is already in existence. In these countries, the right-wing Social-Democrats support the Constituent Assembly as against the Soviets and encourage the proletarians to support parliament as the only organ capable of achieving socialism, while the centrists (Kautskyists, etc.) strive to get Parliament to "legalize" the Soviets and thus arrive at a State system with two chambers – one political (Parliament) and the other economic (the Congress of Soviets). In Italy, Soviets do not yet exist, indeed there has not even been any concrete attempt to promote their organic formation. Hence to abstain from parliamentary elections in Italy has no Sovietist significance; it does not amount to a "choice". As long as it is not possible to choose, one cannot abstain from participating in parliamentary elections, in which the differences between political forces and their relative strengths are recorded. As long as Soviets do not exist, the cry "All power to the Soviets" is inane and indeed could actually damage the fortunes of the revolution, by discrediting the Soviet movement itself.

Signed A. G., Piedmont edition of *Avanti!*, 23 August 1919, Vol. XXIII, No. 232.

23. THE DEVELOPMENT OF THE REVOLUTION

The basic theses of the Communist International can be summarized as follows.

1. The 1914–18 World War represents the coming to pass on a tremendous scale of that moment in the process of development of modern history which Marx summed up in the expression: the catastrophe of the capitalist world.

2. Only the working class can save society from plunging into the abyss of barbarism and economic ruin towards which the enraged and maddened forces of the propertied class are driving it. It can do this by organizing itself as the ruling class, to impose its own dictatorship in the politico-industrial field.

3. The proletarian revolution is imposed rather than proposed. The conditions created by the war – utter exhaustion of the economic resources needed to satisfy the basic requirements of collective and individual life; concentration of the international means of production and exchange in the hands of a tiny clique of shareholders; colonial subjection of the whole world to Anglo-Saxon capitalism; within individual nation states, concentration of the propertied class's political forces – can lead to three possible outcomes. Either a conquest of social power on the part of the working class, using its own methods and instruments, in order to put a stop to the dissolution of the civilized world and lay the foundations of a new order, an order which will favour a resumption of productive activities and the generation of a drive towards higher forms of production and social existence. Or the death of the majority of the workers through starvation and exhaustion. Or an endless slaughter in society until a balance has been restored between capitalistically managed production and the consumer masses.

* * * * *

Meanwhile, what adhering to the Communist International means in practical terms is this: it means being convinced of the urgent need to organize the dictatorship of the proletariat, i.e. to equip the proletarian movement with the appropriate structures and procedures for the proletarian political system to become a normal and necessary phase of the class struggle waged by the worker and peasant masses. And by contrast with what is asserted in the programme of the Italian Socialist Party adopted at Genoa in 1892, it further implies that "the proletariat's activity and strength" should take the following two forms:

1. Organization of the workers and peasants on a production unit basis (factory, farm, village, city, region, nation) in order to allow the masses to become accustomed to self-government both in the industrial and political fields.

2. The waging of a systematic and incessant propaganda campaign on the part of communist elements to win over these proletarian organs as fast as possible and centralize them into a new type of State (the State of Workers' and Peasants' Councils) – a State which will embody the dictatorship of the proletariat, after the dissolution of the bourgeois politico-industrial system.

These fundamental innovations need to be inserted into the 1892 Programme as a result of the concrete experiences of the workers of Russia, Hungary, Austria and Germany in their revolutionary activities. They may be assumed to be a necessary, intrinsic aspect of the industrial development of world capitalist production, for they have been carried out by English and American workers, quite independently from the consequences of general political circumstances (military defeat, etc.), as a normal reflection of the class struggle in the most intensely capitalist countries.

* * * * *

The concrete revolutionary experiences of the international working class can be summarized in the following theses.

1. The dictatorship of the proletariat, which must establish communist society by eliminating classes and the incurable conflicts of capitalist society, is the moment of most intense activity in the class organization of the workers and peasants.

2. The existing system of organization of the proletarian class – combination on a craft basis (trade unions), on an industrial basis (federations), and on a local and national basis incorporating all trades (Chambers of Labour and the General Confederation of Labour) – which arose in response to the need to organize competition in the sale of the labour-commodity, is not suited, on account of its essentially competitive nature, to administer production along communist lines, nor to embody the dictatorship of the proletariat. Organization on a craft basis has been an effective instrument for defence of the workers,

since it has successfully limited the great power and freedom of the capitalist class, by forcing recognition of the rights of the oppressed on the questions of hours and wages. This form of organization will continue to fulfil a similar function under the proletarian dictatorship and communist society, functioning as the technical organ which settles conflicts of interest between categories of workers, and standardizes levels of communist retribution on a national and international scale.

3. The workers' organization which will exercise communist social power and embody the proletarian dictatorship can only be a system of Councils, elected on a work-place basis and linked flexibly in such a way that they correspond to the process of industrial and agricultural production. They will have to be co-ordinated and graduated on a local and national basis, in such a way as to realize the unity of the working class, over and above the various categories determined by the division of labour.

Even today this process of unification is taking place within the Chambers of Labour and the Confederation; but it has not resulted in any effective cohesion of the masses, for it consists merely of irregular and haphazard contacts between headquarters and individual leaders. At the work-place, on the other hand, this unification will have great and permanent effectiveness, since it will be a product of the harmonious and articulated system of the industrial process in its living immediacy; since it will be based on creative activity, which binds men's wills together in brotherhood and unites the interests and feelings of the producers.

4. Only on the basis of this type of organization will it ever be possible to make the work units aware of their capacity to produce and exercise sovereignty (sovereignty must be a function of production), without need for the capitalist and an indefinite delegation of political power. To make the producers aware in other words of the fact that, within the general process of production of material goods and hence within the process of historical creation, their organized community can replace the proprietor or his hired thugs in the running of industry and responsibility for production.

5. The various work units will have to be co-ordinated via higher organs, which will be linked on a local basis or on the basis of different industrial sectors within the same territorial unit of production (provinces, regions, nations), the whole making up the system of Councils. The replacement of individual proprietors by productive communities, linked and intertwined in a tight-knit network of mutual

relations designed to protect all the rights and interests deriving from labour, will result in the elimination of competition and false freedom, thereby laying the foundations for the organization of communist freedom and civilization.

6. Once they are bonded together in productive communities, the workers will be led automatically to express their will to power in terms of principles which are strictly organic to the relations of production and exchange. All mythical, utopian, religious and petty-bourgeois ideologies will drop away from the average proletarian psychology. A communist psychology will become rapidly and lastingly consolidated, as a constant leaven of revolutionary enthusiasm, tenacious perseverance in the iron discipline of work and resistance against any open or underhand assault of the past.

7. The communist party can have no competitors within the world of work itself. In this current phase of the class struggle, pseudo-revolutionary parties are flourishing: the Christian socialists (who find a ready reception among the peasant masses); the "true" socialists (war veterans, petty-bourgeois elements, and all those restless spirits who are eager for any kind of novelty); the individualist libertarians (noisy conventicles of unsatisfied vanities and capricious, chaotic tendencies). These parties have come out onto the street and are deafening the electoral markets with their empty and inconclusive speech-mongering, their amazing and irresponsible promises, and their loud appeals to the lowest passions of the people and their narrowest selfish interests. These parties would have no hold whatsoever over individual workers, if the latter were to express their social preferences within the work community, face to face with the machine that enslaves them today but must become their slave tomorrow, instead of in the tumult and carnival atmosphere of Parliament.

8. The revolution is not a thaumaturgical act, but a dialectical process of historical development. Every industrial or agricultural workers' Council that arises around the work unit is a point of departure for this development: it is a step on the road to communism. What communists have to do now is campaign for the establishment and diffusion of workers' and peasants' Councils; ensure that they are linked and co-ordinated systematically in such a way that they culminate in a general congress at their apex expressing their national unity; and finally wage an intensive propaganda campaign to win a majority within them. The pressure of this new flowering of strength arising irresistibly from the ranks of the broad masses will lead to a

violent clash between the two classes and the advent of the proletarian dictatorship. If the foundations of the revolutionary process are not rooted within productive life itself, the revolution will remain a sterile appeal to the will, a false mirage – and chaos, disorder, unemployment and hunger will swallow up and crush the finest and most vigorous proletarian forces.

Unsigned, *L'Ordine Nuovo*, 13 September 1919, Vol. I, No. 18.

24. TO THE WORKSHOP DELEGATES OF THE FIAT CENTRO AND BREVETTI PLANTS

The new form which the internal commission has assumed in your plants with the election of workshop delegates, together with the discussions that led up to and accompanied this transformation, have not passed unnoticed amongst the workers and bosses of Turin. On the one hand, the workers in other plants in the city and province are preparing to follow your lead. On the other hand, the owners and their direct agents, the managers of the great industrial enterprises, are watching the movement with mounting interest: they are asking themselves and asking you what can be the ultimate goal of all this, what can be the programme that the Turin working class is pursuing.

We are well aware of the fact that our newspaper has played a substantial part in bringing this movement into existence. In its pages, not only has the question been examined from a theoretical and general point of view, but we have also brought together and analysed the results of experiences in other countries, to furnish material for the study of practical applications. We know, however, that our work has been of value to the extent that it has satisfied a need, and has helped to give concrete expression to an aspiration that was latent in the consciousness of the working masses. This is why we were so rapidly understood; this is why the transition from discussion to realization was effected so rapidly.

We believe that this need and this aspiration, whence the movement to renew working-class organization initiated by you draws its origins, are inscribed in reality; that they are a direct consequence of the point reached, in the process of its development, by the social and economic system based on private appropriation of the means of production and exchange. Today the worker on the shopfloor and the peasant in the fields, the English miner and the Russian muzhik – all the workers of the whole world – are sensing more or less certainly, and experiencing more or less directly, that truth which studious men had foreseen, and about which they are growing more and more certain when they observe the events of this phase in the history of humanity. We have reached the point at which the working class, if it does not wish to fail in the task of reconstruction which is inherent in its actions and its will, must begin to organize itself positively and appropriately for the ends to be accomplished.

Now if it is true that the new society will be based on work and on co-ordination of the producers' energies, then tomorrow the work-places where the producers live and function together will be the centres of the social organism and will have to take the place of the directive bodies of present-day society. In the early stages of the workers' struggle, organization along craft lines was most suitable for the purposes of defence, for the requirements of the struggle for immediate improvements in economic conditions and the work régime. So too today, when reconstructive aims are beginning to emerge and take on increasing coherence in the minds of the workers, it is essential that a factory organization should arise parallel to and in support of the craft one, as a true school for developing the reconstructive capacities of the workers.

The working masses must take adequate measures to acquire complete self-government, and the first step along this road consists in disciplining themselves, inside the work-shop, in the strictest possible, yet autonomous, spontaneous and unconstrained manner. Nor can it be denied that the discipline which will be established along with the new system will lead to an improvement in production – but this is nothing but the confirmation of one of the theses of socialism: the more the productive human forces acquire consciousness, liberate themselves and freely organize themselves by emancipating themselves from the slavery to which capitalism would have liked to condemn them forever, the better does their mode of utilization become – a man will always work better than a slave. So to those who object that by this method we are collaborating with our opponents, with the owners of the factories, we reply that on the contrary this is the only means of letting them know in concrete terms that the end of their domination is at hand, since the working class is now aware of the possibility of *doing things itself*, and doing them well. Indeed from one day to the next it is acquiring an ever clearer certainty that it alone can save the entire world from ruin and desolation. Hence every action that you undertake, every battle that is waged under your leadership, will be illuminated by the light of that ultimate goal which is in all of your minds and intentions.

And so even the acts of apparently little importance in which the mandate conferred upon you is concretized will acquire an enormous value. Since you were elected by a work-force in which there are still many unorganized elements, your first concern naturally will be to bring these into the ranks of the workers' organizations – a task which, moreover, will be facilitated by the fact that these people will see in you their ready defenders, their guides, their initiators into the life of the factory. You will show them through example that a worker's strength lies wholly in union and solidarity with his comrades.

You will also have the job of ensuring that the rules of work fixed by the trade federations and accepted in the agreements are respected in the workshops; for in this area too, the slightest departure from the established principles can constitute a grave threat to the worker's rights and person – and you will be his inflexible and tenacious defenders and guardians. And since you yourselves will be living continuously on the job in the midst of the workers, you will be in a position to know what modifications should be made in the rules from time to time, as a result of technological progress or the improved consciousness and capacity of the workers themselves. In this way a shop-floor *way of life* will be established, initial germ of a true and effective labour legislation, i.e. laws which the producers will enact and lay down for themselves. We feel sure that the importance of all this does not escape you, and that it is equally clear to all the workers who have promptly and enthusiastically grasped the value and significance of the task you have set yourselves. The era of the active intervention of the labour forces themselves in the fields of technique and discipline has begun.

In the technical field you can, on the one hand, do an extremely useful job of collecting precious data and factual material for both the trade federations and the central directive bodies of the new factory organizations. In addition, you will see to it that the shop-floor workers acquire more and more skill, and that the petty feelings of craft jealousy that still divide them are banished forever. In this way you will prepare them for the day when they are no longer working for the boss but for themselves, and will have to be united and in solidarity if the strength of the great proletarian army, whose first units they represent, is to be enhanced. Why could you not set up, inside the factory, appropriate instruction departments, real vocational schools, in which every worker, rousing himself from the fatigue that brutalizes, may open his mind to knowledge of the processes of production and so better himself?

Certainly, if all this is to be accomplished then discipline will be needed, but the discipline you will require from the working masses will be quite different from the kind imposed and demanded by the boss, who derived his strength from the property rights that gave him a position of privilege. You will derive your strength from another right, the right of labour: this has for centuries been an instrument in the hands of its exploiters, but today it is ready to redeem itself and govern itself on its own. Your power, as opposed to that of the bosses and their officials, represents not the forces of the past, but the free forces of the future – which await their hour and are preparing for it, in the knowledge that it will be the hour of redemption from all slavery.

And so the central organs that will be created for every group of workshops, every group of factories, every city and every region, right up to a supreme national Workers' Council, will pursue and broaden and intensify the job of controlling and preparing and organizing the whole class for the tasks of conquest and government.

We realize that the road will not be short or easy: many difficulties will arise and be placed in your path. To overcome them, you will have to draw on great ability, perhaps at times you will have to appeal to the strength of the organized working class, you will always have to be inspired and stimulated to action by a supreme faith in our cause. But what is most important, comrades, is that under your guidance and under the guidance of those who will follow your lead, the workers should acquire a deep certainty that now, secure in their goal, they are marching on the great road of the future.

Signed L'ORDINE NUOVO, *L'Ordine Nuovo*, 13 September 1919, Vol. 1, No. 18.

25. UNIONS AND COUNCILS

The proletarian organization which, as a global expression of the worker and peasant masses, is centred on the headquarters of the Confederation of Labour, is passing through a constitutional crisis that is similar in nature to the crisis in which the democratic-parliamentary State is vainly floundering. It is a crisis of power and a crisis of sovereignty. The solution of one will be the solution of the other, in the sense that, by resolving the problem of the will to power within the sphere of their own class organization, the workers will succeed in creating the organic framework of their own State and will victoriously counterpose it to the parliamentary State.

The workers feel that "their" organization has become such an enormously complex apparatus, that it has ended up obeying only laws of its own, inherent in its structure and complicated functioning, but alien to the masses who have acquired a consciousness of their historical mission as a revolutionary class. They sense that their will to power is not being expressed clearly and precisely enough through the current institutional hierarchies. They feel that even in their own house, in the house they built with tenacious and patient efforts, cementing it with blood and tears – even in this house, the machine crushes man and bureaucracy crushes any creative spirit. A banal and verbose dilettantism vainly attempts to conceal the absence of clear ideas on the needs of industrial production and the failure to understand in any way the psychology of the proletarian masses. The workers are angered by this state of affairs, but individually they are powerless to change them. The words and intentions of individual men are too puny to stand up to the iron laws inherent in the bureaucratic structure of the trade-union apparatus.

* * * * *

The organization's "leaders" are oblivious of this profound and widespread crisis. The more obvious it becomes that the working class is not organized into forms which accord with its real historical structure, and is not mobilized into a formation that is ceaselessly adapting itself to the laws governing the inner process of the real historical development of the class itself, the more these "leaders" persist in their blindness and attempt to settle disputes and conflicts on a "legalistic" basis. Eminently bureaucratic in spirit, they believe that an objective condition, rooted in a psychology that develops out of living experiences on the shop floor, can be over-ruled by emotional speeches and slogans adopted unanimously in mass meetings stupefied by uproar and tedious oratorical performances. Today, they are making efforts to keep "abreast of the times"; to show that they too are capable of "tough thinking", they hark back to the old and out-worn syndicalist ideologies. They laboriously state over and over again that the Soviet is the same as the trade union, and that the current system of trade-union organization itself constitutes the framework of communist society and the system of forces which must embody the proletarian dictatorship.

In its current expression within the countries of Western Europe, the trade union is a kind of organization that not only differs essentially from the Soviet, but also differs considerably from the trade union as it is steadily developing in the Russian Communist Republic.

The craft unions, the Chambers of Labour, the industrial federations and the General Confederation of Labour are all types of proletarian organization specific to the period of history dominated by capital. It can be argued that they are in a sense an integral part of capitalist society, and have a function that is inherent in a régime of private property. In this period, when individuals are valued only to the extent that they own commodities and trade their property, the workers too have had to obey the iron laws of general necessity and have become traders in the only property they possess, their labour power and their professional skills. Since they are more exposed to the risks of competition, the workers have accumulated their property into ever larger and more comprehensive "firms"; they have created these enormous apparatuses for concentrating living labour, and have set prices and hours and disciplined the market. They have hired from outside or have thrown up from their own ranks a trusted administrative personnel that is expert in this kind of transaction, capable of controlling market conditions, of drawing up contracts, assessing commercial risks and initiating economically profitable operations. The trade union has an essentially competitive, not communist, character. It cannot be the instrument for a radical renovation of society. It can provide the proletariat with skilled bureaucrats, and with technical experts on general industrial matters, but it cannot form the basis of proletarian power. It offers no scope for the selection of proletarian individuals who are capable and worthy of running society. It cannot throw up the hierarchies which will embody the *élan vital* and the rhythm of progress of communist society.

* * * * *

The proletarian dictatorship can only be embodied in a type of organization that is specific to the activity of producers, not wage-earners, the slaves of capital. The factory Council is the nucleus of this organization. For all sectors of the labour process are represented in the Council, in proportion to the contribution each craft and each labour sector makes to the manufacture of the object the factory is producing for the collectivity. The Council is a class, a social institution. Its *raison d'être* lies in the labour process, in industrial production, i.e. in something permanent. It does not lie in wages or class divisions, i.e. in something transitory and, moreover, the very thing we are trying to supersede.

Hence the Council realizes in practice the unity of the working class; it gives the masses the same form and cohesion they adopt in the general organization of society.

The Factory Council is the model of the proletarian State. All the problems inherent in the organization of the proletarian State are inherent in the organization of the Council. In the one as in the other, the concept of citizen gives way to the concept of comrade. Collaboration in effective and useful production develops solidarity and multiplies bonds of affection and fraternity. Everyone is indispensable, everyone is at his post, and everyone has a function and a post. Even the most ignorant and backward of workers, even the most vain and "civil" of engineers, will eventually convince himself of this truth in the experience of factory organization. All eventually acquire a communist consciousness that enables them to comprehend what a great step forward the communist economy represents over the capitalist. The Council is the most effective organ for mutual education and for developing the new social spirit that the proletariat has successfully engendered from the rich and living experience of the community of labour. Whereas in the union, workers' solidarity was developed in struggle against capitalism, in suffering and sacrifice, in the Council this solidarity is a positive, permanent entity that is embodied in even the most trivial moments of industrial production. It is a joyous awareness of being an organic whole, a homogeneous and compact system which, through useful work and the disinterested production of social wealth, asserts its sovereignty, and realizes its power and its freedom to create history.

* * * * *

The existence of an organization in which the proletariat is structured homogeneously as a productive class, and which encourages a free and spontaneous flowering of worthy and capable leaders and individuals, will have important and fundamental effects on the constitution and spirit that informs the activity of the trade unions.

The Factory Council too is organized on a craft basis. On the shop floor the workers are divided into crews, and every crew constitutes a work unit (a craft unit). The Council itself is precisely made up of the delegates the workers elect on a craft (crew) basis in each shop. While the trade union is based on the individual, the Council is based on the concrete, organic unity of the craft as it is realized in the discipline of the industrial process. The crew (craft) senses its distinction within the homogeneous body of the class, but at the same time it feels enmeshed in the system of discipline and order that renders the development of production possible through the crew's functioning in a precise and exact manner. As an economic and political interest, the craft is absolutely indistinguishable from the body of the class; it is distinct from it as a technical interest and as a development of the particular instrument it uses in its job. In the same way, all industries are homogeneous and in solidarity in their aim to perfect the production, distribution and social accumulation of wealth; but each industry has distinct interests as far as the technical organization of its specific activity is concerned.

Once the Councils exist, they give the workers direct responsibility for production, provide them with an incentive to improve their work, instil a conscious and voluntary discipline, and create a producer's mentality – the mentality of a creator of history. The workers will carry this new consciousness into the trade unions, which in place of the simple activity of the class struggle will dedicate themselves to the fundamental task of stamping economic life and work techniques with a new pattern; they will elaborate the form of economic life and professional technique proper to communist civilization. In this sense the unions, who are made up of the best and most conscious workers, will realize the highest moment of the class struggle and the dictatorship of the proletariat: they will create the objective conditions in which classes will no longer be able to exist or re-emerge.

This is what the industrial unions are doing in Russia. They have become the organs in which all the individual enterprises within a particular industry are amalgamated, linked up and articulated so that they form one, vast industrial unit. Wasteful competition is being eliminated, and the main services of administration, supply, distribution and storage are being unified into mammoth centres. Work systems, manufacturing secrets, and new applications become the immediate property of everyone in the industry. The multiplicity of bureaucratic and disciplinary functions inherent in private property relations and the individual firm are reduced to the bare industrial necessities. The application of trade-union principles to the textile industry in Russia has enabled the bureaucracy to be reduced from 100,000 employees to 3,500.

Factory organization will bind the class (the whole class) into a homogeneous and cohesive unit corresponding perfectly to the industrial process of production and controlling it by taking it over once and for all. In other words, organization based on the factory embodies the proletarian dictatorship, the communist State, that destroys class domination in the political superstructures and throughout its entire fabric.

Craft and industrial unions are the rigid backbone of the great proletarian body. They build on individual and local experience, store it up and so achieve that national equalization of the conditions of work and production on which communist equality is concretely based.

But to make it possible to imprint on the unions this positive class and communist direction, it is essential that workers should direct all their will-power and faith to the building up and spreading of the Councils, i.e. to the organic unification of the working class. On this solid and homogeneous basis, all the higher structures of the dictatorship and the communist economy will flourish and develop.

Unsigned, *L'Ordine Nuovo*, 11 October 1919, Vol. 1, No. 21.

26. TRADE UNIONS AND THE DICTATORSHIP

The international class struggle reached its highest point yet in the victory of the workers and peasants of two national proletariats. In Russia and Hungary the workers and peasants established a proletarian dictatorship, and in both countries the dictatorship had to wage a bitter battle not only against the bourgeois class, but against the trade unions as well. Indeed, the conflict between the dictatorship and the trade unions was one of the causes of the collapse of the Hungarian Soviet.[36] For the trade unions, although they never openly attempted to overthrow the dictatorship, consistently played the part of the revolution's "defeatists"; they continuously sowed demoralization and cowardice amongst the ranks of the red workers and soldiers. An examination, however brief, of the reasons and conditions bringing about this conflict cannot help but be useful to the revolutionary education of the masses. For if the masses must be persuaded that the trade union is perhaps the most important proletarian organism of the communist revolution, since the socialization of industry must be based upon it and since it must create the conditions in which private enterprise will disappear never to re-emerge, so too must they be persuaded of the need to create, prior to the revolution, subjective and objective conditions under which there could not possibly be any conflict or power dualism between the various organs in which the proletarian class struggle against capitalism is embodied.

* * * * *

In all the countries of Europe and the world, the class struggle has obviously assumed a revolutionary character. The perspective championed by the IIIrd International, namely that the aim of the class struggle should be to establish the dictatorship of the proletariat, has triumphed over the ideology of democracy and is spreading irresistibly through the masses. The Socialist Parties are joining the IIIrd International, or at least they are acting in accordance with the fundamental principles enunciated by the Moscow Congress. The trade unions, on the other hand, have remained faithful to "true democracy", and they never miss an opportunity to induce or force the workers into declaring that they are against the idea of a dictatorship and refuse to demonstrate solidarity with Soviet Russia. This attitude on the part of the trade unions was rapidly overcome in Russia, since the development of Factory Councils kept pace with and even outstripped the development of craft and industrial organizations. On the other hand, it eroded the proletariat's power base in Hungary; in Germany it led to the mass slaughter of communist workers and the rise of the Noske phenomenon; in France it led to the failure of the general strike called for 20–21 July and the strengthening of the Clemenceau régime;[37] in England it has so far forestalled any direct intervention by the workers into political struggle – and in all countries it threatens to drive a dangerous and deep wedge between the forces of the proletariat.

The character of the Socialist Parties is becoming increasingly revolutionary and internationalist; the trade unions, on the other hand, are increasingly embodying the theory (!) and tactics of reformist opportunism and becoming merely national bodies. This is resulting in an intolerable situation, a state of permanent confusion and chronic weakness on the part of the working class – both of which contribute to the general instability of society and encourage the proliferation of tendencies towards moral disintegration and a new barbarism.

* * * * *

The trade unions organized the workers in accordance with the principles of the class struggle and were themselves the first organic expression of this struggle. Trade-union organizers always claimed that the proletariat could emancipate itself only through class struggle, and that the aim of trade-union organization was precisely to do away with individual profit and the exploitation of man by man, since the unions set themselves the task of eliminating the capitalist (the private property owner) from the industrial process of production, and thereafter of eliminating classes. But the trade unions could not accomplish this goal at once, and in the meantime directed all their energies to the immediate one of improving the proletariat's living conditions, demanding higher wages, shorter hours of work and a body of social legislation. Movement followed movement, strike followed strike, and the workers' living conditions gradually improved. But all the achievements, all the victories of trade-union action, are based on the same old foundations: the principle of private property remains intact and powerful; the régime of capitalist production and the exploitation of man by man remain intact and indeed expand into new forms. The eight-hour day, wage increases, the benefits of social legislation – all this does not touch profit. Any disturbance in the profit rate as a direct result of trade-union action is corrected and a new equilibrium found, through the play of free market forces in the case of nations with a global economy (like England and Germany) and through protectionism in the case of nations with a restricted economy (like France and Italy). In other words, capitalism passes the increase in its general expenses of industrial production back either to the amorphous masses of the nation concerned or to those in the colonies.

Thus trade-union action, within its own sphere and using its own methods, stands revealed as being utterly incapable of overthrowing capitalist society; it stands revealed as being incapable of leading the proletariat to its emancipation, of leading it to accomplish the lofty and universal goal it had itself initially proposed.

* * * * *

According to syndicalist doctrines, the job of the trade unions should have been to train the workers for control over production. Because industrial unions are an integral reflection of a particular industry, it was argued, they will become the worker cadres competent to run that particular industry; trade-union responsibilities will serve to ensure that the best workers are selected – those who are most studious, most intelligent and most likely to master the complex mechanism of production and exchange. The working-class "leaders" of the leather industry will be the men most capable of running that industry, the same goes for the metal industry, the book industry, etc.

What a terrible illusion! The selection of trade-union leaders has never been made on the basis of industrial competence, but rather simply on the basis of juridical, bureaucratic and demagogic competence. And the more the organizations expanded, the more frequently they intervened in the class struggle and the more massive and widespread their activity became, the more they found it necessary to reduce their headquarters to a purely administrative and accounting centre; the more technical and industrial capacities became redundant and bureaucratic, commercial capacities came to predominate. Thus a veritable caste of trade-union officials and journalists came into existence, with a group psychology of their own absolutely at odds with that of the workers. This eventually came to occupy the same position *vis-à-vis* the working masses as the governing bureaucracy *vis-à-vis* the parliamentary State: it is the bureaucracy that rules and governs.

* * * * *

The proletarian dictatorship is designed to do away with capitalist production and private property, because only in this way can the exploitation of man by man be eliminated. The proletarian dictatorship is designed to do away with class differences and class struggle, because only in this way can the social emancipation of the working class be accomplished. To achieve this end the communist party teaches the proletariat how to organize its class power, and how to make use of this armed power to hold sway over the bourgeoisie and create the conditions in which the exploiting class may be suppressed, never to rise again. So the task facing the communist party during the period of the dictatorship is this: it must organize the class of workers and peasants once and for all into the ruling class, ensure that all the organs of the new State actually carry out their revolutionary mission, and destroy the ancient rights and relations connected with the principle of private property. But this destructive and supervisory activity must be immediately followed up by positive achievements of creation and production. If these do not succeed, then political power is to no avail – the dictatorship cannot survive. For no society can survive without production, least of all a dictatorship which is actually dependent on an intensification of production, coming into being as it is in conditions of economic chaos brought about by five years of desperate war and by months and months of armed bourgeois terrorism.

So this is the mammoth but glorious task confronting the industrial trade unions. It is they who must carry out a socialization programme; who must bring a new régime of production into being, in which each enterprise is based not on the profit motive, but on the common interests of society, which in the case of each productive sector lose their indistinct, generic, character and are made concrete in the appropriate workers' union.

* * * * *

In the Hungarian Soviet, the trade unions abstained from any creative work. In political terms, the trade-union officials raised continual obstacles to the dictatorship, forming a State within the State; in economic terms they remained inert. On more than one occasion, the factories had to be socialized against the wishes of the trade unions, even though socialization was their obligation *par excellence*. But the "leaders" of the Hungarian organizations were of limited intelligence; they had a bureaucratic-reformist mentality, and were continuously afraid of losing the power they had exercised up to that point over the workers. Since the role for which the trade unions were developed prior to the dictatorship presupposed the domination of the bourgeois class, and since the union officials had no technical or industrial expertise, they claimed that the proletarian class was not yet mature enough to run production directly. They supported the idea of "true democracy", in other words, the continuation of the bourgeoisie in its dominant position as the property-owning class. They wished to perpetuate and intensify the era of agreements, work contracts, social legislation, in order to enlarge their own sphere of competence. They advocated waiting around for the ... international revolution, unable to grasp the fact that in Hungary the international revolution was taking the form of the Hungarian revolution, in Russia that of the Russian revolution, and in Europe as a whole the form of general strikes, military revolts and living conditions which, as a result of the war, had become intolerable for the working class.

* * * * *

At the final session of the Budapest Soviet, one of the most influential "leaders" of the Hungarian trade unions expounded the point of view of the revolution's defeatists in these words: "When the Hungarian proletariat seized power and proclaimed the Soviet Republic, it rested its hopes on three things: 1. on the imminent explosion of the world revolution; 2. on the support of the Russian Red Army; 3. on the spirit of sacrifice of the Hungarian proletariat. But the world revolution was slow to explode, the Russian red troops failed to reach Hungary, and the Hungarian proletariat's spirit of sacrifice was no greater than that of the Western European proletariat. At this current historical juncture, the [Hungarian] Soviet government has withdrawn to give the country an opportunity of entering into negotiations with the Entente. It has withdrawn to save the Hungarian proletariat from a blood-bath; to save it and preserve it in the interests of the world revolution – for *some day* the great hour of the world socialist revolution must *still* strike."

In the final issue (2 August) of the Communist newspaper *Voros Ujsàg*, the situation created for the Hungarian proletariat by its traditional organs was surveyed as follows: "Does the Hungarian proletariat know what is in store for it, if it fails to wipe out immediately the assassins it is harbouring within its own ranks? Does the Budapest proletariat know what destiny awaits it, if it fails to find the strength to get rid of this gang of plunderers who have made their way into the proletarian State? The White terror and the Rumanian terror will unite their forces to conquer the Hungarian proletariat – disease will sweeten the tortures of hunger, and productive labour will be facilitated by the pillage of our machinery and destruction of our factories. The 'aristocracy' of the working class, *all those people* who addressed the proletariat *once only* during the life of the proletarian dictatorship, will account for their actions to the bayonets and artillery of the Rumanians. 'True' democracy will be established in Hungary, since all the people with anything to say will have achieved equality in the graveyard, and the others will enjoy the same rights under the lash of the Boyars' whips. The dispute between the Party and trade unions will cease, because for a long time there will be neither Party nor trade unions in Hungary. The dispute over whether the dictatorship should use force or persuasion will cease, because the bourgeoisie and the Boyars will be in no doubt as to the methods of *their* dictatorship: hundreds of gallows will announce that the dispute ended in favour of the bourgeoisie, due to the weakness of the proletariat."

Unsigned, *L'Ordine Nuovo*, 25 October 1919, Vol. 1, No. 23.

27. SYNDICALISM AND THE COUNCILS

Are we syndicalists? Is the movement of workshop delegates which began in Turin nothing but one more local variation of syndicalism? Can this movement really be seen as the minor disturbance which heralds the devastations of the tornado of home-produced syndicalism – that conglomeration of demagogy, insistent pseudo-revolutionary verbalism, undisciplined, irresponsible enthusiasm and maniacal excitement on the part of a few individuals of limited intelligence (little brains but big mouths) who have in the past sometimes succeeded in pillaging the will of the masses – and will it take its place in the annals of the Italian workers' movement labelled: Italian syndicalism?

*　　*　　*　　*　　*

In the concrete experience of proletarian revolutions, syndicalism has been an utter failure. The trade unions have shown that they are organically incapable of embodying the proletarian dictatorship. The union's normal course of development is marked by a continuous decline in the revolutionary spirit of the masses. The union increases their material strength, but weakens or completely destroys their appetite for conquest; their *élan vital* wilts, and heroic intransigence is succeeded by the practice of opportunism – "bread and butter" demands. An increase in quantity results in a decrease in quality, and a facile accommodation to capitalist forms; it results in the workers acquiring a stingy, narrow, petty- and middle-bourgeois mentality. And yet the basic task of the union is to recruit the masses in their "entirety", and absorb all the workers in industry and agriculture into its ranks. So the means are not adapted to the ends – and since means are anyway nothing but a moment of the end which is accomplished, which is realized, one must conclude that trade unionism is not a means to revolution, is not a moment of the proletarian revolution, is not the revolution in the process of being accomplished and realized: trade unionism is revolutionary only to the extent that it is grammatically possible to link the two expressions.

*　　*　　*　　*　　*

Trade unionism stands revealed as nothing other than a form of capitalist society, not a potential successor to that society. It organizes workers not as producers, but as wage-earners, i.e. as creatures of the capitalist, private property régime, selling the commodity labour. Trade unionism combines workers on the basis of the tools they use or the material they transform; in other words, trade unionism combines workers on the basis of the form that the capitalist régime, the régime of economic individualism, impresses on them. The use of one tool rather than another, and the transformation of one material rather than another, brings to light different capacities and attitudes to work and to earnings; the worker becomes fixed in his particular capacity and attitude, and sees his job not as a moment of production, but simply as a means of earning a livelihood.

The industrial or craft union, by combining the worker with his comrades in the same craft or industry, with men who use the same tools or transform the same material as himself, helps to foster this mentality, so that the worker is even less likely to see himself as a producer. He is led instead to consider himself as a "commodity" whose price, whose value, is set by the free play of competition in a national and international market.

The worker can see himself as a producer only if he sees himself as an inseparable part of the whole labour system which is concentrated in the object being manufactured, and only if he experiences the unity of the industrial process which *in toto* demands collaboration between manual workers, skilled workers, administrative employees, engineers and technical directors. The worker will see himself as a producer if – after he has become psychologically part of a particular productive process in a particular factory (e.g. in a car plant in Turin) and has come to think of himself as a necessary and indispensable factor in the activity of the social complex producing the car – he can now go one stage further and comprehend the whole of the Turin car-manufacturing process. If he can comprehend Turin as one production unit characterized by the car; see a large part of the general productive activity of Turin as existing and developing simply as a result of the existence and development of the car industry; and so see the workers in these general productive activities as themselves belonging to the car industry, for the simple reason that they create the necessary and sufficient conditions for that industry's existence. Starting off from this original cell, the factory, seen as a unit, as an act that creates a particular product, the worker proceeds to the comprehension of ever vaster units, right up to the level of the nation itself – which is in its entirety a gigantic apparatus of production, characterized by its exports, by the sum of wealth it exchanges for an equivalent sum of wealth coming in from every part of the world, from the various other gigantic apparatuses of production into which the world is divided. At this point the worker has become a producer, for he has acquired an awareness of his role in the process of production, at all its levels, from the workshop to the nation and the world. At this point he is aware of his class; he becomes a communist, because productivity does not require private property; he becomes a revolutionary, because he sees the capitalist, the private property owner, as a dead hand, an encumbrance on the productive process, which must be done away with. At this point he arrives at a conception of the "State", i.e. he conceives a complex organization of society, a concrete form of society, because this is nothing but the form of the gigantic apparatus of production which reflects – through all the novel, superior links and relations and functions inherent in its very enormity – the life of the workshop: which represents, in a harmonized and hierarchical fashion, the complex of conditions needed for the survival and development of his industry, his workshop, and even his person as a producer.

* * * * *

The Italian practice of pseudo-revolutionary syndicalism, like the practice of reformist trade unionism, is negated by the Turin movement of workshop delegates; in fact, it is negated twice over, since reformist trade unionism represents an advance over pseudo-revolutionary syndicalism. For if the trade union is alone in being able to get "bread and butter" for the workers; in being able to guarantee, within the context of a bourgeois régime, a stable wage market and eliminate some of the most dangerous uncertainties as far as the worker's physical and moral integrity is concerned; then it is obvious that reformist and not pseudo-revolutionary practice has obtained these results. To try to squeeze more out of an instrument than it can give, or to foster the belief that it can deliver more than its nature would allow it, is simply to commit blunders and indulge in purely demagogic activity. The pseudo-revolutionary syndicalists in Italy are frequently to be found discussing (as for instance in the railwaymen's union) whether they should restrict membership of their union to "revolutionaries" only, to the audacious minority dragging the cold and indifferent masses after it. In other words, these people end up by rejecting the basic principle of trade unionism, which is organization of the masses in their entirety. For deep down and unconsciously they are aware of the inanity of "their" propaganda; aware that the trade union is incapable of giving the worker's consciousness a concretely revolutionary form. For they have never considered the problem of the proletarian revolution in clear and precise terms and, although they uphold the "producers" theory, they have never experienced the mentality of producers. These people are demagogues, not revolutionaries; they are agitators stirring the flood that they have excited with their fatuous fiery speeches; they do not educate the worker or shape his consciousness.

* * * * *

Would the delegates' movement have arisen and developed simply to replace Buozzi and D'Aragona by Borghi?[38] The delegates' movement is the negation of every form of individualism and personalism. It is the beginning of a great historical process, a process in which the working masses will acquire consciousness of their indissoluble unity based on production and on the concrete activity of labour, and will provide this consciousness with an organic form, by building up their own leadership, by throwing up these leaders from the depths of their own ranks, so that they will be as it were the conscious expression of a precise goal to be accomplished, of a great historical process which—notwithstanding the errors that individuals may commit and the crises that national and international conditions may precipitate – must and will culminate in the dictatorship of the proletariat, in the Communist International.

Syndicalism has never once expressed such a conception of the producer, nor of the process of historical development of the producer society; it has never once indicated that this leadership, this line, should be impressed upon the workers' organization. It has theorized a particular form of organization – the craft and industrial union – and has built, to be sure, on a reality, but a reality that was given its form by the capitalist régime of free competition and private ownership of labour-power. Therefore it has simply constructed a Utopia, a great castle of abstractions.

The idea of the Councils system, based on the power of the working masses organized around their place of work, around production units, arose as a result of the concrete historical experiences of the Russian proletariat; it is the fruit of the theoretical labours of Russian communist comrades, who are revolutionary socialists, not syndicalists.

Unsigned, *L'Ordine Nuovo*, 8 November 1919, Vol. 1, No. 25.

Appendix

28. THE PROGRAMME OF THE WORKSHOP DELEGATES

PREAMBLE

This is the programme adopted by the first quasi-general assembly of the Turin factory delegates. It is more than just a programme; it is meant to be an exposition of the concepts which have underpinned the rise of a new form of proletarian power. The exposition is propagandist in intention, and is designed to establish a basis for discussion with the proletarian organs which emerged earlier.

This first assembly, therefore, does not reserve to itself the right to formulate a definitive programme, because this is a programme for revolutionary activity and ought therefore to be open to continuous radical innovation. Its purpose rather is to set in train in Italy a practical experiment in the achievement of communist society.

It is first-comers who characteristically claim all rights for themselves; this is the practice of some of those men who would like to embody in themselves all the activities of the trade unions and to convince everyone that the union with its various functions can cover the whole of social life.

We ourselves, through the reality of our power and our functions, are a primary negation of this theory. It is not a theoretical negation, not an artificial construct of the human mind. Our power has arisen through the spontaneous will of the factory proletariat, which is tired of having to submit – despite all the fine talk of democracy – to a discipline and a formulation of guiding concepts in which it has no say. It is tired of always having to be on its guard against being carried down a road which is not that of revolution, as a result of the tendencies or weaknesses of individual men.

It is this sharp reaction which has resulted in factory delegates appearing in every single nation. The rise of the delegates shows that negotiation about prices in the context of bourgeois competition, and administration of the means of production and masses of men, are two different functions. The first has what might be called a commercial objective: it consists in establishing the value of the labour of a category of workers, on a given bourgeois market, in order to sell it at the best possible price (a function exercised by the trade unions). The second has the potential objective of preparing men, bodies and concepts, through a continuous pre-revolutionary process of scrutiny, so that they may be equipped to replace the employer's authority in the factory and impose a new discipline on social life. This is the function of the delegates who, through the very mechanism whereby they are formed, represent the most democratic kind of power. It is with the aim of establishing precise demarcations between the activities and competence of these two functions that the programme has been preceded by a declaration of fundamental principles.

The example of the fatal conflict between trade-union leaders and the power of the councils in Hungary has led us to attempt to prevent a repetition of the phenomenon in the Italian revolution, by defining at the outset the relations between the two functions and allotting to each the tasks that its constitution, governing principle and daily practice warrant.

The principle of the democratic mandate must prevail in every form of power: the elected must be nothing other than the executors of the will of the masses. This principle is faithfully put into practice by the delegates.

In this system there is not yet universal suffrage, as a result of a variety of contingent factors. For example, there still exists a bourgeoisie with numerous agents; there still exist unconscious proletarians, who are not members of a trade union. While these latter can and must have the right to express their will by voting, they should not have the right to stand for election: they cannot be invested with authority over the unions, of which they are unconscious, or over social life, which they do not understand.

But the delegates, precisely because they are elected by all the proletarians, constitute a social power; and because they are union members elected by all the proletarians (who as conscious workers will undoubtedly win authority over the masses) they can represent the will of the union members themselves within the organizations.

The programme, we repeat, cannot be and will never be definitive. Successive regional and then national assemblies will have to revise it continuously and develop the ideas contained in it.

In the meantime, to secure its widespread distribution and discussion, the delegates' assembly has adopted the following resolutions.

1. The factory delegates of Turin, meeting in an assembly held on 31 October 1919, drew up the enclosed programme concerning the powers of councils and delegates. They decided:

(a) to request its publication in all proletarian newspapers and journals;

(b) to distribute it in factories all over Italy;

(c) to form industrial commissions on the basis of the former internal commissions, to examine its application in different industries;

(d) to have it discussed and eventually adopted by all organizations and co-operatives whose watchword is the class struggle.

2. The assembly of the Turin factory delegates resolves to call a regional assembly, as soon as delegates have appeared throughout the region, to review the programme and prepare a first regional or national congress.

Declaration of Principles

1. The factory delegates are the sole and authentic social (economic and political) representatives of the proletarian class, by virtue of their being elected by all workers at their workplace on the basis of universal suffrage. At the various levels of their constitution, the delegates embody the union of all workers as realized in organs of production (work-crew, workshop, factory, union of the factories in a given industry, union of the productive enterprises in a city, union of the organs of production in the mechanical and agricultural industry of a district, a province, a region, the nation, the world) whose authority and social leadership are invested in the councils and council system.

2. The workers united in the council system recognize the part played by the craft and industrial unions in the history of the class struggle, together with the need for them to carry on in their role of organizing individual categories of workers to obtain improvements in wages and hours for as long as the competitive labour market, as constituted under the capitalist régime, survives. They see the unions as an indispensable form of organization, in that they represent a higher union of workers who share the same individual interests stemming from their exercise of the same functions within the order of capitalist production. They maintain that all workers should belong to a trade union.

3. The objectives of the workers' movement must arise directly from the workers organized at the point of production, and be expressed via the factory delegates.

The craft and industrial unions should continue to exercise their present function, which is to negotiate with employer organizations on behalf of the collectivity to obtain satisfactory wages, hours and working conditions for entire categories, dedicating all the competence they have acquired in past struggles to drawing up clear, effective agreements that faithfully reflect the current requirements of labour and the consciousness of the factory workers.

On the other hand, the councils embody the power of the working class organized on a plant basis, as the antithesis to the employer's authority which is manifested within the plant itself. In social terms, they embody the action of the whole of the solidarized proletariat in its struggle to conquer public power and eliminate private property.

4. Union members within the councils accept without question that discipline and order in economic movements (whether partial or collective) must be maintained by the unions – provided, however, that the objectives for the unions are given by the factory delegates, as representatives of the working masses. They reject as artificial, parliamentarist and false any other system that the unions might wish to follow in determining the wishes of their membership. Workers' democracy is not based on numbers and the bourgeois concept of citizen, but on the functions of labour and the order that the working class adopts naturally in the process of skilled industrial production and in the factories.

5. The factory delegates proclaim themselves ready to confront any resistance whatsoever which seeks to curtail the right of their specific organs to scrutinize the internal affairs of the proletarian trade organizations within the factory.

6. The representatives undertake to direct all their propaganda energies to bring about the merger into a single national union of all the organizations in a particular category which are not yet confederated, but which base their actions on the class struggle to achieve the aims of the communist revolution.

All the craft and industrial unions of the Italian proletariat must affiliate to the General Confederation of Labour. The delegates appeal to all working comrades who voted for them in a spirit of communist consciousness, to use all their powers of personal persuasion to strengthen the organizations of which they are members. If, as they proclaim, workers have really attained a fully mature class consciousness, they must convince themselves of the need to build a single great union of all Italian proletarian forces. They must play a greater role in the affairs of the unions, infuse them with the ides that govern the council system and work towards eliminating all the difficulties that stand in the way of proletarian unity at this stage. When the workers have infused today's various dissenting organizations with that same spirit of conquest and desire for self-government and proletarian power that governs the council system, the fusion of these organizations will require no more than a simple administrative act. On the other hand, the delegates call upon working comrades to break with organizations that are based on religious or nationalist principles, both of which are utterly foreign to the functions and tasks of workers' organizations.

7. The assembly of all the Turin plant delegates asserts with pride and assurance that their election and the establishment of the council system represents the first concrete indication of the communist revolution in Italy. The assembly pledges to devote all the means at the disposal of individual representatives and the council system to ensure that the system of workers' councils, made up of delegates elected on a shop and work-crew basis, should spread irresistibly throughout Italy, and that within the shortest possible time a national congress of worker and peasant delegates from all over Italy should be called.

GENERAL REGULATIONS

Appointment of Delegates and their Powers

1. Delegates are appointed on a factory workshop basis, in accordance with the number of work-crews; their number, fixed provisionally for the moment by the internal commissions, will be determined finally by the factory council, which will carry out a thorough survey of work operations. Council assemblies will lay down what the ratio should be between numbers of workers and numbers of candidates.

Management personnel will be divided into the following categories: engineers, technical supervisors, designers, departmental secretaries, and clerical staff attached to internal administration, sales, accounts and auxiliary services. The precise weight of the various specialized categories in this sector of the productive process will be determined by the factory assembly.

2. All the proletarians in the factory, both manual and intellectual workers, have the right to vote.

3. Members of any trade union that is committed to the class struggle are eligible as candidates. A delegate whose mandate is

revoked is ineligible for three successive assemblies; his right of candidature is thus suspended for one election.

4. The first elections are to be held under the auspices of the old-style internal commissions. The commissions elected will normally remain in office for six months; in the course of this period they may be replaced in part (in some shops) or *en bloc* throughout the factory, through the resignation of the delegates. It is up to the outgoing delegates' assembly to establish the norms for holding new elections, subject to their being in line with the general principles.

5. The delegate must enjoy the confidence of his electorate at all times: he is therefore subject to instant recall. If he is repudiated by a half plus one of his electorate, or by a majority of the factory assembly, the delegate is obliged to seek renewal of his mandate. If under these circumstances he fails to have his mandate renewed, the factory assembly will refuse to recognize his delegate's rights.

6. Voting will take place by secret ballot during working hours. Counting must begin at once and in public, and the results be announced immediately. The candidate's name on the ballot slip must be handwritten. While voting takes place, no worker from another part of the factory may enter the shop. If the result and its validity are in doubt, the vote must be taken again in the presence of the Council secretary.

7. The factory council must meet within two days of the elections. Temporarily, the council will meet in the rooms of the nearest socialist club. When the council wins recognition in the factory, the assembly should be held in the factory itself. Rules for the convening of council meetings will be drawn up by the council itself.

8. The delegate has a twofold responsibility: (a) he represents the trade-union members in his workshop and is responsible for the affairs of the particular organization of which he is a member; (b) he represents all the workers in his shop, being responsible for their defence in economic matters and for their social activity.

9. The factory council therefore represents the whole of the proletariat in the factory. Delegates choose from their own number the factory executive committee, which they invest with an executive mandate within the factory itself, and a representative mandate in the council assemblies.

10. In the general assembly of all the local delegates, on the other hand, delegates represent the interests of their own category and of local production.

11. In the assemblies of all the executive committees of an area, on the other hand, delegates represent the interests of the whole of the factory proletariat and of production in social life.

12. Delegates in a particular district who are members of the same craft or industrial union will meet in craft and industrial assemblies. The assemblies will appoint from their own number the executive committee of the local branch of the union.

Delegates and Unions

13. Assemblies of workers in a particular category are convened either on the initiative of delegates representing more than one tenth of union members or by the branch council. They must be called as a matter of course whenever a dispute arises affecting the category.

14. Secretaries of union administrative and propaganda sections must have proven capacity to conduct negotiations with employer organizations, and they must be seen as the executors of the will of the trade-union members, as it is expressed in the union and the factory council. They are responsible to the executive committees.

15. The drawing up of agreements and the negotiations with the employer organizations are delegated to the secretaries themselves, assisted by representatives of the executive committees.

The ratification of economic agreements concerning a category is effected by the category assembly.

No agreement can be seen as valid until it has been ratified.

16. Before an agreement is put to the assembly for approval, one copy must have been sent to each factory concerned.

17. Thus agreements will be discussed in the delegates' assembly, and delegates who are not members of the union which led a particular agitation will also have the right to vote on the agreement reached in it. In the category assemblies, on the other hand, the delegates do not enjoy the right to criticize the members and procedures of a union which is not their own.

18. However, the delegates gathered in a category assembly do have the right to discuss and criticize the procedures of unions which are not committed to the class struggle.

The Duties of the Factory Delegates

1. The most important and delicate of the delegate's duties is inside the factory. He must at all times be the faithful interpreter of the feelings

of his comrades before representatives of the employer's authority and within the council.

The workshop is the source of his power, which resides in the solidarity his comrades express in supporting his actions and in standing by his recommendations in a disciplined fashion. Such solidarity and discipline are forthcoming only when the electorate see him as a genuine exponent of their feelings.

2. The delegates work. The assertion of their power in the factory should be limited, in this sense, to ensuring that they may down tools in particular circumstances which demand their presence outside the workshop.

3. The role of the delegate during working hours may be summed up in the word control.

He must exercise control:[39]

(a) to ensure that existing work agreements are faithfully adhered to, and to resolve any disputes that might arise between the work-force in the shop and representatives of management;

(b) to defend the interests and personal feelings of the workers in the event of foremen abusing their power, by mis-assessing work unjustly or through incapacity, in the event of changes in the work process or in the event of a crisis of production on the market;

(c) to maintain order on the job, in the face of either management provocation or bad conduct on the part of dissenters from the wishes of the majority;

(d) to obtain precise intelligence on: (i) the value of capital employed in his own shop; (ii) the output of his shop in relation to all known costs; (iii) the possible increase in output that could be achieved;

(e) to prevent the capitalists from removing any of the fixed capital invested in the plant.

4. The delegate should study and encourage his comrades to study the bourgeois systems of production and work processes, inviting criticisms and suggestions that will facilitate work by speeding up production. It must be driven home to all that communist equality can be won only through an intensive productive effort, and that higher living standards will flow not from disorder in production and a relaxation of work discipline, but rather from an improved and more equal distribution of social obligations and rewards, obtained through making labour compulsory and equalizing rates of pay.

5. In the light of the above considerations, the delegates should study internal technical innovations proposed by management, and not take a

decision before having discussed the question with their comrades; they should invite them to accept such innovations, so long as any temporary damage to the workers' interests is balanced by similar sacrifices on the part of the industrialists, and provided the innovation will result in an improvement in the process of production. Hence they should put pressure on management to force it to respect legislation concerning safety, hygiene and workshop facilities.

Towards Workers' Schools

6. It is up to the council to organize a school on the factory premises for all workers who wish to perfect their professional skills. Capable teachers must be found in the factory itself, and rooms and equipment must be provided by management.

7. It is also up to the council to ensure that management provides an organic system of education for apprentices, and to be vigilant in defence of their interests.

8. The council will also have to intervene when workers are promoted, to unmask cases of favouritism and denounce it as a weapon of class struggle employed by the bosses.

9. Backward or indifferent workshop delegates need to be shaken up by frequent elections and referenda. All delegates are obliged to hold frequent referenda in their shops on social and technical issues and to hold frequent meetings to explain the principles and advice emanating from proletarian organs.

10. No council has the right to break a work agreement without having first obtained the approval of the assembly of category delegates, and through it the executive committee of the branch.

11. When a dispute with management in a workshop has been settled by the delegate, or becomes a matter of principle, or is due to a conflict of interest between workshops, the delegate must report the case at once to the factory commissariat's office. Throughout the period of the dispute he is excused work.

THE EXECUTIVE COMMISSARIAT OF A FACTORY

Appointment, Functions, Powers

1. The factory council will appoint a certain proportion of its member delegates to execute decisions and negotiate with management: these will form the executive commissariat of the factory. This body will

take the place of the former internal commission, and should receive corresponding recognition from the management of the factory.

2. The proportionality and election arrangements will be decided by the individual councils and assemblies.

3. A fixed number of members delegated to serve on the commissariat will be excused work for their term of duty and stationed permanently in an appropriate executive commissariat office, to receive complaints from delegates, examine them, reject or accept them, support them where necessary with the power which the force of the entire factory confers upon them.

4. Delegates of the commissariat should be present at all conversations between union secretaries and employers' bodies in the factory.

5. Every evening the members of the commissariat are called upon to assess the situation in the factory and the work done by their comrades.

6. Delegates to the E.C. must give all possible support to the work of control, study and propaganda carried out by the delegates, encouraging and driving the slow and accusing the inept and incapable before the council.

7. Members of the E.C. may remain in office continuously for the duration of the council: they remain in office during elections and for the period immediately following, in order to hand over their powers and current business to the incoming commissariat.

Members who suffer a vote of no confidence in the council automatically lose their mandate.

8. The E.C. and management have equal rights to post notices in the factory.

9. The E.C. should ensure that newspapers are freely distributed inside the factory during workbreaks.

10. The E.C. should try to publish a fortnightly factory bulletin that will gather together statistics designed to extend the workers' knowledge of factory operations, explain the work done by the E.C. and the factory council, reprint news items concerning the factory from sectional journals, etc.

If the factory is too small it can join with others in the same industrial sector.

11. The E.C. should also try to set up a factory social and savings fund, with the aim of establishing a co-operative factory canteen in conjunction with the local Co-operative Alliance.

12. The E.C. should keep a daily log-book recording its own activities and submit it weekly to the council for its approval.

13. The E.C. will distribute propaganda and research duties between its own members and the delegates.

14. The factory council should be convened by the E.C. each week if possible (Saturday half-day)[40] to hear the E.C.'s report, to assess the situation in the factory and the morale of the workforce, and to make recommendations to the E.C. on matters concerning the external interests of the factory or the category.

In exceptional circumstances the council could meet daily.

Publications, Notices, Reports, Meetings

1. The Turin delegates' assembly resolves to recognize the newspaper *Avanti!* as the sole political daily of the region and to seek space in it for the publication of notices, reports and agenda of delegates' meetings. It has no confidence in the publication of other newspapers, which would drain the social assets.

2. The assembly resolves, moreover, to request publication of articles propagating these new ideas in all proletarian periodical publications. The replies of the periodicals to the delegates' request should be read at the next assembly.

Unsigned, *L'Ordine Nuovo*, 8 November 1919, Vol. I, No. 25. (On 25 July 1920, Gramsci referred to this text as being written by the "Gruppo di Studio" of the Factory Delegates movement, though his own influence admits of no doubt.)

III

The Coming Confrontation

29. REVOLUTIONARIES AND THE ELECTIONS

What do conscious revolutionaries, those workers and peasants who see the Parliament of deputies elected by universal suffrage (i.e. by the exploiters and the exploited) and according to territorial constituencies as the mask of bourgeois dictatorship, expect from the elections?[41] They certainly do not expect to win one more than half the seats; nor do they expect the sort of legislature that will issue a whole series of laws and decrees tending to blunt sharp edges and make it easier for the two classes – the exploiters and the exploited – to get on together. On the contrary they expect the electoral effort of the proletariat to succeed in sending a strong force of Socialist Party militants into parliament; and they expect this group to be numerous and aggressive enough to prevent any bourgeois "leader" from forming a powerful and stable government. In this way the bourgeoisie will be forced to abandon its democratic equivocation, to abandon legality and thereby foment an uprising of the broadest and deepest strata of the working class against the exploiters' oligarchy.

Conscious revolutionaries, the workers and peasants who are already convinced that the communist revolution will be achieved only by a proletarian dictatorship embodied in a system of workers' and peasants' Councils, have struggled to send a great number of socialist deputies to Parliament, because they have reasoned in the following manner.

The communist revolution cannot be carried out through a coup. Even if a revolutionary minority were to succeed in violently taking over power, this minority would be overthrown the next day by a counter coup launched by capitalism's mercenary forces, for the uninvolved majority would allow the cream of the revolutionary forces to be massacred. They would allow all the evil passions and barbarities stirred up by capitalist gold and corruption to run riot. Therefore, the proletarian vanguard needs to organize this majority of indolent and sluggish people, in both material and moral terms. Using its own means and systems, the revolutionary vanguard needs to bring into being the material and moral conditions that will prevent the propertied class from peacefully governing the broad masses; conditions that will force it, through the intransigence of the socialist deputies under Party discipline and control, to terrorize the broad masses, strike them blindly and so make them rise up in arms. Such a goal can only be pursued today through parliamentary action, understood in the sense of action which immobilizes Parliament, strips the democratic mask away from the ambivalent face of the bourgeois dictatorship and reveals it in all its horrible and repugnant ugliness.

The communist revolution is a necessity in Italy more for international reasons than for reasons inherent in the process of development of the national apparatus of production. The reformists and the whole gang of opportunists are right when they say that in Italy the objective conditions for revolution do not exist: they are right in so far as they think and speak as nationalists, in so far as they see Italy as an entity that is independent of the rest of the world, and see Italian capitalism as a purely Italian phenomenon. They do not see internationalism as a living reality, operating in the history of capitalism and the proletariat alike.

But if, by contrast, one sees conditions in Italy in the wider context of an international system, as a function of this international system, then one's historical point of view changes. Every conscious socialist, every worker and peasant who is aware of his class's revolutionary mission, is led to the following practical conclusion: we must be prepared, we must be armed for the conquest of social power. The fact that the revolutionary process is laid down by the prevailing conditions within the international capitalist system makes the task of the Italian revolutionary vanguard more complicated and difficult – but these complications and difficulties should drive us to be better armed and prepared, rather than delude us and fill us with doubts.

Precisely: the revolution finds the broad masses of the Italian people still shapeless, still atomized into an animal-like swarm of individuals lacking all discipline and culture, obedient only to the stimuli of their bellies and their barbarian passions. It is precisely for this reason that conscious revolutionaries have accepted the electoral challenge. They see the need to create a unity and elemental form within this multitude; they see the need to bind it to the activity of the Socialist Party; and they see the need to provide its instincts and passions with a direction and a glimmer of political consciousness. But for this very reason too the revolutionary vanguard does not want these multitudes to be deluded; it does not want them given to believe that it is possible to overcome the present crisis through parliamentary and reformist action. The division between the classes needs to be hardened; the bourgeoisie needs to demonstrate its utter inability to satisfy the demands of the multitudes; the latter need to be convinced through their own experience that they face two clear and brutal alternatives: either death by starvation, servitude beneath a foreign heel forcing the worker and the peasant to die at their machines or on their strips of land; or a heroic effort, a superhuman effort on the part of the workers and peasants of Italy to create a proletarian order, to do away with the class of property-owners and eliminate every source of waste, unproductiveness, indiscipline and disorder.

It is only for these revolutionary reasons that the conscious vanguard of the Italian proletariat has entered the electoral lists and solidly planted itself in the parliamentary circus. It has not done so through any democratic illusion or reformist tenderness, but strictly in order to create the conditions for the triumph of the proletariat; in order to ensure the success of the revolutionary effort directed towards installing a proletarian dictatorship embodied in the system of Councils, outside and against Parliament.

Unsigned, *L'Ordine Nuovo*, 15 November 1919, Vol. I, No. 26. Under the heading "The Week in Politics".

30. THE PROBLEM OF POWER

The present historical position of the class of the exploited in Italy can be summarized in the following general terms.

Political Order

A movement of about three and a half million factory workers, peasants and office workers, corresponding to about fifteen million of the Italian population, represented in parliament by 155 socialist deputies.

Within the political order, the Italian class of producers who do not own the instruments of labour and the means of production and exchange which form the national economic apparatus, has succeeded in marshalling a concentration of forces which has put an end to the utility of parliament as the basis of State power and as the constitutional form of political government. The class of the exploited in Italy has thus struck a crippling blow at the political apparatus of capitalist supremacy, founded as it is on a rotation of conservative and democratic parties, an alternation in government of the various political outfits who paint capitalist robbery and the dominion of the strong-box in a diversity of colours.

Economic Order

The corporative movement in its various tendencies:

1. the movement of vanguard industrial workers (because employed in the most advanced sectors of industry) and agricultural workers from the intensive farming regions, concentrated in the CGL;

2. the movement of workers in the backward sectors of industry, who tend to be restless and undisciplined, substituting revolutionary rhetoric for permanent, concrete, revolutionary activity, and who camp under the nomadic tents of the *Unione Sindacale Italiana*;

3. the railwaymen's union, an amorphous mass of vanguard industrial workers, petty-bourgeois white-collar workers, politically apathetic technicians and a vague and uncertain number of wage and

salary earners, clinging to the coffers of the State as only the Italian petty bourgeois and small peasant can;

4. the Catholic peasant unions, which stand in the same relation to the CGL land workers as do USI to CGL industrial workers: they represent a mass of backward proletarian elements, who introduce alien or contradictory principles into trade unionism (religion, vague and chaotic libertarian aspirations);

5. peasant leagues and Chambers of Labour scattered here and there throughout Italy, but especially in the South and the Islands: these are a symptom of the lack of cohesion in the national economic and political apparatus; they arise as the result of individual initiative and stagger along from one day to the next, wearing themselves out in chaotic activities that lack any permanent, concrete direction;

6. proletarian leagues of war-wounded and veterans, free associations of veterans and ex-servicemen: these represent the first grandiose attempt to organize the peasant masses.

The corporative movement, in these its various forms and tendencies, has concentrated a mass of nearly six million Italian workers (corresponding to about twenty-five million of the national population). It has banished the "free" worker from the economic scene, and so paralysed the capitalist labour market. The conquest of the 8-hour day and a minimum wage are the outcome of this state of affairs in the labour market. The capitalist order of production has been rocked to its foundations by these achievements; the "freedom" to exploit, to extract surplus-value from labour-power (profit for the capitalist, rent to the landowner, taxes to the State, tribute to the newspapers and hired killers of the big banks), has been limited and placed under the – albeit indirect – control of the proletariat. The economic foundations of capitalist organization, which reaches its apex in the bureaucratic-parliamentary State, have been destroyed, through the sabotage of the primary source of capitalist power: the freedom to extract surplus-value.

The electoral triumph of the Socialist Party, the election of 155 Socialist deputies who will paralyse the functioning of Parliament as the constitutional form of political government, is simply a reflection of this basic and fundamental economic phenomenon, viz. the paralysis of the functioning of the labour-power market as the constitutional form of economic-capitalist government, of the capitalist's power over the process of production and exchange.

* * * * *

The vanguard workers and peasants have realized that such a situation was forming in Italy during the war and has been consolidated in this first post-war period. They have realized that the gains won can be preserved only if they press forward; if the 8-hour day becomes a workers' and peasants' law, a "way of life" for communist society; if the minimum wage becomes a law which recognizes the right of the peasants and workers to satisfy, with the fruits of their labour, all the demands of a particular standard of civil and intellectual life – a law which emanates from the power of the worker and peasants, which in turn is the political reflection of a transformed order in the process of industrial and agricultural production; if the control of the combined masses of workers and peasants over the source of bourgeois power (the formation of surplus-value) develops from its present brute and confused form of mass pressure and mass resistance into an economic and political technique, embodied in a hierarchy of economic and political institutions culminating in the workers' and peasants' State, the workers' and peasants' government, the workers' and peasants' central power; if the conquest of the land on the part of the peasants develops from mere possession of the basic instrument of labour into the conquest of the fruits which that instrument can produce – develops, that is to say, into control over the forms in which the goods produced circulate and over the economic organs that represent the various stages of this circulation: the banks, the banking consortia, the commercial agencies and the network of rail, river and maritime transport.

If a workers' State does not give the peasants a guarantee of immunity from the predatory assaults of capitalism and high finance, the war will be paid for by a "glorious" agrarian revolution carried out by the bourgeois State and the lesser capitalist organizations: viz. the introduction of agricultural machinery, coupled with expropriation of the peasants and their reduction to the rank of agricultural wage-labourers, without trade-union experience and hence more severely exploited and robbed of their wealth of labour-power than the workers in urban industry.

To advance along the road of revolution to the point of expropriation of the expropriators and the foundation of a communist State is in the immediate interests of the two most numerous orders of the class of Italian producers. For the urban workers it means preserving the gains they have won up to this point, rather than seeing them swept away in a collapse of the apparatus of industrial production and a disintegration of society, culminating in a permanent state of disorder and terrorism with no foreseeable end; in addition, it means taking over the national apparatus of production and directing it in the interests of working-class well-being and intellectual improvement. For the peasants, it means keeping the land they have won, extending their own property, freeing the land from the burdens of capitalist mortgages and taxes and starting the industrial revolution, with communist methods and systems, in close collaboration with the urban workers.

The vanguard workers and peasants have realized that all these things are necessities inherent in the current economic situation, the catastrophic tension between the forces and organs of production. And they have done all that they could do in a democratic society, a society that is politically defined: they have pointed to the Socialist Party, which represents the ideas and programmes to be accomplished, as their natural political leader; and they have pointed out to the Party the road to power, the road to government – based constitutionally not on a Parliament elected by a universal suffrage encompassing both exploited and exploiters, but on a system of workers' and peasants' Councils embodying the rule of industrial as well as of political power: bodies which, in other words, are instruments for the expulsion of the capitalists from the process of production, and instruments for the suppression of the bourgeoisie, as dominant class, from all the nation's institutions of control and economic centralization.

* * * * *

Thus the immediate, concrete problem confronting the Socialist Party is the problem of power; the problem of how to organize the whole mass of Italian workers into a hierarchy that reaches its apex in the Party; the problem of constructing a State apparatus which internally will function democratically, i.e. will guarantee freedom to all anti-capitalist tendencies and offer them the possibility of forming a proletarian government, and externally will operate as an implacable machine crushing the organs of capitalist industrial and political power.

There exists the great mass of the Italian working people. Today it is divided politically into two dominant tendencies – the Marxist socialist masses and the Catholic socialist masses – and into a multitude of secondary tendencies: anarcho-syndicalists, social-democratic ex-servicemen and various local groupings with revolutionary tendencies. This mass represents more than twenty-five million of the Italian population; in other words, it represents a stable and secure foundation for the proletarian apparatus.

There exist a series of trade-union organs and semi-proletarian associations, which represent a gradation of technical and political capacities within the broad masses of the working people.

There exists the Socialist Party and, within the Party, the revolutionary communist tendency, which represents the mature form of the present historical consciousness of the proletarian masses.

For revolutionaries, the outstanding concrete problem of the present moment is this: 1. to organize the broad masses of the working people into a social configuration appropriate to the industrial and agricultural production process (formation of factory and village Councils, with the right to vote extended to all workers); 2. to ensure that the majority in the Councils is represented by comrades in the Party and workers' organizations together with sympathetic comrades, but without excluding the possibility that temporarily, in the first moments of uncertainty and immaturity, it may fall into the hands of the *popolari*, the anarcho-syndicalists or the reformists, in so far as they are wage-workers elected at their work-place and in so far as they support the workers' State.

In the higher urban and (for the countryside) district hierarchies, representation in the urban and district Councils will have to be given not only to the production centres, i.e. to the working masses as such, but also to Party sections, clubs, trade unions, proletarian associations and cooperatives. The socialist majority should be impressive in these local authorities, and overwhelming in the great industrial cities – i.e. where the workers' State will truly be a proletarian dictatorship (of factory workers) and will be faced by the greatest difficulties, since it will have to take over the nerve-centres of the capitalist system, the capitalist organs that grip the whole nation in their tentacles.

Unsigned, *L'Ordine Nuovo*, 29 November 1919, Vol. I, No. 28.

31. THE EVENTS OF 2–3 DECEMBER [1919]

Petty Bourgeoisie

The events of 2–3 December represent a high point in the class struggle.[42] The struggle was not between proletarians and capitalists (that struggle develops organically, as a struggle over wages and hours, and as a tenacious and patient attempt to build up an apparatus – to control production as well as masses of men – which will replace the present apparatus of the bourgeois State); it was between proletarians and the petty- and middle-bourgeois. In the final analysis, the struggle was over the defence of the liberal-democratic State, over the liberation of the liberal-democratic State from the stranglehold of a section of the bourgeoisie, the worst, vilest, most useless and most parasitical section: the petty and middle bourgeoisie, the "intellectual" bourgeoisie (called "intellectual" only because, after an undemanding secondary schooling, it has got hold of minor or intermediate general educational qualifications), the bourgeoisie of civil servants father-and-son, shopkeepers, industrial and agricultural small owners, urban merchants and rural usurers. This struggle took place in the only way it could take place: it was disordered and tumultuous, like a sweep through the streets and squares to free them of a plague of putrid and voracious locusts. But this struggle was connected, albeit indirectly, to the other, higher class struggle between capitalists and workers. The petty and middle bourgeoisie is in fact the barrier of corrupt, dissolute and rotten humanity that capitalism uses to defend its economic and political power: a servile, abject horde of hirelings and lackeys, that has now become a *serva padrona*[43] and wants to extort a booty from production that is not only larger than the wages paid to the working class, but larger even than the booty grabbed by the capitalists themselves. To drive them out of society – in the way a plague of locusts is driven from a half-devastated field – with steel and fire would have the effect of relieving the national apparatus of production and exchange of a leaden harness that suffocates it and prevents it from functioning. It would have the effect of clearing the social atmosphere and bringing the workers face to face with their real adversary: the class of capitalists who own the means of production and exchange.

The war gave the petty and middle bourgeoisie their great opportunity. Because of the war, the capitalist apparatus of political and economic control was militarized: the factory became a barracks, the city became a barracks, the whole nation became a barracks. All activities serving the public interest were nationalized, bureaucratized, militarized. To effect this monstrous construction, the State and the lesser capitalist groupings brought about the mass mobilization of the petty and middle bourgeoisie. Completely lacking in any cultural or intellectual preparation, tens and tens of thousands of individuals came flocking in from the depths of villages and hamlets in the South: from the back of father's store, from benches warmed in vain in the middle and upper schools, from the editorial offices of blackmailing newspapers, from the trash of the city suburbs, from all those ghettoes where there rot and decompose the indolence, cowardice and arrogance of the social debris and rubbish deposited by centuries of servility and the domination of priests and foreigners over the Italian nation. They were given the wages of indispensable and irreplaceable men, and were entrusted with power over the masses in the factories, the cities, the barracks and the trenches at the front. [Well armed, well fed, subject to no control, in a position to satisfy the three passions which pessimists claim are inherent and insuppressible in human nature: the passion for absolute power over other men, dominion over the life and death of other men; the passion to possess many women; the passion to possess much money to buy pleasure and luxury – these tens and tens of thousands of the corrupt, the crooked and the dissolute bound themselves to the monstrous military-bureaucratic apparatus built during the war. They want to go on governing masses of men, to be invested with absolute authority over the life and death of masses of men; they organize *pogroms* against proletarians, against socialists, they hold the streets and squares in a reign of terror.][44]

The parliamentary elections have shown that the masses want to be governed and led by socialists; that the masses want a social order in which whoever does not produce, whoever does not work, does not eat. Those gentlemen who continue to take a cut of a million a month from the national product and the State's foreign credit, who shout their nationalist ardour from the rooftops and get the homeland to maintain them;

[two lines censored]

these gentlemen, terrified by the imminent danger, at once organized a *pogrom* against the Socialist deputies. And from the factories, the building sites, the workshops, the arsenals in every Italian city, all at once, as if at a command – just as happened in Russia and Poland, when the Black Hundreds attempted to stir up *pogroms* against the Jews and drown each tiny yearning for liberty in a swamp of barbarity and dissolution[45] – the workers burst into the streets in the city centre and swept away these petty-bourgeois locusts, these *pogrom* organizers, these professional idlers.

At bottom, this was an episode of "liberalism". A way had been found of earning a living without work or responsibility or risk; but today this way too has its risks, its worries and its dangers.

* * * * *

A Hypothesis . . .

And if it had succeeded? . . . The hypothesis is not an abstract one. In the great Northern cities, during the days of the strike, there were certainly moments when even calm and temperate men had the distinct impression that decisive events could occur at any moment: that any minor incident could have sufficed to give the course of events a different turn and disrupt the balance of forces between the people and the authorities, so turning insurrection into revolution. This really is the best indication of the fact that we are living in a revolutionary period: *one senses* that something new and different could crop up at any moment, one waits, one questions the unknown and one counts to some extent, too, on chance.

[three lines censored]

True, revolt is made up largely of imponderables, and revolt too must count on chance, on a group of youths going farther than other people intended or a young tough who perhaps will have to be shot a couple of days later for looting or killing.

The element of order is provided by the existence of groups of revolutionaries, in the true sense of the word: i.e. nuclei of people who are not afraid of events, of the unknown and unexpected, who are strong-willed and have a precise goal, who are ready and capable of acting in accordance with their will. An insurrection signifies the dissolving of one form of social organization; revolution begins when the society as a whole, prodded by conscious, courageous and capable people, moves in the direction of acquiring a new structure. The purely negative stage of insurrection lasts for as long as it takes the vanguard groups to remove the difficulties in their path, place themselves at the head of the movement and give organic form to the masses whom the movement of revolt has rendered fluid and formless.

In Russia, one can say that this transitional period lasted for eight long months, from the March to the October revolution, from the petty-bourgeois revolution to that of the workers and peasants. Eight months that were filled with the efforts of the petty-bourgeois intellectuals to keep their place at the head of a mass movement increasingly discontented and disillusioned with their untrustworthy leadership. Eight months in which the capitalists and landowners employed every means available to them, from sabotage of the factory to armed counter-revolution, to press the human masses back into the old forms of oppression and slavery, after the revolt had stirred them down to the deepest layers of society and turned them into the active agents of history. And during these months, the great majority of the people learn to make the revolution; they sense at once, even before having any theoretical conviction, that they must form their own organs of power. They detach themselves from the democratic leaders and gather around the communists. They form organs of control and self-government that automatically proceed to eliminate the organs of the old power – the power of the bosses, the generals, the politicians and the traitors – and divest them of any authority.

In October 1917, while the Kerensky government was still standing, the executive committee of the Congress of Soviets issued orders that were followed by a mass of workers and peasants ranked and organized with iron discipline; it called whole regiments, whole cadres of armed factory workers, into the streets and directed their movements; it was, in short, at the head of an apparatus that acted with the precision and implacable regularity of a machine.

It would be absurd to maintain that in Italy we should make no move until we had reached that point, but we should certainly seek to reach it, through the experience of movements like that of 2–3 December and the others which will undoubtedly follow it. These movements must serve to smash the bond of apparent legality which still unites the majority of the population within the form of bourgeois institutions; they must serve to set in motion the human masses who still, through either the force of habit or fear, accept the old social system; they must serve to confront everyone with the problem of preparing to make the revolution.

We have not had and perhaps will never have a March revolution that opens up the way for us, initiating the period of turmoil, uncertainty and open confrontation outside the limits of the law between the forces striving for dominion in the economic and political sphere. Negative parliamentary action can and must in effect replace this initial rupture. Hence street demonstrations are a necessary complement to it. . . .

And in the meantime we have to confront the problem I mentioned above, the problem of "what next", the problem that would have confronted us yesterday had the Mantua events occurred in Milan or Turin, where there exists a mass of revolutionary workers disposed to go to the very end. It is a hypothesis: but if we are revolutionaries, we have to make this hypothesis too, that some day or other the revolution may succeed. . . .

Class Struggle, Peasant War

Purely by chance, the period of general strike and serious disturbances in upper and central Italy coincided with the spontaneous outbreak of a popular insurrection in the territory of Andria, typical of the Italian South.[46] The notice attracted by the insurrection of the urban proletariat against that section of the petty-bourgeois caste which acquired a militaristic countenance during the War and does not want to lose it now, and against the police, has deflected attention away from Andria. As a result, due weight has not been given to these southern events and their significance has not been fully appreciated. We hope to be able to provide our readers with important information from eye-witnesses on why these events occurred and on the actual course they took. For the moment, we shall confine ourselves to the observation that chance, by making these two disturbances coincide, has provided virtually a model of what the Italian revolution should be like.

On one side the proletariat, in the strict sense of the word, i.e. the workers in industry and industrialized agriculture; on the other, the poor peasants: these are the two wings of the revolutionary army. The urban workers are revolutionary as a result of their education – their consciousness has slowly matured within the context of the factory, the cellular unit of the exploitation of labour. Today the urban workers see the factory as the place where the process of liberation must start, as the centre from which the movement of insurrection will radiate outwards. Hence their movement is sound, strong and will be victorious. In the urban insurrection, the workers are destined to play the part of the extreme element and simultaneously that of the ordering element: the element that will not allow the machine, once it has been set in motion, to stop and that will hold it on the right course. The workers represent the intervention here and now of the broad masses in the revolution; they are the living personification of the interests and the will of the masses themselves.

In the countryside, we must count above all on the action and support of the poor peasants, the "landless". They will be driven into activity, like the peasants at Andria, by the need to resolve the problem of how to live, by the need to struggle for bread. And this is not all: they will be obliged by the same perpetual need, the ever-present danger of death from hunger or bullets, to put pressure on the other sectors of the agricultural population, to make them set up organs for collective control over production in the countryside as well. These organs of control, the peasants' Councils, despite the fact that they will leave intermediate forms of private land ownership (small holdings) in existence, will have to carry out a psychological and technical transformation of the countryside and become the basis of a new communal life-style: centres through which the revolutionary elements will be able to enforce their will in a continuous and concrete fashion.

Today, the peasants too need to know what has to be done; their actions must put down deep and tenacious roots that adhere, as in the case of the workers, to the process of the production of wealth. Just as the workers look to the factory, so the peasants must start to look to the fields as their future work community.

The Andria uprising informs us that this problem is ripe for solution. At bottom, it is the problem of the whole of the Italian South: the problem of how those who work the land should win it for themselves. It is the responsibility of our Party to confront this problem and resolve it. The take-over of the land is being organized today with the same weapons the workers will use to take over the factories: i.e. through the formation of organs that will enable the working masses to govern themselves, at their place of work. The workers' and peasants' movements are flowing naturally in the same direction, towards the creation of organs of proletarian power.

The Russian revolution derived its strength and salvation from the fact that the workers and peasants there, though starting from opposite points and motivated by different feelings, found themselves united with a common aim in a common struggle. For both became convinced through experience that they would never liberate themselves from the oppression of the bosses, unless they gave their own organization of conquest a form that enabled them to eliminate the exploiter directly from the sphere of production. This form was the Council, the Soviet. In this way, class struggle and peasant war fused their destinies inseparably and had a common outcome in the establishment of directive organs for the whole activity of the country.

In our country, the problem is identical. Workers and peasants must collaborate in concrete fashion by organizing their forces in a single body. The latest upsurge found them united, perhaps by chance; the revolution must find them united on a conscious and fully-agreed basis. Factory control and land seizure must be seen as a single problem. North and South must work together, and together lay the preparations for the nation's transformation into a productive community. It must become more and more obvious that today only the workers are in a position to give a "complete" solution to the problem of the South. The problem of unity, which three bourgeois generations have left unsolved, will finally be resolved by the workers and peasants collaborating in a common political structure – the political structure in which they succeed in organizing their dictatorship and making it triumph.

Unsigned, written in collaboration by Antonio Gramsci and Palmiro Togliatti, *L'Ordine Nuovo*, 6–13 December 1919, Vol. I, No. 29.

32. THE PARTY AND THE REVOLUTION

The Socialist Party, with its network of sections (which in turn in the great industrial centres are the pivot of a solid and powerful system of local branches); with its provincial Federations, tightly unified by the currents of ideas and activities radiating out from the urban sections; with its annual congresses which embody the Party's supreme authority, exercised by the mass of members through well-defined delegations, limited in their powers – congresses that are always convoked to discuss and resolve immediate and concrete problems; with its leadership, which emanates directly from the congress and constitutes its permanent executive and administrative committee – taken all in all, the Socialist Party constitutes an apparatus of proletarian democracy which could easily, in political fantasy, be seen as "exemplary".

The Socialist Party is a model of a "libertarian" society, voluntarily disciplined by an explicit act of consciousness. To imagine the whole of human society as one huge Socialist Party, with its applications for admission and its resignations, inevitably excites the fondness for social contracts of many subversive spirits who were brought up more on J. J. Rousseau and anarchist pamphlets, than on the historical and economic doctrines of Marxism. The Constitution of the Russian Soviet Republic is based on exactly the same principles as the Socialist Party; the Russian government of popular sovereignty functions in ways which are impressively similar to the government of the Socialist Party. Hence it is not surprising that these analogies and instinctive aspirations should give rise to the revolutionary myth that equates proletarian power with a dictatorship of the system of Socialist Party sections.

* * * * *

This view is at least as Utopian as that which sees the trade unions and Chambers of Labour as expressing the process of revolutionary development. Communist society can only be viewed as a "natural" formation inherent in the instruments of production and exchange, and the revolution can be seen as the act of historical recognition of how "natural" this formation is. Hence the revolutionary process can only be identified with a spontaneous movement of the working masses brought about by the clash of contradictions inherent in the social system characterized by the régime of capitalist property. Caught in the pincers of capitalist conflicts, and threatened by condemnation without appeal to the loss of civil and intellectual rights, the masses break with the forms of bourgeois democracy and leave behind them the legality of the bourgeois constitution. Society could fall apart, all production of useful wealth could collapse and men could plunge into a dark abyss of poverty, barbarism and death, if the historical consciousness of the popular masses is not aroused and if they do not find a new framework, create a new order in the process of production and distribution of wealth. The proletariat's organs of struggle are the "agents" of this colossal mass movement, and the Socialist Party is undoubtedly the primary "agent" in this process of destruction and neo-formation – but it is not and cannot be seen as the form of the process, a form malleable and plastic to the leaders' will. German Social-Democracy (understood as a totality involving trade-union and political activity) effected the paradox of violently forcing the process of the German proletarian revolution into the form of its own organization, believing it was thereby dominating history. It created *its own* Councils, by fiat, and made sure its own men would have a majority on them. It shackled and domesticated the revolution. Today it has lost all contact with historical reality, save for the beating of Noske's fist on the worker's nape, and the revolutionary process pursues its own uncontrolled and still mysterious course, to well up again from unknown depths of violence and pain.

The Socialist Party achieves the same results through its intransigence in the political domain as the trade unions do in the economic field: it puts an end to free competition. With its revolutionary programme, the Socialist Party pulls out from under the bourgeois State apparatus its democratic basis in the consent of the governed. Its influence sinks deeper and deeper into the mass of the people, and assures them that the hardship in which they are floundering is not something trifling, nor a sickness without end, but corresponds to an objective necessity: it is the ineluctable moment of a dialectical process which must debouch in a blood-letting, a regeneration of society. And so the Party comes to be identified with the historical consciousness of the mass of the people, and it governs their spontaneous, irresistible movement. This is an incorporeal government that is transmitted through millions and millions of spiritual links; it is a radiation of prestige, that can become a truly effective government only in climactic moments, when it is expressed as a summons into the streets, as a physical marshalling of militant forces who are ready to fight to ward off danger or dissolve a cloud of reactionary violence.

Once the Party has succeeded in paralysing the functioning of the legal government over the mass of the people, the phase of its most difficult and delicate activity opens before it – the phase of positive activity. The views propagated by the Party operate autonomously in the individual consciousness, and they cause new social patterns to emerge in line with these views. They produce organs that function in accordance with their own inner laws, they produce an embryonic apparatus of power in which the masses exercise their own government and acquire a consciousness of their own historical responsibility and their own particular mission: to create the conditions for a regenerative communism. As a compact and militant ideological formation, the Party exerts an influence over this inner elaboration of new structures, this activity on the part of millions and millions of social infusoria building up the red coral reefs which one day in the not too distant future will burst forth above the waves and still them, and lull the oceanic tempest, and establish a new balance between the currents and climes. But this influx is organic, it grows from the circulation of ideas, from the maintenance of an intact apparatus of spiritual government, from the fact that millions and millions of workers know that, as they establish new systems and a new order, the historical consciousness that moves them has its living embodiment in the Socialist Party, that it is justified by the doctrine of the Socialist Party, that it has a powerful bulwark in the political strength of the Socialist Party.

The Party remains the leading apparatus within this irresistible mass movement, and exercises the most effective of dictatorships, a dictatorship based on prestige, on the conscious and spontaneous acceptance of an authority that workers see as indispensable if their mission is to be accomplished. It would be disastrous if a sectarian conception of the Party's role in the revolution were to prompt the claim that this apparatus had actually assumed a concrete form, that the system for controlling the masses in movement had been frozen in mechanical forms of immediate power, forcing the revolutionary process into the forms of the Party. The result would be to successfully divert a number of men, to "master" history: but the real revolutionary process would slip from the control and influence of the party, which would unconsciously become an organ of conservatism.

* * * * *

The Socialist Party's propaganda today stresses the following irrefutable theses. The traditional relations of capitalist appropriation of the products of human labour have been radically altered. Before the war, Italian labour consented without serious explosive resistance to the appropriation of 60 per cent of the wealth produced through work, at the hands of a tiny capitalist minority and the State, while the tens of millions of the working population had to be content with a meagre 40 per cent to satisfy their basic needs together with their higher cultural requirements. Today, after the war, a new situation has emerged. Italian society produces only half of the wealth it consumes. The State is charging colossal sums to future labour, i.e. it is gradually enslaving Italian labour to international plutocracy. To the two extortionists of a slice of production (the capitalists and the State) a third, purely parasitic element has been added: the petty bourgeoisie of the military-bureaucratic caste that came into existence during the war. This caste appropriates precisely that half of non-produced wealth that is being charged to future labour; it extorts it directly in the form of stipends and pensions, and indirectly because its parasitic role presupposes the existence of a whole parasitic apparatus. If Italian society produces goods worth only 15 billion Lire while it consumes 30, and these 15 are produced by the 8 hours daily labour of the tens of millions of working people who receive six to seven billion in wages, the capitalist budget can normally be balanced in only one way: by forcing the tens of millions of working people to take the same wages but work an extra one, two, three, four or five hours overtime – overtime which is unpaid, and serves to enrich capital and allow it to resume its accumulatory function, and serves to fill the coffers of the State so that it can pay off its debts. Finally, it consolidates the economic position of the pensioned petty bourgeoisie and rewards it for its armed service to the State and to Capital in forcing the working population to exhaust itself on machines and patches of land.

In this general situation of capitalist relations, class struggle can have no other aim than the conquest of State power on the part of the working class, which can turn that vast power against the parasites and force them to take up work again and abolish at a stroke the monstrous booty they extort at present. To this end the whole of the working masses must co-operate; they must adopt a conscious structure in accordance with the position they occupy in the process of production and exchange. Thus within the context of the Council, every worker and peasant is summoned to collaborate in the effort of regeneration, to build the apparatus of industrial government and the dictatorship. The present form of the class struggle for power is embodied in the Councils. This, then, is the network of institutions in which the revolutionary process is unfolding: the Councils, the trade unions, the Socialist Party. The Councils, historical products of society, brought into being by the need to master the apparatus of production; products born of the newly achieved self-awareness of the producers. The trade unions and the Party, voluntary associations, driving forces of the revolutionary process, the "agents" and "administrators" of the revolution: the trade unions coordinating the productive forces and impressing a communistic form on the industrial apparatus; the Socialist Party, the living and dynamic model of a social system that unites discipline with freedom and endows the human spirit with all the energy and enthusiasm of which it is capable.

Unsigned, *L'Ordine Nuovo*, 27 December 1919, Vol. I, No. 31.

33. WORKERS AND PEASANTS

Industrial production has to be controlled directly by the workers organized on the basis of firms; the process of control has to be unified and co-ordinated by means of purely working-class trade-union bodies. Workers and socialists cannot see control over industry exercised by the (corrupt, venal and non-revocable) functionaries of the capitalist State as being in accordance with their interests or their aspirations: any such form of control over industry can signify nothing but a re-emergence of the committees of industrial mobilization that would benefit only capitalist parasitism.[47]

The slogan "the land to the peasants" must be understood in the sense that the modern agricultural holdings and farms should be controlled by the agricultural workers organized on the basis of individual holdings and farms; it must mean that large-scale agricultural holdings should be administered by the Councils of poor peasants in the villages and agricultural hamlets. Agricultural workers, revolutionary poor peasants and conscious socialists cannot view the propaganda about "uncultivated or poorly cultivated lands" as being in accordance with their interests and aspirations, or in the interests of proletarian education – which is a necessity for a communist republic. This propaganda can have no other effect than a dissolution of revolutionary consciousness and confidence, and its results can be nothing but a monstrous defamation of socialism. What can a poor peasant achieve by occupying uncultivated or poorly cultivated lands? Without machinery, without accommodation on the place of work, without credit to tide him over till harvest-time, without co-operative institutions to acquire the harvest (if – long before harvest time – the peasant has not hung himself from the strongest bush or the least unhealthy-looking wild fig in the undergrowth of his uncultivated land) and preserve him from the clutches of the usurers – without all these things, what can a poor peasant achieve by occupying? Momentarily he can satisfy his land-holder's instincts and slake his primitive thirst for land. But subsequently, when it dawns on him that his arms are not equal to the task of breaking open ground that only dynamite can rip apart; when it dawns on him that he needs seeds, fertilizers and tools;

when he realizes that no one is going to give him this indispensable equipment; when he sees a future succession of days and nights to be spent on a piece of land without a house, without water, infested by malaria – then the peasant becomes aware of his impotence, his solitude and the desperation of his plight. He turns into a bandit, not a revolutionary; he becomes an assassin of the "gentry", not a fighter for communism.

For this reason, revolutionary workers and peasants and conscious socialists have not seen any reflection of their interests or aspirations in these parliamentary initiatives to do with control over industry and "uncultivated or poorly cultivated lands". They have seen in them only parliamentary "cretinism", reformist and opportunist illusions, and counter-revolution. All the same, these parliamentary moves could have served some purpose. They could have served to inform *all* the workers and *all* the peasants of the precise terms of the industrial and agricultural problem, and of the necessary and sufficient requirements to resolve it. It could have served to let the broad masses of the peasants in the *whole* of Italy know that the solution to the agricultural problem lies solely in the hands of the urban workers in Northern Italy, and that the solution will be put into effect only by a dictatorship of the proletariat.

The Northern bourgeoisie has subjugated the South of Italy and the Islands, and reduced them to exploitable colonies; by emancipating itself from capitalist slavery, the Northern proletariat will emancipate the Southern peasant masses enslaved to the banks and the parasitic industry of the North. The economic and political regeneration of the peasants should not be sought in a division of uncultivated or poorly cultivated lands, but in the solidarity of the industrial proletariat. This in turn needs the solidarity of the peasantry and has an "interest" in ensuring that capitalism is not re-born economically from landed property; that Southern Italy and the Islands do not become a military base for capitalist counter-revolution. By introducing workers' control over industry, the proletariat will orient industry to the production of agricultural machinery for the peasants, clothing and footwear for the peasants, electric lighting for the peasants, and will prevent industry and the banks from exploiting the peasants and subjecting them as slaves to the strongrooms. By smashing the factory autocracy, by smashing the oppressive apparatus of the capitalist State and by setting up a workers' State that will subject the capitalists to the law of useful labour, the workers will smash all the chains that bind the peasant to his poverty and desperation. By setting up a workers' dictatorship and taking over the industries and banks, the proletariat will swing the enormous weight of the State bureaucracy behind the peasants in their struggle against the landowners, against the elements and against poverty. The proletariat will provide the peasants with credit, set up co-operatives, guarantee security of person and property against looters and carry out public works of reclamation and irrigation. It will do all this because an increase in agricultural production is in its interests; because to win and keep the solidarity of the peasants is in its interests; because it is in its interests to orient industrial production to work which will promote peace and brotherhood between town and countryside, between North and South.

In this sense, all conscious workers and peasants will wish to see socialist parliamentary action directed towards: launching a campaign of revolutionary education among the broad masses; unifying the feelings and aspirations of the broad masses in an understanding of the communist programme; ceaselessly spreading the conviction that the current problems of the industrial and agricultural economy can be resolved only outside Parliament, against Parliament, by the workers' State.

Unsigned, *L'Ordine Nuovo*, 3 January 1920, Vol. I, No. 32. Under the heading "The Week in Politics".

34. THE HISTORICAL ROLE OF THE CITIES

The communist revolution will be carried out by the working class, understood in the Marxist sense as a social stratum made up of the urban workers unified and moulded by the factory and the capitalist industrial system. Just as the city, this organ of industry and civil life, was the instrument of capitalist economic power and the bourgeois dictatorship, so it will be the instrument of communist economic power and the proletarian dictatorship. The proletarian dictatorship will preserve this magnificent apparatus of industrial and intellectual production, this driving force of civil life, from the ruin that looms over it ever more menacingly. Corrupted and devastated by the imperialistic war and its economic consequences, bourgeois power cannot hide its gradual dissolution in the cities, which are steadily declining *vis-à-vis* the countryside. The city-dwellers are hungry, and before this basic need which can be met only by the countryside, all the historical and intellectual conquests achieved by the cities lose their worth and disintegrate. The proletarian dictatorship will preserve the cities from ruin; it will provoke civil war in the countryside and bind the broadest strata of the poor peasants to the cities. In this way it will prevent these marvellous engines of civil progress, the modern cities, from being destroyed piecemeal by the land-holders and usurers of the countryside, who in their uncouth way loathe and despise modern industrial civilization.

In Italy, the same situation as applied in the national *Risorgimento*, in the development of the bourgeois revolution, is being reproduced today in the development of the communist revolution: the effective historical forces, then as now, are especially the two cities Turin and Milan. The two cities are linked by a multitude of relations. The national *Risorgimento* had its fulcrum in Milan. Bourgeois energies eager for expansion teemed in the region of Milan and Lombardy: for them, the organization of Italy into a unified system was an existential class necessity. They needed a unified system of tariffs, weights and measures, currency, transport, maritime outlets, taxes and civil laws. But the Milanese bourgeoisie would never have been capable of creating a bourgeois State, of liberating itself from the Austrian yoke.

To this end, barricades were not enough, nor individual heroism, nor the Five Days, not yet the liberal city of Milan on its own, crushed as it was by the Austrian-sympathizing countryside.[48] The historical force that was decisive, that was capable of creating an Italian State and unifying the bourgeois class on a firm national basis, was Turin.

The bourgeois population of Piedmont was not as rich or daring as its Lombard counterpart, but it was solidly unified with its own State power, it enjoyed an iron military and administrative tradition and, through the intelligence of its politicians, it had succeeded in becoming a part of the European political system. The Piedmontese State was a tight-knit apparatus of conquest, capable of provoking, through its impact, an Italian neo-formation; it was able to provide the new State with a powerful military and administrative nucleus, and to give the Italian people an organic form – its *own* form. Turin was the nerve-centre of this powerful Piedmontese system. Turin was the force that unified the Piedmontese population. It was the forge of the capitalist revolution in Italy.

Today Turin is not the capitalist city *par excellence*, but it is the industrial city, the proletarian city, *par excellence*. The Turin working class is solid, disciplined and *distinct* as in few other cities in the world. Turin is like one great factory: its working population conforms to a single pattern, being powerfully unified by industrial production.

The Turin proletariat was able to advance so far along the road of Soviet-type mass organization precisely because of this powerfully unified character of the city's industry; precisely because, through its experiences of class struggle, it had acquired a vivid awareness of its homogeneity and solidarity. And a similar awareness could rapidly be acquired by the whole of the working people of Piedmont, for in its traditions of a patient and tenacious approach to work, in its heritage of material and cultural wealth accumulated over many centuries of political independence and self-governing practice, Piedmont continues to form a highly individual and distinct economic unit of an autonomous kind. It produces nearly all the wealth it consumes and exports so much that it is indispensable, not only to Italy, but to Europe itself.

The model of State organization that will encompass the whole nation and embody the dictatorship of the proletariat can only arise from this compact and disciplined system of industrial and agricultural production, magnificently equipped by capitalism to exercise political dominance over the entire nation. (The phenomenon of Giolitti is at bottom nothing other than a consequence of the blind faith Italian capitalism has in the government and leadership traditions of the bourgeoisie of Piedmont.) The conditions of economic ruin in Italy and the poverty of its natural resources will require an enormous productive effort from the proletariat once it takes power. Hence the workers' dictatorship in Italy can be seen as capable of governing and developing as far as the establishment of communism, only if the worker and peasant class succeeds in setting up a tight-knit system of workers' and peasants' Councils that take over the national apparatus of production and exchange, acquiring a keen sense of their economic responsibility and giving the workers a powerful and watchful self-awareness as producers.

The working class can model its national proletarian economic State on the regional economic system of Piedmont – an important producer of foods (grain, rice, potatoes, chestnuts, wine), a region that is rich in natural electric power, boasts a variety of industries (food, textiles and clothing, engineering, building, wood, rubber, leather, chemical industries, etc.), produces more than it consumes locally, and is centralized in the great industrial apparatus of Turin.

By virtue of their particular structure and the well-defined and cohesive character of the proletariat produced by the capitalist mode of production, Turin and Piedmont are called upon to play the same role in the communist revolution and creation of the workers' State as they played in the capitalist revolution and creation of the bourgeois State.

But in the communist revolution too, Milan will be the fulcrum of the movement. The bourgeoisie's most important and powerful financial forces are located in Milan and the proletariat will have to fight its most difficult battles there. The nerve-centre of this immense factory of capitalist profit, the bourgeois State, is located in Milan. From Milan, thousands and millions of threads branch out all over Italy and subjugate the labour of the workers and peasants to high finance. The proletariat will destroy the capitalist dictatorship only by taking over the powerful commercial and financial concerns that have their headquarters in Milan and turning them into an instrument of the economic and political power of the proletariat. The communist revolution in Milan signifies the communist revolution in Italy, for in effect Milan is the capital of the bourgeois dictatorship.

As a service to counter-revolution, the Reggio Emilia weekly *La Giustizia* has reproduced and commented on a passage from J. Wanin's article published in *L'Ordine Nuovo* of 6–13 December, where it says:

"with rare exceptions (which from this point of view are interesting exceptions) the capitalist countries today possess a State apparatus so concentrated that a political revolution can only be conceived as a beheading of this apparatus: the revolution must be carried out in the capitals if it is not to be ground underfoot." *La Giustizia* is concerned with the exception of Rome, not to offer the workers a solution to the problem, but to discourage them, to try and convince them that the revolution is impossible in Italy because the capital "is not an industrial city and is not surrounded by proletarian communities". But the fact is that the Italian State has to be beheaded at Milan, not Rome; for the country's real capitalist governing apparatus is located not in Rome, but in Milan. Rome is the bureaucratic capital; in Rome, the proletarian dictatorship will not have to struggle against the formidable economic power of the bourgeoisie, but merely against the sabotage of bureaucrats. [Rationing of foodstuffs and a solid corps of armed workers in Rome will guarantee the Italian Soviet government normal administration and the security that will be indispensable in carrying out the essential task of transferring the bureaucratic capital to the economic capital.][49] As a city, Rome has no role whatsoever in Italian social intercourse; it represents nothing. Rome will be subjected to the iron laws against parasites that the workers' State will enact.

Unsigned, *L'Ordine Nuovo*, 17 January 1920, Vol. I, No. 3. Under the heading "The Week in Politics".

35. FIRST: RENEW THE PARTY

The Socialist Party is the party of the workers and poor peasants. Having emerged in the field of liberal democracy (the field of political competition, which is a projection of the process of development of capitalism), as one of the social forces striving to create for themselves a governmental basis and conquer State power in order to direct it to the advantage of their own followers, its mission is to organize the workers and poor peasants into a dominant class; to study and promote the conditions that favour the advent of a proletarian democracy.

The Italian Socialist Party has succeeded in accomplishing the easiest and most elementary part of its historical task. It has succeeded in stirring the masses down to their deepest levels; it has succeeded in focusing the attention of the working people on its programme for revolution and a workers' State; it has succeeded in constructing a government apparatus numbering three million citizens which, if it is consolidated and materialized in permanent revolutionary institutions, could well be capable of taking over State power. But the Socialist Party has had no success so far as the essential aspect of its historical task is concerned. It has not succeeded in giving a permanent and solid form to the apparatus it had succeeded in building up by its agitation amongst the masses. It has made no progress and so has given way to a crisis of disorder and lethargy. Built to win power, built as an alignment of militant forces determined to give battle, the Socialist Party's government apparatus is falling to pieces, collapsing. Every day sees the Party lose contact more and more with the broad masses in movement. Events occur and the Party is absent. The country is racked by feverish spasms, the forces eroding bourgeois democracy and the capitalist régime continue to operate implacably and ruthlessly, and yet the Party does not intervene, does not illuminate the broad masses of workers and peasants, does not justify its activity or its non-activity, does not launch slogans to calm impatience, check demoralization, hold serried the ranks and strong the structure of the worker and peasant armies. The Party, which had become the greatest historical force in the Italian nation, has fallen prey to a crisis of political infantilism and is today the most crippling of the social weaknesses of the Italian nation. No wonder then that in such propitious circumstances, the seeds of dissolution of revolutionary unity – opportunist and reformist nihilism and the pseudo-revolutionary phrase-mongering of the anarchists (two aspects of a single petty-bourgeois tendency) – should swarm and multiply with such striking speed.

Daily, the national and international conditions for the proletarian revolution are becoming more clearly and precisely visible and are establishing themselves. But now, at the very moment when it could be decisive, the supreme instrument of the proletarian revolution in Italy – the Socialist Party – is falling apart, attacked and insidiously entangled by parliamentary politicians and national trade-union officials; by individuals who claim a representative authority that has no concrete or serious basis, that is founded on ambiguity, on the absence of any continuity of action and on that mental laziness which is characteristic of the workers as much as of all other Italians. And from the communist wing, the revolutionary wing, the directive organs nominated by the revolutionary majority, no joint action whatsoever to check this decomposition; to disinfect the Party and organize it into a homogeneous unity; to organize it as a section of the IIIrd International, powerfully integrated into the world system of revolutionary forces which are striving in all seriousness to carry through the communist programme.

The resistance of the imperialist bloc, which had succeeded in subjecting the world to a handful of finance houses, has been smashed and broken up by the military victories of the Russian workers' State. Today, the system of the international proletarian revolution, which is based upon the existence and development into a world power of the Russian workers' State, has at its command an army of two million bayonets: an army overflowing with warlike enthusiasm, as a result of its victories and of its consciousness that it is the protagonist of contemporary history. The victories and advances of the army of the IIIrd International are shaking the very foundations of the capitalist system; they are accelerating the process of decomposition of the bourgeois States and exacerbating the conflicts within the western democracies. The English are concerned about India, Turkey, Persia, Afghanistan and China, where hotbeds of revolt are multiplying; they have gently applied pressure to remove Clemenceau from the political arena.[50] The fall of the anti-Bolshevik puppet has at once revealed the cracks in the reactionary French bloc, and has set in train the disintegration of the political State: the communist and intransigent tendency within the workers' movement has been strengthened. The Russian question pits the opportunism of Lloyd George against the counter-revolutionary intransigence of Winston Churchill. But the terrain of British democracy, formerly a marvellous arena for the radical demagogy of Lloyd George, has been completely transformed: the structure of the English working class continues to evolve, slowly but surely, towards higher forms. The workers are clamouring to intervene more frequently and directly in formulating their programmes of action. Trade-union congresses are becoming more numerous and the revolutionaries are making their voices heard there more frequently and effectively. The permanent headquarters of the trade-union congresses is slipping from the grip of the parliamentary Labour group into the hands of a central workers' committee. In Germany the Scheidemann government is falling apart, it feels all popular support fall away, as the white terror brutally rages. The communist and independent workers have regained a certain freedom of movement, and the conviction is spreading that only a proletarian dictatorship can save the German nation from economic collapse and militarist reaction. The international counter-revolutionary system is collapsing, through the sharpening of internal contradictions within bourgeois democracy and the capitalist economy and through the gigantic thrusts of the Russian proletariat. The Italian bourgeois State is falling to pieces, under the impact of the colossal strikes in the public services and the ridiculous failure of its foreign and domestic policies.

The necessary and sufficient conditions for the proletarian revolution are present on both the national and international levels. But at this crucial moment, the Socialist Party is not up to its task. A party of agitators, negators and intransigents in questions of general tactics, a party of apostles of elementary theories, it is incapable of organizing and mobilizing the broad masses into movement; incapable of filling the minutes and days; incapable of finding a sphere of action which will keep it in constant touch with the broad masses. It has not succeeded in organizing its own internal unity. It has none of the theoretical and practical discipline that would enable it to keep in close contact with national and international proletarian conditions in order to master them, to control events and not be overwhelmed and crushed by them. The party of revolutionary workers and peasants, it allows the permanent army of the revolution, the workers' unions, to remain under the control of opportunists who can at will bewitch its ability to manœuvre; who systematically sabotage every revolutionary action;

who form a party within the Party – and the stronger party, because they control the motor ganglions of the working-class body. Two strikes which could have been deadly to the State – and which now will leave long trails of recriminations and polemical attacks from the anarchists – took place without the Party having a word to say, a method to suggest other than the obsolete and worn-out one of the yet more worn-out and obsolete IInd International: the *distinction* between a political and an economic strike.[51] And so, while the State was going through a desperate crisis, while the bourgeoisie, armed and brimming with hatred, could have launched an offensive against the working class, while a militarist *coup* loomed on the horizon, the workers' revolutionary centres were left to their own devices, without a word of a slogan to guide them. The working class found itself trapped and imprisoned in a system of watertight compartments, bewildered, disillusioned, exposed to all manner of anarchoid temptations.

Are we discouraged and demoralized? No – but the naked and raw truth must be spoken; it is essential to expose a situation which can and must be changed. The Socialist Party must renew itself if it is not to be overwhelmed and crushed by events which are almost upon us. It must renew itself, for its defeat would signify the defeat of the revolution. The Socialist Party must be a section of the IIIrd International in earnest, and must start by carrying out the latter's programme within itself, within the united body of the organized workers. The organized masses must become masters of their own struggle organs, must "organize themselves into a ruling class" first of all within their own institutions, and must work together with the Socialist Party. The communist workers, the revolutionaries who are conscious of the tremendous responsibilities of the present period – it is they who must renew the Party, who must give it a precise form and a clear direction, and who must prevent the petty-bourgeois opportunists from reducing it to the level of so many other parties in this land of Pulcinella.[52]

Unsigned, *L'Ordine Nuovo*, 24–31 January 1920, Vol. I, No. 35. Under the heading "The Week in Politics".

36. ACTION PROGRAMME OF THE TURIN SOCIALIST SECTION

The electoral committee has decided to select comrades who can be relied upon to complete and further develop the work of the former executive commission, organizing its revolutionary action in the light of the new demands of the national and international situation.[53] It therefore sets out the basic criteria which have guided it, by virtue of which the list it has compiled represents not simply a collection of names, but a well-defined action programme.

* * * * *

In this latest period of national and international political life, the Party has shown itself to be incapable of giving a firm and precise direction to the class struggle being fought by the Italian working people. The Party's activity has been confused with the action of the parliamentary group – with an action, in other words, that is either openly reformist and opportunist or utterly void of any concrete content that might serve to educate (in the revolutionary sense as laid down by the Congress of Bologna) the widest sectors of the population, in order to rally them to the cause and programme of the proletarian revolution. This confused and aimless situation was highlighted by the discussions held by the Florence session of the National Council:[54] uncertain and confused discussions, from which it is obvious that: 1. the Party's leading bodies are being manipulated more than ever by the opportunists and reformists; 2. the impotence of the maximalists' actions is due to the fact that they have no firm and concrete conception of the stage through which the class struggle is passing, and no method that would enable them to counterpose a permanent activity of their own to the permanent activity carried out by the reformists and opportunists within the highest institutions of the proletarian movement.

If this state of confusion and disorientation is to be overcome, the party must initiate a positive campaign among the masses in pursuit of the theses of the IIIrd International, which were acclaimed by an overwhelming majority at Bologna and then forgotten at once through the attraction of Parliament.

The Turin socialist section must take responsibility for pushing the Socialist Party to promote the establishment of Workers' and Peasants' Councils all over Italy; these would be based in the first instance on an extension of trade-union action, directed no longer at winning improvements in hours and wages, but at bringing to the fore the question of proletarian control over the instruments of labour and over industrial and agricultural production. The demand for control must have the objective of organizing the whole of the working people in their places of work and production; of binding the broadest sections of the masses more solidly together within a primary economic unit and on this concrete and solid basis – the only one which offers freedom of manœuvre so long as Italy has not openly entered the phase of violent civil war – allowing the Party to launch its propaganda and begin the task of building the higher institutions (the political Soviets) in which the dictatorship of the proletariat will be embodied. The Party must therefore resist any attempt on the part of the reformists and opportunists to turn control into a function of the bourgeois State and make the Factory Councils into organs of industrial collaboration, collaboration with the bourgeois State bureaucracy and with Parliament. Control must be exercised by purely proletarian organs, and the working class must make it the vehicle for their mass revolutionary action.

The Turin socialist section, on the existing basis of the healthy and powerful Factory Councils that have been formed, can and must enter the second phase of the revolutionary process referred to. Every energetic action carried out by the Turin section to this end will serve to encourage the working masses in the other industrial centres and to obstruct counterfeit schemes on the part of opportunists, who would like to fool the workers by giving the name of Councils to organs that have no hope of developing or promoting revolutionary action.

In Turin, the Factory Councils have by now established strong bonds of proletarian discipline among the working masses. Now the section must use this solid basis to promote the establishment of a Workers' Council for the city, which will strive to focus the political and revolutionary attention of the masses on itself and to be considered by the masses themselves as the local organ of future proletarian power – for the conquest of which the struggle must now begin. In the transitional period, the Council will have to operate both as an organ of constant criticism of Parliament and the bourgeois State and as an organ for direct control of the municipalities.

The municipal elections will have to be fought on this slogan: all real power of decision to the Workers' Council. The local section will have to win a majority on the Council and ensure that the offices of the presidency, education, propaganda, etc. are entrusted to communist comrades.

Under the prodding of the local section, the Council will have to prepare, discuss and publish draft laws designed to teach the masses the true aims of communism and to show them that the solution to the pressing problems of the current period can be found only by a purely proletarian centre of power, by a workers' State: draft laws designed, therefore, to give a real and immediate significance to the slogan All Power to the Soviets!

In order to give the revolutionary movement full autonomy and freedom of manœuvre, the section must work out an organic solution to the problem of relations between the Party and the trade-union organizations. To this end, the section must set about forming communist groups on a permanent basis in every league and union. These groups will carry out revolutionary propaganda within the organization and constantly criticize and block any opportunist or reformist degeneration within the trade-union movement. In this way, the two major instruments of the class struggle will be brought into close collaboration, based no longer simply on an accidental pact of alliance, but on an inner fusion and identity of their programmes. Through these communist groups within the unions, the section will be able to promote the establishment of industrial unions (for manual workers, white-collar workers, technicians). These will have the task, together with the Factory Councils, of drawing up and creating the higher institutions of workers' control and communist management of production, thereby surpassing in effect the current phase of struggle over hours and wages.

The problem of *Avanti!* will be raised in discussion, so that, in agreement with the competent organs, a solution can be found that is consistent with the ever increasing needs of our region. At the same time, the collection of the necessary funds will have to be intensified, for without them any discussion of technical and administrative improvements is purely academic.

We will have to ensure that the programme of work adopted at the last elections will, as far as possible, be fully carried out. At the same time, we must ensure that the new life we are trying to infuse into our major co-operative institution does not compromise its solidity, but on the contrary accelerates its development, attracting to it ever broader sections of supporters within the mass of the working class – which will come to see it as a valid instrument for defence and class struggle – and preparing its role as the supreme organ for requisition and social distribution.

With the Turin Co-operative Alliance as well, the Executive Committee of the Party should ask the administrative council every six months for a report on the development of the enterprise and on the work done to carry out the approved programme.

The working masses will frequently have to be summoned to consultative assemblies, in the interests of preserving that profitable harmony with the class that has been so fertile of results in the past and constitutes our greatest strength now and in the days to come.

In strict compliance with the decisions of the national leading bodies, we shall have to carry out agitational work among the masses on all questions involving real class interests, with the aim of preserving and intensifying the proletariat's political sensibility and steering it towards communism.

We believe that the bourgeoisie cannot avoid the fate that awaits it other than by having recourse to a reactionary and military dictatorship, and that sooner or later this is what it will do. It is, therefore, imperative that the Party take steps to safeguard its own organization and the proletariat its own gains, not only by means of the range of political and trade-union actions we have referred to above, but also by making specific material preparations.

Such activity obviously cannot be the responsibility of an Executive Committee, precisely because it is only an executive body; but the E.C. must support all positive and serious efforts in this direction by comrades and groups who volunteer for the job. In this work – which is as delicate as it is valuable – the E.C. must be concerned above all to forestall the emergence of isolated and undisciplined movements, more likely to compromise than to hasten our victory.

It is on this main axis, coinciding as it does with the real revolutionary process, that the local section must base all its activity, directed towards 1. solving the problem of arming the proletariat; 2. arousing throughout the province a powerful class movement of poor peasants and smallholders, in solidarity with the industrial movement.

Unsigned, *L'Ordine Nuovo*, 24–31 January 1920, Vol. I, No. 35.

37. THE INSTRUMENTS OF LABOUR

The communist revolution achieves autonomy for the producer both in the economic and in the political field. Political action on the part of the working class (with the aim of establishing the dictatorship, the workers' State) acquires real historical value only when it is a function of the development of new economic conditions, pregnant with possibilities and eager to expand and consolidate themselves once and for all. If political action is to have a successful outcome, it must coincide with economic action. The communist revolution is the historical recognition of pre-existing economic facts: it is these facts which it reveals, which it vigorously defends from all reactionary manœuvres and which it codifies in law – to which, in other words, it gives an organic and systematic form. This is why the construction of *communist* political Soviets cannot help but follow in historical terms the emergence and primary systematization of the Factory Councils. In the first instance, the Factory Council and the system of Councils assay and demonstrate empirically the new positions which the working class has come to occupy in the field of production. The Councils give the working class an awareness of its current value, its true role, its responsibility and its future. The working class draws conclusions from the quantum of positive experience amassed personally by individuals, acquires the character and mentality of a ruling class and organizes itself as such; in other words, it sets up political Soviets and establishes its dictatorship.

In this respect, the reformists and opportunists are vague in the extreme when they assert that the revolution depends on the extent to which the instruments of labour have developed. For the reformists, the term "instruments of labour" is a kind of genie in the lamp. They love the expression "maximalist nihilism", they let it resonate in their mouths and their brains, but they are careful not to be specific in any concrete way, they are careful not to hazard a test of their knowledge on this point. What do they mean by the term "instruments of labour"? Do they mean material objects, the individual machines and tools? These alone, or do they include the relations of hierarchical organization within the work crew operating a machine or group of machines on the shop floor? Or do they mean the shop itself, with all its machinery and equipment and its more comprehensive specification and division of labour? Or the whole factory? Or the system of factories within a particular firm? Or the system of relations between various industrial firms, or between various industries, or between industry and agriculture? Or do they mean the position which the nation state occupies in the world, through its export and import relations? Or do they mean the whole complex of these many-sided and inter-dependent relations, which as a whole constitute the conditions of labour and production?

The reformists and opportunists are very careful not to be concretely specific about anything. These people, with their claims to be the depositaries of political wisdom, holders of the lamp with the genie inside, have never studied the real problems of the working class or the problems of the socialist future. They have lost all physical and spiritual contact with the proletarian masses as well as with historical reality. They are long-winded and vacuous rhetoricians, incapable of undertaking any kind of action or giving any concrete judgment whatsoever. Since they have lost all contact with proletarian reality, it is perfectly understandable how they have ended up by convincing themselves, sincerely and in good faith, that the mission of the working class is accomplished when universal suffrage has led to the formation of a ministry with Turati enacting a law that gives prostitutes the vote and Enrico Ferri reforming the disciplinary régime in the mental asylums and prisons.

* * * * *

Have the "instruments of labour" developed over the past twenty years, the past ten years, from the outbreak of the war to the Armistice, from the Armistice to today? The reformist and opportunist intellectuals, who claim monopolistic private property rights in interpreting Marxism, have always believed that playing *scopone* or parliamentary intrigue were more hygienic than a systematic and profound study of the Italian situation.[55] So it comes about that maximalist "nihilism" cannot boast of even a single book on the development of the Italian economy. So it comes about that the Italian working class cannot be informed about the development of conditions for the Italian proletarian revolution. So it comes about that the Italian working class has no defence against the violent confused irruption of the above-mentioned hare-brained, irresponsible "nihilism".

Yet the working class, even without the contribution of the petty-bourgeois intellectuals who have betrayed their mission as educators and masters, nevertheless manages to reach an understanding and evaluation of the process of development which the instruments of labour, the apparatus of production and exchange, have undergone. The meetings and discussions in preparation for the Factory Councils were worth more for the education of the working class than ten years of reading pamphlets and articles written by the owners of the genie in the lamp. The working class has informed itself about the concrete experiences of its individual members and turned them into a collective heritage. The working class has educated itself in communist terms, using its own means and its own systems.

In order to establish the Council, every worker has had to become conscious of his position in the economic domain. He felt initially that he was part of a basic unit, the shop-floor work crew, and he felt that the introduction of technical innovations to the mechanical equipment changed his relations with the technician: the worker is now less dependent than formerly on the technician, the master craftsman, hence he has acquired greater autonomy and can exercise discipline himself.

The role of the technician too has changed. His relations with the industrialist have been completely transformed. He is no longer a trusted employee, an agent of capitalist interests: since the worker can do without the technician for a great number of jobs, the technician becomes redundant as disciplinary agent. The technician too is reduced to the status of a producer, linked to the capitalist via the naked and savage relationship of exploited to exploiter. His mentality sheds its petty-bourgeois encrustations and becomes proletarian, revolutionary in outlook. Industrial innovations and enhanced professional capacity provide the worker with a greater degree of autonomy, put him in a higher industrial bracket. But the changes in hierarchical relations and degrees of indispensability are not limited to the work crew, the basic unit which animates the workshop and the factory.

In the person of the delegate, each work crew expresses the combined consciousness it has acquired of its own degree of autonomy and self-discipline on the job; it thus assumes a concrete personality in the workshop and in the factory. Every Factory Council (Delegates' Assembly) expresses, through the individuals who make up its executive committee, the combined consciousness which the workers throughout the factory have acquired of their position in the industrial domain. The executive committee will note how the role of the factory's director has changed, just as the workers note how the role of the technician has changed.

The factory is not an independent entity. It is not run by an owner-entrepreneur who possesses the commercial know-how (stimulated by the interest that is inherent in private ownership) to buy the raw materials wisely and sell the manufactured object at a profit. These functions have been displaced from the individual factory and transferred to the system of factories owned by the same firm. And it does not stop here: they are concentrated in the hands of a bank or system of banks, who have taken over real responsibility for supplying raw materials and securing markets for sales.

But during the war, and as a result of the war, was it not the State which supplied raw materials to industry, distributed them in accordance with a pre-established plan and became the sole purchaser of production? So what has happened to the economic figure of the owner-entrepreneur, the captain of industry, who is so indispensable to production and who causes the factory to flourish, through his foresight, his initiatives and the stimulus of his own personal interest? This figure has vanished, has been liquidated in the process of development of the instruments of labour, in the process of development of the technical and economic relations that constitute the conditions in which production and work are carried on.

The captain of industry has become the pirate of industry.[56] He has sought refuge in the banks, in the board-rooms, in the corridors of Parliament and the Ministries, in the stock exchanges. The owner of capital has become a dead branch in the field of production. Since he is no longer indispensable and his historical functions have atrophied, he has become a mere police agent; he has placed his "rights" squarely in the hands of the State, so that it will defend them ruthlessly.

In this way the State has become the sole proprietor of the instruments of labour and has taken over all the traditional functions of the entrepreneur. It has become an impersonal machine, buying and distributing raw materials, imposing a plan of production, buying and distributing the products. It is the bourgeois State that does this, the State of incompetent and non-recallable bureaucrats, of politicians, adventurers and swindlers. The consequences? An expansion of the armed police forces, a chaotic increase in incompetent bureaucracy, an attempt to absorb all the malcontents of the petty bourgeoisie who are looking for an easy job, and the consequent creation of endless parasitical bodies to accommodate them.

The number of non-producers is increasing unhealthily and has certainly exceeded the limits which the apparatus of production can sustain. People work and produce nothing, they work themselves to exhaustion and the level of production falls continuously. The reason is that a gaping abyss has been opened up, a huge maw that swallows the products of labour and reduces them to nothing. The unpaid hours of the worker's labour are no longer used to increase the wealth of the capitalists. They are used to satisfy the hunger and rapacity of the multitude of agents, functionaries and idlers; to satisfy the hunger of those directly employed by this crowd of useless parasites. No one is responsible; no one can be blamed. It is the bourgeois State, with its armed forces, which is present at all times and all places; the bourgeois State, which has become the agent of the instruments of labour as they fragment and fall apart, mortgaged and ready to be auctioned on the international market for worn-out, useless scrap-iron. . . .

* * * * *

This is how the instruments of labour, the system of economic and social relations, have developed. The working class has attained a very high degree of autonomy within the domain of production; for the development of commercial and industrial technology has done away with all the useful functions once fulfilled by private property, by the person of the capitalist.

Now that the private owner has automatically been expelled from the immediate domain of production, he has sought refuge in the power of the State, the monopolizer of the distillation of profit. The working class is being held by armed force in a state of economic and political servitude that has become anti-historical, a source of decay and ruin. The working class is closing ranks around its machines; it is creating its own representative institutions based on labour, based on its newly-won autonomy and its newly-won awareness of self-government. The Factory Council is the foundation for its positive experiences and its appropriation of the instruments of labour. It is the solid foundation for the process which must culminate in the workers' dictatorship and the conquest of State power – a power which can then be used to eliminate chaos, the cancer that threatens to suffocate, corrode and dissolve human society.

Unsigned, *L'Ordine Nuovo*, 14 February 1920, Vol. I, No. 37.

38. GOVERNING PARTY AND GOVERNING CLASS

The Socialist Party is a "governing" party, a party dedicated to the exercise of political power. The Socialist Party is the expression of the interests of the proletarian class, i.e. the class made up of the factory workers who own no property and are never likely to own any. It is on the interests of this group that the Socialist Party bases its real activity; on the interests of whomsoever has no property and is mathematically certain of never having any. The working class does not consist entirely of industrial workers; nevertheless the entire working class is destined to end up like the factory proletariat, as a class that has no property in its possession and is mathematically certain never to have any. Therefore, the Socialist Party addresses the whole of the working class – the clerks, the poor peasants and the small land-holders. It popularizes its doctrine – Marxism – and shows the working people, both manual and intellectual, how they will all be reduced to the state of the working class; how all those democratic illusions about becoming a property-owner are precisely illusions, puerility and petty-bourgeois dreams.

The Liberal Party, representing the industrialists and economic competition, is the model party of capitalist society. It is the governing party of the capitalist class: through the effects of competition, it aims to industrialize the whole of society's organized labour and to mould the entire property-owning class on the model of its economic client, the capitalist industrialist.

The communist party, representing the proletarians and the socialized and internationalized economy, is the model party of proletarian society. It is the governing party of the working class: through the functioning of a central Council of the national economy, which will co-ordinate and unify initiatives in production, it aims to socialize the whole of the labour process that has been industrialized by the capitalists, and to industrialize on a socialist basis all other sectors of labour that have not yet been drawn into the system of capitalist industrialism. It aims to mould all men in society on the model of the proletarian – an emancipated and regenerated proletarian, one who possesses no private wealth but administers the common wealth and receives in return that measure of enjoyment and security of life that are his due for the work he puts into production.

This historical situation imposes clearly-defined obligations upon the Socialist Party. It is a governing party insofar as it essentially represents the proletariat, the class of industrial workers. Private property threatens to strangle the proletariat, to starve it and freeze it to death. After first leading to over-production, the economic competition that is characteristic of the capitalist property régime has now led to monopoly on a national scale, to imperialism, to a bloody clash between imperialist States, to an immeasurable destruction of wealth, to famine, unemployment and death from hunger and cold. The class of those who own no property and are never likely to own any has a vital, a permanently vital interest in socialization, in the advent of communism.

On the other hand, the other sections of the working population could spawn a new capitalism; those forms of production which capitalism has not yet industrialized could dangerously extend the domain of property and the exploitation of man by man. With the destruction of the bourgeois State, and the destruction of the apparatus which finance capital employs to monopolize all labour and production in its own interests, artisans could attempt to exploit the socialist government to improve their businesses, take on wage-workers and become industrialists. If the proletarian government were to block these artisans, they could become rebels, declare themselves anarchists, individualists or whatever, and form the political basis for an opposition party to the proletarian government. The small land-holders (or the poor peasants on the latifundia, the agrarian system of extensive cultivation) could exploit the fact that temporarily, so long as the rationing conditions created by the war persist, a kilo of potatoes can be worth more than a motorcar wheel and a loaf of bread more than a cubic metre of masonry-work, in order to demand in exchange for their non-industrialized and hence economically impoverished labour the tenfold more efficient labour of the proletarian. And if the proletarian government will not allow the peasant to take over from the capitalist in exploiting the worker, then the peasant may rebel, and find among the agents of the bourgeoisie a group to form a peasant opposition party to the proletarian government. From all these sectors of labour, none of which can be denied political rights in the workers' State – from these sectors of labour which have not yet been penetrated by capitalist industrialism and so have not yet been reduced to the state of the proletarian worker, the worker who owns no property and is mathematically certain never to own any – there could emerge after the revolution anti-proletarian political forces working to restore capitalist property relations and exploitation of the working class.

* * * * *

The Socialist Party, insofar as it represents the economic interests of the working class threatened with extinction by capitalist private property, will be mandated by the working class with the revolutionary government of the nation. But the Socialist Party will be a governing party only to the extent that it forces the working class to overcome all these difficulties; only to the extent that it succeeds in reducing all men in society to the fundamental model of a proletarian emancipated and regenerated from his condition of wage-slavery; and finally, only to the extent that it is successful in establishing communist society, in the form of an International of nations not States. The Socialist Party will become a party of revolutionary government only when it sets itself concrete, revolutionary goals and when it is in a position to state: the following problems of modern life that are assailing the human masses and driving them to despair will be resolved in such and such a way by the proletarian revolution. Today, the revolution as such is the maximum programme of the Socialist Party, but it should be its minimum. Its maximum programme should indicate the exact manner in which the working class, through its ordered and methodical proletarian exertions, will succeed in suppressing every antagonism and conflict that may arise from the state of disorder that is the legacy of capitalism and will finally establish communist society. If the working class, which has a vital interest in the establishment of communism, is to be given the preparation it needs to attain its historical goals, it must be organized as the dominant class. The proletariat needs to acquire the sort of mentality that the bourgeois class possesses at present – in the sense that it needs to acquire the art of governing, the art of bringing an initiative or general activity on the part of the workers' State to a successful conclusion, though certainly not in the sense that it needs to acquire the art of exploitation. For that matter, even if it wanted to, the proletariat could never cultivate an exploiter's mentality. The proletarian could never become a proprietor, unless he were to destroy the factories and machines and become the proprietor of a pile of useless scrap metal, only to perish on it the day after. It is precisely because the proletarian, at a certain stage in the development of the technology of industrial production, cannot become a proprietor and exploiter, that he is summoned by history to establish communism and liberate all the oppressed and exploited.

* * * * *

The Socialist Party will not, in fact, become a party of revolutionary government unless the proletariat comes to see its pressing problems of existence as resolvable only by a class government of its own that takes power by revolutionary means.

The working class is aware that it is only by virtue of its being a producing class that it can master society and lead it to communism: for the working class too, production and increasing production are fundamental and ever-pressing problems. But for the working class, these problems are posed in the following manner. How should things be organized to ensure that the working class may carry on producing and be in a physical condition to increase its output? How should things be organized to ensure that the working class is no longer harassed by the problem of getting enough to eat, and is able to regenerate itself both physically and culturally and devote all its revolutionary enthusiasm to the problems of the industrial labour process, production, and the discovery and realization of new labour techniques – new techniques that form so many links in the historical chain leading to communism? The immediate problems of the working class boil down in the last analysis to this single problem: how to get enough to eat, and how to establish a political system in which the supply of provisions is no longer left to the free play of the market, to the mercy of private property, but is linked to the demands of labour and production. The proletarian principle: "He who does not work does not eat!" is daily acquiring an increasingly concrete, historical significance. It is becoming apparent how little this principle has in common with Jacobinism, or mysticism, and how it cannot even remotely be compared to the formula of the bourgeois revolution: "Liberty, equality, fraternity!" The proletarian principle is the explicit recognition of an immediate, organic necessity for human society, now that society itself is in danger of disintegrating and falling apart along with the bourgeois State. Production is a necessity, and to produce, there must exist a working class that is physically and mentally capable of mounting a heroic work effort. Hence food supplies must be directed above all to the sustenance of the working class, the class of producers; and there must exist a power capable of enforcing this priority, of ensuring that the working class has the basic food and other supplies it needs to produce and increase output. If on average only 200 gm of bread is available per citizen per day, there must exist a government that ensures that workers get 300 gm and non-producers have to content themselves with less, or with nothing at all, if they refuse to work and produce. The type of government required could only be a workers' government, a government of the working class turned governing, ruling class.

There can be no workers' government until the working class is in a position to become, in its entirety, the executive power of the workers' State. The laws of the workers' State need to be executed by the workers themselves: only in this way will the workers' State avoid the danger of falling into the hands of adventurers and political intriguers, of becoming a counterfeit of the bourgeois State. Hence the working class must train itself and educate itself in the management of society. It must acquire the culture and psychology of a dominant class, acquire them through its own channels and its own systems – meetings, congresses, discussions, mutual education. The Factory Councils have been an initial expression of these historical experiences on the part of the Italian working class as it moves towards self-government in a workers' State. A second, and most important, step will be the first congress of the Factory Councils – to which all Italian factories will be invited. The congress will be open to the whole of the Italian proletariat, represented by expressly elected delegates and not by union officials. The congress will have to get to grips with the essential problems facing the Italian proletariat and find a solution to them. There are internal problems such as the problem of proletarian unity, the relations between Councils and trade unions, membership of the IIIrd International, acceptance of the individual theses of the IIIrd International (proletarian dictatorship, industrial unions, etc.), and relations between the anarcho-syndicalists and socialist-communists. Then there are problems related to the class struggle: workers' control over industry, the 8-hour day, wages, the Taylor system, labour discipline, etc. Comrades should begin discussing these problems right away in factory assemblies. The whole of the working masses should be involved in these discussions, and in the light of their experience and intelligence should have a contribution to make to the solution of the problems. In all the factory assemblies, comprehensive motions on these problems, supported by argument, should be discussed and put to the vote; and at the congress, reports should represent a distillation of the factory assembly discussions, of the intellectual labour devoted by the whole of the working masses to seeking out the concrete truth. Then and only then will the Turin Congress of Councils be an event of the greatest historical importance. Workers coming from all over Italy would have in their hands a document shedding valuable light on how the Factory Council can lead the working class to its emancipation, its victory. And even more than is the case today, the Turin working class would be led to set an example of revolutionary enthusiasm, of methodical and orderly proletarian exertion to raise itself, educate itself and foster the conditions needed for the triumph and permanent duration of communist society.

Unsigned, *L'Ordine Nuovo*, 28 February–6 March 1920, Vol. I, No. 39. The article consisted of two short pieces "Governing Party" and "Class Party" published together under the same heading: "The Week in Politics".

39. PROLETARIAN UNITY

In the polemic over the present stage of the revolutionary process and over the degree of "maturity" attained by the capitalist organization of the instruments of labour and production, there is one source of facts that the reformists and opportunists (and the anarcho-syndicalists too, come to that) have systematically shrunk from consulting – the masses of workers and peasants. The communists, on the contrary, see the masses as their richest and most reliable source of information. This contrast shows that: 1. the opportunists and reformists, despite their ostentatiously scientific phrase-mongering, have completely abandoned the tradition of Marxist doctrine and represent an infiltration on the part of the ideological agents of capital into the domain of organized working-class struggle; 2. the anarcho-syndicalists, despite their ostentatiously revolutionary phrase-mongering, represent the irresponsible activity within the working-class camp of a clique of political intriguers, who are substituting an uncontrollable Freemasonry for the open and controllable political party of the working class.

For the communists who hold to Marxist doctrine, the masses of workers and peasants are the only genuine and authentic expression of the historical development of capital. By the spontaneous and uncontrollable movements which spread throughout their ranks and by relative shifts in the position of strata due to changes in intellectual outlook, the masses indicate the precise direction of historical development, reveal changes in attitudes and forms, and proclaim the decomposition and imminent collapse of the capitalist organization of society. From the perspective of revolutionary lyricism and of petty-bourgeois morality, these mass manifestations are seen as sublime or grotesque, heroic or barbaric; from the perspective of Marxism, they have to be seen in terms of historical necessity. For communists, they have real value in so far as they reveal among the masses a capacity, the beginnings of a new life, the aspiration to create new institutions and the historical drive to renew human society from the roots upwards. For communists, they have real value in so far as they reveal that the process of development of heavy industry has created the conditions for the working class to acquire an awareness of its own historical autonomy: an awareness of the possibility of constructing, through its own ordered and disciplined work, a new system of economic and juridical relations based on the specific function performed by the working class in the life of the world.

If one becomes estranged from the inner life of the working class, then one becomes estranged from the historical process that is unfolding implacably, in defiance of any individual will or traditional institution. The reformists base the "direction" of their own political action on the official pronouncements of constituted authorities, on the external and superficial appearances of traditional institutions and on the will of bourgeois or trade-union "leaders". The anarcho-syndicalists base their foolish ambition on tumult in the streets artificially provoked at their whim; on the howl which bursts from the throats of a mob whose blood has been violently stirred by the speech of some strident, truculent popular tribune. Both of them, however, refer to the "true" will of the masses; both of them, to the same degree, have the intuition and dialectical capacity of a blindfolded mule.

What communists see as the will of the masses, as their historical and revolutionary will, is what is enacted daily, when the toiling masses are moulded by the technical demands of industrial production, when every individual feels linked to his comrades through his toil and productive activity, when the working class senses the driving force of historical necessity within its own specific domain of activity. The will of the masses is what is stated in an organic and durable fashion, constructing each day a new cell of the new working-class psychology, of the new social organization that will culminate in the Communist International, the supreme regulator of the world's activity.

* * * * *

The period of history we are passing through is a revolutionary period because the traditional institutions for the government of the human masses, institutions which were linked to old modes of production and exchange, have lost any significance and useful function they might have had. The centre of gravity of the whole society has been removed to a new field: the institutions have been left as mere shells, devoid of any historical substance or animating spirit. The bourgeois class no longer governs its vital interests through Parliament. The working class is trying out new avenues in search of its institution of government, outside the trade unions; it has found that institution in the

Factory Council and system of Councils. Parliament was formerly the body in which the higher political relations produced by competition for profit between individuals, groups and sectors were synthesized. But since competition has been wiped out by the imperialist phase of world capitalism, the national Parliament no longer has any historical role. The bourgeoisie now governs itself through the banks and the great capitalist consortia which reflect the combined and unified interests of the whole class. Political government rests squarely on these coalitions, and is reduced to police activity and the maintenance of order on the streets and squares.

But it is not only bourgeois class institutions which have collapsed and fallen apart: working-class institutions too, which emerged while capitalism was developing and were formed as the response of the working class to this development, have entered a period of crisis and can no longer successfully control the masses. The leading figures in these working-class institutions voice their protests at the events which are occurring. They find them irrational and chaotic. They accuse X or Y of having artificially stirred them up. The truth is that the working class too is no longer governing itself through the unions, but is governing itself within the factories, on the job. And if it has not yet succeeded in generating its own governmental organ, if its ranks still lack individuals capable of expressing in clear and precise terms the tumult of feelings and passions that is stirring the working community and of finding a means to organize this tumult, then the masses will improvise a government from untried leaders, from any one of the many Masaniello's roaming the streets and squares in search of excitement and fine revolutionary adventures.[57]

The economic relations of capitalist society have been displaced and the organization of the apparatus of production and exchange has undergone a radical transformation: the whole juridical edifice that arose on the former terrain is collapsing and falling apart. As always happens, the groups of men professionally involved in guarding this edifice have, like fools, become desperate; they grow loutish and arrogant if anyone "dares" to question whether their role is necessary or not, or if anyone "dares" to suggest that industrial progress has made them expendable.

* * * * *

Every day, the task facing the political party of the working class at the present moment, the task facing the working-class vanguard that makes up the Socialist Party, emerges more distinctly. The proletarian dictatorship, the workers' State, has the task of providing the conditions needed for the development of the institutions created by the working class to control production for its own benefit and to govern itself directly. Here and now, the Party is fulfilling this task within the working class: the Party today is a model of what the workers' State will be tomorrow. Today, the Party provides the freedom needed if the toiling masses are to rediscover themselves on their specific terrain, that of production. Through its cultural activities and work of enlightenment, the Party is helping the working class to acquire a consciousness of its historical position. It is helping the working class to give concrete and organic expression to its passionate desire to rise to the challenge created by mankind's new material conditions. Every day, the errors of the theoretical syndicalists and practical syndicalists, reformists or revolutionaries, are becoming more apparent. The political Party, which was supposed to disappear, submerged beneath the trade-union wave, is in fact getting stronger day by day and the workers are more and more openly recognizing it as the supreme instrument of their emancipation. The unions are experiencing a profound crisis – and coping with it only in so far as a working-class vanguard formed inside the Party has carried a fraction of the Party into the unions, turning them into a wider forum for discussion of the problems which the Party has already discussed, clarified and resolved.

Syndicalism has achieved one result and one alone – it has multiplied the number of political parties representing the working class. This multiplicity of parties is precisely the major obstacle (if not the only obstacle) that stands in the way of proletarian unity and the "one big union" which is nevertheless an element of the syndicalist programme.[58]

* * * * *

Proletarian unity actually exists. This is shown conclusively by the way in which every local or corporative movement assumes epidemic proportions. Proletarian unity exists because capitalist unity also exists: it is a consequence of the new phase which the system of economic and political relations of bourgeois society has entered. No formal unity exists as yet, no organizational unity – because the proletariat is still represented by several different political parties.

From this point of view, the problem of proletarian unity must engage the attention of all revolutionaries conscious of the enormous difficulties the proletariat faces if it is to achieve its historical mission. The proletarian revolution demands clear, precise situations and well-defined responsibilities: the working class needs to be placed in a position to make rapid and direct judgments. But syndicalism, in both its reformist and revolutionary guises, has given rise to political parties which are unacknowledged and ambiguous. Small groups of individuals, who have placed themselves at the head of working-class organization as organizational technicians, specialists in one method of struggle rather than another, have enslaved the masses to their particular political tendencies. The masses have been enslaved to clandestine programmes over which they have no control. It is the vested interests of these clandestine and closed groups, frequently of single individuals, that have always prevented the unity of the Italian proletariat from being realized in practice.

Now the historical process of capitalism has created the conditions in which the masses themselves, using their own methods and direct action, can achieve unity. Proletarian unity forged by the workers themselves represents a higher stage of the unity which *de facto* exists: it is the stage in which the workers show that they have acquired a consciousness of their own unity and want to give it a concrete expression, a sanction.

The working-class vanguard organized in the Socialist Party must take responsibility for resolving this problem. It is clear that any effective solution can only come from the masses themselves and only through the Factory Councils. Once the masses have become accustomed, through the activities of the Councils, to the idea that there do not exist a variety of methods of class struggle, but one only – the method the masses themselves are capable of carrying out, through their trusted representatives, who can be recalled at any time – they will not allow themselves to be deceived by the promises of miracles which union leaders make. They will realize that organizational technicians, through the very fact of their being specialists and technicians, cannot be recalled and replaced – and if this is the case, then they should not be allowed to take on anything more than administrative duties, should have no political power whatsoever. The whole of the masses' political power, the power to lead movements, to lead the masses to victory against capital, should be invested in representative organs of the masses themselves, in the Council and system of Councils. These are responsible to the masses. They are made up of delegates who can be recalled at any time and who, if they belong to the Socialist Party as well as to union organizations, are also controlled by the Party, which is subject to a discipline established by the congresses in which the revolutionary vanguard of the whole nation has participated.

Proletarian unity is blocked by opportunists of every hue, who defend the vested interests of cliques, material interests and especially interests derived from political power over the masses. The masses have nothing to lose and everything to gain from achieving their unity. Hence they alone can develop the activities needed to accomplish this revolutionary goal.

Unsigned, *L'Ordine Nuovo*, 28 February–6 March 1920, Vol. I, No. 39.

40. THE PROBLEM OF FORCE

There are two powers in Italy, the power of the bourgeois State and the power of the working class: the second is gradually destroying the first. Today the bourgeois State survives in only one role – its self-defence, the preparation of arms and armed men for its defence. It stands with its rifle ever at the shoulder, ready to fire the moment its enemy has adopted a concrete form and is embodied in an institution that begins to exercise the new power. The power of the working class grows more and more massive every day; it flourishes in the strikes, the agitation, the fear of the governing class, the convulsions of the government officials, the trepidation of the capitalists, and the endless, rabid snarling of all the strongroom's watchdogs. Tomorrow or even today, the power of the working class could be embodied in a system of Councils, if all that were necessary were the revolutionary enthusiasm of the proletariat and a majority of the population on the proletarian side.

Today the struggle between these two powers centres around armed and organized force. The bourgeois State survives only because it possesses a co-ordinating centre for its military might and because it still has freedom of initiative: it is in a position to manœuvre its troops and concentrate them at a moment's notice upon revolutionary hotbeds, drowning them in a torrent of blood.

This problem of force is being resolved in the process of revolutionary development. Every day, new sectors of the working population become involved in the united movement of the national and global proletarian revolution. Italian capitalism has its deepest roots and the seat of its hegemony in Northern Italy, in the industrial centres of Northern Italy. The communist revolution, which in Italy takes the form of a revolution in industrial technique, and is expressed in the problem of equalizing the conditions of agricultural and industrial labour, will take place predominantly in the North. As a result of the war, the class of factory workers will find itself confronted by the following tremendous problem: how can it succeed in building a State organization that will have the means to industrialize agriculture, and will succeed in putting the peasant on the same labour footing as the worker, so that it will be possible to exchange one hour of agricultural labour for one hour of industrial labour, and so that the proletariat is not destroyed by the countryside in the exchange of commodities produced in absolutely non-comparable conditions of labour? This problem, which the capitalist industrialists are incapable of solving, and which, if left unresolved, will destroy the bourgeois State, can be resolved only by the workers, by a workers' State, here in Italy just the same as in Russia where it has been and is being resolved by the workers' State. It will finally be resolved by the urban industrial workers who will become the principal agents of the communist revolution.

If the workers, concentrated in the industrial cities, are to be the principal actors in the communist revolution, the principal actors in the pre-revolutionary action will instead be the peasant masses. Rural mass movements will smash the power of the bourgeois State once and for all, because they will smash its military might. No army is enough to subdue the countryside when it is up in arms: regiments that seem invincible when lined up in the streets of a city, become a plaything in the wide open fields; the cannons, machine-guns and flame-throwers that would scythe down crowds of workers in closed streets and squares, are impotent in the immensity of the open spaces of the countryside.

The bourgeois State is aware of the imminent danger: the countryside is going over to the revolution. From Apulia to Novara, from Novara to Brescia and Bergamo, the peasant masses are abandoning their torpor and launching magnificent actions. The Popular Party is deeply shaken by these gigantic clashes: driven on by the poor peasants militating under its banners, the left wing of the Popular Party is adopting extremist and revolutionary stances. The bourgeois State senses the danger and would like to precipitate events in the industrial cities, the solidly communist centres. For these will become the fulcrums of the revolution, they will give it a soul and an aim, and will construct the new society from the ruins of the old. And so an internal commission only has to move the hands of a factory clock to set hundreds of Royal Guards and *carabinieri* in motion and threaten an Armageddon.[59] The working class must be on its guard, must maintain discipline in its revolutionary trenches, a discipline born of patience, proletarian critical sense and trust in its own forces and future. The revolutionary process is developing implacably, destroying the bourgeois State and doing away with capitalist power; the working class will win, but as its conscious contribution to the revolution, it must concern itself with making it's victory long-lasting, with winning *once and for all*. It is the depository of the future, the living energy of history. It must not expose itself to repression that would put it out of action for too long; the bourgeois State would be only too happy to withdraw its mercenary troops from the cities and send them against the peasants, after having crushed the workers and secured its rear. The working class is the most politically educated section of the whole of the working people; it must confront the problem of force and realize that it can be largely resolved by the actions of the peasant masses. The Russian working class was able to wait from July to November in 1917. In those months, the Russian peasants destroyed the stability of Kerensky's State; then the workers launched their assault and resolutely seized power.

* * * * *

The normal development of the revolution largely resolves the problem of armed force and the victory of the working class over bourgeois State power. But part of this problem must be resolved by the general political action of the proletariat and of its political party, the Socialist Party. The bourgeois State is currently changing the national army into a mercenary army. According to a minutely worked out plan, soldiers have been transferred from their regiments to the *carabinieri* legions, while retaining their special skills. *Carabinieri*-corps of artillerymen, mortarmen, machine-gunners, flame-throwers and others have been formed. Parliament shows no concern about this activity on the part of the government, which exceeds its powers and the limits of the constitution. Parliament must demand an explanation for this activity from the government, if for no other reason than to force it to unmask its intentions; than to demonstrate with the clearest proof how the bourgeois dictatorship functions, blithely ignoring basic charters and devoting the whole administrative apparatus and all its financial resources to a single end: its defence against the majority of the population, whose supreme representative and sovereignty it claims to be.

Unsigned, *Avanti!*, Piedmont edition, 26 March 1920, Vol. XXIV, No. 74.

41. TURIN AND ITALY

These last few days, proletarian Turin has been experiencing its Holy Week. Sectional struggles are broadening and becoming more intense; new battles are being undertaken, which demand novel tactics, which are being fought out on new bases and whose outcome is not yet certain. On the one hand, there persists a lucid and complete awareness of rights and, on the other, there is a strengthening of the resolve to resist. And the situation is becoming critical. All the workers sense it – with varying degrees of clarity they sense that they are living through a moment which could be decisive for the history of their class, a moment when everything is staked, everything risked and perhaps everything lost. Never before has participation in class action been so close to what it should be as it is today: an effort to master reality, an effort not to be overwhelmed by a mechanism acting independently of ourselves, a straining of every will, a tension in every mind. Never before, then, has one thing been so necessary as it is today: we must not blinker our vision, but open our eyes to reality and approach it with an open mind. When everything is at stake, we must be coldly logical in our reasoning and conclusions.

In part, the symptoms are plain to all: metal-workers, shoemakers, tailors, State employees – in all, 90,000 workers are idle. This is the way Turin responds to the appeals for production, in a manner befitting a socialist city, by the producers intensifying their struggle for liberation. And of the 90,000 who are idle, 50,000 are openly fighting for this goal. For 50,000 of the workers, this goal is no longer merely a word, no longer a vague dream that can only be clarified and given a concrete and tangible form through an inner struggle within themselves. It is now something precise, an explicit programme of continuous action, a guide for day-to-day activities. The struggle is over the attainment of this goal; it is a struggle of will against will, force against force. Should the credit for this new situation go to the Factory Councils? In part, yes, but in part it is the revolutionary and insurrectional traditions of this city which have assumed a new form, become embodied in a programme of action and achieved thereby a new consistency. It is against this spirit that today the guns are being got ready.

It is the government that is getting them ready, and even before the government, the industrialists. Indeed it is symptomatic that the industrialists have gone with their requests for defence directly to the central government, over the heads of the local political authorities. It is obvious that they are determined upon attack. And today, Turin is a garrisoned fortress. It is said that there are 50,000 soldiers in the city, that artillery is drawn up on the hills, that reinforcements are waiting on the outskirts of the town and armoured cars in the city. Machine-guns are positioned on private houses, in those districts which are considered to be most eager to revolt, at bridge-heads, by cross-roads and factories.

For this we thank the honourable industrialists. We thank them for having made it obvious to all – if there was still anyone who needed convincing – just what the real balance of forces is. If there was still someone in our midst who cherished illusions, if any of our workers still thought it right and proper to limit the scope of revolutionary and insurrectional action to the factory or the town, if anyone found difficulty in making that last step to the point where power in the factory can be seen as just one element in relation to State power – if such doubters, such deluded people still existed, then this lesson was for them. The struggle is over discipline in the factory and here at once is the power of the State, actively intervening, as yet insuperable.

So it is a general problem, a problem that must be confronted in all its aspects. Today we are face to face with reality. Today a certain self-questioning is called for. What has brought about this concentration of forces in Turin if not the fact that in our city the signal for battle has been given, or rather the battle has begun, over a question whose terms are such as to engage the interests of the whole of the Italian proletariat and draw it into the struggle? Revolutionary energies have been intensifying and accumulating in our city over the past few months, tending at all costs to expand and seek an outlet. And this outlet must not for the moment be a localized bloodletting that would be dangerous and perhaps even fatal, but rather a stepping-up of the campaign of preparation all over the country, an extension of our forces and a general acceleration of the process of development of the elements which must all come together in a common enterprise.

Today in Turin we have had a test. Tomorrow we shall see whether we are to be victorious or defeated. But let one thing remain, one lesson, one spur to further action. The fight is not only in Turin, but all over Italy, all over the world – and if anything assists in making intentions more steadfast and determination more dogged, then this is a tool in the preparation of the masses, even if it is won at the cost of sacrifices and apparent losses. Even dashed hopes, even disappointment, even the rage in our hearts when we go back into the factories – this too will be a weapon for our victory.

Unsigned, *Avanti!*, Piedmont edition, 3 April 1920, Vol. XXIV, No. 82.

42. ADDRESS TO THE ANARCHISTS

The Italian anarchists are very touchy because they are very presumptuous: they have always been convinced that they are the guardians of the revealed revolutionary truth. This has been a "monstrous" conviction ever since the Socialist Party, under the impact of the Russian revolution and Bolshevik propaganda, mastered certain fundamental points of Marxist doctrine which it is now propagating in simple, popular terms to the masses of workers and peasants. For some time now the Italian anarchists have done nothing but reiterate complacently the statement "We always said so! We were right all along!", without ever bothering to face up to the following questions. Why, if we are right, have we not been followed by the majority of the Italian proletariat? Why has the majority of the Italian proletariat always followed the Socialist Party and its associated trade unions? (Why has the Italian proletariat always allowed itself to be "cheated" by the Socialist Party and its associated trade unions?) The Italian anarchists could have replied at length to these questions only after making a great gesture of humility and contrition – only after abandoning the anarchist point of view, the point of view of absolute truth, and recognizing that they were wrong when . . . they were right. Only after recognizing that absolute truth is not enough to draw the masses into action, to infuse them with a revolutionary spirit, but that what is needed is a *given, particular* "truth" – after recognizing that for the purpose of human history, the only "truth" is the truth that is embodied in action, that becomes a passionate, driving force in people's minds and is translated into profound movements and real conquests on the part of the masses themselves.

The Socialist Party has always been the party of the Italian working people; its errors and shortcomings are those of the Italian working people itself. But things have not stood still: Italian standards of living have improved, the class consciousness of the proletariat has developed, the Socialist Party has acquired a more distinctive political position and attempted to forge a specific doctrine of its own. But the anarchists have stood still and continue to stand still. They are hypnotized by their conviction of having been in the right and of still being in the right. The Socialist Party has changed along with the proletariat: it has changed because the class consciousness of the proletariat has changed. This shifting of the Party reveals the profound truth of the Marxist doctrine it has now made its own; it also reveals the Party's "libertarian" character, a point which should not escape the notice of intelligent anarchists and which should give them food for thought. On reflection, the anarchists might well conclude that freedom, understood as the real historical development of the proletarian class, has never been embodied in the libertarian groups, but has always been on the side of the Socialist Party.

Anarchism is not a conception that belongs to the working class and to the working class alone – herein lies the reason for the anarchists' permanent "triumph", for their permanently being "correct". Anarchism is the basic subversive conception that any oppressed class generates; it is a consciousness propagated by every ruling class. Since all class oppression has been embodied in a State, anarchism is the basic subversive conception that lays all the sufferings of the oppressed class at the feet of the State. Upon becoming dominant, every class substantiates its own anarchist conception, by substantiating its own freedom. The bourgeois was anarchist before his class won political power and imposed on society the State system that was most suitable for defending the capitalist mode of production. Even after his revolution, the bourgeois continues to be an anarchist, because the laws of his State are not a constraint upon him – they are his own laws, so that the bourgeois can say he lives without laws, that he lives a libertarian existence. And the bourgeois will become anarchist again after the proletarian revolution: then he will once more become aware of the existence of a State, of the existence of laws foreign to his will and hostile to his interests, his habits and his freedom. He will become aware that the State is synonymous with constraint; for the workers' State will deprive the bourgeois class of the freedom to exploit the proletariat. The workers' State will be the bulwark of a new mode of production that, as it develops, will destroy all traces of capitalist property relations and all possibility of their re-emergence.

But the conception which belonged to the bourgeois class was not anarchism, but liberalism, just as the conception which belongs to the working class is not anarchism, but Marxist communism. Every particular class has had its own, and no one else's, particular conception. Anarchism has been the "marginal" conception of every oppressed class, but Marxist communism is the particular conception of the modern working class and of this class alone. The revolutionary theses of Marxism become a cabalistic cipher if they are formulated outside the context of the modern proletariat and the capitalist mode of production (of which the modern proletariat is the consequence). The proletariat is not hostile to the State as such, just as the bourgeois class was not hostile to the State as such. The bourgeois class was hostile to the despotic State, to aristocratic power; but it was in favour of the bourgeois State, of liberal democracy. The proletariat is hostile to the bourgeois State, to power in the hands of the capitalists and bankers; but it is in favour of the proletarian dictatorship, of power in the hands of the workers and peasants. The proletariat is in favour of the workers' State as a stage – the final stage – in the class struggle: the stage when the proletariat finally gains the upper hand as an organized political force. But classes will continue to exist, as will the society divided into classes and the form that is proper to all class-divided societies – the State. But this time the State will be in the hands of the workers and peasants, and they will make use of it to secure their own freedom of development and to completely eliminate the bourgeoisie from history. They will consolidate the sort of material conditions that will prevent class oppression from ever re-emerging.

* * * * *

Is it possible to reach a settlement in this polemical dispute between communists and anarchists? It is possible – but only in the case of anarchist groups made up of class-conscious workers. There is no hope of any settlement in the case of anarchist groups made up of intellectuals, of professional ideologues. For the intellectuals, anarchism is an idol: it is a *raison d'être* for their particular activity, present and future. So in the eyes of anarchist agitators, a workers' State will still be a "State", a limitation on freedom, a constraint, just as it will for the bourgeoisie. But for libertarian workers, anarchism is a weapon in the struggle against the bourgeoisie. Their revolutionary spirit transcends their ideology. The State against which they go into battle is really only the bourgeois capitalist State and not the State as such, the idea of the State. The property relations they want to destroy are not "property relations" in general, but the capitalist form of property relations. For anarchist workers, the coming of the workers' State will be the coming of the freedom of their class and hence of their own personal freedom as well; it will open the way to every experiment and every attempt at realizing proletarian ideals in practice. The work of creating the revolution will absorb them and transform them into a vanguard of devoted and disciplined militants.

In the positive act of proletarian creation, no differences will persist between worker and worker. Communist society cannot be built by fiat, through laws and decrees: it arises spontaneously from the historical activity of the working class, which has gained freedom of initiative in industrial and agricultural production and is impelled to reorganize production along new lines, in accordance with a new order. The anarchist worker will then appreciate the existence of a centralized power, that acts as a permanent guarantee of his newly won freedom and relieves him of the need to interrupt his activities and run to the defence of the revolution at any moment. He will then appreciate the existence of a great party made up of the best elements in the proletariat: a highly organized and disciplined party that can act as a spur to revolutionary creativity, that can offer an example of sacrifice and, through this example, draw behind it the broad mass of workers and lead them to overcome more rapidly the state of humiliation and prostration to which capitalist exploitation reduced them.

* * * * *

The socialist conception of the revolutionary process is characterized by two fundamental features that Romain Rolland has summed up in his watchword: "pessimism of the intellect, optimism of the will". Anarchist ideologues, on the other hand, declare that they "are concerned" to repudiate Karl Marx's pessimism of the intellect (see L. Fabbri, *Lettere ad un socialista*, Florence 1914, p. 134) "to the effect that a revolution that comes about as a result of an excess of poverty or oppression would demand the establishment of an authoritarian dictatorship, which perhaps even (!) might bring us to the stage of a sort of State socialism (!?) but never to anarchist socialism". Socialist pessimism has found terrible confirmation in recent events: the proletariat has been plunged into the deepest abyss of poverty and oppression that the mind of man could ever conceive. To such a situation, anarchist ideologues have nothing to counterpose but vacuous and irrelevant pseudo-revolutionary demagogy, interwoven with the most tired themes of street-level, simple-minded optimism. The socialists, on the other hand, counterpose an energetic organizing campaign using the best and most conscious elements in the working class. In every way open to them, the socialists are striving via these vanguard elements to prepare the broadest possible sectors of the masses to win freedom and the power that can guarantee this freedom.

Today the proletarian class is scattered at random throughout the cities and countryside, alongside machines or on scraps of land. It works without knowing why, forced to labour in servitude by the ever-pressing threat of death through starvation or cold. Proletarians do combine in unions and co-operatives, but in response to the demands of economic resistance and not through any spontaneous choice on their part, not through following their own freely generated impulses. Of necessity, all the actions undertaken by the proletarian masses adopt a form that is established by the capitalist mode of production, by the State power of the bourgeois class. To expect masses who are reduced to such conditions of bodily and spiritual slavery to express their own autonomous historical will; to expect them spontaneously to initiate and sustain a revolutionary action – this is purely an illusion on the part of the ideologues. To rely solely on the creative capacity of such masses and not work systematically to organize a great army of disciplined and conscious elements, ready for any sacrifice, trained to carry out slogans as one man, ready to assume effective responsibility for the revolution and become its agents – this is complete and utter betrayal of the working class. It is the beginnings of unconscious counter-revolution.

* * * * *

The Italian anarchists are touchy because they are presumptuous. They easily lose their temper when subjected to proletarian criticism. They prefer to be adulated and told in flattering tones that they are the champions of revolutionism and absolute theoretical coherence. We are convinced that the Italian revolution requires collaboration between socialists and anarchists – a frank and loyal collaboration between two political forces, based on concrete proletarian problems. However, we believe that the anarchists too must subject their traditional tactical criteria to a searching examination, as the Socialist Party has done, and must justify their political assertions in terms of present realities, at a particular time and place. The anarchists need to become a little freer intellectually – not an excessive demand, one would think, of someone who claims to want freedom and nothing but freedom.

Unsigned, *L'Ordine Nuovo*, 3–10 April 1920, Vol. I, No. 43.

43. TOWARDS A RENEWAL OF THE SOCIALIST PARTY

The following report was presented to the National Council meeting of the PSI in Milan, by the representatives of the Turin city Section and provincial Federation; it served as a basis for their criticism of the Party leadership's work and policies.

1. In Italy at the present moment, the character of the class struggle is determined by the fact that industrial and agricultural workers throughout Italy are irresistibly set upon raising the question of the ownership of the means of production in an explicit and violent form. The intensification of the national and international crises which are steadily annihilating the value of money demonstrates that capital is *in extremis*. The present order of production and distribution can no longer satisfy even the basic necessities of human life, and survives only because it is ferociously defended by the armed might of the bourgeois State. In the long run, all these movements on the part of the Italian working people will effect a gigantic economic revolution that will introduce new modes of production, a new order in the productive and distributive process, and give the power of initiative in production to the class of industrial and agricultural workers, by seizing it from the hands of the capitalists and landowners.

2. The industrialists and landowners have achieved a maximum of class discipline and power: an order issued by the general Confederation of Industry (*Confindustria*) is carried out at once in every factory in the land. The bourgeois State has created a body of armed mercenaries,[60] ready to act as an executive instrument of the will of this new and powerful organization of the propertied classes. Its aim is to restore capitalist power over the means of production through the widespread use of lock-outs and terrorism, forcing the workers and peasants to submit to the expropriation of an increased quantity of unpaid labour. The recent lock-out in the Turin engineering plants was an episode in this determination of the industrialists to crush the working class underfoot. They exploited the lack of any revolutionary co-ordination and concentration in the Italian workers' forces in a bid to smash the solidarity of the Turin proletariat and blot out from the workers' minds the prestige and authority of the factory institutions

(Councils and shop-floor delegates) that had begun the struggle for workers' control. The long-drawn-out agricultural strikes in the Novara and Lomellina areas show how the landowners are prepared to stop production altogether in order to reduce the agricultural proletariat to despair and starvation, subjecting it implacably to the harshest and most humiliating conditions of life and work.

3. The present phase of the class struggle in Italy is the phase that precedes: either the conquest of political power on the part of the revolutionary proletariat and the transition to new modes of production and distribution that will set the stage for a recovery in productivity – or a tremendous reaction on the part of the propertied classes and governing caste. No violence will be spared in subjecting the industrial and agricultural proletariat to servile labour: there will be a bid to smash once and for all the working class's organ of political struggle (the Socialist Party) and to incorporate its organs of economic resistance (the trade unions and co-operatives) into the machinery of the bourgeois State.

4. The worker and peasant forces lack revolutionary co-ordination and concentration because the leading organs of the Socialist Party have shown no understanding at all of the stage of development that national and international history is currently passing through, nor of the mission incumbent on revolutionary proletarian organs of struggle. The Socialist Party watches the course of events like a spectator; it never has an opinion of its own to express, based on the revolutionary theses of Marxism and the Communist International; it never launches slogans that can be adopted by the masses, lay down a general line and unify or concentrate revolutionary action. As political expression of the vanguard section of the working class, the Socialist Party should develop a comprehensive action designed to put the whole of the working class in a position to win the revolution, and win it permanently. Since it is composed of those members of the working class who have not allowed themselves to be demoralized and prostrated by the physical and mental oppression of the capitalist system, but have succeeded in preserving their own autonomy and a spirit of conscious and disciplined initiative, the Socialist Party should embody the vigilant revolutionary consciousness of the whole of the exploited class. Its task is to focus the attention of all the masses on itself, so that its directives may become theirs; so that it may win their permanent trust and thus become their guide and intellect. Hence it is essential that the Party should immerse itself in the reality of the class

struggle as waged by the industrial and agricultural proletariat, to be in a position to understand its different phases and episodes, its various forms, drawing unity from this manifold diversity. It needs to be in a position to give real leadership to the movement as a whole and to impress upon the masses the conviction that there is an order within the terrible disorder of the present, an order that, when systematized, will regenerate society and adapt the instruments of labour to make them satisfy the basic needs of life and civil progress. But even after the Congress of Bologna,[61] the Socialist Party has continued to be merely a parliamentary party, immobilizing itself within the narrow limits of bourgeois democracy, and concerning itself only with the superficial political declarations of the governing caste. It has not acquired its own autonomous stance as a party typical of the revolutionary proletariat – and the revolutionary proletariat alone.

5. After the Congress of Bologna the central organs of the Party should immediately have mounted and carried through an energetic campaign to give uniformity and cohesiveness to the Party's revolutionary membership, to give it the specific and distinct features of a communist party belonging to the IIIrd International. But a polemic with the reformists and opportunists was not even started; neither the Party leadership nor *Avanti!* counterposed a genuinely revolutionary conception to the incessant propaganda which the reformists and opportunists were disseminating in Parliament and in the trade-union bodies. Nothing was done by the central Party organs to give the masses a communist political education, to induce the masses to eliminate the reformists and opportunists from the leadership of the trade unions and the co-operative institutions, or to give individual sections and the most active groups of comrades a unified line and tactics. And so while the Party's revolutionary majority has found no mouthpiece for its thoughts or executor of its intentions in the Party's leadership or press, the opportunist elements for their part have been powerfully organized and have exploited the Party's prestige and authority to consolidate their positions in Parliament and the trade unions. The leadership has allowed them to concentrate their forces and to vote for resolutions that contradict the principles and tactics of the IIIrd International and are hostile to the Party line. The leadership has given lower-echelon bodies a free hand to pursue actions and propagate ideas that are opposed to the principles and tactics of the IIIrd International. The Party leadership has had no contact whatsoever with the life and activities of the sections, the organizations and individual

comrades. The confusion that existed in the Party prior to the Congress of Bologna, and which could be explained by the wartime conditions, has not disappeared; on the contrary, it has increased to an alarming extent. It is quite understandable that in such conditions the masses' confidence in the Party should have waned, and that in many places anarchist tendencies should have tried to gain the upper hand. The political party of the working class justifies its existence only to the extent that, by powerfully centralizing and co-ordinating proletarian action, it counterposes a *de facto* revolutionary power to the legal power of the bourgeois State and limits its freedom of initiative and manœuvre. If the Party fails to unify and co-ordinate its efforts, and reveals itself as simply a bureaucratic institution, with no soul or will, the working class will instinctively move to form another party and shift its allegiance to the anarchist tendencies, the very ones that bitterly and ceaselessly criticize the centralization and bureaucracy of political parties.

6. The Party has played no part in the international movement. Throughout the world the class struggle has assumed gigantic proportions. Everywhere workers are being driven to renew their methods of struggle and frequently, as in Germany after the militarist coup, to rise up arms in hand. The Party has made no effort to explain these events to the Italian working people, or to justify them in the light of the ideas of the Communist International. It has made no effort to mount a comprehensive educational campaign designed to make the Italian working people conscious of the fact that the proletarian revolution is a world-wide phenomenon and that each single event must be considered and judged within a global context. The IIIrd International has already met twice in Western Europe: in a German city in December 1919, and in Amsterdam in February 1920. The Italian Party was not represented at either of these two meetings. The Party's militants were not even informed by the central organs of the discussions that took place there and of the decisions that were taken. Polemics rage within the IIIrd International over the doctrine and tactics of the Communist International: these have even led to internal splits (for example, in Germany). The Italian Party has been completely cut off from this vigorous dialogue of ideas – a dialogue that tempers revolutionary consciousness and forges the unity in spirit and action of the proletariats of all countries. The central organ of the Party has no correspondent of its own in France, England, Germany, nor even in Switzerland: a strange state of affairs for the Socialist Party newspaper, that represents the interests of the international proletariat in Italy, and

a strange state of affairs for the Italian working class, which has to obtain its information from the warped and tendentious reports provided by bourgeois papers and news agencies. As the Party organ, *Avanti!* should be the organ of the IIIrd International. There should be space in *Avanti!* for all the reports, polemics and discussions of proletarian problems that are of interest to the IIIrd International. In *Avanti!* there should be conducted, in a spirit of unity, a continuous polemic against all opportunist deviations and compromises; instead, *Avanti!* highlights displays of opportunist thinking, such as the recent speech in Parliament by Claudio Treves which was woven around a petty-bourgeois conception of international relations and expounded a theory that was counter-revolutionary and defeatist of proletarian aspirations.[62] This lack of any concern on the part of the central organs to keep the proletariat informed of the events and theoretical discussions taking place within the IIIrd International can also be observed in the activities of the Party's publishing house. It carries on publishing worthless pamphlets or writings that propagate the ideas and opinions of the IInd International, while it neglects the publications of the IIIrd International. Writings by Russian comrades that are indispensible to an understanding of the Bolshevik revolution have been translated in Switzerland, in England and in Germany, but are unknown in Italy. Lenin's volume *State and Revolution* is just one example among many. Moreover, the pamphlets which are translated are done so badly that they are frequently incomprehensible, with their grammatical errors and violations of common sense.

7. The above analysis has already indicated the kind of effort at renewal and organization which we hold to be indispensable, and which must be carried out by the Party's membership itself. The Party must acquire its own precise and distinct character. From a petty-bourgeois parliamentary party it must become the party of the revolutionary proletariat in its struggle to achieve a communist society by way of the workers' State – a homogeneous, cohesive party, with a doctrine and tactics of its own, and a rigid and implacable discipline. Non-communist revolutionaries must be eliminated from the Party, and its leadership, freed from the preoccupation of preserving unity and balance between various tendencies and leaders, must devote all its efforts to putting the workers' forces on a war footing. Every event in national and international proletarian life should be analysed immediately in manifestos and circulars from the leadership, drawing lessons from them that can be used for communist propaganda and to

form a revolutionary consciousness. The leadership, by keeping constantly in touch with the sections, must become the motor centre for proletarian action in all its manifestations. The sections must promote the formation of communist groups in all factories, unions, co-operatives and barracks which will ceaselessly propagate the Party's ideas and tactics within the masses, and organize the setting-up of Factory Councils to exercise control over industrial and agricultural production. These groups will develop the propaganda needed to conquer the unions, the Chambers of Labour and the General Confederation of Labour in an organic fashion, and so become the trusted elements whom the masses will delegate to form political Soviets and exercise the proletarian dictatorship. The existence of a cohesive and highly disciplined communist party with factory, trade-union and co-operative cells, that can co-ordinate and centralize in its central executive committee the whole of the proletariat's revolutionary action, is the fundamental and indispensable condition for attempting any experiment with Soviets. In the absence of such a condition, every experiment proposed should be rejected as absurd and useful only to those who would slander the idea of Soviets. In the same way we should reject the proposal for a little Socialist parliament, for it would rapidly become an instrument in the hands of the reformist and opportunist majority in the parliamentary group for the dissemination of democratic utopias and counter-revolutionary projects.[63]

8. The leadership should immediately prepare, draw up and distribute a programme of revolutionary government by the Socialist Party, formulating the concrete solutions that the proletariat, when it becomes the dominant class, will give to all the essential problems – economic, political, religious, educational – that beset the various sections of the Italian working population. Basing itself on the idea that the Party's power and activity is founded solely on the class of industrial and agricultural workers who own no private property at all, and that it regards the other strata of working people as auxiliaries of the strictly proletarian class, the Party must issue a manifesto in which the revolutionary conquest of political power is posed in explicit terms, in which the industrial and agricultural proletariat is invited to prepare and arm itself, and in which the elements of communist solutions to current problems are sketched: proletarian control over production and distribution, disarming of mercenary armed bodies, control of local government by working-class organizations.

9. On the basis of these considerations, the Turin Socialist Section has

decided to seek an understanding with all those groups of comrades from other sections who are interested in meeting together to discuss these proposals and approve them; an organized understanding that will lead in a short time to a congress devoted to discussing the problems of proletarian tactics and organization, and which in the meantime will monitor the activities of the Party's executive organs.

Unsigned, *L'Ordine Nuovo*, 8 May 1920, Vol. II, No. 1.

IV

Bordiga's Polemic

44. THE SYSTEM OF COMMUNIST REPRESENTATION – *BORDIGA*

In launching our communist programme, which contained the outlines of a response to many vital problems concerning the revolutionary movement of the proletariat, we expected to see a broad discussion develop on all its aspects.[64] Instead there has been and still is only furious discussion over the incompatibility of electoral participation, which is soberly affirmed in the programme. Indeed, although the electionist maximalists proclaim that for them electoral action is quite secondary, they are in fact so mesmerized by it as to launch an avalanche of articles against the few anti-electionist lines contained in our programme. On our side, apart from the ample treatment given in these columns to the reasons underlying our abstentionism, we have only now begun to use *Avanti!* as a platform to reply to this deluge of electoralist objections.

Hence we are delighted to note that the Turin newspaper *L'Ordine Nuovo* is demanding clarification of the paragraph in the communist programme which states: "Elections to local workers' councils will be held *not in accordance with the trades to which they belong, but on an urban and provincial constituency basis.*" The writer, Comrade Andrea Viglongo, asks whether this was a way of denying that the power of the Soviets should derive from the masses consulted and voting *at the very place where they work*: in the factories, workshops, mines and villages.[65]

What the drafters of the programme had in mind was as follows. The Soviet system is a system of *political* representation of the working class; its fundamental characteristic is denial of the right to vote to anyone who is not a member of the proletariat. It has been thought that Soviets and economic unions were the same thing. Yet nothing could be further from the truth. It may well be that in various countries, in early stages of the revolution, Soviet-type bodies were set up with representation from the craft unions – but this was no more than a makeshift arrangement.

While the trade union has as its object the defence of the sectional interests of the worker in so far as he belongs to a given trade or industry, the proletarian figures in the Soviet as a member of a social class that has conquered political power and is running society, in so far as his interests have something in common with all workers of any trade whatsoever. What we have in the central Soviet is a political representation of the working class, with deputies representing local constituencies. National representatives of the various trades have no place in this schema at all; this should suffice to give the lie simultaneously to trade-unionist interpretations and to the reformist parody of hypothetical constituent assemblies of trades masquerading as Soviet-type institutions.

But the question remains, how should the network of representation be fashioned in the case of local urban or rural village Soviets? If we refer to the Russian system, as expounded in Articles XI, XII, XIII and XIV of the Constitution of the Soviet Republic, we may conclude that the essential feature is that in the cities there is one delegate for every 1,000 inhabitants, and in the countryside one for every 100 inhabitants, elections being held (Art. 66) in accordance with rules established by the local Soviets. So it is not the case that the number of delegates to be elected depends on how many factories or workplaces there are; and we are not told whether the election involves assembling all the electors with the right to a representative, or what the norms should be. But if we refer to the programmes of communists in other countries, it would seem safe to conclude that the nature of the electoral units is not the basic problem of the Soviet order, even though it gives rise to some important considerations.

The network of Soviets undoubtedly has a dual nature: political and revolutionary on the one hand; economic and constructive on the other. The first aspect is dominant in the early stages, but as the expropriation of the bourgeoisie proceeds, it gradually cedes in importance to the second. Necessity will gradually refine the bodies which are technically competent to fulfil this second function: forms of representation of trade categories and production units will emerge and connect with one another, especially as regards technique and work discipline. But the fundamental political role of the network of workers' councils is based on the historical concept of dictatorship: proletarian interests must be allowed free play in so far as they concern *the whole class over and above sectional interests, and the whole of the historical development of the movement for its emancipation*. The conditions needed to accomplish all these are basically: 1. the exclusion of the bourgeois from any participation in political activity; 2. the convenient distribution of electors into local constituencies which send delegates to the Congress of Soviets. This body then appoints the Central Executive Committee, and has the task of promulgating the decisions regarding the gradual socialization of the various sectors of the economy.

Seen in relation to this historical definition of the communist representative system, it seems to us that *L'Ordine Nuovo* slightly exaggerates the *formal* definition of the way the representative bodies intermesh. Which groupings do the voting and where is not a substantive problem: various solutions at a national and regional level can be accommodated.

Only up to a certain point can the factory internal commissions be seen as the precursors of Soviets. We prefer to think of them as precursors of the factory councils, which will have technical and disciplinary duties both during and after the socialization of the factory itself. We should be clear that the civilian political Soviet will be elected wherever convenient, and most probably on the basis of constituencies that are not very different from present electoral seats.

The electoral rolls themselves will have to be different. Viglongo poses the question whether all the workers in the factory should have the right to vote, or just the trade-union members. We would ask him to consider whether some workers, even members of a trade union, should be struck off the electoral roll of the civilian political Soviet where it is found that, in addition to working in a factory, they live on the proceeds from a small capital sum or annuity. This is a not uncommon occurrence amongst us. Again the Russian Constitution clearly takes this into account in the first sentence of Art. 65. Finally the legitimately unemployed and incapacitated must also have a vote.

What characterizes the communist system then is the definition of the right to be an elector, a right which depends not on one's membership of a particular trade, but on the extent to which the individual, in the totality of his social relations, can be seen as a proletarian with an interest in the rapid achievement of communism, or a non-proletarian tied in some way or other to the preservation of the economic relations of private property. This extremely simple condition guarantees the political workability of the Soviet system of representation. In parallel to this system, new and technically competent techno-economic bodies will emerge. They must, however, remain subordinate to whatever the Soviets lay down in terms of broad policy guidelines; for until classes are totally abolished, only the political system of representation will embody the collective interests of the proletariat, acting as the prime accelerator of the revolutionary process. On another occasion we shall discuss the problem whether it is possible or desirable to set up political Soviets even before the revolutionary battle for the conquest of power takes place.

Il Soviet, 13 September 1919, Vol. II, No. 38.

45. IS THIS THE TIME TO FORM "SOVIETS"? – *BORDIGA*

Two of the articles in our last issue, one devoted to an analysis of the communist system of representation and the other to an exposition of the current tasks facing our Party, concluded by asking whether it is possible or appropriate to set up workers' and peasants' councils today, while the power of the bourgeoisie is still intact. Comrade Ettore Croce, in a discussion of our abstentionist thesis in an article in *Avanti!*, asks that we should have a new weapon at the ready before getting rid of the old weapon of parliamentary action and looks forward to the formation of Soviets.

In our last issue we clarified the distinction between the technical-economic and political tasks of the Soviet representative bodies, and we showed that the true organs of the proletarian dictatorship are the local and central political Soviets, in which workers are not sub-divided according to their particular trade. The supreme authority of these organs is the Central Executive Committee, which nominates the People's Commissars; parallel to them, there arises a whole network of economic organs, based on factory councils and trade unions, which culminate in the Central Council of the Economy.

In Russia, we repeat, whereas there is no trade representation in the CEC and Soviet of Soviets, but only territorial representation, this is not the case as regards the Council of the Economy, the organ which is responsible for the technical implementation of the socialization measures decreed by the political assembly. In this Council, trade federations and local economic councils play a role. The 16 August issue of *L'Ordine Nuovo* contained an interesting article on the Soviet-type system of socialization. This article explained how in a first stage, dubbed anarcho-syndicalist, the factory councils would take over the management of production, but that subsequently, in later stages involving centralization, they would lose importance. In the end they would be nothing more than clubs and mutual benefit and instruction societies for the workers in a particular factory.

If we shift our attention to the German communist movement, we see in the programme of the Spartacus League that the Workers' and Soldiers' Councils, the bodies which are to take the place of the bourgeois parliaments and municipal councils, are quite different from factory councils, which (Art. 7 of Section III) *regulate working conditions and control production, in agreement with the workers' councils, and eventually take over the management of the whole enterprise.*

In Russian practice, factory management was made up to the extent of only one-third by representatives from the factory council, one-third by representatives from the Supreme Council of the Economy, and one-third by representatives from the Central Federation of Industry (the interests of the work-force, the general interests of society, and the interests of the particular industrial sector).

In Germany again, elections to the Workers' Councils are arranged in accordance with the formula: one council member to every 1,000 electors. Only the large factories with over 1,000 workers constitute a single electoral unit; in the case of small factories and the unemployed, voting takes place in accordance with methods established by the electoral commission in agreement with various trade organizations.

It seems to us that we have marshalled enough evidence here to be able to declare ourselves supporters of a system of representation that is clearly divided into two divisions: economic and political. As far as economic functions are concerned, each factory will have its own factory council elected by the workers; this will have a part to play in the socialization and subsequent management of the plant in accordance with suitable criteria. As far as the political function is concerned, that is to say the formation of local and central organs of authority, elections to proletarian councils will be held on the basis of electoral rolls in which (with the rigorous exclusion of all bourgeois, i.e. people who in any way whatsoever live off the work of others) all proletarians are included on an equal footing, irrespective of their trade, and even if they are (legitimately) unemployed or incapacitated. Bearing all this in mind, is it possible, or desirable, to set up Soviets now?

If we are speaking of factory councils, these are already spreading in the form of internal commissions, or the English "shop stewards" system. As these are organs which represent the interests of the work-force, they should be set up even while the factory is still in the hands of private capital. Indeed it would certainly be to our advantage to urge the setting up of these factory councils, although we should entertain no illusions as to their innate revolutionary capacity. Which brings us to the most important problem, that of political Soviets. The political Soviet represents the collective interests of the working class, in so far as this class does not share power with the bourgeoisie, but has succeeded in overthrowing it and excluding it from power. Hence the full significance and strength of the Soviet lies not in this or that structure, but in the fact that it is the organ of a class which is taking the management of society into its own hands. Every member of the Soviet is a proletarian conscious that he is exercising dictatorship in the name of his own class.

If the bourgeois class is still in power, even if it were possible to summon proletarian electors to nominate their delegates (for there is no question of using the trade unions or existing internal commissions for the purpose), one would simply be giving a formal imitation of a future activity, an imitation devoid of its fundamental revolutionary character. Those who can represent the proletariat *today*, before it takes power *tomorrow*, are workers who are conscious of this historical eventuality; in other words, the workers who are *members of the Communist Party*. In its struggle against bourgeois power, the proletariat is represented by its *class party*, even if this consists of no more than an audacious minority. The Soviets of tomorrow must arise from the local branches of the Communist Party. It is these which will be able to call on elements who, as soon as the revolution is victorious, will be proposed as candidates before the proletarian electoral masses to set up the Councils of local worker delegates.

But if it is to fulfil these functions, the Communist Party *must abandon its participation in elections to organs of bourgeois democracy*. The reasons supporting this statement are obvious. The Party should have as members only those individuals who can cope with the responsibilities and dangers of the struggle during the period of insurrection and social reorganization. The conclusion that we should abandon our participation in elections only when we have Soviets available is mistaken. A more thorough examination of the question leads one instead to the following conclusion: for as long as bourgeois power exists, the organ of revolution is the class party; after the smashing of bourgeois power, it is the network of workers' councils. The class party cannot fulfil this role, nor be in a position to lead the assault against bourgeois power in order to replace parliamentary democracy by the Soviet system, unless it renounces the practice of despatching its own representatives to bourgeois organs. This renunciation, which is negative only in a formal sense, is the prime condition to be satisfied if the forces of the communist proletariat are to be mobilized. To be unwilling to make such a renunciation is tantamount to abandoning our posture of readiness to declare class war at the first available opportunity.

Il Soviet, 21 September 1919, Vol. II, No. 39.

46. LETTERS TO THE IIIrd INTERNATIONAL – *BORDIGA*

I

Abstentionist Communist Fraction of the
Italian Socialist Party

Central Committee — Borgo San Antonio Abate 221
Naples

To the Moscow Committee of the IIIrd International.

Our fraction was formed after the Bologna Congress of the Italian Socialist Party (6–10 October 1919),[66] but it had issued its propaganda previously through the Naples newspaper *Il Soviet*, convening a conference at Rome which approved the programme subsequently presented to the Congress. We enclose a collection of issues of the journal, plus several copies of the programme together with the motion with which it was put to the vote.

It should be noted at the outset that throughout the war years a powerful extremist movement operated within the Party, opposing both the openly reformist politics of the parliamentary group and the General Confederation of Labour and also those of the Party leadership, despite the fact that they followed an intransigent revolutionary line in accordance with the decisions of the pre-War congresses. The leadership has always been split into two currents *vis-à-vis* the problem of the War. The right-wing current identified itself with Lazzari, author of the formula "neither support nor sabotage the war",[67] the left-wing current with Serrati, the editor of *Avanti!*. However, the two currents presented a united front at all meetings held during the war, and although they had reservations concerning the attitude of the parliamentary group, they did not come out firmly against them. Left elements outside the leadership struggled against this ambiguity, being determined to split the reformists of the group away from the Party and to adopt a more revolutionary attitude.

Not even the 1918 Congress of Rome, held just before the Armistice, was able to break with the transigent politics of the deputies. The leadership, despite the addition of extremist elements like Gennari and Bombacci, did not effect much change in its line; indeed, this was weakened by a soft attitude towards some of the activities of a right wing hostile to the orientation of the majority of the Party.

After the war, apparently the whole Party adopted a "maximalist" line, affiliating to the IIIrd International. However, from a communist point of view, the Party's attitude was not satisfactory; we beg you to note the polemics published in *Il Soviet* taking issue with the parliamentary group, the Confederation (in connection with the "constituent assembly of trades")[68] and with the leadership itself, in particular concerning the preparations for the 20–21 July strike. Together with other comrades from all over Italy, we at once opted for electoral abstentionism, which we supported at the Bologna Congress. *We wish to make it clear that at the congress we were at variance with the Party not only on the electoral question, but also on the question of splitting the Party.*

The victorious "maximalist electionist" faction too had accepted the thesis that the reformists were incompatible with the Party, but failed to act on it for purely *electoral* calculations – notwithstanding the anti-communist speeches of Turati and Treves. This is a powerful argument in favour of abstentionism: *unless electionist and parliamentary activity is abandoned, it will not be possible to form a purely Communist Party.* Parliamentary democracy in the Western countries assumes forms of such a character that it constitutes the most formidable weapon for deflecting the revolutionary movement of the proletariat. The left in our Party has been committed to polemicizing and struggling against bourgeois democracy since 1910–11, and this experience leads us to the conclusion that in the present world revolutionary situation, all contact with the democratic system needs to be severed.

The present situation in Italy is as follows: the Party is waging a campaign against the war and the interventionist parties, certain of deriving great electoral advantages from this policy. But since the present government is composed of bourgeois parties which were hostile to the war in 1915, a certain confluence results between the Party's electoral activity and the politics of the bourgeois government. As all the reformist ex-deputies have been readopted as candidates, the Nitti government, which has good relations with them as may be seen from the most recent parliamentary episodes, will trim its behaviour to ensure that they are preferred. Then the Party, exhausted as it is by the enormous efforts it has made in the present elections, will become bogged down in polemics against the transigent attitude of the deputies. Then we will have the preparations for the administrative elections in

July 1920; for many months, the Party will make no serious revolutionary propaganda or preparations. It is to be hoped that unforeseen developments do not intervene and overwhelm the Party. We attach importance to the question of electoral activity, and we feel it is contrary to communist principles to allow individual parties affiliated to the IIIrd International to decide the question for themselves. The international communist party should study the problem and resolve it for everyone.

Today we are resolved to work towards the formation of a truly communist party, and our fraction inside the Italian Socialist Party has set itself this goal. We hope that the first parliamentary skirmishes will bring many comrades towards us, so that the split with the social-democrats may be accomplished. At the congress, we received 3,417 votes (67 sections voting for us), while the maximalist electionists won with 48,000 votes and the reformists reeceived 14,000. We are also at variance with the maximalists on other issues of principle: in the interests of brevity we enclose a copy of the programme adopted by the congress, which is the Party's programme today (not one member left the Party as a result of the changes in the programme), together with some comments of our own.

It should be noted that we are not collaborating with movements outside the Party, such as anarchists and syndicalists, for they follow principles which are non-communist and contrary to the dictatorship of the proletariat. Indeed, they accuse us of being more authoritarian and centralist than the other maximalists in the Party. See the polemics in *Il Soviet*. What is needed in Italy is a comprehensive clarification of the communist programme and tactics, and we will devote all our efforts to this end. Unless a party that concerns itself solely and systematically with propagandizing and preparing the proletariat along communist lines is successfully organized, the revolution could emerge defeated.

As far as the question of tactics is concerned, in particular the setting up of Soviets, it appears to us that errors are being committed even by our friends; what we are afraid of is that nothing more will be accomplished than to give a reformist twist to the craft unions. Efforts are in fact being made to set up workshop committees, as in Turin, and then to bring all the delegates from a given industry (engineering) together to take over the leadership of the trade union, by appointing its executive committee. In this way, the political functions of the workers' councils for which the proletariat should be prepared are not being tackled; whereas, in our view, the most important problem is to organize a powerful class-based party (Communist Party) that will prepare the insurrectionary seizure of power from the hands of the bourgeois government.

It is our earnest desire to know your opinion concerning:

(a) parliamentary and municipal electionism and the prospects for a decision on this question by the Communist International; (b) splitting the Italian party; (c) the tactical problem of setting up Soviets under a bourgeois régime, and the limits of such action.

We salute both yourselves and the great Russian proletariat, the pioneer of universal communism.

Naples, 10 November 1919.

II

Abstentionist Communist Fraction of the Italian Socialist Party

Central Committee

Borgo San Antonio Abate 221
Naples 11 January 1920

To the Central Committee of the Communist IIIrd International, Moscow.

Dearest Comrades,

We sent you a previous communication on 11 November. We are writing in Italian in the knowledge that your office is run by Comrade Balabanov, who has an excellent knowledge of the language.

Our movement is made up of those who voted in favour of the abstentionist tendency at the Bologna congress. We are again sending you our programme and its accompanying motion. We hope you received the collection of our newspaper *Il Soviet*, and this time we are sending you copies of Numbers 1 and 2 of the new series which began this year. The object of this letter is to let you have some comments of ours on Comrade Lenin's letter to the German communists, published by *Rote Fahne* on 20 December 1919 and reproduced by *Avanti!* on the 31st, to give you a clearer idea of our political position.[69]

First of all, let us draw your attention once again to the fact that the Italian Socialist Party still contains opportunist socialists of the Adler and Kautsky ilk, of whom Lenin speaks in the first part of his letter. The Italian party is not a communist party; *it is not even a revolutionary party.* The "maximalist electionist" majority is closer in spirit to the German Independents. At the congress we differentiated ourselves from this majority *not only on the issue of electoral tactics*, but also on the question of excluding the reformists led by Turati from the party. Hence the division between ourselves and those maximalists who voted in favour of Serrati's motion at Bologna is not analogous to the division between the supporters of abstentionism and the supporters of electoral participation within the German Communist Party, *but corresponds rather to the division between Communists and Independents.*

In programmatic terms our point of view has nothing in common with anarchism and syndicalism. We favour the strong and centralized Marxist political party that Lenin speaks of; indeed we are the most fervent supporters of this idea in the maximalist camp. We are not in favour of boycotting economic trade unions but of communists taking them over, and our position corresponds to that expressed by comrade Zinoviev in his report to the Congress of the Russian Communist Party, published by *Avanti!* on 1 January.

As for the *workers' councils*, these exist in only a few places in Italy and then they are exclusively factory councils, made up of workshop delegates who are concerned with questions internal to the factory. Our proposal, on the other hand, is to take the initiative in setting up rural and municipal Soviets, elected directly by the masses assembled in the factories or villages; for we believe that in preparing for the revolution, the struggle should have a predominantly political character. We are in favour of participating in elections to any representative body of the working class when the electorate consists exclusively of workers. On the other hand, we are against the participation of communists in elections for parliaments, or bourgeois municipal and provincial councils, or constituent assemblies, because we are of the opinion that it is not possible to carry out revolutionary work in such bodies; we believe that electoral work is an obstacle in the path of the working masses, forming a communist consciousness and laying the preparations for the proletarian dictatorship as the antithesis of bourgeois democracy.

To participate in such bodies and expect to emerge unscathed by social-democratic and collaborationist deviations is a vain hope in the current historical period, as is shown by the present Italian parliamentary session. These conclusions are reinforced by the experience of the struggle waged by the left wing in our Party from 1910–11 to the present day against all the manœuvrings of parliamentarism, in a country which has supported a bourgeois democratic régime for a long time: the campaign against ministerialism;

against forming electoral political and administrative alliance with democratic parties; against freemasonry and bourgeois anti-clericalism, etc. From this experience we drew the conclusion that the gravest danger for the socialist revolution lies in collaborating with bourgeois democracy on the terrain of social reformism. This experience was subsequently generalized in the course of the war and the revolutionary events in Russia, Germany, Hungary, etc.

Parliamentary intransigence was a practical proposition, despite continual clashes and difficulties, in a non-revolutionary period, when the conquest of power on the part of the working class did not seem very likely. In addition, the more the régime and the composition of parliament itself have a traditional democratic character, the greater become the difficulties of parliamentary action. It is with these points in mind that we would judge the comparisons with the Bolsheviks' participation in elections to the Duma after 1905. The tactic employed by the Russian comrades, of participating in elections to the Constituent Assembly and then dissolving it by force, despite the fact that it did not prove to be the undoing of the revolution, would be a dangerous tactic to use in countries where the parliamentary system, far from being a recent phenomenon, is an institution of long standing and one that is rooted firmly in the consciousness and customs of the proletariat itself.

The work required to gain the support of the masses for the abolition of the system of democratic representation would appear to be – and is in fact – a much greater task for us in Italy than in, say, Russia or even Germany. The need to give the greatest force to this propaganda aimed at devaluing the parliamentary institution and eliminating its sinister counter-revolutionary influence has led us to the tactic of abstentionism. To electoral activity we counterpose the violent conquest of political power on the part of the proletariat and the formation of the Council State: hence our abstentionism in no way diminishes our insistence on the need for a centralized revolutionary government. Indeed, we are against collaborating with anarchists and syndicalists within the revolutionary movement, for they do not accept such criteria of propaganda and action.

The general election of 16 November, despite the fact that it was fought by the PSI on a maximalist platform, has proved once again that electoral activity excludes and pushes into the background every other form of activity, above all illegal activity. In Italy the problem is not one of uniting legal and illegal activity, as Lenin advises the German comrades, but of beginning to reduce *legal* activity in order to make a start on its *illegal* counterpart, which does not exist at all. The new parliamentary group has devoted itself to social-democratic and minimalist work, tabling questions, drafting legislation, etc.

We conclude our exposition by letting you know that in all likelihood, although we have maintained discipline within the PSI and upheld its tactics until now, before long and perhaps prior to the municipal elections, which are due in July, our fraction will break away from the party that seems set on retaining many anti-communists in its ranks, to form the Italian Communist Party, whose first act will be to affiliate to the Communist International.

Revolutionary greetings.

47. TOWARDS THE ESTABLISHMENT OF WORKERS' COUNCILS IN ITALY – *BORDIGA*

I

We have now collected quite a lot of material concerned with proposals and initiatives for establishing Soviets in Italy, and we reserve to ourselves the right to expound the elements of the argument step by step. At this stage we wish to make a few preliminary observations of a general nature, to which we have already referred in our most recent issues.

The system of proletarian representation that has been introduced for the first time ever in Russia has a twofold character: political and economic. Its political role is to struggle against the bourgeoisie until the latter has been totally eradicated. Its economic role is to create the whole novel mechanism of communist production. As the revolution unfolds and the parasitic classes are gradually eliminated, the political functions become less and less important in comparison with their economic counterparts: but in the first instance, *and above all when it is a question of struggling against bourgeois power*, political activity must come first.

The authentic instrument of the proletariat's struggle for liberation, and above all of its conquest of political power, is the *communist class party*. Under the bourgeois régime, the communist party, the engine of the revolution, needs organs in which it can operate; these organs are the workers' councils. To declare that they are the proletariat's organs of liberation, without mentioning the role of the party, after the fashion of the programme adopted at the Congress of Bologna, seems mistaken in our view.[70] To maintain, after the fashion of the Turin *L'Ordine Nuovo* comrades, that even before the collapse of the bourgeoisie the workers' councils are organs, not only of political struggle, but of technico-economic training in the communist system, can only be seen as a return to socialist gradualism. This latter, whether it is called reformism or syndicalism, is defined by the mistaken belief that the proletariat can achieve emancipation by making advances in economic relations while capitalism still holds political power through the State.

We shall now expand on the criticism of the two concepts we have mentioned.

* * * * *

The system of proletarian representation must be rooted in the whole of the technical process of production. This is a perfectly valid principle, but it corresponds to the stage when the proletariat is organizing the new economy after its seizure of power. Apply it without modification to the bourgeois régime, and you accomplish nothing in revolutionary terms. Even at the stage which Russia has reached, Soviet-type political representation – i.e. the ladder that culminates in the government of the people's commissars – does not start with work-crews or factory shops, but from the local administrative Soviet, elected directly by the workers (grouped if possible in their respective workplaces). To be specific, the Moscow Soviet is elected by the Moscow proletariat in the ratio of one delegate to every 1,000 workers. Between the delegates and the electors there is no intermediary organ. This first level then leads to higher levels, to the Congress of Soviets, the executive committee, and finally the government of commissars.

The *factory council* plays its part in quite a different network, that of workers' *control* over production. Consequently the factory council, made up of one representative for every workshop, does not nominate the factory's representative in the local political-administrative Soviet: this representative is elected directly and independently. In Russia, the factory councils are the basic unit of another system of representation (itself subordinate of course to the political network of Soviets): the system of workers' control and the people's economy. Control *within the factory* has a revolutionary and expropriative significance only after central power has passed into the hands of the proletariat. While the factory is still protected by the bourgeois State, the factory council controls nothing. The few functions it fulfils are the result of the traditional practice of: 1. parliamentary reformism; 2. trade-union resistance, which does not cease to be a reformist way of advancing.

To conclude: we do not oppose the setting up of internal factory councils if the workers themselves or their organizations demand them. But we insist that the communist party's activity must be based on another terrain, namely the struggle for the conquest of political power. This struggle may well be advanced fruitfully by the setting up of workers' representative bodies – but these must be urban or rural workers' councils elected directly by the masses, waiting to take the place of municipal councils and local organs of State power at the moment the bourgeois forces collapse. Having thus advanced our thesis, we promise to give it ample documentation and factual support, and to present our work in a report to the next meeting of the communist fraction.

II

Prior to getting down to discussing the practical problems of setting up workers', peasants' and soldiers' councils in Italy, and bearing in mind the general considerations contained in the article we published in our last issue, we wish to examine the programmatic guidelines of the Soviet system as they are developed in the documents of the Russian revolution and in the declarations of principle issued by some of the Italian maximalist currents, such as the programme adopted by the Bologna Congress, the motion proposed by Leone and other comrades to the same congress;[71] and the writings of *L'Ordine Nuovo* on the Turin factory council movement.

The Councils and the Bolshevik Programme

In the documents of the IIIrd International and the Russian Communist Party, in the masterly reports of those formidable exponents of doctrine, the leaders of the Russian revolutionary movement – Lenin, Zinoviev, Radek, Bukharin – there recurs at frequent intervals the idea that the Russian revolution did not *invent* new and unforeseen structures, but merely confirmed the predictions of Marxist theory concerning the revolutionary process.

The core of the imposing phenomenon of the Russian revolution is the conquest of political power on the part of the working masses, and the establishment of their dictatorship, as the result of an authentic class war.

The Soviets – and it is well to recall that the word *soviet* simply means *council*, and can be employed to describe any sort of representative body – the Soviets, as far as history is concerned, are the system of representation employed by the proletarian class once it has taken power. The Soviets are the organs that take the place of parliament and the bourgeois administrative assemblies and gradually replace all the other ramifications of the State. To put it in the words of the most recent congress of the Russian communists, as quoted by Comrade Zinoviev, "the Soviets are the State organizations of the workers and poor peasants; they exercise the dictatorship of the proletariat during the stage when all previous forms of the State are being extinguished".

In the final analysis, this system of State organizations gives representation to all producers in their capacity as members of the working class, and not as members of a particular trade or industrial sector. According to the latest manifesto of the Third International, the Soviets represent "a new type of mass organization, one which embraces the working class in its entirety, irrespective of individual trades or levels of political maturity". The basic units of the Soviet administrative network are the urban and rural councils; the network culminates in the government of commissars.

And yet it is true that during the phase of economic transformation, other organs are emerging parallel to this system, such as the system of workers' control and the people's economy. It is also true, as we have stressed many times, that this economic system will gradually absorb the political system, once the expropriation of the bourgeoisie is completed and there is no further need for a central authority. But the essential problem during the revolutionary period, as emerges clearly from all the Russian documents, is that of keeping the various local and sectional demands and interests subordinate to the general interest (in space and time) of the revolutionary movement.

Not until the two sets of organs are merged will the network of production be thoroughly communist, and only then will that principle (which in our view is being given exaggerated importance) of a perfect match between the system of representation and the mechanisms of the productive system be successfully realized. Prior to that stage, while the bourgeoisie is still resisting and above all while it still holds power, the problem is to achieve a representative system in which the general interest prevails. Today, while the economy is still based on individualism and competition, the only form in which this higher collective interest can be manifested is a system of *political* representation in which the communist political party is active.

We shall come back to this question, and demonstrate how the desire to over-concretize and technically determine the Soviet system, especially when the bourgeoisie is still in power, puts the cart before the horse and lapses into the old errors of syndicalism and reformism. For the moment we quote these non-ambiguous words of Zinoviev: "The communist party unifies that vanguard of the proletariat which is struggling, in conscious fashion, to put the communist programme into effect. In particular it is striving to introduce its programme into the State organizations, the Soviets, and to achieve complete dominance within them."

To conclude, the Russian Soviet Republic is led by the Soviets, which represent ten million workers out of a total population of about eighty million. But essentially, appointments to the executive committees of the local and central Soviets are settled in the sections and congresses of the great Communist Party which has mastery over the Soviets. This corresponds to the stirring defence by Radek of the revolutionary role of minorities. It would be as well not to create a majoritarian-workerist fetishism which could only be to the advantage of reformism and the bourgeoisie. The party is in the front line of the revolution in so far as it is potentially composed of men who think and act like members of the future working humanity in which all will be producers harmoniously inserted into a marvellous mechanism of functions and representation.

The Bologna Programme and the Councils

It is to be deplored that in the Party's current programme there is no trace of the Marxist proposition that the class party is the instrument of proletarian emancipation; there is just the anodyne codicil: "decides (Who decides? Even grammar was sacrificed in the haste to decide – in favour of elections.) to base the organization of the Italian Socialist Party on the above-mentioned principles".

As regards the paragraph which denies the transformation of any State organ into an organ of struggle for the liberation of the proletariat, there are certain points to be made – but it will have to be done on another occasion, after an indispensable previous clarification of terms. But we dissent still more strongly from the programme where it states that the new proletarian organs will function initially, under the bourgeois régime, as instruments of the violent struggle for liberation, and will subsequently become organs of social and economic transformation; for among the organs mentiond are not only workers', peasants' and soldiers' councils, but also *councils of the public economy*, which are inconceivable under a bourgeois régime.[72] Even the workers' political councils should be seen primarily as vehicles for the communists' activity of liberating the proletariat.

Even quite recently Comrade Serrati, in flagrant opposition to Marx and Lenin, has undervalued the role of the class party in the revolution. As Lenin says: "Together with the working masses, the Marxist, centralized political party, the vanguard of the proletariat, will lead the people along the right road, towards the victorious dictatorship of the proletariat, towards proletarian not bourgeois democracy, towards Soviet power and the socialist order." The Party's current programme smacks of libertarian scruples and a lack of theoretical preparation.

The Councils and the Leone Motion

This motion was summarized in four points expounded in the author's evocative style.[73]

The first of these points finds miraculous inspiration in the statement that the class struggle is the real engine of history and that it has smashed social-national unions. But then the motion proceeds to exalt the Soviets as the organs of revolutionary synthesis, which they are supposed to bring about virtually through the very mechanism of their being created; it states that only Soviets, rather than schools, parties or corporations, can bring the great historical initiatives to a triumphant conclusion.

This idea of Leone's, and of the many comrades who signed his motion, is quite different from our own, which we have deduced from Marxism and from the lessons of the Russian revolution. What they are doing is over-emphasizing a *form* in place of a *force*, just as the syndicalists did in the case of the trade unions, attributing to their minimalist practice the magical virtue of being able to transform itself into the social revolution. Just as syndicalism was demolished in the first place by the criticism of true Marxists, and subsequently by the experience of the syndicalist movements which all over the world have collaborated with the bourgeois régime, providing it with elements for its preservation, so Leone's idea collapses before the experience of the counter-revolutionary, social-democratic workers' councils, which are precisely those which have not been penetrated successfully by the communist political programme.

Only the party can embody the dynamic revolutionary energies of the class. It would be trivial to object that socialist parties too have compromised, since we are not exalting the virtues of the party *form*, but those of the dynamic content which is to be found only in the *communist* party. Every party defines itself on the basis of its own programme, and its functions cannot be compared with those of other parties, whereas of necessity all the trade unions and even, in a technical sense, all the workers' councils have functions in common with one another. The shortcoming of the social-reformist parties was not that they were parties, but that they were not communist and revolutionary parties. These parties led the counter-revolution, whereas the communist parties, in opposition to them, led and nourished revolutionary action. Thus there are no organs which are revolutionary by virtue of their form; there are only social forces that are revolutionary on account of their orientation. These forces transform themselves into a party that goes into battle with a programme.

The Councils and the initiative of L'Ordine Nuovo *in Turin*

In our view, the comrades around the newspaper *L'Ordine Nuovo* go even further than this. They are not even happy with the wording of the Party's programme, because they claim that the Soviets, including those of a technical-economic character (the factory councils), not only are already in existence and functioning as organs of the proletarian liberation struggle under the bourgeois régime, but have already become organs for the reconstruction of the communist economy.

In fact they publish in their newspaper the section of the Party's programme that we quoted above, leaving out a few words so as to transform its meaning in accordance with their own point of view: "They will have to be opposed by new proletarian organs (workers', peasants' and soldiers' councils, councils of the public economy, etc.) . . . organs of social and economic transformation and for the reconstruction of the new communist order."[74] But this article is already a long one, so we postpone to our next issue the exposition of our profound dissension from this principle; in our view, it runs the risk of ending up as a purely reformist experiment involving modification of certain functions of the trade unions and perhaps the promulgation of a bourgeois law on workers' councils.

III

At the end of our second article on the establishment of Soviets in Italy, we referred to the Turin movement to establish factory councils. We do not share the point of view which inspires the efforts of the *L'Ordine Nuovo* comrades, and while appreciating their tenacity in making the fundamentals of communism better known, we believe that they have committed major errors of principle and tactics.

According to them, the essence of the communist revolution lies in the setting up of new organs of proletarian representation, whose fundamental character is their strict alignment with the process of production; eventually these organs are to control production directly. We have already made the point that we see this as over-emphasis on the idea of a formal coincidence between the representative organs of the working class and the various aggregates of the technico-economic system of production.[75] This coincidence will in fact be achieved at a much more advanced stage of the communist revolution, when production is socialized and all its various constituent activities are subordinated in harmonious fashion to the general and collective interests.

Prior to this stage, and during the period of transition from a capitalist to a communist economy, the groupings of producers are in a constant state of flux and their individual interests may at times clash with the general and collective interests of the revolutionary movement of the proletariat. This movement will find its real instrument in a working-class representative institution in which each individual participates in his capacity as a member of the working class, and as such interested in a radical change in social relations, rather than as a component of a particular trade, factory or local group.

So long as political power remains in the hands of the capitalist class, a representative organ embodying the general revolutionary interests of the proletariat can only be found in the *political* arena. It can only be a class party that has the personal adherence of the sort of people who, in order to dedicate themselves to the cause of the revolution, have managed to overcome their narrow selfish, sectional and even sometimes class interests (the latter case obtaining when the party admits deserters from the bourgeois class into its ranks, provided they are supporters of the communist programme).

It is a serious error to believe that by importing the formal structures which one expects to be formed to manage communist production into the present proletarian environment, among the wage-earners of capitalism, one will bring into being forces which are in themselves and through inner necessity revolutionary. This was the error of the syndicalists, and this too is the error of the over-zealous supporters of the factory councils.

The article published by comrade C. Niccolini in *Communismo*[76] comes at an opportune moment. He notes that in Russia, even after the proletarian seizure of power, the factory councils frequently placed obstacles in the path of revolutionary measures; to an even greater extent than the trade unions, they counterposed the pressures of narrow interests to the unfolding of the revolutionary process. Even within the network of the communist economy, the factory councils are not the principal determinants of the production process. In the organs which fulfil this function (Councils of the People's Economy), the factory councils have fewer representatives than the trade unions or the proletarian State authorities; it is this centralized political network that is the instrument and the dominant factor in the revolution – understood not only as a struggle against the political resistance of the bourgeois class, but also as a process of socializing wealth.

At the juncture we have reached in Italy, viz the juncture where the proletarian State is still a programmatic aspiration, the fundamental problem is the conquest of power on the part of the proletariat, or better the communist proletariat – i.e. the workers who are organized into a class-based political party, who are determined to make the historical form of revolutionary power, the dictatorship of the proletariat, into a concrete reality.

* * * * *

Comrade A. Tasca himself, in *L'Ordine Nuovo* No. 22, clearly expounds his disagreement with the programme of the maximalist majority adopted at the Bologna Congress, and his even greater disagreement with us abstentionists, in the following passage that deserves to be reproduced. "Another point in the Party's new programme deserves to be considered: the new proletarian organs (workers', peasants' and soldiers' councils, councils of the public economy, etc.) functioning *initially* (under the bourgeois régime) as instruments of the violent struggle for liberation, are *subsequently* transformed into organs of social and economic transformation, for reconstruction of the new communist order. At an earlier session of the Commission, we had stressed the shortcomings of such a formulation, which entrusted different functions to the new organs *initially* and *subsequently*, separated by the seizure of power on the part of the proletariat. Gennari had promised to make an alteration, along the lines of '. . . initially *predominantly* as instruments . . .', but it is evident that he eventually abandoned this idea, and as I was unable to attend the last session of the Commission, I could not make him adopt it again. There is in this formulation, however, a veritable point of disagreement which, while bringing Gennari, Bombacci and others closer to the abstentionists, puts a greater distance between them and those who believe that the new workers' organs cannot function as 'instruments of the violent struggle for liberation' except and to the degree that they become 'organs of social and economic transformation' *at once* (rather than subsequently). The proletariat's liberation is achieved through the manifestation of its ability to control in an autonomous and original fashion the social processes it created by and for itself: liberation consists in the creation of the sort of organs which, if they are active and alert, by virtue of this fact alone provoke the social and economic transformation which is their goal. This is not a question of form, but of substance. In the present formulation, we repeat, the compilers of the programme have ended up adhering to Bordiga's conception, which attaches more importance to the conquest of power than to the formation of Soviets; for the present period, Bordiga sees the Soviets as having more of a 'political' function, in the strict sense of the word, than an organic role of 'economic and social transformation'. Just as Bordiga maintains that the complete Soviet will come into being only during the period of the dictatorship of the proletariat, so Gennari, Bombacci, etc., argue that only the conquest of power (which thereby acquires a political character, and so brings us back full circle to the 'public powers' that had already been superseded) can provide the Soviets with their true, full functions. It is this which is in our opinion the nub of the argument, and it must lead us, sooner or later, to a further revision of the newly adopted programme."[77]

According to Tasca, then, the working class can project the stages of its liberation, even before it has wrested power from the bourgeoisie. Moreover Tasca lets it be understood that this conquest could occur even without violence, once the proletariat had completed its work of technical preparation and social education: here we have the concrete revolutionary method of the *L'Ordine Nuovo* comrades. We will not proceed at length to demonstrate how this idea eventually coincides with that of reformism and becomes foreign to the fundamentals of revolutionary Marxism; according to Marxist doctrine, the revolution does not occur as a result of the education, culture or technical capacity of the proletariat, but as a result of the inner crises of the system of capitalist production.

Like Enrico Leone, Tasca and his friends attach too much importance to the appearance in the Russian revolution of a new social representative organ, the *Soviet*, and endow it with an inner force such that its mere establishment constitutes a wholly novel historical solution to the proletariat's struggle against capitalism. But the Soviets – most successfully defined by comrade Zinoviev as the State organizations of the working class – are nothing other than organs of proletarian power, exercising the revolutionary dictatorship of the working class; it is this latter which is the lynchpin of the Marxist system, and whose first positive experiment was the Paris Commune of 1871. The Soviets are the form, not the cause, of the revolution.

* * * * *

In addition to this disagreement, there is another point which separates us from the Turin comrades. The Soviets, State organizations of the victorious proletariat, are not at all the same as the factory councils, nor do these latter constitute the first step or rung of the Soviet political system. This confusion is also present in the declaration of principles adopted by the first assembly of workshop delegates from the factories of Turin, which begins as follows: "The factory delegates are the sole and authentic social (economic and political) representatives of the proletarian class, by virtue of their being elected by all workers at their work-place on the basis of universal suffrage. At the various levels of their constitution, the delegates embody the union of all workers as realized in organs of production (work-crew, workshop, factory, union of the factories in a given industry, union of the productive enterprises in a city, union of the organs of production in the mechanical and agricultural industry of a district, a province, a region, the nation, the world) whose authority and social leadership are invested in the councils and council system."[78]

This declaration is unacceptable, since proletarian power is formed directly within the municipal Soviets of town and country, without passing via factory councils and committees, as we have repeated many times; this fact also emerges from the lucid expositions of the Russian Soviet system published by *L'Ordine Nuovo* itself. The factory councils are organs whose task will be to represent the interests of groups of workers during the period of revolutionary transformation of production. They represent not only a particular group's determination to achieve liberation through socialization of the private capitalist's firm, but also the group's concern for the manner in which its interests will be taken into account during the process of socialization itself, a process disciplined by the organized will of the whole of the working collectivity.

The workers' interests have until now been represented by the trade unions, throughout the period when the capitalist system appeared stable and there was scope only for putting upward pressure on wages. The unions will continue to exist during the revolutionary period, and naturally enough there will be a demarcation dispute with the factory councils, which only emerge when the abolition of private capitalism is seen to be imminent, as has happened in Turin. However, it is not a matter of great revolutionary moment to decide whether non-union members should participate or no in the elections for delegates. If it is logical that they should in fact participate, given the very nature of the factory council, it certainly does not appear logical to us that there should be a mingling of organs and functions between councils and unions, along the lines of the Turin proposals – compelling, for example, the Turin section of the Metalworkers' Federation to elect its own executive council from the workshop delegates' assembly.

At any rate, the relations between councils and unions as representatives of the special interests of particular groups of workers will continue to be very complex; they will be settled and harmonized only in a very advanced stage of the communist economy, when the possibility of the interests of a group of producers being at variance with the general interest in the progress of production will be reduced to a minimum.

* * * * *

What is important to establish is that the communist revolution will be led and conducted by an organ representing the working class *politically*; prior to the smashing of bourgeois power, this is a political party. Subsequently, it is the system of political Soviets elected directly by the masses, with the aim of choosing representatives who have a general political programme and are not merely the exponents of the narrow interests of a trade or firm.

The Russian system is so contrived that a town's municipal Soviet is composed of one delegate for every group of proletarians, who vote for a single name only. The delegates, however, are proposed to the electors by the political party; the same process is repeated for the second and third degrees of delegation, to the higher organs of the State system. Thus it is always a single political party – the Communist Party – which seeks and obtains from the electors a mandate to administer power. We are certainly not saying that the Russian system should be adopted in an uncritical fashion elsewhere, but we do feel that the principle underlying the revolutionary system of representation – viz. the subjection of selfish and sectional interests to the collective interest – should be adhered to even more closely than in Russia.

Would it usefully serve the communists' revolutionary struggle if the network of a political system of representation of the working class were instituted now? This is the problem we shall examine in the next article, when we discuss the relevant proposals elaborated by the Party leadership. We shall remain unshaken in our conviction that such a representative system would be quite different from the system of factory councils and committees that has begun to form in Turin (and indeed this is partially recognized in the Party's proposals).

IV

We believe we have already said enough concerning the difference between factory councils and politico-administrative councils of workers and peasants. The factory council represents workers' interests which extend no farther than the narrow circle of an industrial firm. Under a communist régime, it is the basic unit of the system of "workers' control" which has a certain part to play in the system of "Councils of the Economy", a system which will eventually take over the technical and economic management of production. But the factory council has nothing to do with the system of political Soviets, the depositaries of proletarian power.

Under the bourgeois régime, therefore, the factory council, or for that matter the trade union, cannot be viewed as an organ for the conquest of political power. If, on the other hand, one were to view them as organs for the emancipation of the proletariat via a route that does not involve the revolutionary conquest of power, one would be lapsing into the syndicalist error: the comrades around *L'Ordine Nuovo* are hardly correct when they maintain, as they have done in polemic with *Guerra di Classe*,[79] that the factory council movement, as they theorize it, is not in some sense a syndicalist movement.

Marxism is characterized by its prediction that the proletariat's struggle for emancipation will be divided into a number of great historical phases, in which political activity and economic activity vary enormously in importance: the struggle for power; the exercise of power (dictatorship of the proletariat) in the transformation of the economy; the society without classes and without a political State. To identify, in the role of the liberation organs of the proletariat, the stages of the political process with their economic counterparts is to lapse into the petty-bourgeois caricature of Marxism called economism (which in turn can be classified into reformism and syndicalism). Over-emphasis on the factory council is just a resurrection of this hoary old error, which unites the petty-bourgeois Proudhon with all those revisionists who believe they have transcended Marx.

Under a bourgeois régime, then, the factory council represents the interests of the workers in a particular enterprise, just as it will do under a communist régime. It arises when circumstances demand it, through changes in the methods of proletarian economic organization. But perhaps to an even greater extent than the trade union, the council opens its flank to the deviations of reformism.

The old minimalist tendency that argues in favour of compulsory arbitration and profit-sharing by workers (i.e. their participation in the management and administration of the factory) could well find in the factory council the basis for the drafting of an anti-revolutionary piece of social legislation. This is happening in Germany at the moment, where the Independents are opposing not the principle, but the manner of the draft legislation, in stark contrast to the Communists who maintain that the democratic régime cannot grant the proletariat any form of control whatsoever over capitalist functions. It should thus be clear that it makes no sense to speak of workers' *control* until political power rests in the hands of the proletarian State. Such control can only be exercised, as a prelude to the socialization of firms and their administration by appropriate organs of the collectivity, in the name of the proletarian State and on the basis of its power.

* * * * *

Councils of workers – industrial workers, peasants and, on occasion, soldiers – are, as is clear, the political organs of the proletariat, the foundations of the proletarian State. The urban and rural local councils take the place of the municipal councils under the bourgeois régime. The provincial and regional Soviets take the place of the present provincial councils, with this difference, that the provincial Soviets are not elected directly, but indirectly from the local Soviets. The State Congress of Soviets, together with the Central Executive Committee, take the place of the bourgeois parliament, with the difference again that they are not elected directly, but by third or even fourth degree suffrage.[80]

There is no need here to emphasize the other differences, of which the most important is the electors' right of recall of any delegate at any time.

If the mechanism to cope with these recalls is to be flexible, then the elections in the first place should not be based on lists of candidates, but should involve giving a single delegate to a grouping of electors who, if possible, should live and work together. But the fundamental characteristic of this whole system does not reside in these technicalities, which have nothing magical about them, but rather in the principle which lays down that the right to vote, both actively and passively, is reserved to the workers alone and denied to the bourgeois.

As far as the formation of municipal Soviets is concerned, two errors are commonly encountered. One is the idea that delegates to the Soviets are elected by factory councils and committees (executive commissions of the councils of workshop delegates), whereas in fact, as we make no apology for repeating, the delegates are elected directly by the mass of electors. This error is reproduced in the Bombacci proposal for establishing Soviets in Italy (Para. 6).

The other error consists in thinking that the Soviet is a body composed of representatives simply nominated by the Socialist Party, the trade unions and the factory councils. Comrade Ambrosini, for example, makes this error in his proposals. Such a system might perhaps be useful in order to form Soviets quickly and on a provisional basis, but it does not correspond to their definitive structure. It is true that in Russia a small percentage of delegates to the Soviet are added to those elected directly by the proletarian electors. But in reality the Communist Party, or any other party, obtains its representation by standing tried and proven members of its organization as candidates, and by campaigning around its programme before the electorate. In our view, a Soviet can only be called revolutionary when a majority of its delegates are members of the Communist Party.

All of this, it should be understood, refers to the period of the proletarian dictatorship. Now we come to the vexed question: what should be the role and characteristics of the workers' councils while the power of the bourgeoisie is still intact?

* * * * *

In central Europe at the moment, workers' councils co-exist with the bourgeois-democratic State, which is all the more anti-revolutionary in that it is republican and social-democratic. What is the significance of this proletarian representative system, if it is not the depositary and foundation of State power? At the very least, does it act as an effective organ of struggle for the realization of the proletarian dictatorship?

These questions are answered by the Austrian comrade Otto Maschl in an article we came across in the Geneva journal, *Nouvelle Internationale*.[81] He states that in Austria the councils have brought about their own paralysis and have handed over their power to the national bourgeois assembly. In Germany on the other hand, according to Maschl, once the Majoritarians and Independents had left the councils, these latter became true foci of the struggle for proletarian emancipation, and Noske had to smash them in order to allow social-democracy to govern. In Austria, however, Maschl concludes, the existence of councils within the democratic system, or rather the existence of democracy *in spite of the councils*, proves that these workers' councils are far from playing the role of what are called Soviets in Russia. And he expresses the doubt that perhaps at the moment of the revolution, alternative, truly revolutionary Soviets may emerge and become the depositaries of proletarian power in place of these domesticated versions.

* * * * *

The Party programme adopted at Bologna declares that Soviets should be set up in Italy as organs of revolutionary struggle. The object of the Bombacci proposal is to concretize this aim.

Before getting down to details, let us discuss the general ideas which have inspired Comrade Bombacci. First of all, and let no one accuse us of being pedantic, let us request a formal clarification. In the phrase: "only a national institution that is broader than the Soviets can usher the present period towards the final revolutionary struggle against the bourgeois régime and its democratic mask: parliamentarism", does it mean that parliamentarism is the aforementioned *broader institution*, or is it the *democratic mask*? We fear that the first interpretation must be the right one, a feeling which is confirmed by the paragraph on the Soviets' programme of action, which is a strange mixture of the functions of the latter with the Party's parliamentary activity. If the councils to be set up are to carry out their activities on this ambiguous terrain, then it would certainly be better not to set them up at all.

The idea that the Soviets should have the role of working out *proposals for socialist and revolutionary legislation* which socialist deputies will place before the bourgeois State – here we have a proposal that makes a fine pair with the one on communal-electionist Sovietism which was so well demolished by our own D.L.[82] For the moment we shall go no further than remind the comrades who put forward such proposals of one of Lenin's conclusions in the declaration adopted by the Moscow Congress: "Put a distance between yourselves and those who delude the proletariat by proclaiming the possibility of their victories within the bourgeois framework, and propose that the new proletarian organs should combine with or collaborate with the instruments of bourgeois domination."[83] If the former are the social-democrats (who are still members of our Party), should we not recognize the latter in the electionist maximalists, concerned as they are with justifying their parliamentary and communal activity by monstrous pseudo-Soviet projects?

Are the comrades in the faction which was victorious at Bologna blind to the fact that these people are not even in line with that form of communist electionism which may legitimately be opposed – on the basis of the arguments of Lenin and certain German communists – to our own irreducible, principled abstentionism?

V

With this article we propose to conclude our exposition, though we may resume the discussion in polemic with comrades who have commented on our point of view in other newspapers. The discussion has now been taken up by the whole of the socialist press. The best articles we have come across are those by C. Niccolini in *Avanti!* These articles were written with great clarity and in line with genuine Marxist principles; we fully concur with them.

The Soviets, the councils of workers, peasants (and soldiers), are the form adopted by the representative system of the proletariat, in its exercise of power after the smashing of the capitalist State. Prior to the conquest of power, when the bourgeoisie is still politically dominant, it can happen that special historical conditions, probably corresponding to serious convulsions in the institutional arrangements of the State and society, bring Soviets into existence – and it can be very appropriate for communists to facilitate and stimulate the birth of these new organs of the proletariat. We must, however, be quite clear that their formation in this manner cannot be an artificial procedure, the mere application of a recipe – and that in any case the simple establishment of workers' councils, as the *form* of the proletarian revolution, does not imply that the problem of the revolution is resolved, nor that infallible conditions have been laid for its success. The revolution may not occur even when councils exist (we shall cite examples), if these are not infused with the political and historical consciousness of the proletariat – a consciousness which is condensed, one might almost say, in the communist political party.

The fundamental problem of the revolution thus lies in gauging the proletariat's determination to smash the bourgeois State and take power into its own hands. Such a determination on the part of the broad masses of the working class exists as a direct result of the economic relations of exploitation by capital; it is these which place the proletariat in an intolerable situation and drive it to smash the existing social forms. The task of the communists, then, is to direct this violent reaction on the part of the masses and give it greater efficiency. The communists – as the *Manifesto* said long ago – have a superior knowledge of the conditions of the class struggle and the proletariat's emancipation than the proletariat itself. The critique they make of history and of the constitution of society places them in a position to make fairly accurate predictions concerning the developments of the revolutionary process. It is for this reason that communists form the class's political party, which sets itself the task of unifying the proletarian forces and organizing the proletariat into the dominant class through the revolutionary conquest of power. When the revolution is imminent and its pre-conditions have matured in the real world, a powerful communist party must exist and its consciousness of the events which lie ahead must be particularly acute.

As regards the revolutionary organs which will exercise proletarian power and represent the foundations of the revolutionary State on the morrow of the collapse of the bourgeoisie, their consciousness of their role will depend on the extent to which they are led by workers who are conscious of the need for a dictatorship of their own class – i.e. communist workers. Wherever this is not the case, these organs will concede the power they have won and the counter-revolution will triumph. Thus if at any given moment these organs are required and communists need to concern themselves with setting them up, it should not therefore be thought that in them we have a means of readily outflanking the bourgeoisie and almost automatically overcoming its resistance to the ceding of power.

Can the Soviets, the State organs of the victorious proletariat, play a role as organs of revolutionary struggle for the proletariat while capitalism still controls the State? The answer is yes – in the sense, however, that at any given stage they may constitute the right terrain for the revolutionary struggle that the Party is waging. And at that particular stage, the Party has to fashion such a terrain, such a grouping of forces, for itself.

Today, in Italy, have we reached this stage of struggle? We feel that we are very close to it, but that there is one more stage to go through. The communist party, which has to work within the Soviets, does not yet exist. We are not saying that the Soviets will wait for it before they emerge. It could happen that events occur differently. But then we will run this grave risk, that the immaturity of the party will allow these organs to fall into the hands of the reformists, the accomplices of the bourgeoisie, the saboteurs and falsifiers of the revolution. And so we feel that the problem of forging a genuine communist party in Italy is much more urgent than the problem of creating Soviets. To study both problems, and establish the optimal conditions in which to tackle both without delay – this too is acceptable, but without setting fixed and schematic dates for an almost official *inauguration* of Soviets in Italy.

To accomplish the formation of the genuine communist party means sorting out the communists from the reformists and social-democrats. Some comrades believe that the very proposal to set up Soviets would also facilitate this sorting out process. We do not agree – for the very reason that the Soviet, in our view, is not in its essence a revolutionary organ. In any case, if the rise of Soviets is to be the source of political clarification, we fail to see how this may be accomplished on the basis of an understanding – as in the Bombacci proposal – between reformists, maximalists, syndicalists and anarchists! On the contrary, the forging of a sound and healthy revolutionary movement in Italy will never be accomplished by advancing new organs modelled on future forms, like factory councils or soviets – just as it was an illusion to believe that the revolutionary spirit could be salvaged from reformism by importing it into the unions, seen as the nucleus of the future society.

We will not effect the sorting-out process through a new recipe, which will frighten no one, but by abandoning once and for all the old "recipes", the pernicious and fatal methods of the past. For well-known reasons, we feel that if a method has to be abandoned, and expelled along with non-communists from our ranks, then it should be the electoral method – and we see no other route to the setting up of a communist party that is worthy to affiliate to Moscow.

Let us work towards this goal – beginning, as Niccolini puts it so well, with the elaboration of a consciousness, a political culture, in the *leaders*, through a more serious study of the problems of the revolution, with fewer distractions from spurious electoral, parliamentary and minimalist activities.

Let us work towards this goal. Let us issue more propaganda concerning the conquest of power, to build awareness of what the revolution will be, what its organs will be, how the Soviets will really function. Then we can say we have done truly valuable work towards establishing the councils of the proletariat and winning within them the revolutionary dictatorship that will open up the radiant road to communism.

Il Soviet, Vol. III, Nos. 1, 2, 4, 5, 7; January 1, 11, February 1, 8, 22 1920.

Appendix

The Leone statement (see p. 216 above).

"The Bologna Congress of the Socialist Party proclaims and recognizes that the Russian revolution, which it salutes as the most magnificent event in the history of the world proletariat, has sparked the necessity to facilitate its expansion into all the countries of capitalist civilization; it believes that the methods and forms of this revolutionary expansion, destined to transform the Russian upheaval into a total social revolution, are to be sought in the models of a revolution which, although it is called Russian in reference to geography, is universal in character – a revolution founded on the principle of uniting the proletarians of the world. The lessons we may learn from this revolution of the Soviets, a revolution which has realized in practice all the expectations of the authentic champions of the cause of socialism, may be summarized in the following points.

1. The class struggle has been revealed as the true engine of the present history of mankind, demonstrating its capacity to smash the social-national union, to which bourgeois governments with their mystifications intended to entrust the task of eliminating or delaying it.

2. The socialist revolution has manifested a twofold movement in practice: (a) a movement of *erosion* and *emptying* of State powers and negation of the fundamental institutions which democratic forms utilize to deflect the historical mission of the proletariat; i.e. constituent assemblies, which place oppressed and oppressors on a sham footing of

legal equality, and the parliaments which emerge from them – complementary organs of State sovereignty and not expressions of the popular will; (b) a movement of *construction*, thanks to a class organ of new creativity – the *Soviet of workers, peasants and soldiers* – which, as an organ linking all the oppressed desirous of attaining the giddy heights already reached by the Russian pioneers, should henceforth be established throughout Italy and western Europe, and whose social composition should consist of the masses of workers and peasants and also (without abandoning their individual specificity) the parties which conduct a revolutionary campaign for the abolition of private ownership and the powers of the bourgeois State; the trade unions, which will operate on a more elevated and revolutionary socio-political level within the Soviet than they have hitherto achieved on account of their corporative structure; the members of the co-operative movement, who in the Soviet will be able to struggle against the capitalist régime as allies of the wage-earners, making up for the revolutionary inactivity of their organization; and the working-class Leagues of war veterans.

3. The political struggle against the State, a military organ of war, in every political form open to it, must as in Russia have passion and rebellious *élan*, because socialism has been transformed from a pure problem in social logic into a furnace of ardour and enthusiasm, by implanting in the civil and military proletariat the confidence that they can effect the transfer of power to the Soviets and subsequently defend them against any revolutionary attack. This and nothing else is the summons to violence that the Russian pioneers challenge us with. It is a debt of honour and a necessity for us to take it up, rather than the conflict and chaos against which socialism in Russia has become the guarantee, as the bearer of a new order.

4. The Russian Bolshevik Party, and equally the Italian Socialist Party, will not give up its existence until the Soviet experiment has reached full maturity – an experiment which must at once be initiated – though it must subordinate all its activities to the principles suggested by the Russian revolutionary experience, which teaches that only the proletariat grouped in Soviets, which are superior to parties, schools, corporations, may take great historical initiatives and bring them to a triumphant conclusion."

48. SEIZE POWER OR SEIZE THE FACTORY? – *BORDIGA*

The working-class disturbances of the past few days in Liguria have seen yet another example of a phenomenon that for some time now has been being repeated with some frequency, and that deserves to be examined as a symptom of a new level of consciousness among the working masses.

Instead of abandoning their jobs, the workers have so to speak taken over their plants and sought to operate them for their own benefit, or more precisely without the top managers being present in the plant. Above all, this indicates that the workers are fully aware that the strike is not always the best weapon to use, especially under certain circumstances.

The economic strike, through the immediate harm it inflicts on the worker himself, derives its utility as a defensive weapon for the worker from the harm the work-stoppage inflicts on the industrialist by cutting back the output which belongs to him.

This is the state of affairs under normal conditions in the capitalist economy, when competition and price-cutting force a continual increase in production itself. Today the profiteers of industry, in particular the engineering industry, are emerging from an exceptional period in which they were able to amass enormous profits for a minimum of effort. During the war the State supplied them with raw materials and coal and, at the same time, acted as sole and reliable purchaser. Furthermore, through its militarization of factories, the State itself undertook to impose a rigorous discipline on the working masses. What more favourable conditions could there be for a fat profit? But now these people are no longer disposed to deal with all the difficulties arising from shortages of coal and raw materials, from the instability of the market and the fractiousness of the working masses. In particular, they are not disposed to put up with modest profits which are roughly the same or perhaps a bit below their pre-War level.

This is why they are not worried by strikes. Indeed they positively welcome them, while mouthing a few protests about the absurd claims and insatiability of the workers. The workers have understood this, and through their action of taking over the factory and carrying on working instead of striking, they are making it clear that it is not that they have no wish to work, but that they have no wish to work the way the bosses tell them to. They no longer want to be exploited and work for the benefit of the bosses; they want to work for their own benefit, i.e. in the interests of the work-force alone.

This new consciousness that is emerging more clearly every day should be held in the highest regard; however, we would not want it to be led astray by vain illusions.

It is rumoured that factory councils, where they were in existence, functioned by taking over the management of the workshops and carrying on the work. We would not like the working masses to get hold of the idea that all they need do to take over the factories and get rid of the capitalists is set up councils. This would indeed be a dangerous illusion. The factory will be conquered by the working class – and not only by the workforce employed in it, which would be too weak and non-communist – only after the working class as a whole has seized political power. Unless it has done so, the Royal Guards, military police, etc. – in other words, the mechanism of force and oppression that the bourgeoisie has at its disposal, its political power apparatus – will see to it that all illusions are dispelled.

It would be better if these endless and useless adventures that are daily exhausting the working masses were all channelled, merged and organized into one great, comprehensive upsurge aimed directly at the heart of the enemy bourgeoisie.

Only a communist party should and would be able to carry out such an undertaking. At this time, such a party should and would have no other task than that of directing all its activity towards making the working masses increasingly conscious of the need for this grand political attack – the only more or less direct route to the take-over of the factory, which if any other route is taken may never fall into their hands at all.

Il Soviet, 22 February 1920, Vol. III, No. 7.

V

The Debate with Tasca

49. POLITICAL AND TRADE-UNION SIGNIFICANCE OF THE FACTORY COUNCILS

(Report by Comrade Angelo Tasca to the Congress of the Turin urban and provincial Chamber of Labour)

At the Extraordinary Congress of the Turin Chamber of Labour, held on the 14th and 15th of last December, there was a unanimous decision in favour of setting up factory councils; on the other hand, the motion granting the vote to unorganized workers and proposing to fight at the Confederation Congress for immediately beginning propaganda "for the establishment of producers councils all over Italy" merely obtained a majority.

From that moment on, the question was debated among ever wider circles of workers; in fact it became the question of the day, a question on which everyone had to adopt a position. Let us be unstinting in our recognition of the fact that the discussions of that time were extremely productive, for they allowed all those who had initially been supporters or opponents of the new trade-union structures to profit from the day to day experiences within the Turin factories and the rank and file of the organization. Every one of us had discarded something of our previous opinions, for the very reason that they were merely opinions. The experience of the workers' movement has enriched the various polemics with its abundant juices, making them at once more dispassionate and more conclusive. We shall not waste time, therefore, repeating here the theoretical formulation of the new movement, but shall content ourselves with making some observations which might help clarify any ambiguities which remain.

By now we are all agreed on the need to democratize the proletarian organizations, to bring them closer to the reality of the workshop than to that of an office, to re-order them on the basis of a system which allows the leading bodies to be brought into rapid contact with the needs and tendencies of the masses, placing the two in permanent and close collaboration. The internal commissions had already emerged in the past precisely in response to a need for decentralization of trade-union action; for years, these commissions usefully represented the traditional form of trade-union action. But these same commissions were no longer adequate to the task of protecting the workers' interests in the factory. In the Agreement of 1 March 1919, Art. 4, it is recognized that: "When necessary, a representation of three shopfloor workers may be heard in a consultative capacity in discussions of a technical character between the Firm and the Internal Commission." (See *Report on the general FIOM movement*, from 1 January 1918 to 30 June 1919, page 32.)

The new system of elections, arranging for the internal commission to be elected directly by the workshop delegates and endowing the latter with trade-union duties within the confines of the workshop itself (duties which are not recognized by the industrialists and will not be recognized until we have endured a bitter, and perhaps lengthy, struggle), gave a systematic ordering to the direct representation of the workers in such a way as to allow them to be present or be able to intervene effectively on all questions, large and small, affecting the interests of the workers themselves at the workplace. In this way the problem of creating democracy inside the factory was resolved; there remained the problem of democratizing the unions themselves.

That such a process of democratization is necessary is recognized even by those who differ from us on the question of granting the vote to unorganized workers. In the "Proposal concerning the establishment of factory councils and the reordering of economic organizations" presented by the presidency of the executive committee of the Milan Chamber of Labour, on the basis of Schiavello's report, one reads: "The Union ought to be the authentic expression of the thinking of the masses . . . the genuine expression of the Factory; it should fuse itself with the factory. It should vibrate, speak, act in tune with the collective will of the masses working, fretting and hoping within the factory. Hence what is needed is a transformation of the Unions; of the Chamber of Labour; of the Federations, which we would like to have an industrial rather than a craft basis; and of the General Confederation of Labour, which we would like to be closer to us – a preparatory general staff, a driving influence, an agitator of our great army, this army which belongs entirely to us. The present constitution of the organizations corresponds to conditions which obtained in the past, when the members were only a minority representing, as it were, the aristocracy of the proletariat. At that time, the members' general meeting could act as the basis of contact between the leaders and this *élite* of workers who participated in the Union more as 'citizens' than as 'producers', i.e. participating in a purely social-democratic activity no longer compatible with the new forms of thought and action of the proletariat. At the present juncture, with the mass entry of the proletariat into the Unions, the leaders have lost all contact with the masses. Now the Milan comrades are determined that their proposals should enable the proletariat at its natural source – the factory – to draw closer to the Union and make its voice heard there and in the Chamber of Labour, if for no other reason than to avoid a state of affairs in which its strength of action may degenerate into a negative form of selfish shop, plant or sectional particularism, wholly damaging to the general interests of the class." We are in complete agreement with these proposals. They bring us to the central problem in our report: the relations between Factory Councils and trade unions.

In the past, the two extreme wings of our movement have held that it was convenient to keep the two bodies absolutely distinct, giving each of them well-defined functions. Thus at the Extraordinary Congress of the Turin Chamber of Labour, Garino maintained that "the trade union's principal function is not to form a producer's consciousness in the worker, but to defend his interests as a wage-earner" (see *Avanti!*, 16 December 1919) – in other words, confusing a state of affairs created by historical events (which are now well behind us) and by the reformist degeneration of the trade-union movement with a fatal impotence and limitation which would weigh down the unions, in the future as in the past.

Now we, in accordance with Zinoviev's thesis, reject the conception of the union as "a firm combination of wage earners in a particular industry formed to improve working conditions and oppose their deterioration, within the limits posed by the capitalist economy" (see *Avanti!*, 7 January 1920); we see it instead as the organ which, by defending the wage worker within the framework of the bourgeois system, ultimately liberates the proletariat from its enslaved station under capitalism, driving it to overcome the limits of the capitalist economy and replace it with its own proletarian economy. Thus our criticism of the errors and mistakes of the trade-union movement should not lead us to condemn the unions, but to strengthen them, by restoring to them all the functions they were formed to fulfil during the period of the First International. If the unions' function today were to be limited to discussing wages and hours, their action would be both useful and indispensable (even under these circumstances we could say that if the unions did not exist, they would have to be invented) but hardly effectual, because the present economic system does not provide the remotest possibility of stable, long-lasting links being established between its constituent elements: capital and labour.

Now if it is unable to form long-term contracts, and is unable to negotiate particular agreements for particular industries, the Union, if confined within the limits to which both its critics and defenders wish to keep it, would find itself condemned to taking action that has no hope of spreading or developing. And it would be strange indeed if the whole enormous apparatus of the trade unions, this mountain of membership cards, could only give birth to a tiny mouse feeding off *chiffons de papier* [scraps of paper].

On the other hand capitalism, vitiated as it is as a result of war practices, is tending to move its field of operations from the factory to the bank, from production to circulation, from individual groups to political trusts which have to dominate the central authorities and control the whole of national life – from the ministries to the borders, from the banks to the army. So it comes about that politics, which has seemingly been (and should have been, in the eyes of friends and adversaries) excluded from the unions, thrown out of the window by pacts of alliance and motions to congresses,[84] returns by the back door and forces the union, like other bodies today, to submit to the iron law: renewal or extinction. Thus our conclusion is as follows: the unions are not going to be suppressed, but raised to the level of the demands of the class struggle in this period of history.

On the extreme right (we make use of this expression even though we recognize that it is extremely relative) it seems that people would like to maintain a clear distinction, no longer for workshop delegates over and above the trade unions, but for trade unions above the Factory Councils. The anarchists would leave the unions with nothing other than the role of resistance; the reformists (see Colombino's article in *Avanti!*, 18 February 1920) would reduce the Factory Councils to mere technical organs educating the workers for the future management of the factory itself; they would reduce their competence to questions concerning the factory alone, allowing them to play only a consultative role in questions of a general or national character. We do not accept either the Garino or the Colombino thesis. We do not believe it is possible to create two distinct organs, both of which live on the same tissue: the working class.

Sooner or later they would clash and come to blows, and this pointless struggle would demand too much of the energy of the working class. To think like Comrade Colombino, for instance, in whose eyes the problem of direct control can be left to the individual factory councils and excluded from the competence of the unions, or to think like those who argue that it is possible to make a distinction between questions concerning the workshop and general and national questions, without being aware that at any moment the most insignificant of issues concerning a particular establishment (moving the hands of the clock, for instance)[85] can become a general and national issue – to think in such a way is simply a desire to resolve the problem through a convenient, but utterly unreal, simplism. Factory Councils and trade unions cannot possibly operate on the basis of a "pact of alliance" defining their respective functions. They can only have one function, that is common to both of them – the liberation of the proletariat and the creation of a new order in which the revolutionary class, having conquered political power, may establish its own economy.

Now everyone, from all shades of opinion, is convinced of the need to transform the system of organization along craft lines into an organization along industrial lines. Yet the Factory Council – formed on a topographical basis but most assuredly a part of the industrial trade union – cannot help but be the vital element in this transformation. As the factory councils or committees spread to all industries, the individual factories or firms will become sections and sub-sections of the trade union in each locality; the Metalworkers' Federation will number its sections in terms of factories, instead of in terms of individual members; the headquarters will remain in being not as a substitute for the sections (factories), but purely for administrative purposes. We must insist that once this transformation is complete, the trade union too will be the natural organ of the class struggle – not only in terms of defence or resistance, but of conquest and production as well.

We believe that the thesis proposed by one of our number at the December Congress is mistaken (see the speech by Gramsci, *Avanti!*, 15 December 1919). According to this thesis, the Factory Council has to function as an extension of the trade-union domain, because it must adapt itself to the "present pre-revolutionary conditions". The trade union does not belong to the "pre-revolutionary" phase except in so far as it preserves the methods of the Second International – just as any other organ can preserve them, the Socialist Party for instance, or the Factory Councils, too, were they to be considered as organs of collaboration for the gradual conquest of the factory. But if the trade union is transformed, reacts against the forces of inertia which strive to keep it on the old tracks and accepts the programme of the revolution, for the very reason that the class struggle today cannot help but rapidly debouch into revolution, we should not regard it with mistrust or accept it as a sort of necessary evil, but should see it as a formidable tool of revolutionary action.

Now let us proceed to examine some of the most interesting problems to do with the Councils movement. These are in our view: 1. the possibility of extending the Councils to all industries; 2. industrial unions and craft unions; 3. electoral procedures, legislative and executive organs; 4. the possibility of drafting legislation on factory councils; 5. economic councils.

I

It may be observed that the Councils system is applicable to industries in inverse proportion to the ease with which they may be directly controlled. In other words, the more the industry is centralized and the work in it specialized and divided, and the more gigantic it is in terms of plants and its employment of motive force and labour power, the more readily do the workers feel the need to orient themselves within this colossal technical apparatus and seek to mould their own organization for defence and attack in such a way as to follow the lines of industrial organization, maintaining a continuous contact with the "enemy". The need for councils is felt less in small-scale industry, in the grey zone of artisanal production which still survives or vegetates on the margins of the modern centralized and technically advanced industrial organization.

Then there are a few industries where the councils have made little impact by virtue of the pre-capitalist character of most of them: among printers for instance, where the great industrial plant has not yet entirely killed off the small workshop and factory. This factor, combined with other historical factors which it would be out of place to go into here, preserves within the printing trade something of the spirit of the old corporations, which were famous for the finely detailed regulations with which they defined the relations between employer and worker. In the printing industry it is unusual for labour relations to be as tense as they are in other industries, since the employer almost invariably works directly in the print-shop etc. and the worker's mentality is certainly formed at the point of production – indeed, too much so, since he loses his own individuality, becomes one with his work, which frequently requires individual aptitudes that cannot easily be replaced or communicated. This is why the Councils have such little importance in the eyes of the printworkers (see *Avanti!*, 9 March 1919); they see them as irrelevant, because they have already been established and even surpassed in their own industry. For this category, as for others where a fragmenting individualism snaps the threads of technical-industrial organization as much as of the class consciousness of the worker, the problem of the Councils cannot come to life or acquire significance other than through industrial transformation and through the extinction of the traditional corporative spirit. It is this spirit which oozes the soporific poison from an antiquated and obstinately conservative technology over the worker's consciousness. Large-scale typography and big printing plants are an essential condition for the creation of a revolutionary consciousness in this category too. On the other hand, given the present state of this industry, direct control on the part of the workers would be anything but difficult. In almost every case, the personnel involved in a printing shop would be capable of carrying on production smoothly even without the boss, who would have to be replaced not as a capitalist, since he hardly ever is a big capitalist, but often as a worker, skilled in some of the most delicate operations.

Another category worthy of consideration is the building industry. In this case too we are confronted with the near impossibility of creating factory councils as a permanent feature of the workers' organization. Bricklayers (when they do not have a stable job in some other industry carrying out repairs or maintenance work, in which case they would belong to the trade union relevant to the factory where they are working), decorators and other building workers change their place of work at least once a year, and some of them every month or even every day. So where does that leave workplace organization? And what about the fact that decorators migrate (or used to migrate before the war) to the coast in winter and bricklayers flock to Switzerland in the spring, in both cases to "do the season", moving from village to village, from one construction site to another? In this connection, see the discussion on Councils which took place at the Milan Building Congress (see *Avanti!*, Piedmont edition, 13 March 1920). We have to conclude that for this category, the enterprise Council can only replace the entrepreneur and become the administrative Council of a production co-operative. In other words, in this category, the very nature of the work (which could be modified in time by a process of industrialization which we cannot foresee, although such a process is likely) precludes the creation of Councils along the lines of those in heavy industry.

For that matter, we may say that the Councils are not uniform dies which must stamp the whole of the diverse material of working-class life; they are simply a vital principle, which can and must give birth to as many creations as there are raw materials to be moulded. For, we repeat, in the categories in which councils are applicable only with difficulty, there is a correspondingly greater opportunity for the workers to take over direct control of production.

The Councils movement has frequently been compared with that of the English guilds, in order to bring out their common features and their differences. Indeed, the valuable study by Schiavi on "Socialization and Enterprise Councils" counterposes the political character of the guilds to the more strictly trade-union character of the Councils. Now, since we argue that the Factory Councils too should have political aims, since they are organs of power and of struggle against the bourgeois system, surely it would not be heretical to suggest that in those categories where the present organization of work does not present the "Councils" with any avenue of development, it is guilds which could oppose the entrepreneur on the model of the factory councils' opposition to the capitalist in large-scale industry.

II

One question which has not yet been raised to my knowledge, is that of how useful it would be to allow the various categories to maintain a certain distinctive profile within the unions. In particular, I maintain that within the unions embracing a particular industry, *category commissions* should remain in being in a purely *consultative* capacity, to examine questions peculiar to each work process, and that category meetings should also be held occasionally for the same purpose. Let us take an example: the pattern-makers. According to *Avanti!* of 26 October 1919, they wanted to transform their former category commission into a council for pattern-makers. Such a council would be composed of the delegates elected by the small firms and those elected by the pattern-making departments in large-scale industry. We consider this to be a splendid innovation; however, we feel it would be a good idea to preserve the name "category commission", precisely because the term "council" should always be used for organic formations based on a work-place (either a factory or single firm).

At this point we are compelled to examine a much more serious problem concerning the organization of white-collar workers (clerks and technicians). Past experience and especially recent events make us more than ever convinced of the need for white-collar workers and technicians to co-operate with workers in the factory council, and consequently for them to take part in the industrial organization which embraces the factory where they work. Category commissions (grouping engineers, technical supervisors, designers, departmental secretaries, and clerical staff in internal administration, sales, accounts and auxiliary services, as some would propose – see *Impiego Privato*, 22 December 1919 – though this appears a too detailed subdivision in our eyes) could and should remain in existence; moreover, they could come to some arrangement with the commissions of the same category in another industry or another group. But it is essential for the trade-union and political aims which lie behind our movement that they should be merged into a single whole in the shortest possible time.

And what about the union of clerks and shop assistants? It should be transformed into a union of commercial enterprises, to include all workers in firms not engaged in production – banks, commercial offices, shops: all workers, I repeat, from the director to the office boy, from the travelling salesman to the driver.

III

The problem of the mode of election to the factory councils and to the branch executive councils of trade federations and unions was examined by myself in detail in the written report presented to the Socialist Party section. The conclusions of that examination are summarized below in a few propositions:

1. the factory or enterprise council, as the body acting in the interests of and in accordance with the wishes of all the producers, gathered together in the work-place, should be elected by all the producers;

2. the Council is elected indirectly, however, by the workshop delegates, who should be members of the union.

3. the Federation recognizes the Council as the body taking the place of the former internal commission;

4. the branch executive (formerly directive) committee is elected only by members of the union, on the basis of a list proposed by the workshop delegates, who will nominate for the purpose an electoral committee;

5. if the executive committee is in agreement with the workshop delegates, it may adopt at once the decisions arising from that agreement;

6. in cases of disagreement or doubt, the executive committee can and must call a meeting of the branch General Council, the highest legislative organ, which has the advantage of being less numerous;

7. the branch General Council is made up of the plenary assembly of the factory executive committees in those factories in which more than 75 per cent of the workers are organized in the union, and of the federal committees – i.e. the commissions elected by the trade-union members only and therefore distinct from the factory executive committees – in those factories where less than 75 per cent of the workers belong to the union;

8. as the primary responsibility of the workshop delegates is to organize their own electorate into the union, the factory executive committee will have the right to represent the factory in the branch General Council when the number of trade-union members in the factory passes the 75 per cent mark. In short, the branch General Council will become identical with the plenary assembly of the factory executive committees.

IV

We must strive to ensure that organization on an industrial basis does not lead to collaboration with the capitalist inside the factory. In other words, we must preclude any form of collaboration other than the kind imposed by the fact that, until the proletariat conquers power, its labour-power must collaborate in creating the bourgeoisie's commodities and its political power. We do not know how much truth there is in the rumours that credit the government with the intention of enacting legislation on the factory and enterprise councils; what is certain is that the clerical party will come to the Chamber shortly with a draft law, which is very understandable in view of the fact that its representatives voted at the time for the Reyna Bill and secured its passage.[86] Now we must oppose any attempt whatsoever to regulate from above the relations between workers and employers inside the factory. The workers are moving towards control of production, indeed to its direct management (which is the only possible form of control) – but they alone, through their organizations, have the right to select the best method of protecting their interests, whether on the level of resistance or on that of production.

All these draft laws, such as the one on plant councils in Austria and Germany and the Whitley Report in England, have the effect of leaving property relations intact.[87] The profit-sharing scheme proposed by the clericals, a rehash of unsuccessful specific remedies that go back to the time when Louis Blanc wrote his *Organisation du Travail*, has nothing to do with the goals of the working class. The proletariat is not driven by a thirst to get some sort of a share in the cake represented by the profits of a firm; it has no wish to share in the booty accruing to theft, speculation and privilege. It does not wish to diminish in this way the gulf separating it from the capitalist. What it wishes to discuss is the legitimacy, from its own point of view, of the relations created by capital in the sphere of production. The proletariat does not wish to enter into solidarity with, and hence become the accomplice of, a social organization based on the individual, on the random play of particular interests; it wishes to enter the sphere of production in control of all its own class capacities, making itself act as a class and thus bringing into being a productive force that is absolutely new and superior to that developed by the so-called free competition of the bourgeois class. The communist economy: this is the factor the proletariat wishes to import into the sphere of production; this is the sort of economy it wishes to have a stake in. Its task is to take in hand a society in which the process of production is bound to develop in ever more centralized and interlocking forms as a result of being increasingly directed from a single centre, and to apply to it a system of social relations perfectly suited to the maximum development of production. The proletariat enters history (not the factory, to share the profits with the owner) with all the baggage of the economy which it alone, in its capacity as a revolutionary class, can attain in practice, and which is attainable only in its entirety.

V

Now let us briefly summarize the structure of the political and trade-union organs, in the relations with one another which they could most naturally and usefully assume at this time. With factory, enterprise and agricultural community councils being formed rapidly, one would have the foundations of the system of councils which, in the view of us communists, must embody all the forces of the revolution and be identified tomorrow with the framework of communist society. The factory and agricultural community councils would be so many branches of the industrial and agricultural unions; control over production inside the factory or agricultural community would in part be entrusted to them. We say in part, because this control would also be exercised from outside the factory, by the union, which would thus have ultimate control over production in that particular industrial sector. In addition, the union is concerned with questions of hours and wages, and under a communist régime would have the job of mobilizing the workforce into the army of labour. At this juncture membership in a trade union would be compulsory, for the ranks of the unions will have to coincide with those of the army of labour.

The great economic problems – raw materials, exchange, large-scale transformations of the process of production, its limitation or intensification in accordance with the needs of the communist State, the utilization of sources of power, etc. – will have to be discussed in economic councils, in which the industrial and agricultural trade unions and co-operatives will be represented as well as the central political organ (the Soviet). On the other hand, the Soviets will be the organs of political power, the real columns supporting the State edifice: the unions will become the industrial and agricultural mobilizing organs of the communist State, just as the co-operatives will become its distributive organs. The general technical problems of production and distribution will be tackled by the economic councils, under the control of and with the participation of the political authorities (Soviets).

Let us translate into the following diagram the fundamental features of the system we are describing, which more or less reproduces the structure of the Russian State:

Co-operative Industrial Union Agricultural Union Soviet	economic councils

Organs of the communist State under the control of the Soviets	industrial union	industrial production	factory	SOVIETS
	Nat. Fed. of Ag. Workers	agricultural production	farm	
	Nat. Co-op League	distribution	Co-op	
	Nat. Fed. Red Guard	defence	regiment	

There is just one further feature in this system that we should note, namely that just as any disturbance in the basic elements, the cells, needs to reach the central organs quickly, so the individual elements need to be open to the direct intervention of the central organ, which represents the interests of the community.

CONCLUSION

It must not be forgotten that what is essential in the communist system is that every part of the organization should keep in step with the rhythm of the whole and reproduce in itself all the general features of the system as a whole, if necessary in opposition to features which may be peculiar to any particular part. The latest Russian experiences seem to have made it necessary to entrust the administration of the individual factories, not only to the workers in the factory, but also to direct representatives nominated by the Councils of the People's Economy. Today we do not have the knowledge to extract from this news all the light we should expect. It holds no surprises, however, for anyone who, like us, is convinced that the factory councils are not an end in themselves: they are instruments in the revolutionary class struggle. If in the way they have been established by the Russian proletariat, and in the way the Turin proletariat wishes to establish them, they respond, as we firmly believe they will, to the goal advanced by the communists (and to which everything else is subordinate): the social revolution – if this is the case, we shall continue to create them and strengthen them, and be ready to transform them or suppress them on the day that they become a danger or obstacle to the cause of communism. The councils are not a recipe designed to meet all difficulties for all time, but a formidable and essential tool of the revolution – essential at least, as far as we believe, in hastening its advent and in consolidating the results after its triumph.

We present the Congress with the following motion:

I

The Congress of the Turin Chamber of Labour reaffirms the need to create workers' and peasants' councils in industry and agriculture, with the aim of achieving the following results, which should be seen as the effective tasks of the new bodies.

1. The "council" represents a more rational and profitable

articulation of the trade-union movement, since the work-place provides a natural basis for the mobilizing of the proletarian masses. To this end the "council", assisted by the delegates, can speedily and effectively protect the interests of the proletariat in the disputes which may arise at any moment in the complex affairs of the factory and enterprise. These interests, in so far as they are ongoing and permanent, can reach the central organs via the council and furnish the material for the demands on which to base the trade-union struggles.

2. The "council" is the organ of proletarian power at the work-place and helps give the wage-worker awareness of being a producer; hence it raises the class struggle from the level of resistance to that of conquest. Such a transformation has its origins in the work-place, but it must invest trade-union action in its entirety. For this reason, the "council" is the element which will transform the pattern of organization on a craft and category basis into a system of organization on an industrial basis. This transformation is not simply a change of form, but a genuine shift of activity, as a result of which the trade-union organizations will opt for the communist revolution and prepare themselves to become the constituent elements of the new régime on the morrow of their victory.

II

As far as relations between councils and unions are concerned, Congress approves the points made in the Tasca report and the modifications proposed therein to the system of election currently employed by the Turin metal-workers. Congress affirms that it is not a question of two distinct bodies of different character, whose competence and limits need to be defined, *but of a single body*, since the "council" is nothing but the expression of trade-union activity at the work-place and the union is the master body grouping the councils by productive sector, co-ordinating and disciplining their action. The "council" is the cellular unit of a whole – the trade union. The tasks of the former are different from the latter only in terms of the territorial division of their single activity – the class struggle. Such a division is not to the detriment of the unity of the whole – on the contrary, it gives it effective value, because it makes it rest on the whole of the working class organically drawn up in ranks.

III

Congress deems inapposite and contradictory any struggle for recognition of Factory Councils, because their task, viz control, if it is to have any significance, must be political in scope. In fact, control over production cannot help but debouch into the struggle to eliminate the capitalists as a class, i.e. it is bound to destroy the bourgeois State and instal a communist State. Hence the struggle for the total recognition of the Councils will take place, and must take place, but this struggle cannot be other than the revolution.

Congress calls for an intensive campaign of propaganda and activity on the part of all trade-union bodies in favour of setting up councils, emphasizing their political value. But after these preparations, the struggle which the organizations wage should be limited to demanding maximum freedom of movement within the work-place for the Factory Committees, which in the industrialists' eyes will still be internal Commissions. Such freedom of movement will undoubtedly bear fruit. It is not possible to trace here with a resolution the limits of the role of the councils inside the plant, because the benefit the working masses obtain from the freedom won will depend on their political capacity and on how good was their choice of delegates. The struggle to win this freedom should be waged now: the workers' consciousness must be made to bear fruit.

No conquest (it is our duty not to delude ourselves nor to delude others) can occur on the presumption that "strips of power" are being torn away from the capitalist: let the factory council draw all its power from the fact of its being the expression of the will of a conscious mass, and not from the impossible and absurd recognition of a capitalist, who cannot be expected to commit suicide. "Political" recognition should not be demanded; this can come about only unilaterally, as a result of one force imposing itself victoriously on the other. The two sides are, on this terrain, mortal enemies – the victory of one is the death of the other.

It may be (and indeed it is likely) that even this struggle (for freedom of functioning of the Internal Commissions, elected under the new system) will meet with determined resistance from the capitalists, who have understood its full importance. Hence it will be necessary to make serious preparations for it.

Congress expresses its profound conviction that, if the revolution in Italy were to break out as a result of a clash provoked even on the elementary terrain of trade-union freedom, no cause would be more worthy of hazarding all the forces of the proletariat. In this case, the victory of the revolution would be won on the very terrain of revolution itself – that of communist proletarian power seeking to take the place of the anarchic power of the bourgeoisie.

L'Ordine Nuovo, 29 May 1920, Vol. II, No. 3.

50. THE TASCA REPORT AND THE CONGRESS OF THE TURIN CHAMBER OF LABOUR

In our last number, we published the whole of the report on the Factory Councils that Comrade Angelo Tasca drew up on behalf of the Executive Committee of the Turin Chamber of Labour and delivered at the Chamber's congress.[88] However, this report is in no sense a statement from *L'Ordine Nuovo*, and therefore it does not represent an authorized or accepted exposition, in practical terms, of the theses that *L'Ordine Nuovo* has developed in order to construct and propagate an idea and theory of the Councils movement. *L'Ordine Nuovo* published it, and was bound to publish it, for the same reasons as it published the manifesto-programme that Comrade Ercole Bucco issued to the workers organized in the Bologna Chamber of Labour: it had to be published as a document representing an important stage in the Councils' process of development, as a document representing the attitude that, at a given moment, certain representative individuals and trade union delegations can and do adopt, in theory and practice, towards this novel working-class institution.

Comrade Tasca saw fit to accept the post of Congress rapporteur without having a mandate from any trade-union organization. He saw fit to accept the post of official rapporteur of the Executive Commission of the Chamber of Labour without actually being its official rapporteur. In this way he adopted a position and role which, while they might have been, and were, extremely interesting and picturesque from an abstract and intellectualist point of view (a position and role in which are interwoven the characteristic traits of the bishop *in partibus infidelium*[89] and the teacher standing above the petty contingencies of the struggle between political tendencies), could not in practice have helped to do anything other than promote ambiguities and illusions, and encourage opportunist intrigues and manœuvres. It was a position and role that could have led, as it did, to only one possible result: the value and historical importance which the Congress of the Turin Chamber of Labour could and should have had was reduced to nothing.

Comrade Tasca's report is a hurried document. There is no underlying central idea to give the treatment as a whole direction and life. Comrade Tasca has not got his facts right concerning the development of the Factory Councils in Russia, even though this information is not difficult to come by. He states, for example, that "the latest Russian experiences seem to have made it necessary to entrust the administration of the individual factories, not only to the workers in those factories, but also to direct representatives nominated by the Councils of the People's Economy".

Now in its issue of 16 August 1919, *L'Ordine Nuovo* published an article, *The Soviet Mechanism of Nationalization*, in which this reorganization of management functions in the Russian factory was described, given a historical justification and projected as the next stage in a development advanced and aided by the communists. In the chapter "From Control of Industry to Government" in the book by Bukharin *The Communist Programme* (published in May 1918), this reorganization is proposed as an essential plank in the Bolsheviks' platform, in their bid to check and resist the petty-bourgeois mentality and anarcho-syndicalist tendencies of a backward section of the Russian working class.[90] The "latest" Russian experiences concern the militarization of industry, which in certain cases has carried with it the dissolution of the Factory Council. The fact is that, due to shortages of power and physical equipment, the workers' State has been obliged to import into certain industries vast masses of peasants, whose psychology is anything but proletarian and who therefore have no capacity for industrial self-government. For these backward peasant masses, the Council had no significance (it had no significance in the industrial sphere); the only adequate form of collective discipline was the discipline of the revolutionary Army, with its slogans and warlike enthusiasm.

These shortcomings and imprecisions on the part of Comrade Tasca as far as the "bibliography" of the problem of the Councils is concerned, are also shown up in documents which are nearer to us in time and space. In his motion summarizing the discussions that took place at the Congress (published in *Avanti!*), Tasca credits Schiavello with the formulation of the workshop delegates' responsibilities, whereas the formulation was due in fact to the delegates from the Turin factories themselves. Schiavello simply lifted them from the General Regulations, published in *L'Ordine Nuovo* on 8 November 1919, and reproduced them in his proposal.[91] Assembling the Turin delegates' immense store of experiences and proposals and organizing them into the General Regulations cost the Councils Study Committee no little effort. It is not right to give Schiavello credit for all this, when he did nothing but copy them out and put them in a final literary form.

In the same way, Tasca polemicizes with Comrade Garino over the statement that "the trade union's principal function is not to form a producer's consciousness in the worker, but to defend his interests as a wage-earner". This was the thesis advanced in the editorial article, *Syndicalism and the Councils*,[92] which *L'Ordine Nuovo* published on that same date, 8 November 1919. When the anarcho-syndicalist Garino defended this thesis at the extraordinary Congress of the Turin Chamber of Labour in December 1919, and defended it with great dialectical skill and warmth, we, unlike Comrade Tasca, were very agreeably surprised and moved. Since we see the Factory Council as the historical beginning of a process that must lead necessarily to the founding of the workers' State, this attitude on the part of the libertarian and syndicalist Comrade Garino was a confirmation of a profound conviction we have always nourished, namely that in the course of the actual revolutionary process the whole of the working class would forge a theoretical and practical unity of its own, and that every worker, in so far as he is a sincere revolutionary, could not help but collaborate with the whole of his class in meeting a challenge that arises from within capitalism and in no sense can be considered as a freely-willed goal on the part of individuals.

But the conception of the Factory Council that we have had in the past and still have today is entirely missing from Comrade Tasca's report – and he offers nothing in its place. We see the Factory Council as an absolutely original institution. We see it arising from the conditions created for the working class in this present historical period by the structure of capitalism. We see it as an institution that cannot possibly be confused with, co-ordinated with or subordinated to the trade union; on the contrary, through its emergence and development, it effects radical changes in the form and structure of the unions. In the present period, capitalism is characterized by the predominance of finance over industrial capital, of the bank over the factory, of the stock exchange over the production of commodities, of monopoly over the traditional captain of industry. This is a development that comes from within capitalism; it is entirely normal and certainly not "a vice contracted as a result of War practices", as Comrade Tasca maintains. In this he agrees with Kautsky and contradicts the fundamental thesis of the Communist International. The theorists of the IIIrd International (Lenin, Zinoviev, Bukharin, Rosa Luxemburg, A. Pannekoeck, etc.) all defended this economic thesis even before the World War, basing themselves mainly on the data and conclusions contained in Hilferding's volume, *Finance Capital.* They defended it in a polemic with Kautsky and the other literary "leaders" of German Social-Democracy – who during and after the war became the "centrists" of the international workers' movement. The theorists of the International used this economic thesis even then as the basis for other theses on colonialism, imperialism and the civil war that was bound to follow the expected conflagration over a new partition of the globe and the conquest of world hegemony on the part of England or Germany. Civil war; creation of their own States by the national proletariats; acknowledgment throughout the International that the Council and system of Councils is the natural form of the workers' State as it arises spontaneously from the economic and political conditions created for the proletariat by the current phase of development of capitalism – this is the logical sequence of ideas that informs the Communist International, and in the light of which the birth of new workers' institutions should be considered. Mouthing communist and revolutionary phrases, Comrade Tasca has actually come to the aid of the opportunists and reformists who have always tried to undermine the Factory Council – whose goal is to carry the class struggle beyond the limits of industrial legality – by appealing to bureaucratic "discipline": i.e. by projecting themselves as custodians of that form of industrial legality which means giving a factory codification to the relations between exploiter and exploited.

Thus, as a result of this intervention by Comrade Tasca, who was not qualified either from the general theoretical point of view or from the point of view of the theory of the Councils to discuss the problem – as a result of this "official but unofficial" intervention, warmly received by the Congress delegates as being disinterested and above the internal struggles rending the trade-union movement – the Congress of the Turin Chamber of Labour has served only to generate fresh ambiguities and confusions and perpetuate a state of affairs that is highly damaging to the trade-union movement in general and to the unity of the unions and the Chamber of Labour.

When, together with Comrade Tasca, we started to publish *L'Ordine Nuovo*, we all promised one another that we would stand for the right and obligation of mutual checking and criticism, especially between ourselves; for the right and obligation to speak the truth frankly and mercilessly. We aimed to establish within our group a higher form of reciprocal relations. Accordingly, would Comrade Tasca allow us to state that in the two or three hours of his intervention, he ruined efforts to educate and raise the level of working-class culture that had cost the journal *L'Ordine Nuovo* and the group around it a whole year of labour and struggle.

Unsigned, *L'Ordine Nuovo*, 5 June 1920, Vol. II, No. 4.

51. THE FACTORY COUNCIL

The proletarian revolution is not the arbitrary act of an organization that declares itself to be revolutionary, or of a system of organizations that declare themselves to be revolutionary. The proletarian revolution is a prolonged historical process that manifests itself in the rise and development of given forces of production (which we summarize by the expression "proletariat") in a given historical context (which we summarize by the expressions "régime of private property, capitalist mode of production, factory system, organization of society in a democratic-parliamentary State"). At a given stage in this process, the new forces of production are no longer able to develop or organize themselves on an autonomous basis within the official framework of the human community. It is at this given stage that the revolutionary act occurs: it consists in an effort aimed at violently smashing this framework, at destroying the whole apparatus of political and economic power in which the revolutionary productive forces are oppressively contained. It consists in an effort aimed at shattering the bourgeois State machine and forming a new type of State in whose framework the liberated productive forces find an adequate form for their further development and expansion; in whose organization they find strong defences and the necessary and sufficient arms to suppress their adversaries.

* * * * *

The actual process of the proletarian revolution cannot be identified with the development and activity of revolutionary organizations of a voluntary and contractual nature, such as political parties and trade unions. These organizations arise in the sphere of bourgeois democracy and political liberty, as affirmations and developments of this political liberty. In so far as they embody a doctrine that interprets the revolutionary process and predicts its development (within certain limits of historical probability), and are recognized by the broad masses as their expression and embryonic apparatus of government, these organizations are currently – and increasingly – the direct and responsible agents for the successive acts of liberation which the entire working class will attempt in the course of the revolutionary process. But all the same they do not embody this process. They do not supersede the bourgeois State; they do not and cannot embrace the whole spectrum of teeming revolutionary forces that capitalism throws up in the course of its implacable development as a machine of exploitation and oppression.

During the period in which the bourgeois class is economically and politically dominant, the actual unfolding of the revolutionary process takes place subterraneously, in the murky depths of the factory and of the minds of the countless multitudes that capitalism subjects to its laws. This unfolding cannot be controlled or documented: it will be so in the future when the elements that constitute it (feelings, desires, mores, the stirrings of initiative and of a new way of life) are developed and purified with the development of society and the position that the working class comes to occupy in the sphere of production. Revolutionary organizations (political parties and trade unions) arise in the sphere of political liberty and bourgeois democracy, as affirmations and developments of liberty and democracy in general, and where relations of citizen to citizen still exist. The revolutionary process takes place in the sphere of production, in the factory, where the relations are those of oppressor to oppressed, exploiter to exploited, where freedom for the worker does not exist, and democracy does not exist. The revolutionary process takes place where the worker is nothing but intends to become all, where the power of the proprietor is unlimited, where the proprietor has power of life or death over the worker, and over his wife and children.

* * * * *

When we say that the historical process of the workers' revolution which is inherent in the capitalist social system, which obeys its own intrinsic laws and develops of necessity through the confluence of a multiplicity of actions, all of which are uncontrollable since they arise from a situation that the worker neither willed not foresaw – when we say that this historical process has exploded into the light of day, does this mean it can now be controlled and documented?

We say it can be when the whole of the working class has become revolutionary – no longer in the sense that it refuses in a general way to collaborate with the governing institutions of the bourgeois class and to function as an opposition within the framework of democracy, but in the sense that the whole of the working class, as it is to be found in a factory, launches a movement that must necessarily result in the founding of a workers' State and the shaping of human society in an absolutely original and universal form that embraces the whole workers' International, and hence the whole of humanity. And we say the present period is revolutionary because we can see that the working class, all over the world, is beginning to create, is beginning with all its energies (albeit with the mistakes, gropings and impediments natural in an oppressed class that has no historical experience and must do everything for the first time) to generate working-class institutions of a new type, representative in character and constructed on an industry basis. We say the present period is revolutionary because the working class is beginning to exert all its strength and will to found its own State. This is why we say that the birth of the workers' Factory Councils is a major historical event – the beginning of a new era in the history of the human race. For now the revolutionary process has burst into the light of day, and entered the phase where it can be controlled and documented.

* * * * *

In the liberal phase of the historical evolution of the bourgeois class and the society dominated by the bourgeoisie, the basic unit of the State was the proprietor subjugating the working class to his profit in the factory. In this liberal phase, the proprietor was also an entrepreneur and industrialist. Industrial power, the source of industrial power lay in the factory, and the worker could not succeed in freeing himself from the conviction that the proprietor was necessary: his person was identified with that of the industrialist, with that of the manager responsible for production and hence also for the worker's wages, his bread, his clothing and the roof over his head.

In the imperialist phase of the historical evolution of the bourgeois class, industrial power is divorced from the factory and concentrated in a trust, a monopoly, a bank, the State bureaucracy. Industrial power does not have to answer for what it does and becomes more autocratic, ruthless and arbitrary. But the worker, freed from the boss's subjection and from the servile mentality generated by a hierarchy, and driven too by the new social conditions resulting from the new historical phase, achieves priceless gains in terms of autonomy and initiative.

In the factory, the working class becomes a given "instrument of production" in a given organic system. Each worker comes to play a part in this system "by chance" – by chance as regards his own intentions, but not by chance as regards the job he does, since he represents a given necessity in the labour and productive process. This is the only way he is taken on, and it is the only way he can earn his bread. He is a cog in the division-of-labour machine, in the working class constituted as an instrument of production. If the worker acquires a clear consciousness of this "given necessity" that he represents, and builds upon it a representative apparatus that has all the hallmarks of a State (i.e. an apparatus that is not voluntary or contractual, organized around membership cards, but is absolute, organic, closely corresponding to a reality that must be recognized if bread, clothing, housing and industrial production are to be guaranteed) – if the worker, the working class does this, it achieves something of deep significance. It begins a new history, the era of workers' States that must coalesce to form a communist society: a society organized on the model of a large engineering works, a communist International in which every people, every part of humanity acquires a character in so far as it carries out a particular form of production and no longer in so far as it is organized in the form of a State with particular frontiers.

In so far as it constructs this representative apparatus, the working class in effect completes the expropriation of the *primum mobile*, of the most important instrument of production of all – the working class itself. It thereby rediscovers itself, acquiring consciousness of its organic unity and counterposing itself as a whole to capitalism. The working class asserts in this way that industrial power and its source ought to return to the factory. It presents the factory in a new light, from the workers' point of view, as a form in which the working class constitutes itself into a specific organic body, as the cell of a new State – the workers' State – and as the basis of a new representative system – the system of Councils. The workers' State, since it arises in accordance with a given pattern of production, has within it the seeds of its own development, of its own dissolution as a State and of its organic incorporation into a world system – the Communist International.

Just as today, in the Council of a large engineering plant, every work crew (by craft) is amalgamated, from the proletarian point of view, with the other crews in the same shop; just as every stage of the industrial process is merged, from the proletarian point of view, with the other stages, throwing into relief the productive process – so on a world scale, English *coal* will merge with Russian *oil*, Siberian *grain* with Sicilian *sulphur*, *rice* from Vercelli with *wood* from Styria . . . in a single organism, subject to an international administration governing the riches of the world in the name of all humanity. In this sense the workers' Factory Council is the first step in a historical process that should lead eventually to the Communist International, no longer as a political organization of the revolutionary proletariat, but as a reorganization of the world economy and of the whole human community, on a national as well as a world level. The value and historical reality of every revolutionary action today depends on whether it fits into this process, and is designed successfully to free it from the bourgeois superstructures that restrict and obstruct it.

* * * * *

The relations that should link the political party and the Factory Council, the trade union and the Factory Council, are implicitly contained in the argument presented above. The party and trade unions should not project themselves as tutors or as ready-made superstructures for this new institution, in which the historical process of the revolution takes a controllable historical form. They should project themselves as the conscious agents of its liberation from the restrictive forces concentrated in the bourgeois State. They should set themselves the task of organizing the general (political) external conditions that will allow the revolutionary process to move at maximum speed, and the liberated productive forces to find their maximum expansion.

Unsigned, *L'Ordine Nuovo*, 5 June 1920, Vol. II, No. 4.

52. UNIONS AND COUNCILS

The trade union is not a predetermined phenomenon. It *becomes* a determinate institution, i.e. it takes on a definite historical form to the extent that the strength and will of the workers who are its members impress a policy and propose an aim that define it.

Objectively, the trade union is the form which labour as a commodity is bound to assume in a capitalist system, when it organizes itself in order to control the market. This form consists in an office staffed by functionaries, organizational technicians (when they can be called technicians), specialists (when they can be called specialists) in the art of concentrating and guiding the workers' forces in such a way as to establish a favourable balance between the working class and the power of capital.

The development of trade-union organization is characterized by two facts: 1. the union embraces an ever increasing number of workers; 2. the union concentrates and generalizes its scope until the movement's power and discipline is focused in a central office. This office becomes divorced from the masses it has regimented, and removes itself from the eddies and currents of fickle whims and foolish ambitions that are to be expected in the excitable broad masses. The union thus acquires the ability to negotiate agreements and take on responsibilities. In this way it obliges the employer to acknowledge a certain legality in his dealings with the workers, a legality that is conditional on his faith in the union's *solvency* and its capacity to secure respect for contracted obligations from the working masses.

The emergence of an industrial legality is a great victory for the working class, but it is not the ultimate and definitive victory. Industrial legality has improved the working class's standard of living but it is no more than a compromise – a compromise which had to be made and must be supported until the balance of forces favours the working class. If the trade-union officials regard industrial legality as a necessary, but not a permanently necessary compromise; if they deploy all the means at the union's disposal to improve the balance of forces in favour of the working class; and if they carry out all the spiritual and material preparatory work that will be needed if the working class is to launch at any particular moment a victorious offensive against capital and subject it to its law – then the trade union is a tool of revolution, and union discipline, even when used to make the workers respect industrial legality, is revolutionary discipline.

The relations which should prevail between the trade unions and Factory Councils need to be judged in the light of the following question: what is the nature and value of industrial legality?

The Council is the negation of industrial legality: it strives at all times to destroy it, to lead the working class to the conquest of industrial power and make it the source of industrial power. The union represents legality, and must aim to make its members respect that legality. The trade union is answerable to the industrialists, but only in so far as it is answerable to its own members: it guarantees to the worker and his family a continuous supply of work and wages, i.e. food and a roof over their heads. By virtue of its revolutionary spontaneity, the Factory Council tends to spark off the class war at any moment; while the trade union, by virtue of its bureaucratic form, tends to prevent class war from ever breaking out. The relations between the two institutions should be such that a capricious impulse on the part of the Councils could not result in a set-back or defeat for the working class; in other words, the Council should accept and assimilate the discipline of the union. They should also be such that the revolutionary character of the Council exercises an influence over the trade union, and functions as a reagent dissolving the union's bureaucracy and bureaucratism.

The Council strives at all times to break with industrial legality. The Council consists of the exploited and tyrannized masses who are obliged to perform servile labour: as such, it strives to universalize every rebellion and give a resolutive scope and value to each of its acts of power. The union, as an organization that is jointly responsible for legality, strives to universalize and perpetuate this legality. The relations between union and Council should create the conditions in which the break with legality, the working-class offensive, occurs at the most opportune moment for the working class, when it possesses that minimum of preparation that is deemed indispensable to a lasting victory.

* * * * *

The relations between unions and Councils cannot be stabilized by any other device than the following: the majority or a substantial number of the electors to the Council should be organized in unions. Any attempt to link the two institutions in a relation of hierarchical dependence can only lead to the destruction of both.

If the conception that sees the Councils merely as an instrument in the trade-union struggle takes material form in a bureaucratic discipline and a hierarchical structure in which the union has direct control over the Council, then the Council is sterilized as a force for revolutionary expansion – as a form of the actual development of the proletarian revolution, tending spontaneously to create new modes of production and labour, new modes of discipline and, in the end, a communist society. Since the rise of the Council is a function of the position that the working class has achieved in the sphere of production, and a historical necessity for the working class, any attempt to subordinate it hierarchically to the union would sooner or later result in a clash between the two institutions. The Council's strength consists in the fact that it is in close contact – indeed identified – with the consciousness of the working masses, who are seeking their autonomous emancipation and wish to put on record their freedom of initiative in the creation of history. The masses as a whole participate in the activity of the Council, and gain a measure of self-respect in the process. Only a very restricted number of members participate in the activity of the trade union; its real strength lies in this fact, but this fact is also a weakness that cannot be put to the test without running very grave risks.

If, moreover, the unions were to lean directly on the Councils, not to dominate them, but to become their higher form, then they would reflect the Council's own tendency to break at all times with industrial legality and unleash the final phase of the class war. The union would lose its capacity to negotiate agreements, and would lose its role as an agent to regulate and discipline the impulsive forces of the working class.

If its members establish a revolutionary discipline in the union, a discipline which the masses see as being necessary for the triumph of the workers' revolution and not as slavery to capital, this discipline will undoubtedly be accepted and made its own by the Council. It will become a natural aspect of the Council's activity. If the union headquarters becomes a centre for revolutionary preparation, and appears as such to the masses by virtue of the campaigns it succeeds in launching, the men who compose it and the propaganda it issues, then its centralized and absolutist character will be seen by the masses as a major revolutionary strength, as one more (and a very important) condition for the success of the struggle to which they are committed all the way.

* * * * *

In Italian conditions, the trade-union official sees industrial legality as a permanent state of affairs. Too often he defends it from the same perspective as the proprietor. He sees only chaos and wilfulness in everything that happens amongst the working masses. He does not universalize the worker's act of rebellion against capitalist discipline as rebellion; he perceives only the physical act, which might in itself be trivial. Thus the story of the "porter's raincoat" has been as widely disseminated and has been interpreted by stupid journalists in the same way as the myth of the "socialization of women in Russia".[93] In these conditions, the trade-union discipline can be nothing other than a service rendered to capital; in these conditions any attempt to subordinate the Councils to the trade unions can only be judged as reactionary.

The communists would like the revolutionary act to be, as far as possible, a conscious and responsible act. Hence they would like to see the choice of the moment in which to launch the working-class offensive (to the extent that such a moment can be chosen) resting in the hands of the most conscious and responsible section of the working class – the section organized in the Socialist Party and playing the most active part in the life of the organization. For this reason, the communists could not possibly want the union to lose any of its disciplinary energy and systematic centralization.

By forming themselves into permanently organized groups within the trade unions and factories, the communists need to import into these bodies the ideas, theses and tactics of the IIIrd International; they need to exert an influence over union discipline and determine its aims; they need to influence the decisions of the Factory Councils, and transform the rebellious impulses sparked off by the conditions that capitalism has created for the working class into a revolutionary consciousness and creativity. Since they bear the heaviest historical responsibility, the communists in the Party have the greatest interest in evoking, through their ceaseless activity, relations of interpenetration and natural interdependence between the various working-class institutions. It is these relations that leaven discipline and organization with a revolutionary spirit.

Unsigned, *L'Ordine Nuovo*, 12 June 1920, Vol. II, No. 5.

53. POLEMICS OVER THE *L'ORDINE NUOVO* PROGRAMME – *TASCA*

I

The appeal made by Comrade Gramsci to our freedom to criticize each other and keep each other in line is superfluous, for this freedom goes without saying. On the other hand, the following observation is not superfluous: as managing editor of *L'Ordine Nuovo*, before separating the outcast from the elect he should have taken the time to examine carefully our respective positions with regard to the problems of the revolution; prior to doing so he had no right to label me as a deserter. This lengthy epistle, which we may hope will have a more propitious fate than my long speech to the Chamber of Labour congress, would then perhaps have been unnecessary.

* * * * *

I am admonished for having accepted "the post of congress rapporteur without having a mandate from any trade-union organization", and for the ambiguity of an "official but unofficial" intervention. Gramsci is trying to steal Chignoli's job and make himself a champion of due procedure.[94]

I must take readers back to the preamble to the "official" report of the Executive Commission of the Chamber of Labour, published on pp. 41–50 of the volume containing the reports on the Employment Office, the Medico-Legal Institute and the Factory Councils; in this preamble it is explained how the E.C. asked me, as someone who has studied the problem (in the words of the invitation), if I would present draft proposals (the invitation did not use the phrase "draft proposals") clearly indicating "the aims, functions and means required to bring factory councils into being and to define their relations with the local trade-union bodies – the union branches and the Chamber of Labour".

Furthermore, the E.C. laid down that in case any of its members "disagreed with the Tasca report, there was a clear right for the resulting minority to deliver its own separate report". As it turned out, once the E.C. had examined my proposals, it concluded *officially* as follows: "... we must firmly place our dissatisfaction on record. In our view the Tasca report completely lacks the arguments which it should have contained; it lacks above all any indication as to what should be the relationship between factory councils and trade unions; and it lacks guidelines for putting factory councils into operation in the locality".

Could this be more explicit? Not explicit enough for Gramsci, who demands to know whom I represented at the congress, in the name of whom I spoke. In my own name, dear comrade, in the name of my own ideas, my own convictions, in my capacity as a socialist. In the same capacity as at all the other meetings, delegates' assemblies, etc., where I have made an intervention, seeing it as my duty to take advantage of any opportunity that presents itself to "make propaganda".

But Gramsci has sought to bring into the limelight and give formal expression to the judgment of certain comrades who, when they heard that I had accepted the invitation from the Chamber of Labour to give a report on the councils (though I had not yet written a line of it), went around whispering that I had become a reformist, because I had aligned myself with "*those* people from the Chamber of Labour". Gramsci – a deceiver casting out the Beast Triumphant[95] – has made himself the interpreter of these rumours. When they reached my ears, I felt a deep sense of indignation to which I gave full vent – at those who see the Chamber of Labour as the "leper's tower", at which you throw stones from a distance and at best hand in your membership dues on the end of a long stick to avoid infection – unless you are a *monatto*[96] who, like me, has nothing to lose and may carouse and sing or even, let us suppose, deliver a report in the plague-ridden house. Indignation also at those who judge comrades on the basis of a queer application of the proverb, "tell me your friends, and I will tell you who you are", whereby it is enough that one is seen in the company of this or that person, no matter for what reason or purpose, whether for an hour or a year, for one to avoid disqualification or earn it.

* * * * *

My report aimed deliberately to leave "the theoretical formulation of the new movement" to one side, in order to deal with some concrete problems: in particular, relations with the unions; the possibility of extending the councils to all industries; and the struggle for their recognition.

I shall now deal with some of the "philological" charges brought against me by Comrade Gramsci, who has retained some of the pedantry proper to a school-room, where one easily acquires fame by demonstrating that such and such a person forgot to quote a certain book or left out one of the hundred extant interpretations of a certain text.

The "motion" on which Congress voted was the one which concluded my written report, and this was the "summary of the discussions that took place in the course of the congress"; *Avanti!* published as a motion an "outline of the tasks to be accomplished": while I was expounding this, I told the congress clearly that the proposals contained in the Schiavello motion were the Turin proposals (I had them in front of me, on the rostrum from which I was speaking), with the omission of section (e) that gives the workshop delegates responsibility for ensuring "that the capitalists are prevented from removing fixed capital goods from the factory" – a responsibility which, given the present relations between industrialists and workers, could not be put into effect other than through the conquest of power on the part of the working class. And I also explained that I mentioned the Schiavello motion solely because it emanated from Milan, the headquarters of the Confederation, and a place whose trade-union initiatives can hope for a much greater reponse than those of Turin – a fact which *L'Ordine Nuovo* comrades have noted many times in discussions amongst themselves.

Garino's statement to last December's congress is literally identical to the editorial *Syndicalism and the Councils* in *L'Ordine Nuovo* No. 25.[97] But I referred to it as the "Garino thesis" because at the congress itself Gramsci maintained that in order for the council to adapt itself to the present pre-revolutionary conditions, it was bound "to function as an extension of the trade-union domain: the trade union must underpin the council of delegates" (*Avanti!*, 16 December 1919). Now if an extension of the trade-union domain is possible (it being understood that we mean a functional, not a topographical extension), then it must be possible for the union to take on other tasks in addition to defending the worker as wage-earner. Garino in fact goes further than Gramsci, even if the thesis is in a literal sense the same in both cases; for the former denies that the union has any possibility of developing, while the latter admits it, if only as a contingent necessity.

* * * * *

Comrade Gramsci makes out that I argue that "the predominance of financial over industrial capital" is "a vice contracted as a result of War practices", rather than a natural development of capitalism. And he puts me in the company of Kautsky, "in opposition to the fundamental thesis of the Third International". The relevant passage in my report reads as follows: "Capitalism, vitiated as it is as a result of War practices, is tending to move its field of operations from the factory to the bank, from production to circulation, from individual groups to political trusts which have to dominate the central authorities and control the whole of national life – from the ministries to the borders, from the banks to the army."[98]

Now, in the Manifesto of the Third International, we read: "Financial capital, which precipitated mankind into the abyss of war, has itself undergone a catastrophic change in that war. The dependence of paper currency on the material basis of production has been completely disturbed. Paper money, more and more diminishing in importance as an instrument and regulator of capitalist barter, finally became an instrument of requisition, of confiscation and of military and economic violence" (see *Comunismo*, pp. 26–7).[99] So the Manifesto of the Third International is also in agreement with Kautsky! The fact is that Gramsci is besotted by "centrism": some day he will have a go at Jesus Christ, vile centrist that he was, because he let himself be crucified between two thieves.

To argue that the "economic thesis" according to which this is the era of predominance of finance over industrial capital, is the exclusive property of the theoreticians of the Third International, is a polemical *canard* in the worst possible taste. In 1913 in a student magazine I wrote a review of Arturo Labriola's book on capitalism (Bocca, 1910)[100] in which I summarized the chapters where the author examines the era in which capital, "once its ability to employ labour is exhausted, becomes parasitical on capital itself and from the sphere of production returns to the sphere of circulation, whence it had emerged at the start of the industrial revolution" (*Corriere Universitario*, No. 4–5, April 1913, p. 4). It should be noted that Labriola's book was not the product of original research, but a manual of intelligent compilation, and that Labriola examined the post-liberal era of capitalism in relation to colonialism, imperialism, etc. In the struggle against the war at that time, these theses were advanced countless times by ourselves – in perfect agreement, without our being aware of it, with the theoreticians of the future Third International. Since we have upheld these theses all this time, we need say no more to defend ourselves against Gramsci's accusation that we are ignorant of them.

* * * * *

In the editorial of the last issue,[101] Comrade Gramsci gave us his theory of the factory councils as the foundations of the "workers' State". In this article we are treated to a descriptive gloss of Proudhon's concept of "the workshop replacing the government"; the concept of the State that is expounded in the article is an anarchist and syndicalist, not a Marxist concept. He identifies communist society with the "workers' State", and assigns to the Party and trade unions the task of "organizing the general 'political' external conditions" governing the strengthening and development of that State. What does Gramsci mean by these "conditions"? Do they represent the bourgeois organization that must be conquered, and from whose assaults the process of formation of the councils must be safeguarded? Or are they something inherent in the State itself, something occurring as an element in its structure and its functioning, in which case the expression " organizing the general (political (?)) external (?) conditions" would amount to the following: "bring into existence the working class's own State"?

For the State system of councils is not just the system of factory and farm councils. These form the foundations, the pre-conditions for the workers' State, but they are not the workers' State itself. The more the "social" significance of the factory councils is confirmed – in terms of what is "determined" in their formation – the more does it become impossible for the structure of the communist State to be reduced to them or their federation (a libertarian thesis). The communist State is made up of Soviets, of workers' and peasants' councils, all of which are bodies of a "voluntary" nature, and so are the only possible bodies which can provide us with a State.

The factory council is nothing but the antithesis of capitalist power, as it is organized in the work-place. The council is the negation of its power, and as such is incapable of transcending it. In order for the process of liberation to be accomplished, the antithesis must give way to the synthesis – the Soviet. In terms of State structure, the Soviet stands in relation to the factory council in the same way as economic determinism stands to class consciousness. The proletariat finds in the capitalist system the conditions which "determine" its emergence, but this is not sufficient to give us a class. A class exists only when it becomes conscious of itself as a class. Marx puts it in the *Manifesto*: "But with the development of industry the proletariat not only increases in number: it becomes concentrated in greater masses, its strength grows, and it feels that strength more."[102]

Now another element is superimposed over the deterministic

element: the voluntaristic element. The factory council makes the class adhere to the productive process, it shapes it and moulds it in its likeness. In the Soviet, on the other hand, the class dominates the productive process and in a certain sense rises above it. For the class itself is the essential moment of the productive process – and in so far as it is "conscious" of itself as a class, it preserves all its freedom of manœuvre, its power of initiative to express in an increasingly stable and organic fashion its own intervention in the productive process, becoming the agent of its own intervention, its engine.

Comrade Gramsci writes that "the workers' State, since it arises in accordance with a given pattern of production, has within it the seeds of its own development and of its own dissolution as a State, of its organic incorporation into the world system of the Communist International".[103]

Now it is true that the factory council system, which Gramsci improperly (in our view) calls a "workers' State", creates the "conditions" needed for the process to debouch into the International, but the councils cannot be identified with that process itself. In order for the councils to develop into the International, the voluntarist element of the class needs to come into play – the element which *strives* to construct its own State. This element embodies not only the necessary "conditions" for the International, but also the will, embodied in a programme – a myth[104] that is "sufficient" to develop those conditions, set them in motion and in operation, until the final victory of the revolution.

Otherwise, one would lapse into the ingenuous abstractism of Norman Angell, who used to prove that war was impossible by showing how the various capitalisms were enmeshed in a complex system of interlocking interests, no longer reducible to individual national groups; one would thus prove the reality of the Communist International solely by the fact that the proletariat has experienced the international structure of the productive phenomenon – within which it lives and of which it feels itself to be a "determinate" constituent.

II

So far as the "process of revolution" is concerned, Comrade Gramsci did not discuss the "imperialist" phase of capitalism in all its aspects. The phenomenon of the transformation of capital, which is at first tied rigidly to the work-place and then breaks free, grows wings and hovers above the sphere of production – this phenomenon is not wholly contrary to the interests of production itself. Banks, credit, joint-stock companies, trusts – these have all helped to give an enormous thrust to the development of industry and commerce. It was these instruments that provided the bourgeoisie with the capacity to organize, in a powerful and rapid fashion, the conditions which, on the one hand, provided it with a maximum return on its capital and, on the other, ensured the continued survival of its own class dictatorship.

Had the bourgeoisie remained at the primitive "liberal" stage of its development, it would by now have been swept away. In other words, had the capitalist continued to be an entrepreneur, and had the structure of industrial organization continued to be tied rigidly to the "work-places", and had each capital continued to live symbiotically with the instruments of labour – the individual factory, mine or field – then the bourgeoisie would have failed to accomplish its great mission. That revolution in production from which the modern world originated would never have occurred.

And so we see that the "fusion" of products of different origin, which Gramsci correctly describes as the culmination of the process triggered by the intervention of the proletariat in the sphere of production, was in fact initiated by the bourgeoisie. Recall the words of the *Manifesto*: "The bourgeoisie has through its exploitation of the world market given a cosmopolitan character to production and consumption in every country. To the great chagrin of reactionaries, it has drawn from under the feet of industry the national ground on which it stood. All old-established national industries have been destroyed or are daily being destroyed. They are dislodged by new industries, whose introduction becomes a life and death question for all civilized nations, by industries that no longer work up indigenous raw material, but raw material drawn from the remotest zones; industries whose products are consumed, not only at home, but in every quarter of the globe. . . . The bourgeoisie keeps more and more doing away with the scattered state of the population, of the means of production, and of property. It has agglomerated population, centralized means of production, and has concentrated property in a few hands. The necessary consequence of this was political centralization."[105]

The crisis of the bourgeoisie is not due to the fact that it has continued to develop these tendencies and productive forces; on the contrary, it is due to its inability to drive the development it initiated on to its conclusion – a "single administration" of the world economy. And this is because, as Marxist theory predicts, and as has been amply verified, the bourgeoisie is incapable of coming to terms with "those dark forces which its own activities conjure up". But let us not forget that "imperialism" is the measure of the scale of effort the bourgeoisie has made in the past, and is still prepared to make now, to keep itself abreast of the demands of production, and to sanction its role as the "demiurge" of the economic world by capitalizing on its position as victorious and dominant class. Its success in this enterprise was bought at the cost of detaching itself from the sphere of production to such an extent that it has largely lost contact with it. Now it feels cut off, an intruder in the world of the economic forces that it unleashed (and which, at an earlier period, it adequately controlled) – and so is forced to strengthen its own dictatorial political apparatus.

Hence the "workers' State" is not achieved by a simple harking back to the "liberal" phase, i.e. to the phase in which capital "adheres" tightly to the location and techniques of production; in this case, the idea of the "factory councils" that Gramsci has tried to give us would have only a historical sense – anachronistic, but historical. The "workers' State", let us repeat, must indeed negate bourgeois organization, in the sense that today the proletariat is the only class that is capable of bringing capital back to production, of moulding the world of the economy in accordance with the relations of production. But it must also synthesize in itself the vital *revolutionary* aspect of the second phase of the capitalist process, the stage when the owners of the means of production and exchange have achieved a fuller freedom to dispose of these – to serve and enhance their own class dominion, of course, but also to develop the forces of production themselves.

It is this "transcendence" of the bourgeois economy that the proletariat as a class succeeds in accomplishing, through negating it at a certain stage and appropriating its vital elements. It does so by setting up its own State, in which the economy is newly organized according to the proletariat's own requirements at that stage of its development. But also the means of production and exchange are utilized to the limits of their capacity, an indispensable condition if a rational division of labour is to be achieved within the framework of the Communist International.

For the very reason that the factory council adheres strictly to the "point of production" (which does not quite mean "production" itself as yet), it represents the beginning of the historical process by which the proletariat succeeds the bourgeoisie in the management of the social heritage. The council is an indispensable factor, and hence its emergence has all the historical significance which Gramsci attributes to it. In other words, the factory council is the first truly characteristic (Comrade Gramsci would say "original") moment of the process by which the proletariat as a class makes its presence felt with all the might and confidence of its mission. And so the bourgeoisie is expelled in a disoriented state from that world to which it was born and to which it gave birth; for, as the *Manifesto* puts it, "the history of industry and commerce is but the history of the revolt of modern productive forces against modern conditions of production, against the property relations that are the conditions for the existence of the bourgeoisie and of its rule".[106] To the bourgeoisie there is counter-posed the proletariat, whose conditions of existence and dominion coincide perfectly with the demands of production and the conditions of existence of the whole of humanity, with the exception of a minority of exploiters.

It is the proletariat, and only the proletariat, that is capable of bringing the work of the bourgeoisie to a conclusion, for it is not hampered by the idea and the institution of bourgeois property. The proletariat constituted itself as a class before it had any possessions; hence it has everything to gain and nothing to lose in the revolution. It is the youthful class which, because it has no past (or rather its past is the bourgeoisie, and is destroyed along with it), can fashion the relations of ownership in accordance with the relations of production. At the present time, the "factory council" is attracting capital back to production; in the Soviets, the workers' and peasants' councils, we now have a communist State which, by basing itself on the process of production and aligning itself on it in a flexible fashion, is in a position to organize that same process in such a way as to achieve the total emancipation of the class, that is to say, the Communist International.

* * * * *

Since Comrade Gramsci accuses me of lacking a "central idea" which might give my treatment of the councils an inner logic and character of its own, I propose to examine our different ideas with regard to the revolution and the opposing practices which are implied by them.

That the Revolution is nothing other than the triumph of the proletariat; and that this triumph cannot be called definitive until the proletariat can melt away as a class and identify itself with humanity, to which it will have given the social organization that corresponds to its needs and maximum development (as they are felt and foreseen today);

that the Revolution is not completed until the proletariat can place its seal on its handiwork and disappear – taken up to a new life and redeemed, together with the whole world, for a new liberty – into the Communist International: all this is perfectly true and in line with what socialists have always expressed. Now the construction that Gramsci *describes* in his editorial on the factory councils is nothing but an exemplification of the idea of the new order that socialists and communists hold in common – a new order that the proletariat would like to create, and will have to create. But the attractive feature of this idea is that it is not a dream concerning the year 2000, but a myth that lives in the consciousness of the class at this hour, on this fervid eve. The "myth" has unleashed precious forces, and it is being translated into the creation of new proletarian institutions in which, as Gramsci says, "the historical process of the Revolution is assuming a controllable historical form".

However, bearing in mind the different scope of factory and enterprise councils and workers' and peasants' councils, we maintain that the Revolution (with a capital R) is accomplished only through the medium of the dictatorship of the proletariat, which must hold social power in its hands for years or even decades if the international organization of production is to become a reality. In other words, the revolution (with a small r) has to be made – the revolution that will strip the bourgeoisie of its power and its ability to intrigue, that will place at the disposal of the proletariat all the means presently at the disposal of the bourgeoisie, so that it may use them to further its own Revolution.

If the proletariat is to be able to construct the new order in which a single administration disposes of English coal, Russian oil, Siberian wheat, Sicilian sulphur, rice from Vercelli and wood from Styria, then the proletariat in Italy, England, Austria, etc., will have had, as in Russia, to dispossess the bourgeoisie and carry through that revolution which is no less indispensable to the "historical process of the Revolution" than the successive realizations of the communist programme with regard to social organization – indeed, it is its essential condition. And if we are not to feed off words, and are not to lose our sense of historicity, that is to say, of reality, then before we view the factory councils as the foundations of the communist State, we must view them as instruments (yes, as means, because all things are means; only the working class is an end, and an end unto itself) of struggle for that revolution without which the communist State . . . will never be any more than a set of foundations. And what I would call Gramsci's abstract and anti-historical view of the factory councils derives precisely from his viewing them essentially as the beginnings of the workers' State, whose development both Party and trade unions should strive to ensure; whereas I see them on the same level as [. . .][107] to make the revolution, not that which will be realized after the conquest of political power, but that which will permit us to take this power.

Hence my treatment is based squarely on the following idea – an idea which I have repeated a thousand times over and which I belaboured at the congress of the Chamber of Labour: that the creation of the factory councils would have no significance if we were not living through a revolutionary period, if we were not on the eve of the revolution. This idea, or rather this historical intuition, puts the problem of the councils in perspective far more successfully than the "logical sequence of ideas" that Comrade Gramsci sees as underpinning the Communist International.

No, dear comrade, underpinning the Communist International you will not find a "sequence of logical notions", but a reality that has nothing in common with logic. What underpins the Communist International is the effective will of the various proletariats to have done with the bourgeois régime, and hence to make the revolution. All the rest has its significance – and I would be the last to deny the significance of the culture and ideas we share, that allow us to understand the process in which we participate and in which we intervene on a conscious basis (provided we understand it). But to think that underpinning the Communist International there exists "a sequence of notions" is proof of the abstractism that Gramsci is infused with – an abstractism that prevents him, as we shall see below, from making even a minimal contribution to the practical problem of the revolution.

It is not people who are familiar with the "contents and conclusions contained in a volume by Hilferding on *Finance Capital*" who join the Third International, but people who are working to make the proletariats of the different countries, and everyone in his own home, conscious of the need to wrest from the hands of the bourgeoisie as fast as possible those weapons it employs to hang onto power and stifle the Russian revolution. It is this revolution that is the real beginning of the process of liberation of the proletariat – a beginning which is both historical and historically controllable. Our task is to safeguard the Russian revolution, by making the revolution in our respective countries, i.e. by ensuring that the proletariat as a class comes rapidly to power: this is the task in whose light one should view the relations between factory councils, Party and trade unions.

In an editorial published in this same journal ("Seeking the Truth", No. 20, and see also another editorial, "The War Veterans", No. 27), I argued that the problem of the revolution had to be resolved by the proletariat in time to forestall the inevitable advent of the bourgeois dictatorship and to capitalize on the psychological after-effects of the war. And in my report on the councils, written for the Socialist Section, I said with regard to the question of giving the vote to non-union members: "Today revolutionaries do not have an unlimited period of time stretching before them, accommodating the gradual stages of their own advance; *the problem of the revolution is no longer only a problem of method, but also of time*. In other words, the usefulness of a tactic can no longer be considered purely in the light of its correspondence to the general aims of socialism; it should be judged good or bad according to whether it offers the possibility of bringing into being – in the shortest time possible, i.e. before the bourgeoisie attempts a military coup or the mob forces our hand – a revolutionary state of affairs in which the conscious and dominant will of the communists may be brought into play."

Could it be clearer? Comrade Gramsci was present at the Section when I read my report. He was also present at the Chamber of Labour congress when I began my speech with similar observations. And yet he believes he can argue that I lack a "conception" of the factory councils. To which I may reply that the factory councils have as their premise that which I have expounded a thousand times – and without which all "logical notions" become schemas allowing the proletariat, if it read everything that Comrade Gramsci has the good fortune to be able to read, at best to console itself for its own impotence to act and free itself from its bondage to capital.

The proof that it is not "logical notions" which underpin the Communist International (I belabour this point, because it has to do with a fundamental antithesis between my concept and that of Gramsci's) lies in these comments of Comrade Sadoul's, contained in the same issue of *L'Ordine Nuovo* where Gramsci set off with lance in rest to scatter the barbarians from the land blessed by the councils: "comrades, for us the unity of doctrine cannot be other than the union of workers determined to initiate at once the social transformation and follow it through, until a communist society has been thoroughly established. The unity of tactics cannot help but bring determined communists closer to making use of revolutionary action, the direct action of the masses, in order to forcibly wrest from the bourgeoisie their political power and the capitalistic means of production, in order to set up the dictatorship of the proletariat and the Soviet régime, in order to put doctrine into practice, in order to execute the programme of the Third International."[108]

The "notions" which underpin the Third International are therefore essentially notions of revolutionary action, of the violent conquest of political power, of the setting up of the dictatorship of the proletariat. "To put doctrine into practice", "to execute the programme of the Third International", etc. – this is the watchword of communist action. It is in this light that the problem of the councils needs to be considered. Otherwise one runs the risk of confusing the actual revolution with the theory, the myth, of the revolution. This is what Gramsci has done, and this explains his comic desperation at seeing the councils movement, viz. the beginning of the revolution, compromised because the Chamber of Labour congress was concerned less with formulae than with practical action.

Gramsci has even lagged behind the syndicalists, who mistakenly, in our view, identified the process of development of the unions with that of the revolution, as Gramsci now identifies the emergence of the factory councils with the creation of the "workers' State". But the syndicalists accompanied their conception with its companion idea of the "expropriating general strike", so that the myth of the future society advanced in step with that of the struggle to be undertaken against the bourgeoisie. In other words, Gramsci has repeated the error of the syndicalists and made it worse. For in the first place, industrial unions are more suited to the direct management of production than factory councils, in accordance with the demands of production such as we inherit it from the bourgeoisie and such as we shall have to develop. In the second place, the syndicalist programme boasted a method of its own, so-called "direct action", a method which is quite definitely absent from Comrade Gramsci's "programme". This explains the weakness of his position and the contradictions into which he has fallen. We shall seek to demonstrate some of the contradictions in the editorial he wrote in the last issue, *Unions and Councils*, where he examined the problem of the relations between these two bodies.

Editorial Note

Comrade Tasca will conclude his reply with an article which he has promised us for the next issue, and so Comrade Gramsci will postpone his reply to the subsequent issues. We should like to point out, however, that our friend Tasca has already begun in earnest to "grow wings and hover above the sphere of polemic". Above all, we should like to demand of him greater precision in expounding the thought of his friends.

Attentive readers will no doubt have given scant credence to Tasca's gross blunder of claiming that Gramsci argues that the communist State will usher in a return to the "liberal phase" of the economy. In any case we invite them to read attentively last week's column "The Week in Politics", published under the heading: *Giolitti in Power*, where the question is expounded in the simplest and clearest possible fashion. Furthermore there is not a little difference between a "logical sequence of notions" and a "sequence of logical notions".

We should not like to be forced to indulge in any further philology, but if this is to be possible, each one of us will have to make certain to penetrate and interpret in a close and precise fashion the thought of the comrade who is being polemicized against.

The Review

III

Although Comrade Gramsci presented my action at the Chamber of Labour congress as a sudden defection, a non-authorized adaptation of the *L'Ordine Nuovo* theses, he knew, and many comrades who are closer to us were aware of this, that for a long time I have been studying together with others the possibility of creating a non-artificial but rational systematization of the relations between factory councils and trade unions, such as would be of most use to the cause of the revolution. The workshop delegates echoed these concerns in their Programme: "The example of the fatal conflict between trade-union leaders and the power of the councils in Hungary has led us to attempt to prevent a repetition of the phenomenon in the Italian revolution, by defining at the outset the relations between the two functions and allotting to each the tasks that its constitution, governing principle and daily practice warrant."[109]

In the Study Committee nominated by the Socialist Section we got down first of all to formulating a more precise definition of the limits, competences, etc., of the two bodies, for the committee had been formed with the precise mandate "of specifying and recommending what relations should exist between factory councils and the workers' resistance organizations, in order to avoid disputes over demarcation of competence and to prevent the present organizations from being weakened, or rather to ensure that their prestige should be enhanced in the eyes of the masses" (*Avanti!*, 12 December 1919). Well, it was precisely the workers' delegates from Fiat Centro, that is to say from the very plant where the new proletarian institutions had been tried out before anywhere else and had been further developed than anywhere else, who on several occasions pointed out to us that our efforts were in vain and our attempts absurd, so that in the end we abandoned them, having become aware and convinced that we were on the wrong track.

These were the premises governing the proposals concerning statutory modifications that were presented to the Chamber of Labour congress. It is on the basis of these, it seems to me, that the congress come to recognize the need for trade-union organizations to be able at all times to keep in touch with the masses, to feel their pulse and be able to count on their collaboration and spontaneous discipline. If this goal was to be attained, then an essential feature of the organizations had to be workshop delegates at the work-place, or meeting in factory and general assemblies. On the other hand, what was equally necessary was that the trade-union organization should retain overall responsibility for the movement, i.e. its leadership and control. In this way the General Council of the Federation or union, made up of the factory executive committees and officers – a less numerous and more selective body than the delegates' assembly – would be able to inject whenever necessary its own aims into the movement, aims peculiar to the particular organization. This is the systematization which genuinely responds, or attempts to respond, to the necessity of creating a situation "such that a capricious impulse on the part of the councils could not result in a setback or defeat for the working class; in other words, the council should accept and assimilate the discipline of the union. They should also be such that the revolutionary character of the council exercises an influence over the trade union, and functions as a reagent dissolving the union's bureaucracy and bureaucratism" (see *L'Ordine Nuovo*, Vol. II, No. 5, *Unions and Councils*), as Comrade Gramsci so well puts it.

Not that I am deluded enough to believe that such a situation can be brought into being as the result of a set of norms. I maintain that the situation should be mirrored in norms, norms which are not rigid and immutable like the Tablets of the Law, but like a snapshot of a situation where the "de facto position" is set in the context of the concern and conscious efforts of the communists to capitalize on the fertile elements and warn against the dangers. If the norms were simply to represent a drawing-board project, a draft proposal – one out of many, then they would stand condemned *a priori*; but if they represent the results or the fruits of lived experience, then they derive their legitimacy from the vital facts which they have taken into account and *expressed*.

It is beyond doubt that some set of norms must eventually be reached. Comrade Gramsci can insist all he likes on his point that the council strives to break with legality and the union to remain within it. But the fact is that when the council departs from legality, the employer calls in the Royal Guard and makes it . . . depart from the factory. And then the workers come to the union, to the Chamber of Labour; the event falls within the province of the organization, which can no longer and can *never* be uninvolved. And if this is the case, then the organization must be in a position to intervene and not just to throw sand on the flames and "bury the dead": it cannot merely "give aid" to the workers in a given factory when they decide to "depart from legality", but, indirectly, at once receives the full blast of the fate the workers have suffered in their clash with the industrialist. Of course, Comrade Gramsci has a formula, a peremptory and infallible formula, at the ready: "The relations between union and council should create the conditions in which the break with legality, the working-class offensive, occurs at the most opportune moment for the working class, when it possesses that minimum preparation that is deemed indispensable to a lasting victory."

Many thanks! This point will certainly have to be reached, but if it is to be reached then much hard work will have to be done, and relations will have to be provisionally systematized in such a way as to make possible a common activity that will succeed in providing us with those "conditions" which mean applying to the revolution the law of maximum return for minimum cost. To obtain this it is not sufficient to print resolutions against "strike-breakers" or satirical attacks on "revolutionary adventurers"; one must concern oneself also with such petty-bourgeois items as norms, conventions, regulations. Always with the proviso that this sort of work must not substitute for the rest of the work, which is much more substantial: revolutionary trade-union activity, which is the terrain on which the two bodies can live in mutual interdependence.

I was perfectly aware of this when, in the report I wrote for the Socialist Section, although I argued that the executive committee of the organization should be elected by the General Council of the organization itself, I observed that "if an executive committee could not collaborate with the Assembly of workshop delegates, this would imply that the committee did not enjoy the trust of the masses and was unable to impose itself by giving them the feeling that it was defending their interests. A dispute between the executive committee and the workshop delegates would indicate that the situation was compromised, and that no code of regulations would avail, but only new men and enlightened action."

* * * * *

Comrade Gramsci reproaches me with not having taken account of publications on the functioning of factory councils in Russia. In this he is right, although my starting-point was the experience of the local movement and I deliberately restricted myself to this frame of reference when writing the report. However, I can conclude, now that I have been able to read systematically through everything important which has been published on the subject by *L'Ordine Nuovo*, *Avanti!* and *Comunismo*, that my position as regards the problem of the factory councils corresponds perfectly to the theory and practice of the Russian movement.

I argued that the "factory council" is the basis of the "workers' State", but that its development cannot autonomously produce the whole of the structure of the workers' State. The workers' State is a State in which the working class, through the medium of its dictatorship, has been able to organize production along communist lines, its organization being expressed as a wholly novel form of State structure, namely the Communist International. Indeed, since the basis of the proletarian dictatorship has to reside in its capacity to organize production, both during and after the climactic crisis, and since the attainment of this capacity is the task attaching to the unions, the reponsibilities of these latter cannot be minimized to merely ensuring, along with the Socialist Party, that the factory councils can operate freely. *The unions are just as important* to the workers' State, and to the proletarian dictatorship, its precondition, *as the factory councils*; if anything, they are more important, because it is possible to conceive of the unions' managing production without the factory councils, but not the other way round.

"So this is the mammoth but glorious task confronting the industrial trade unions. It is they who must carry out a socialization programme;

who must bring a new régime of production into being, in which each enterprise is based not on the profit motive, but on the common interests of society, which in the case of each productive sector lose their indistinct, generic character and are made concrete in the appropriate workers' union" (an article by Gramsci on *Trade Unions and the Dictatorship, L'Ordine Nuovo*, Vol. I, No. 33).[110] In other words, if it is true that the trade unions can realize "the highest moment of the class struggle and of the dictatorship of the proletariat" (*L'Ordine Nuovo*, Vol. I, No. 21, and Gramsci cites the example of the industrial unions in Russia); if they represent "the rigid backbone of the great proletarian body"; if, for their part, they constitute "the higher structures of the dictatorship and the communist economy": how is it possible, without contradiction, to conceive of the workers' State as an extension of the factory councils, apart from or at most under the protection of the unions?[111]

Hence it is my opinion that Comrade Gramsci has allowed himself to be seduced by a "myth" that has very little historical substance to it, when he states that the unions, along with the Party, must set themselves the task of "organizing the general (political) external conditions" in which the revolutionary process, i.e. the process of development of the factory councils, can achieve its maximum expansion.

Either the "higher structures of the dictatorship and the communist economy" are viewed as "external political conditions" (*L'Ordine Nuovo*, Vol. II, No. 4) – which would be an idiotic thing to say – or one of them is quite different from the other. In this case, the "position" of the unions *vis-à-vis* the factory councils is seen to have a quite different basis than the one pointed to by Gramsci. For the task of realizing those structures, of carrying out the necessary transformations for them, becomes of prime importance and ensures that the unions take part as essential elements in the "revolutionary process". In other words, the development of the capacity of the unions to take over management of production in their industrial sector is just as important for this as the development of the councils' capacity to control production in the individual factories.

In Russia, the unions played an overwhelming role in the nationalization of production, i.e. in the consolidation of the proletarian dictatorship. Indeed Bela Kun saw fit to state in a speech that "the Russian system may be summarized in the following way: the apparatus of socialized industry must be based on the unions embracing at first the majority, and subsequently the whole of the workers in a given industry" (*L'Ordine Nuovo*, Vol. I, No. 25).[112] From being the "stagnant bog" as Lenin defined them in 1917, the unions became the "auxiliary organs of the proletarian dictatorship" (Glebov, "The Role of the Workers' Unions in the Russian Revolution", *L'Ordine Nuovo*, Vol. I, No. 27). Indeed, Zinoviev defines them as "a long-lasting activity on the part of all workers in a particular industry"; they "form one of the principal organizational bases of the proletarian dictatorship" (*L'Ordine Nuovo*, Vol. I, No. 34: "The Party and the Unions").

The unions cannot fulfil this role unless two conditions are satisfied: 1. they are led by communists; 2. they are transformed from craft unions into industrial unions. The first condition is met by the action of communist groups attempting to gain control of the organizations, while the second calls for a methodical and rational programme of gathering the necessary data and ordering it systematically in such a way that trade-union topography may faithfully coincide with the topography of production. In Russia, as Comrade Glebov informs us in the article quoted above, "throughout the eight months of democratic bourgeois power, the proletariat worked assiduously on the task of organizing its unions" on an industrial basis. And it was the creation of central administrations, linked to the unions and sometimes formed by them, which made possible "the transition from workers' control to total administration of the factories and plants on the part of the workers' State" (C. Larin, "The Economic Practice of Soviet Power", *L'Ordine Nuovo*, Vol. I, No. 33). In Russia the unions function, as we read in the last issue of *L'Ordine Nuovo*, "as part of the State mechanism", and a very powerful current wishes to turn them into "an organic part of the Soviet government".

On the other hand, the factory councils, or rather the factory committees, play only a secondary role in the management of production. This was explained in the correspondence from *The Economist* concerning the Soviet mechanism of nationalization, translated in *L'Ordine Nuovo*: "The workers nominate their representatives through their factory committee, a body which enjoyed full powers under the anarcho-syndicalist régime. . . . But today the workers' committees do not possess very great powers and are little more than factory clubs, or mutual benefit and recreation societies" (No. 14).[113] And Comrade Niccolini affirmed this more recently in *Comunismo*: "When one reads the various measures and decrees of the Soviet Republic, one always observes the predominance and importance attached to the representatives of the proletariat *organized into the Association. In the end, the factory committees in Russia have become part of the trade-union organization*" (No. 6, "The Factory Committees").

It is true that Comrade Niccolini too has been "failed" by Professor Gramsci on the theory and practice of the Third International, but this does not prevent his testimony from carrying considerable weight in our eyes. As we have argued many times, the significance of the factory councils is essentially political; their importance is very great during the period of revolutionary struggle, while it declines step by step as the workers' State is consolidated and becomes capable of taking over the management of production, a stage which it reached through the struggle for control. But just as in the workers' State "the clash between the factory committees and the trade-union organizations was resolved in Russia in favour of the trade-union organizations, which according to the principles of collectivity represent the interests of the workers in the whole of industry as against local individual interests" (C. Niccolini, op. cit.), so in the present period it is up to the unions to carry the class struggle from the field of resistance to that of conquest.

When Comrade Gramsci states that the factory council "cannot be co-ordinated with or subordinated to the trade union", but "through its emergence and development, it effects radical changes in the form and structure of the unions" (*L'Ordine Nuovo*, Vol. II, No. 4), I reply: either this makes no sense, or it means that the factory council is responsible for the transformation of the union into an industrial organ. In this case, the unions could not play mid-wife to the fledgling factory councils, as Gramsci would have us believe; on the contrary, the relations between the two bodies should be determined by their functional links, which I expressed as follows in the motion presented to the Chamber of Labour congress: "The 'council' is the organ of proletarian power at the work-place and helps give the wage-worker awareness of being a producer; hence it raises the class struggle from the level of resistance to that of conquest. Such a transformation has its origins in the work-place, but it must invest trade-union activity in its entirety. For this reason, the 'council' is the element which will transform the pattern of organization on a craft and category basis into a system of organization on an industrial basis. This transformation is not simply a change of form, but a genuine shift of activity, as a result of which the trade-union organizations will opt for the communist revolution and prepare themselves to become the constituent elements of the new régime on the morrow of their victory."

If the cultural changes that Comrade Gramsci has in mind are different from the ones stated above, let him explain them to us when he replies. But all the same, let us observe that, since factory committees are just as much elements of the communist State as the unions, by virtue of their being elements of communist production, I ask whether it is possible to conceive of them as being separate and in no way co-ordinated or subordinate, once they have taken their place in the organic hierarchy that constitutes the workers' State.

* * * * *

In a note on the second instalment of my reply, Comrade Gramsci recommends me to "penetrate and interpret in a close and precise fashion the thought of the comrade being polemicized against". He informs us that the "intelligent reader" will have spotted a "gross blunder" of mine in "claiming that Gramsci argues that the communist State will usher in a return to the 'liberal' phase of the economy". I am sorry, but this time it is Gramsci himself who is making the "gross blunder", and in this case he makes it worse by clothing it in editorial impartiality.

In the relevant instalment I wrote: "The 'workers' State' is not achieved by a simple harking back to the 'liberal' phase, i.e. to the phase in which capital 'adheres' tightly to the location and techniques of production; in this case, the idea of the 'factory councils' that Gramsci tried to give us *would have* only a historical sense – anachronistic, but historical" (p. 276 above). In other words, what this means is that Gramsci's idea *would make* historical sense if the workers' State consisted in a pure and simple return to the liberal phase; but since the workers' State does not consist in this – not even for Gramsci – so his idea does not correspond to the characteristics of the economy during the liberal phase. And because Gramsci would not wish to identify the "workers' State" with the individual councils or their federation, neither does it correspond to the characteristics of the imperialist economy, because he identifies the workers' State with a (not very well-defined or concrete) process of development of the factory councils, and banishes the unions – the real productive instruments suited to the monopolistic phase – to non-participation in the workers' State.

My polemic is based here on a dilemma: either the workers' State does nothing but reintroduce capital into production via the councils, in which case we are going back about two centuries; or else it is seriously concerned with controlling production and with obtaining that "full freedom to dispose of the means of production and exchange that is indispensable if a rational division of labour is to be attained within the framework of the Communist International", in which case it must make use of other organs as well as the councils – i.e. unions, economic councils, etc. The rational division of labour is not achieved, as Gramsci argues, because the workers' State, having emerged along with the factory councils in accordance with the pattern of productive industry, "has within it the seeds of its own development, of its own dissolution as a State and of its organic incorporation into a world system – the Communist International" (*L'Ordine Nuovo*, Vol. II, No. 4). On the contrary, this division of labour is achieved because the workers' State possesses the organs capable of controlling production in all its complexity and of determining its selection *on a voluntary basis* in relation to the requirements of the world economy. The workers' State is delineated in accordance with the pattern of productive industry, but the factory council is no more patterned in accordance with the productive process than the industrial union. The only difference is that one is patterned on the basis of the work-place alone, and the other in accordance with the whole of its own branch of industry. Hence the productive pattern upon which the industrial union bases the workers' State reproduces in itself the pattern of the whole system, from a much closer range than would be possible for the individual council or councils.

* * * * *

In conclusion, I hold that Comrade Gramsci's outburst could well be put in quarantine, if it has helped to open up a polemic that was necessary, but which I hope will not drag on into a never-ending dialogue, giving little pleasure either to the readers or to ourselves.

These "family rows" will no doubt give satisfaction in certain quarters, and to this we can only oppose our constant, impassioned, disinterested effort to gain a clearer perspective on the reality in which we participate, and thus to make a contribution which will enable the class to which we have consciously bound our fate to confront the problems of the revolution better prepared; and which will also enable our party with sure insight to dominate the historical situation from which its own triumph and that of the proletariat must spring.

L'Ordine Nuovo, Vol. II, Nos. 5, 6, 7; 12 and 19 June, 3 July 1920.

54. ON THE *L'ORDINE NUOVO* PROGRAMME

I

When in the month of April 1919, three or four or five of us got together and decided to begin publishing this review *L'Ordine Nuovo* (and the transcripts of those discussions and decisions of ours should still be in existence – yes, the actual transcripts . . . they were written up and a fair copy made – for history!), none of us (perhaps) thought in terms of changing the face of the world, of renewing the hearts and minds of the human multitudes, of starting a new historical cycle. None of us (perhaps: some dreamed of 6,000 subscribers in a few months) entertained rosy illusions as to the success of the enterprise. Who were we? What did we represent? Of what new tidings were we the bearers? Ah well! The only sentiment that united us, in those meetings of ours, was the sentiment aroused by a vague passion for a vague proletarian culture. We wanted to *do* something. We felt desperate, disoriented, immersed in the excitement of life in those months after the Armistice, when the cataclysm in Italian society appeared imminent. Ah well! The one original word that was uttered at those meetings was stifled. Someone who was a technician said: "We need to study the organization of the factory as an instrument of production. We should devote the whole of our attention to capitalist systems of production and organization, and we should work to focus the attention of the working class and Party on this subject." Someone else who was interested in the organization of men, in the history of men, in the psychology of the working class, said: "We need to study what happens among the working masses. Is there any working-class institution in Italy that can be compared to the Soviet, that shares some of its characteristics? . . . Something that would allow us to say: the Soviet is a universal form, not a Russian, and only a Russian, institution; wherever there exist proletarians struggling to win for themselves industrial autonomy, the Soviet is the form in which the working class manifests this determination to emancipate itself; the Soviet is the form of self-government of the working masses. Is there any germ, a vague hope or hint of such Soviet-style self-government in Italy, in Turin?" A third person, who had been struck by the following question put to him bluntly by a Polish comrade:[114] "Why hasn't a congress of the internal commissions ever been held in Italy?" answered the same questions at our meetings: "Yes, a germ of a workers' government, of a Soviet, does exist in Italy, in Turin – it is the internal commission. Let us study this working-class institution; let us inquire into it. And let us study the capitalist factory as well, but not as an organization to produce materials, for we don't have the specialist knowledge that would be needed. Let us study the capitalist factory as a necessary form of the working class, as a political organ, as the 'national territory' of workers' self-government." This struck a new note – and it was Comrade Tasca who rejected it.

What did Comrade Tasca want? He wanted us not to launch any propaganda directly among the working masses. He wanted an agreement with the general secretaries of the federations and unions. He wanted us to work for a convention to which these secretaries would be invited and to draw up a plan for official action. The "Ordine Nuovo" group would thus have been reduced to the level of an irresponsible clique of conceited coachman-flies.[115] What then was the actual programme of *L'Ordine Nuovo* in its first numbers? The programme was the absence of a concrete programme, just a vague and hopeless aspiration to deal with concrete problems. What was the *idea* of *L'Ordine Nuovo* in its first numbers? There was no central *idea*, no inner organization of the literary material published. What did Comrade Tasca mean by "culture" – what did he mean in concrete, not abstract, terms? This is what Comrade Tasca meant by culture: he meant "recollection" not "thought" – and recollection of the discarded, useless junk of working-class thought. He meant letting the Italian working class know, "recalling" for the benefit of the worthy Italian working class – which is so retarded, so rough and uncultured – that Louis Blanc had some thoughts on how work should be organized and that these ideas were tried out in actual experiments. He meant "recalling" that Eugène Fournière compiled a careful scholastic treatise for dolloping out plans for a socialist State nice and hot (or nice and cold). He meant "recalling", in the spirit of Michelet (or of the worthy Luigi Molinari), the Paris Commune, without dropping the least hint that the Russian communists, in the footsteps of Marx, are currently linking the Soviet or system of Soviets to the Paris Commune. Without dropping the least hint that the Russian communists had made use of Marx's notes on the "industrial" character of the Commune in their theorization of the Soviet; in their elaboration of the *idea* of the Soviet; in drawing up their Party's programme of action, once it had become the ruling party.

What was *L'Ordine Nuovo* in its first numbers? It was an anthology, nothing but an anthology. It was a review like any other that could have come out in Naples, Caltanisetta or Brindisi, a journal of abstract culture, abstract information, with a strong leaning towards horror stories and well-meaning woodcuts. This is what *L'Ordine Nuovo* was in its first numbers: a mess, the product of a mediocre intellectualism, which sought on all fours an ideal place to land and march on to action. This was *L'Ordine Nuovo* as it was launched following the meetings we held in April 1919: meetings which were duly recorded and in which Comrade Tasca rejected, on the grounds that it was a breach with the fine traditions of the respectable and peaceable little family of Italian socialism, the proposal that we devote our energies to "unearthing" a Soviet tradition within the Italian working class, to digging out the thread of the real revolutionary spirit in Italy – real because at one with the universal spirit of the workers' International, the product of a real historical situation and an achievement of the working class itself.

Togliatti and I staged an editorial *coup d'état*. The problem of the internal commissions was raised explicitly in issue number 7 of the review.[115] A few evenings before writing the article, I had developed its line to Comrade Terracini who had expressed his full agreement with it in terms of theory and practice. The article, written in collaboration with Togliatti and cleared by Terracini, was published, with results more or less as we had foreseen. Togliatti, Terracini and myself were invited to give talks to study groups and factory assemblies; we were invited by the internal commissions to discussions at meetings restricted to officers and dues collectors. We carried on; the problem of the development of the internal commission became the central problem, the *idea*, of *L'Ordine Nuovo*. It came to be seen as the fundamental problem of the workers' revolution; it was the problem of proletarian "liberty". For ourselves and our followers, *L'Ordine Nuovo* became the "journal of the Factory Councils". The workers loved *L'Ordine Nuovo* (this we can state with inner satisfaction) and why did they love it? Because in its articles they rediscovered a part, the best part, of themselves. Because they felt its articles were pervaded by that same spirit of inner searching that they experienced: "How can we become free? How can we become ourselves?" Because its articles were not cold, intellectual structures, but sprang from our discussions with the best workers; they elaborated the actual sentiments, goals and passions of the Turin working class, that we ourselves had provoked and tested. Because its articles were virtually a "taking note" of actual events, seen as moments of a process of inner liberation and self-expression on the part of the working class. This is why the workers loved *L'Ordine Nuovo* and how its *idea* came to be "formed". Comrade Tasca took no part whatsoever in this process of formation, in this elaboration. *L'Ordine Nuovo* developed its own *idea* independently of his intentions and his "contribution" to the revolution. This to me explains his attitude today; it explains the "tone" of his polemic. He has not put any effort into reaching "his conception", and I am not surprised that it was an abortion, since it was unloved. I am not surprised that he has treated the argument with such crudity and intervened in our activity with such lack of consideration and inner discipline, seeking to restore to it that *official* character which he had supported and formulated a year before.

II

In the preceding instalment, I sought to locate the origin of Comrade Tasca's attitude to the *L'Ordine Nuovo* programme. As a result of our contact with the intellectual and practical demands of the working class, this programme came to be organized around the central problem of the Factory Council. Since Comrade Tasca took no part in this experience, and indeed was hostile to its taking place, he has failed to grasp the problem of the Factory Council in its actual historical terms and in the organic development which, despite a few hesitations and quite understandable mistakes, it was given by myself, Togliatti and the other comrades who wished to help us. For Tasca, the problem of the Factory Councils was simply a problem in the arithmetic sense of the word: the problem of how to organize at once the *whole* of the class of Italian workers and peasants. In one of his polemical pieces, Tasca writes that he sees the communist party, the trade union and the Factory Council all on the same level.[117] At another point he shows he has failed to understand the meaning of the adjective "voluntary" that *L'Ordine Nuovo* pins on the party and trade-union organizations in order to distinguish them from the Factory Council, which is assumed to be a "historical" form of association of the kind which today can only be compared with that of the bourgeois State. According to the conception developed by *L'Ordine Nuovo* – a conception which being worthy of the name was organized around an idea, the idea of freedom (and in concrete terms, on the level of actual historical creation, around the hypothesis of the working class carrying out an autonomous revolutionary action) – the Factory Council is an institution with a "public" character, while the Party and the unions are associations with a "private" character.

In the Factory Council, the worker participates as a producer, i.e. as a consequence of his universal character and of his position and role in society, in the same way that the citizen participates in the democratic parliamentary State. In the Party and trade unions, the worker participates "voluntarily", by signing a written undertaking, a "contract", that he can back out of at any time. As a result of this "voluntary", "contractualist" character of the Party and trade unions, they can in no way be confused with the Council. This latter is a representative institution, that develops morphologically not arithmetically and, in its higher forms, has the effect of impressing a *proletarian* pattern on the apparatus of production and exchange that *capitalism* created for the purpose of making profits.

It was for this reason that *L'Ordine Nuovo* did not employ the political terminology appropriate to a society divided into classes, when referring to the higher forms of the organization of the Councils, but relied instead on references to organization on an industrial basis. According to the conception developed by *L'Ordine Nuovo*, the system of Councils cannot be expressed by the word "federation" or something similar; it can only be represented by transferring the complex of industrial relations that link one job crew to another, one shop to another in a factory, onto the level of an entire industrial zone. For us, Turin was an example ready to hand, and so in one article Turin was assumed to be the historical hearth of the communist revolution in Italy.

In a factory, the workers are producers in so far as they collaborate in the preparation of the object being manufactured; they are ordered in a way that is determined precisely by the industrial technique being used, which in turn is independent (in a certain sense) of the mode of appropriation of the values that are produced. All the workers in a motor vehicle factory, whether they be metalworkers, masons, electricians, carpenters or whatever, all take on the character and role of producers in so far as they are equally necessary and indispensable in the fabrication of a motor vehicle: in so far as they form a historically necessary and absolutely indivisible body, organized as they are on an industrial basis. Turin developed historically as a city in this way: as a result of the transfer of the capital to Florence and then Rome and the fact that the Italian State was formed initially as an extension of the

Piedmont State, Turin was deprived of a petty-bourgeois class, whose elements provided the personnel for the new Italian apparatus.[118] But this transfer of the capital, and the sudden disappearance of a characteristic element in modern cities, did not cause a decline in the city. On the contrary, it began to develop – and the new development occurred organically in line with the growth of the mechanical engineering industry, the system of FIAT factories. Turin provided the new State with its class of petty-bourgeois intellectuals; the development of the capitalist economy, by ruining Italy's small-scale industry and handicrafts, caused a compact proletarian mass to converge on Turin, giving the city its present character, perhaps one of the most original in all Europe. The city was and still is shaped as a matter of course around a single industry that "controls" all the city's movements and regulates its outlets. Turin is the *motor car* city, just as Vercelli is characterized economically by *rice*, the Caucasus by *oil*, South Wales by *coal*, etc. Just as in a *factory* the workers form a pattern – being ordered in accordance with the production of a particular object that unites and organizes metal- and wood-workers, masons, electricians, etc. – so in the *city* the proletarian class forms a pattern in accordance with the prevailing industry, which through its existence orders and governs the whole urban complex. So, too, on a national level, a people forms a pattern in accordance with their exports, with the actual contribution they make to the economic life of the world.

Comrade Tasca, a most inattentive reader of *L'Ordine Nuovo*, has grasped nothing of this theoretical development, which for that matter was nothing other than a translation into Italian historical conditions of ideas developed by Comrade Lenin in several texts which *L'Ordine Nuovo* itself published, and of the ideas of the American theoretician of the revolutionary syndicalist organization IWW, the Marxist Daniel De Leon. In one passage, Comrade Tasca gives a purely "commercial" and accounting interpretation to the representation of the economic production complexes expressed by the words "rice", "wood", "sulphur", etc. In another passage, he asks himself how the Councils should be linked to each other. In a third passage, he locates in Proudhon's idea of the factory destroying the government, the source of the idea developed by *L'Ordine Nuovo*[119] – whereas in that very issue of 5 June that published the article "The Factory Council" and the comment on the Congress of the Chamber of Labour, an extract from Marx's text on the Paris Commune was also reproduced, in which Marx explicitly pointed to the *industrial* character of the communist society of producers. It was in this text that both De Leon and Lenin found the fundamental source of inspiration for their ideas. The *L'Ordine Nuovo* articles were prepared and elaborated on the basis of these elements: once again, and particularly in the case of this issue which gave rise to the polemic, Comrade Tasca showed he had read the articles extremely superficially and without any understanding of their historical and intellectual substance.

It is not my wish to repeat, for the benefit of the readers of this polemic, all the arguments already advanced to develop the idea of workers' freedom being realized in practice initially in the Factory Council. All I wanted to do was point to certain fundamental themes to demonstrate how Comrade Tasca has completely failed to grasp the inner process of development of the *L'Ordine Nuovo* programme. In an appendix which will follow these two brief articles, I shall analyse some of the points made by Tasca in his exposition, in so far as it seems opportune to clarify them and demonstrate their inconsistency.[120] One point, however, should be clarified at once. This occurs in Tasca's discussion of finance capital, where he writes that capital "takes off", becomes divorced from production and hovers above it. . . . This whole muddle about paper money (!) taking off and hovering has nothing whatever to do with the elaboration of the theory of the Factory Councils. We emphasized that the *person* of the capitalist had become divorced from the world of production – not capital, whether financial or otherwise. We emphasized that the factory is no longer controlled by the person of the proprietor but by the bank, through an industrial bureaucracy which tends to lose its interest in production in the same way that the State functionary loses his interest in public administration. This served as starting-point for a historical analysis of the new system of hierarchical relations which have become established in the factory, and for locating the emergence of one of the most important historical preconditions of the working class's industrial autonomy, whose factory organization tends to embody in itself the power of initiative over production. This whole "flight" and "hovering" business is a somewhat unfortunate fantasy on the part of Comrade Tasca. While he refers to his recent review of Arturo Labriola's book *Capitalism*, published in *Corriere Universitario*, to show that he is "alive" to the question of finance capital (and it should be noted that Labriola supports precisely the opposite thesis to that maintained by Hilferding, which in turn was adopted by the Bolsheviks), so far as the facts are concerned he shows he has understood nothing at all of the matter and has merely built a pathetic castle out of vague reminiscences and empty words.

The polemic has been useful in showing that the points I raised in connection with the Tasca report were absolutely fundamental. Tasca had a superficial smattering of the problems raised by the Councils, but was consumed by a craving to produce his "own" ideas on them, to initiate an action of his "own", to open a new era in the trade-union movement. The comment on the Congress of the Chamber of Labour, and on Comrade Tasca's intervention designed to influence the voting on a motion of an executive character, was dictated by our determination to keep our review's programme intact. The Factory Councils are subject to their own laws; they cannot and should not accept the legislation of the very trade-union organs it is their immediate aim to renew fundamentally. Similarly, the Factory Councils movement holds that the workers' representatives should be elected directly by the masses and should be bound to them by an authoritative mandate. The intervention of Comrade Tasca at a workers' congress, as rapporteur, without a mandate from anyone, in connection with a problem that concerns the whole of the working masses and whose authoritative resolution would have been binding on the masses, was in such marked contrast to the whole spirit and tenor of *L'Ordine Nuovo* that the comment, and all its bitterness, was perfectly justified and absolutely necessary.

Signed ANTONIO GRAMSCI, *L'Ordine Nuovo*, 14 August 1920, Vol. II, No. 12; and 28 August 1920, Vol. II, No. 14.

VI

Towards the Communist Party

55. THE COLONIAL POPULATIONS

Today, after the historical experience of the Russian revolution and with the increasing number and scale of insurrections taking place among the populations subjected to the colonial régime, we have an opportunity to attach a more or less precise significance and scope to the following Marxist proposition: By emancipating itself, the proletariat will liberate along with itself all other oppressed classes.

The subjugation of the colonial populations was the characteristic feature of the stage of development that the capitalist system had reached before the war. The efforts on the part of the bourgeois States to bring this process of subjugation to completion, the efforts at imperialist expansion were the characteristic feature of the phase in the history of capitalism ushering in the global conflagration, during which the relations of class struggle were turned upside down and the forces thrown up by capitalism acquired the capacity to overthrow their oppressor and liberate themselves.

During the process of its historical development, the industrial bourgeoisie has repeatedly had to find new solutions to the following problems: how to buy raw materials for the factory at low prices; how to enable the working class to feed itself cheaply, in order to keep wages low; how to create a supply situation in which it would be possible to absorb a growing proportion of the rural population in the factories. These problems have been resolved by the industrial bourgeoisie by the use of State power in several new forms, but always on the basis of an ever more implacable subjugation of a growing proportion of the world's population, incorporated as direct colonies, protectorates or spheres of influence in the metropolitan States' systems of domination.

In the European countries, relations between the urban and rural population were turned upside down between 1870 and 1914. In 1871, France was still a predominantly agricultural country and defeat enabled government power to pass from the hands of the middle industrial bourgeoisie to the clerical and reactionary landed nobility. In 1913 the rural population accounted for only 40 per cent of the population of France, and during the war this percentage diminished further. Before the war, the whole of Western Europe was becoming one great industrial workshop: competition for the colonial markets in raw materials and foodstuffs had become endemic and could only end in war.

The hierarchy of capitalist exploitation of the classes subjected to servile labour had been consolidated in the following fashion: the factory worker, by transforming the raw materials plundered from the colonies and living off the foodstuffs produced by the peasant class enslaved to the demands of the cities, creates a profit on capital. The peasant is reduced to a state of permanent hunger, because he has to produce foodstuffs cheaply for the cities and produce rent for the landlord. The colonial population is subjugated to the interests of the mother-country: it has to produce cheap raw materials for industry – in other words, it has to allow the soil and subsoil of its own country to be impoverished for the benefit of European civilization. It has to produce cheap foodstuffs to make up the deficit in agricultural production in the mother-country caused by the drift of the rural masses into the cities, into the direct service of capital. In this way the colonial populations become the foundation on which the whole edifice of capitalist exploitation is erected. These populations are required to donate the whole of their lives to the development of industrial civilization. For this they can expect no benefit in return; indeed, they see their own countries systematically despoiled of their natural resources, i.e. of the necessary conditions for their own autonomous development.

This struggle of capitalism against the requirements of life of the working people all over the world reached its climax during the war; the colonial peasants came to be stripped of their all, to be starved to death to provide the food that would enable the warring European States to resist to the very end. In Russia, these conditions of colonial exploitation took place within the State itself; by conquering political power and emancipating itself, the proletariat liberated the peasant class as well. Thc Russian peasant, who had always suffered from hunger and through his hunger had always enabled Western Europe to feed itself better, at last became his own master and fed himself. This fact on its own represents a death blow to the interests of Western European capitalism, which requires for its own existence and development the hunger of millions and millions of Russian peasants. By overthrowing Tsarism, the Russian proletariat has smashed one of the heaviest chains that held the peoples of Asia Minor and Persia in thrall and shaken the British colonial system to its very foundations. They have called into question the existence of the whole capitalist system. Therefore, the insurrections that are taking place among the peoples subjected to the colonial régime also enable us to determine, with ever greater precision, the actual historical import of these violent predictions concerning the international proletariat struggling to achieve its own emancipation, conscious of its lofty historical mission. The Russian revolution is the first stage in the world-wide defeat of the capitalist economic régime and the parliamentary political régime; the liberating movement of the Russian working people has been the first step in an absolute and thorough-going revolution, a revolution that will radically transform the social face of the whole world.

The uprising of the Moslem world against the European States has brought in its wake the following results: the Senegalese are refusing to fight their religious co-thinkers who have rebelled against France; Indian troops are refusing to fight for the English against the insurgent Moslem populations in Mesopotamia and Persia.[121] The global repercussions of the Russian revolution, that has acted as a positive historical thrust driving all the oppressed and exploited peoples into movement, have made themselves felt in Italy as well, with the Moslem insurrection in Albania. In England there is already a question of having to enlist British military forces to protect the colonies; this fact on its own is giving the rulers of the English State sleepless nights. In Italy, the Albanian events have at once brought about a state of unrest and open conflicts.[122]

The problem of how to continue exploiting the colonial populations to the same extent as hitherto is now forcibly being brought to the attention of the bourgeois States; this is a problem they will be unable to resolve. Western Europe has blockaded Russia and brought down the Russian industrial system, which was linked more closely to England and Germany than to the local national markets. Petrograd no longer rates as a great industrial city and Russian production is slowly starting to build up again upon the basis whence every industrial formation has sprung, in the actual centres of raw materials. But now the colonial uprising is already starting to realize its potential as a blockade of the Western European capitalist States. By freeing themselves of foreign capitalist exploitation, the colonial populations would deprive the European industrial bourgeoisies of raw materials and foodstuffs, and bring down the centres of civilization that have lasted from the fall of the Roman Empire till today.

Capitalism, in the extreme form that is characteristic of its imperialist phase today, has presented the world with two fundamental problems:

1. how to industrialize agriculture on a vast scale; 2. how to extend industrial civilization to the whole world, not in the form of European suppression of the colonies, but in the form of the autonomous development of all populations.

These two problems can be resolved only by the revolutionary proletariat: i.e. by the class that is not burdened by any property or national interests, but stands to benefit by the development of all the world's productive forces in order to expand and secure its freedom once and for all.

Unsigned, *L'Ordine Nuovo*, 26 June 1920, Vol. II, No. 7. Under the heading "The Week in Politics".

56. TWO REVOLUTIONS

Every form of political power can only be historically conceived and justified as the juridical apparatus of a real economic power. It can only be conceived and justified as the defensive organization and condition of d velopment for a given order in the relations of production and distribution of wealth. This fundamental (and elementary) canon of historical materialism sums up the whole complex of theses we have sought to develop in an organic fashion around the problem of the Factory Councils. It sums up the reasons why, in dealing with the real problems of the proletarian class, we have given a central and pre-eminent place to the positive experience which the broad movement of the working-class masses to create, develop and co-ordinate the Councils has generated. We have therefore maintained: 1. that the revolution is not necessarily proletarian and communist simply because it proposes and achieves the overthrow of the political government of the bourgeois State; 2. nor is it proletarian and communist simply because it proposes and achieves the destruction of the representative institutions and administrative machinery through which the central government exercises the political power of the bourgeoisie; 3. it is not proletarian and communist even if the wave of popular insurrection places power in the hands of men who call themselves (and sincerely are) communists. The revolution is proletarian and communist only to the extent that it is a liberation of the proletarian and communist forces of production that were developing within the very heart of the society dominated by the capitalist class. It is proletarian and communist in so far as it advances and promotes the expansion and systematization of proletarian and communist forces that are capable of beginning the patient and methodical work needed to build a new order in the relations of production and distribution: a new order in which a class-divided society will become an impossibility and whose systematic development will therefore eventually coincide with the withering away of State power, i.e. with the systematic dissolution of the political organization that defends the proletarian class, while the latter itself dissolves as a class to become mankind.

* * * * *

The revolution that destroys the bourgeois State apparatus and constructs a new State apparatus, concerns and involves all the classes oppressed by capitalism. Its immediate cause is the brute fact that, in the conditions of famine left by the imperialist war, the great majority of the population (made up of artisans, small land-holders, petty-bourgeois intellectuals, impoverished peasant masses and also backward proletarian masses) no longer has any guarantee of being supplied with the basic requirements of everyday life. This revolution tends to have a predominantly anarchic and destructive character. It manifests itself as a blind explosion of rage, a tremendous release of fury without any concrete objective, and takes shape in a new State power only to the extent that fatigue, disillusionment and hunger finally force recognition of the necessity for a constituted order and a power to enforce respect for that order.

This revolution may consolidate itself simply in a constituent assembly that seeks to heal the wounds inflicted on the bourgeois State apparatus by the people's anger. It may go as far as Soviets – the autonomous political organization of the proletariat and the other oppressed classes – and yet these may not dare go beyond the stage of organization to tamper with economic relations, and so will be thrown back by the reaction of the propertied classes. It may go as far as the complete destruction of the bourgeois State machine and the establishment of a state of permanent disorder, in which the existing wealth and population simply dissolve and disappear, shattered by the impossibility of achieving any autonomous organization. It may go as far as the establishment of a proletarian and communist power that exhausts itself in repeated and desperate attempts to create by fiat the economic conditions it needs to survive and grow stronger, until it is finally overthrown by capitalist reaction.

We have seen all these historical developments in Germany, Austria, Bavaria, the Ukraine and Hungary. The revolution as a destructive act has not been followed by the revolution as a process of reconstructing society on the communist model. The presence of these external conditions – a communist party, the destruction of the bourgeois State, powerful trade-union organizations and an armed proletariat – was not sufficient to compensate for the absence of another condition: the existence of productive forces tending towards development and growth, a conscious movement on the part of the proletarian masses to substantiate their political power with economic power, and a determination on the part of these proletarian masses to introduce proletarian order into the factory, to make the factory the basic unit of the new State, to build the new State as an expression of the industrial relations of the factory system.

* * * * *

This is why we have always maintained that the duty of the communist nuclei which exist in the Party is not to magnify particular points out of all proportion (for example, the problems of electoral abstentionism or the constitution of a "truly" communist Party) but to work to create the mass conditions in which all particular problems can be resolved as problems of the organic development of the communist revolution. In fact, is it possible for a communist party to exist (as a party of action, not an academy of doctrinaires and politicians who think and express themselves "well" where communism is concerned) if there does not exist among the masses that spirit of historical initiative and aspiration towards industrial autonomy that should be reflected and synthesized in the communist party? And since the formation of parties and the rise of real historical forces of which parties are the reflection are events that do not occur at a stroke, out of nothing, but occur in accordance with a dialectical process, should not the major task of the communist forces be precisely that of importing consciousness and organization into the productive forces – communist in essence – which will have to develop and, by their growth, create the secure and lasting economic base of the proletariat's hold on political power?

Similarly, can the Party abstain from participation in electoral struggles to fill the representative institutions of bourgeois democracy, when it has the task of politically organizing all the oppressed classes around the communist proletariat? To achieve this, will it not have to become the "governing" party representing these classes in a democratic sense, given that only for the communist proletariat can it be a party in the revolutionary sense?

In so far as it becomes the trusted "democratic" party of all the oppressed classes, and keeps in permanent contact with all sections of the working people, the communist party induces all these sections to acknowledge the communist proletariat as the ruling class that must replace the capitalist class in State power. It creates the conditions in which the revolution as destruction of the bourgeois State can be identified with the proletarian revolution, the revolution that expropriates the expropriators, and must begin the development of a new order in the relations of production and distribution.

Hence, in so far as it projects itself as the specific party of the industrial proletariat, and works to equip the productive forces thrown up by the development of capitalism with a consciousness and precise line, the communist party creates the economic conditions for the communist proletariat's hold on State power. It creates the conditions in which the proletarian revolution can be identified with the popular revolt against the bourgeois state, the conditions in which this revolt becomes an act of liberation on the part of the real productive forces who had been building up within capitalist society.

These various sequences of historical events are not separate and independent; they are moments of a single dialectical process of development in the course of which relations of cause and effect interweave, reverse and interact. But the experience of revolutions has shown that, since Russia, all other two-stage revolutions have failed and the failure of the second revolution has plunged the working classes into a state of prostration and demoralization. This has allowed the bourgeois class to reorganize in strength and begin the systematic extermination of the communist vanguards trying to regroup.

For those communists who are not content to monotonously chew the cud of the basic elements of communism and historical materialism, but live in the reality of the struggle and grasp that reality, as it is, from the viewpoint of historical materialism and communism, the revolution as the conquest of social power on the part of the proletariat can only be conceived as a dialectical process, in which political power makes possible industrial power and vice versa. The Soviet is the instrument of revolutionary struggle that provides for the autonomous development of the communist economic organization from a system of Factory Councils to a Central Economic Council. It settles the plans for production and distribution, and thus succeeds in making capitalist competition redundant. The Factory Council, as an expression of the autonomy of the producer in the industrial sphere and as the basis of communist economic organization, is the instrument for the final struggle to the death with the capitalist order, in that it creates the conditions in which class-divided society is eliminated and any new class division is made "physically" impossible.

But for communists alive to the struggle, this conception will not remain an abstract thought; it will spur them into struggle, into making a greater organizational and propaganda effort. Industrial development has brought about a certain degree of intellectual autonomy and a certain spirit of positive historical initiative among the masses. These elements of the proletarian revolution must be given a form and organization; the psychological conditions for their development and their generalization throughout the whole of the working masses must be created through the struggle for control of production.

We must strive to promote the organic creation of a communist party that is not a collection of dogmatists or little Machiavellis, but a party of revolutionary communist action; a party with a precise consciousness of the historical mission of the proletariat and the ability to guide the proletariat to the accomplishment of that mission – in other words, a party of the masses who, through their own efforts, are striving to liberate themselves autonomously from political and industrial servitude through the organization of the social economy, and not a party which makes use of the masses for its own heroic attempts to imitate the French Jacobins. In so far as it can shape reality, the Party must create conditions in which there will not be two revolutions, but in which the popular revolt against the bourgeois State will find organized forces capable of beginning the transformation of the national productive apparatus from an instrument of plutocratic oppression to an instrument of communist liberation.

Unsigned, *L'Ordine Nuovo*, 3 July 1920, Vol. II, No. 8.

57. THE TURIN FACTORY COUNCILS MOVEMENT

(A report despatched in July 1920 to the Executive Committee of the Communist International)

One of the members of the Italian delegation that has just returned from Soviet Russia reported to the workers of Turin that the platform set up to welcome the delegates at Kronstadt bore the following inscription: "Long live the April 1920 general strike in Turin". It was with great pleasure and satisfaction that the workers greeted this piece of news. The majority of the members of the Italian delegation to Russia had been opposed to the April general strike. In their articles against the strike, they maintained that the Turin workers had been suffering under an illusion and had over-estimated the importance of the strike. So the Turin workers were very pleased to hear of the sympathetic action of the Kronstadt comrades, and they said to themselves: "Our Russian Communist comrades have a better understanding and estimation of the importance of the April strike than the Italian opportunists, and in this way have taught them a good lesson."

The April Strike

The April movement in Turin was in fact a glorious chapter in the history, not only of the Italian, but of the European proletariat – and even, one might claim, in the history of the world-wide proletariat. In fact, this was the first time in history that a proletariat engaged in struggle for control over production, without being driven into action through the privations and sacrifices involved, carried the struggle through to its conclusion. The metal-workers struck for one month; the other categories of workers struck for ten days. In its last ten days, the general strike encompassed the whole of Piedmont, mobilizing about half a million industrial and agricultural workers; this means that it involved about four million of the population.

The Italian capitalists exerted every effort to stifle the Turin workers' movement. All the means of the bourgeois State were placed at their disposal, while the workers had to fight on their own, without any assistance whatsoever either from the leadership of the Socialist Party or from the General Confederation of Labour. Indeed, the leaders of the Party and the Confederation spurned the Turin workers, and did all in their power to prevent the workers and peasants of Italy from taking any revolutionary action that might have enabled them to demonstrate their solidarity with their Turin brothers and give them some effective assistance. But the Turin workers did not lose heart. They bore the whole brunt of the capitalist reaction, but observed discipline right up to the very last moment. And even after the defeat, they remained faithful to the banner of communism and world revolution.

Anarchists and Syndicalists

The propaganda issued by the anarchists and syndicalists against Party discipline and the dictatorship of the proletariat had no influence over the masses, even after the betrayal of the leaders caused the strike to end in a defeat. In fact the Turin workers swore to step up their revolutionary struggle and to wage it on two fronts: on the one hand against the victorious bourgeoisie, and on the other against their own treacherous leaders. The revolutionary consciousness and discipline which the Turin masses demonstrated have their historical roots in the economic and political conditions in which the class struggle developed in Turin.

This city is a purely industrial centre. Nearly three quarters of the population, which numbers half a million inhabitants, is made up of workers – petty-bourgeois elements are insignificant in number. Furthermore, there is a solid mass of clerks and technicians in Turin, all of whom are organized in unions and affiliated to the Chamber of Labour. During all the major strikes they stood by the workers, with the result that, if not all of them, then at least a majority have acquired the mentality of a true proletarian, struggling against capital to achieve the revolution and communism.

Industrial Production

Viewed from outside, the process of production in Turin is perfectly centralized and homogeneous. The engineering industry, which employs about 50,000 shop-floor workers and 10,000 clerks and technicians, is the most important. The FIAT plants alone employ 35,000 workers, clerks and technicians; in this firm's principal plants, 16,000 workers are employed producing motor vehicles of every kind, using the most modern and advanced techniques. The production of motor vehicles is the characteristic feature of the Turin engineering industry. The greater part of the work-force is made up of skilled workers and technicians; these do not, however, share the petty-bourgeois mentality of skilled workers of some other countries – for example, England. Motor vehicle production, which is the dominant feature of the engineering industry, has subordinated other branches of production to itself: for example, the wood-working and rubber industries. The metal-workers form the vanguard of the Turin proletariat. Given the characteristics of this industry, every time the metal-workers take action they spark off a general mass movement that takes on political and revolutionary overtones, even if it began in the pursuit of merely trade-union objectives.

Turin possesses a single important trade-union organization, the Chamber of Labour, which has 90,000 workers affiliated to it. The existing anarchist and syndicalist groups have virtually no influence whatsoever over the mass of workers, who opt firmly and decisively for the Socialist Party section, which in turn is made up for the most part of communist workers. The communist movement has the following battle organizations at its command: the Party section with 1,500 members, 28 clubs with 10,000 members and 23 youth organizations with 2,000 members. There is a permanent and autonomous communist grouping within every one of these organizations. The individual groupings are combined, by area, into ward groupings, which in turn are represented in a steering committee within the Party section. This committee concentrates the whole of the city's communist movement in its hands, as well as the leadership of the mass of the workers.

Turin, the Capital of Italy

Before the bourgeois revolution which created the present order in Italy, Turin was the capital of a small state, comprising Piedmont, Liguria and Sardinia. At that time, commerce and light industry predominated in the city. After the unification of the Kingdom of Italy and the transfer of the capital to Rome, it seemed that Turin stood in danger of losing its importance. But the city soon recovered from its economic crisis and became one of the most important industrial centres in Italy. One can say that Italy now has three capitals: Rome, as administrative centre for the bourgeois State; Milan, as the country's commercial and financial centre (all the banks, commercial offices and finance houses are concentrated in Milan); and finally Turin, as industrial centre. It is in Turin that industrial production has attained its maximum level of development. When the capital was transferred to Rome, the whole of the intellectual petty and middle bourgeoisie emigrated from Turin and furnished the new bourgeois State with the administrative personnel it needed to function. On the other hand, the development of heavy industry in Turin attracted the cream of the Italian working class to that city. The process of development of Turin as a city, both from the point of view of Italian history and from that of the Italian proletarian revolution, is fascinating.

This was how the Turin proletariat came to assume the spiritual leadership of the Italian working masses, who are bound to the city by family ties, ties of history and tradition, as well as intellectual bonds (it is the ideal of every Italian worker to be able to work in Turin). All this explains why the working masses from one end of Italy to the other wanted to demonstrate their solidarity with the general strike in Turin, even at the cost of going against the will of their leaders. They view this city as the centre, as the capital of the communist revolution – the Petrograd of the proletarian revolution in Italy.

Two Armed Insurrections

During the 1914–18 Imperialist War, Turin witnessed two armed insurrections. The first, which broke out in May 1915, had as its aim the prevention of Italy's intervention in the war against Germany (on this occasion the *Casa del Popolo* was sacked). The second, in August 1917, took on the character of a large-scale revolutionary struggle.

The news of the March revolution in Russia was greeted in Turin with indescribable joy. The workers wept with emotion when they heard that the Tsar's régime had been overthrown by the workers of Petrograd. But the Turin workers did not allow themselves to be taken in by the demagogic rhetoric of Kerensky and the Mensheviks. When the mission sent to Western Europe by the Petrograd Soviet arrived in Turin in July 1917, the delegates Smirnov and Goldenberg, who appeared before a crowd of 50,000 workers, were greeted by deafening shouts of "Long live Lenin! Long live the Bolsheviks!" Goldenberg was none too pleased with this reception – he could not fathom how Comrade Lenin had acquired such popularity amongst the workers of Turin. Nor should it be forgotten that this episode occurred after the suppression of the Bolshevik revolt in July, and at a time when the bourgeois press in

Italy was raging against Lenin and the Bolsheviks, denouncing them as bandits, intriguers, agents and spies of German Imperialism. From the date of Italy's entry into the war (24 May 1915), the Turin proletariat had held no mass demonstration.

Barricades, Trenches, Barbed-Wire Entanglements

The impressive gathering that had been organized in honour of the delegates from the Petrograd Soviet signalled the beginning of a new wave of mass movements. Not a month had passed before the workers of Turin rose in arms against Italian Imperialism and militarism. The insurrection broke out on 23 August 1917. For five days the workers fought in the streets of the city. With rifles, grenades and machine-guns at their disposal, the insurgents even managed to occupy several quarters of the city and to make three or four attempts to gain control of the centre, where the government institutions and military command posts were situated.

But two years of war and reaction had weakened the formerly powerful organization of the proletariat, and the workers, with their inferior supply of arms, were defeated. In vain they counted on support from the soldiers – but these latter had allowed themselves to be taken in by insinuations that the revolt had been staged by the Germans. The people erected barricades, dug trenches, and surrounded some of the districts with electrified barbed-wire entanglements. For five days they repulsed all attacks from the troops and police. Over 500 workers were killed and a further 2,000 seriously injured. After this defeat, the best elements were arrested and sent away, and the proletarian movement lost its revolutionary drive. Nevertheless, the communist sympathies of the Turin proletariat were not extinguished.

Evidence of this can be found in the following episode. A short time after the August insurrection, elections were held for the Administrative Council of the Turin Co-operative Alliance (TCA), a vast organization that supplies the basic needs for a quarter of the people of Turin.

The Co-operative Alliance

The TCA is made up of the Railwaymen's Co-operative and the General Association of Workers. For many years the Socialist section in the city had controlled the Administrative Council, but now it no longer had the capacity to carry out any effective agitation amongst the working masses. The capital of the Alliance was made up for the most part of shares in the Railwaymen's Co-operative owned by the railwaymen and their families. The growth registered by the Alliance had increased the value of the shares from 50 to 700 Lire. Nevertheless, the Party succeeded in persuading the shareholders that the aim of a workers' co-operative is not to secure a profit for its individual members, but to strengthen the means of revolutionary struggle; so the shareholders contented themselves with a dividend of $3\frac{1}{2}$ per cent on the nominal value of 50 Lire rather than on the real value of 700 Lire. After the August insurrection, a committee of railwaymen was formed, with the support of the police and the bourgeois and reformist press, to put an end to Socialist Party control of the Administrative Council. Shareholders were promised immediate liquidation of the 650 Lire difference between the nominal and current value of every share. Railwaymen were promised especially favourable treatment in the supply of foodstuffs. The reformist traitors and the bourgeois press wheeled out every means of propaganda and agitation in order to transform the Co-operative from a workers' organization into a commercial business run along petty-bourgeois lines. The working class was exposed to all manner of persecutions. Censorship drowned the voice of the Socialist section. And yet, in spite of all these persecutions and brutalities, the Socialists – who had never at any time abandoned their point of view concerning the workers' Co-operative – i.e. that it was a weapon to be used in the class struggle – obtained a majority once again within the Co-operative Alliance. The Socialist Party received 700 out of 800 votes, despite the fact that most of the electors were white-collar railway workers and might have been expected, after the defeat of the August insurrection, to have wavered in their loyalties and even to have shown reactionary tendencies.

The Post-War Period

After the close of the Imperialist War, the proletarian movement made rapid advances. The working masses of Turin were well aware that the historical period opened up by the war was profoundly different from the pre-war epoch. The Turin working class was quick to perceive the nature of the IIIrd International as a body of the world proletariat, with the role of directing the civil war, seizing political power, setting up the proletarian dictatorship and establishing a new order in economic and social relations.

In all the workers' Assemblies, it was the economic and political problems of the revolution that formed the subject of discussion. The best elements in the working-class vanguard combined to produce a weekly newspaper of communist tendency, *L'Ordine Nuovo*. The columns of this weekly were devoted to discussion of the various problems of the revolution: what sort of revolutionary organization was needed by the masses who had to win the unions for the communist cause; how to shift trade-union struggle out of its narrowly reformist and corporatist framework up to the level of revolutionary struggle, control over production and proletarian dictatorship. The question of Factory Councils too was placed on the agenda.

Small committees of workers were already in existence inside the Turin factories: they were recognized by the capitalists and some of them had already launched a campaign against the bureaucratism, reformist spirit and constitutional tendencies of the unions. But for the most part these committees were nothing more than creatures of the unions. The lists of candidates for the committees (the Internal Commissions) were drawn up by the trade-union hierarchies, who showed a preference for workers of opportunist tendency; workers who would give no trouble to the bosses and would stifle any mass action before it could start. What the followers of *L'Ordine Nuovo* emphasized most in their propaganda was the transformation of the Internal Commissions. They stressed that the lists of candidates should be drawn up by the working masses themselves and not by the upper echelons of the trade-union bureaucracy. The tasks they assigned to the Factory Councils were control over production, the arming and military preparation of the masses, and their political and technical preparation. They were no longer to play their former role of watchdogs protecting the interests of the dominant class, or to hold back the masses in their actions against the capitalist order.

Enthusiastic support for the Councils

Propaganda in support of the Factory Councils was enthusiastically received by the masses. Within six months, Factory Councils had been set up in all the engineering factories and workshops, and communists had won a majority in the metalworkers' union. The principle of Factory Councils and control over production was approved and accepted by the majority of delegates at congress, and by most of the unions belonging to the Chamber of Labour.

The organization of the Factory Councils is based on the following principles: every single factory and workshop establishes its own organism, on a representative basis (and not on a bureaucratic basis, as in the previous system). This organism translates the proletariat's strength into reality; it struggles against the capitalist order, or exercises control over production, by educating the whole of the working masses for revolutionary struggle and the creation of a workers' State. The Factory Council has to be formed in accordance with the principle of organization by industry.[123] In the eyes of the working class, it must represent a model of communist society, which will be attained via the dictatorship of the proletariat. In this society, class divisions will be a thing of the past: all social relations will be regulated in accordance with the technical requirements of production and its corresponding organization, and will not be subordinate to an organized State power. It is vital that the working class should see the full beauty and nobility of the ideal for which it is struggling and making so many sacrifices. It must realize that to attain this ideal, several stages must first be passed through. It must recognize the necessity for revolutionary discipline and dictatorship.

Every factory is subdivided into workshops and every workshop into crews with different skills; every crew carries out a particular part of the work-process. The workers in each crew elect one of their number as delegate, giving him an authoritative and revocable mandate. The assembly of delegates from the entire factory makes up a Council, and this Council elects an executive committee from its own ranks. The assembly of political secretaries of the various executive committees forms in turn a central committee of the Councils, and this central committee elects from its own number an education committee for the whole city, with the task of organizing propaganda, drawing up work plans, approving projects and proposals from individual factories and even individual workers, and finally giving general leadership to the whole movement.

The Councils and Internal Commissions during Strikes

Some of the functions of the Factory Council have a purely technical and even industrial character: for example, control over technical personnel, dismissal of employees who show themselves to be enemies of the working class, the struggle with management to win rights and freedoms and control over the factory's production and financial operations.

The Factory Councils soon took root. The masses greeted this form of communist organization with enthusiasm; they aligned themselves with the executive committees and energetically supported the struggle against capitalist autocracy. Despite the fact that neither the industrialists nor the trade-union bureaucracy were willing to recognize the Councils and committees, they nevertheless obtained some notable successes: they threw out the capitalists' agents and spies; they forged links with the office workers and technicians to get hold of financial and industrial information. In the affairs of the factory, they concentrated disciplinary power in their own hands and showed the disunited and fragmented masses what direct control by workers in industry means.

The activity of the Councils and Internal Commissions was demonstrated most clearly during strikes. Strikes lost their impulsive, fortuitous character and became an expression of the conscious activity of the revolutionary masses. The technical organization and capacity for action of the Councils and Internal Commissions was perfected to such a degree that it was possible within five minutes to get 16,000 workers scattered throughout 42 departments at FIAT to down tools. On 3 December 1919 the Factory Councils provided tangible evidence of their capacity to lead mass movements on a grand scale.[124] Acting on orders from the Socialist section, which held control over the whole of the mass movement in its hands, and without any preparation whatsoever, the Factory Councils were able to mobilize 120,000 workers, called out factory by factory, in the course of just one hour. This armed proletariat was launched like an avalanche into the city centre and soon cleared the streets and squares of all the nationalist and militarist riff-raff.

The Struggle against the Councils

At the head of the movement to form Factory Councils were the communists belonging to the Socialist section and the trade-union organizations. Anarchists took part as well, seeking to counterpose their pompous rhetoric to the clear and precise language of the Marxist communists. However, the movement encountered determined resistance from the trade-union officials and from the leadership of the Socialist Party and *Avanti!*. These people based their polemical assertions on the difference between the concept of a Factory Council and a Soviet. Their conclusions were of a purely theoretical, abstract and bureaucratic character. Behind their high-flown phrases was concealed their desire to prevent the masses from participating directly in the revolutionary struggle; their desire to maintain the unions' hold over the masses. The members of the Party leadership repeatedly refused to take the initiative in launching revolutionary activity, prior to the drawing-up of a co-ordinated plan of action – but they never made the slightest effort to prepare and elaborate this plan.

So the movement did not succeed in establishing itself outside Turin, for the whole machinery of the trade unions was set in motion to prevent the working masses in other parts of Italy from following the Turin lead. The Turin movement was derided, jeered at, insulted and criticized in every possible manner. The bitter criticisms of the union organizations and the Socialist Party leadership provided the capitalists with fresh encouragement and gave them a free rein in their struggle against the Turin proletariat and the Factory Councils. The meeting of industrialists that was held in Milan in March 1920 drew up a plan of attack. But the "guardians of the working class", its economic and political organizations, ignored these activities. Abandoned on all sides, the Turin proletariat was forced to confront the nation's capitalists and the power of the State entirely on its own, with its own resources. Turin was invaded by an army of police; around the city, cannon and machine-guns were placed at strategic points. And when all this military apparatus was ready, the capitalists set about provoking the proletariat. It is true that in face of these extremely adverse battle conditions, the proletariat hesitated in taking up the challenge. But when it was seen that a clash was inevitable, the working class came out boldly from its reserve positions, determined to carry the struggle through to a victorious conclusion.

National Socialist Council in Milan

The metalworkers struck for a whole month and the other categories of workers for ten days. Industry was at a standstill all over the province and communications paralysed. But the Turin proletariat was isolated from the rest of Italy. The central organs did nothing to assist it: they did not even publish a single manifesto to explain the importance of the Turin workers' struggle to the Italian people. *Avanti!* refused to publish the manifesto of the Party's Turin section. The Turin comrades had the labels "anarchist" and "adventurist" hurled at them from all sides. At that time the Party's National Council was due to be held in Turin; however, its venue was transferred to Milan, for a city "in the grip of a general strike" was not thought to be a suitable theatre for socialist discussion.

On this occasion, the bankruptcy of the men who were supposed to be leading the Party was displayed to its full extent. While in the city of Turin the workers were courageously defending the Factory Councils – the first organizations to be based on workers' democracy and embodying proletarian power – in Milan the leaders were chatting about theoretical projects and methods for creating Councils as a form of political power to be won by the proletariat. There were discussions on how to systematize conquests not yet won, while the Turin proletariat was abandoned to its fate and the bourgeoisie given the opportunity of destroying whatever power the workers had already won. The Italian proletarian masses demonstrated their solidarity with the Turin comrades in various ways: the railwaymen of Pisa, Livorno and Florence refused to transport troops bound for Turin, and the dock-workers and sailors of Livorno and Genoa sabotaged transport of materials through the ports. In many cities, the proletariat came out on strike in defiance of their union's orders.

The Turin and Piedmont general strike clashed head-on with the sabotage and resistance of the trade-union organizations and even the Party itself. Nevertheless, it had great educational significance, in that it demonstrated that a union between workers and peasants is possible in practice. Moreover, it highlighted the urgent need to combat the whole bureaucratic mechanism of the trade-union organs, which form the most solid bulwark for the opportunist activities of the parliamentarists and reformists who aim to stifle every revolutionary initiative on the part of the working masses.

Published for the first time in Russian, German and French in *Communist International*, 1920, No. 14. Republished in Italian, unsigned, in the daily edition of *L'Ordine Nuovo*, 14 March 1921, Vol. I, No. 73.

58. EDITORIAL: 21 AUGUST 1920

In his letter published elsewhere in this issue, Comrade D. R. alludes to the thesis in which Comrade Lenin expresses his solidarity with the Turin movement and with *L'Ordine Nuovo*.[125] Here is what Comrade Lenin says: "Concerning the Socialist Party of Italy, the Second Congress of the Third International considers that the criticism of that party and practical proposals submitted to the National Council of the Socialist Party of Italy in the name of the party's Turin section, as set forth in *L'Ordine Nuovo* of 8 May 1920, are in the main correct and are fully in keeping with the fundamental principles of the Third International. Accordingly, the Second Congress of the Third International requests the Socialist Party of Italy to convene a special congress to discuss these proposals and also all the decisions of the two Congresses of the Communist International for the purpose of rectifying the party's line and of purging it, particularly its parliamentary group, of non-Communist elements."[126]

The report which the Turin Socialist section had prepared for the April meeting of the National Council, planned to take place in Turin and moved to Milan at the last moment, is only known to the readers of *L'Ordine Nuovo* and the handful of readers of the pamphlet *Towards a Renewal of the Socialist Party*: the central, responsible bodies of the party have never taken any account of it. By contrast, it has been read in Moscow by the comrades of the Executive Committee of the Third International; it is this report which has served as a basis for the judgment reached on the Italian Socialist Party, and which has been chosen as a useful basis for discussion at an extraordinary congress. This report had been drawn up during the first days of the Turin Metalworkers' strike, at a moment when nobody as yet envisaged a general strike, even if only as a simple possibility. It reflected the sense of anxiety and perturbation which in that period was tormenting the executive committee of the section, which had tried everything to draw the party's attention to what was taking place but without success, and which hoped for more understanding and a keener intuition of the imperatives of the Italian proletarian movement on the part of the National Council. The report is unfortunately still relevant today.

Events then unfolded in accordance with the wishes of the capitalists, and the Turin working class was defeated. The efforts of the Turin section to make the party assume the leadership of the movement were in vain. The section was accused of breaking discipline, of light-mindedness . . . of anarchism. All discussion was systematically avoided. To have discussed this report at the National Council – a report which had been written and brought to the party's attention before the metalworkers' strike became the Piedmont general strike, in other words at a time when an energetic intervention by the central organs was still possible and could have been decisive – would have meant going back on the judgments which had been proclaimed and on the accusations which had been made; it would have amounted to "losing face" in the eyes of the masses.

All that is past. Today, those events seem far away. It even appears that certain of those who raged most against the "Turinese" have now entirely changed their minds! And yet, because of the memory we retain of the dramatic days we lived through last April, it gave us pleasure – as it will no doubt give pleasure to all the comrades of the section and to the mass of workers – to learn that the judgment of the Executive Committee of the Third International is very different from the one, apparently without appeal, pronounced by the most eminent representatives of the Italian party. To learn that it is precisely the opinion of the "four wild men" from Turin which has received the approval of the highest authority in the international workers' movement.

Unsigned, *L'Ordine Nuovo*, 21 August 1920, Vol. II, No. 13.

59. WHAT DO WE MEAN BY DEMAGOGY?

In the 19 August issue of *Umanità Nova*, comrades Ferrero and Garino complain bitterly about a reference to the "notorious demagogic phrasemongering of the anarchists and syndicalists", in the declaration our group published in connection with the elections to the executive committee of the Turin Socialist section. Garino and Ferrero lost their patience when they read this reference: they ask us how we can collaborate with *demagogues* on projects of undoubted importance like the Factory Councils. They reproach us with not having taken due account of the fact that such demagogues have done more loyal work in support of proletarian unity than was perhaps expected (and at this point comrades Garino and Ferrero interpose a parenthetic lament that their work was "only too loyal!", and we in turn ask if there can ever be "too much" loyalty). Finally, they ask us to clarify these ambiguous terms and make them more precise. Now any such clarification must hinge on our "dictatorial" leanings. We are profoundly convinced that the working class will achieve its liberation only by passing through a period of "dictatorship", a period of restrictions, a period characterized as a workers' State.

The war has plunged society into such a state of barbarity and demoralization, heaped so many ruins upon ruins and let loose such a flood of meanness and cowardice, that only a youthful and energetic class, a class that is rich in the spirit of discipline and sacrifice, like the working class, will be able to restore order. Only through its example and through its ability to command, by holding State power firmly in its own hands, will it be able to give back to the apparatus of production and exchange the capacity to feed, clothe and house our people. Anyone – who wishes to pose as a political leader of the working class – who argues under such conditions and in the face of such a spectacle, that a workers' State is not a necessity; any one who affects to believe or spreads abroad the conviction that "individual or group initiative" is enough, that "the people" will manage on their own, that the choice is not between a dictatorship of the bourgeoisie (as in Hungary) and a dictatorship of the proletariat, but simply between dictatorship and freedom – in our view, such a person corresponds, on the political level, to the charlatan who offers a potion of barley water to someone afflicted with typhus. The anarchists saddle the Marxist communists with the label "dictatorial", which is meant to make them a laughing-stock. So why should Marxist communists not call the anarchists demagogues? Perhaps because the anarchists (or at least some of them or even many of them) are in good faith? To the class, it matters little whether a defeat is due to good or bad faith. What matters is not being defeated. What matters is achieving liberation, and so being able to do away with classes – and hence the State – once and for all. Peasants believe that plague is due to an evil "powder", and have recourse to exorcism or killing the "plague-spreader":[127] the charlatan prescribes barley water for typhus. On the political level, the Marxist communists are seeking to organize effective remedies against the plague and typhus of capitalism. Anyone who opposes their "sanitary" propaganda is asking to be called a charlatan or a peasant who believes in evil "powders".

This is our point of view on the anarchist movement in general: this must underpin our judgment on anarchists as propagandists and as politicians. In terms of individuals, the question is different. Individually, Garino and Ferrero are two workers, two fine workers in professional terms, two sincere and loyal militants for the working-class cause. In our view it matters little that they are anarchists, so long as their activity is real and concrete. In the creation of history, all workers are "libertarians". The Bolshevik method is "libertarian". The Russian workers are advancing along the road to communism on a "libertarian" basis. The "Communist Saturday" is a libertarian, spontaneous product of the revolutionary spirit, and as such comrade Lenin exalted it.[128] The Factory Councils in Turin were a "libertarian" creation by the working class; they obey their own inner laws of development and, in so far as they respond to a vital need of the proletariat, in so far as they represent the historical expression of forces and desires existing in the factory working class, they are vital and alive. Marxist communists do not believe in historical creation through administrative or legislative means. The workers' State is the Committee of Public Safety of the proletarian revolution. For the working class, it represents the guarantee that they will be able to work towards the construction of their city. What is the difference between an anarchist and a Marxist communist? The anarchist is like someone who before speaking . . . looks at his tongue. He bases his political programme on freedom, which exists only in so far as it cannot be reduced to a programme. In other words, he confuses freedom with chance, and so in ideological terms is no different from the Christian or bourgeois liberal. The Marxist communist is a historical materialist: for him, freedom signifies the organization of the conditions under which freedom might be achieved. For the working class, therefore, it signifies: 1. organizing the conditions under which the bourgeois class would be incapable of sabotaging the creative labours of the proletariat and would lose all hope of regaining power – this amounts to constructing a proletarian State; 2. organizing the whole of national and international industry on the model of heavy industry, i.e. universalizing the way of life of the proletarian – who can be a "property-owner" only in so far as everyone is a "property-owner", in so far as property is owned in common and the relations between individuals are industrial, productive relations and not political, class relations. Before being anarchists, Garino and Ferrero are proletarians and factory workers, who *sense* within themselves that things must be as we say and cannot be otherwise. Then they are sincere and loyal – why should we not collaborate with them? We hope and trust that the "determinism" of history, at a given moment, will penetrate the veneer of their political "demagogy" and lead them (spontaneously, in a libertarian fashion, as a result of inner conviction) to support the workers' State with loyalty and sincerity.

"The Communist Education Group of the Turin Socialist Section", *Avanti!*, Piedmont edition, 29 August 1920, Vol. XXIV, No. 217.

60. THE OCCUPATION

In Milan, Rome, Naples, Florence, Turin and many other centres, the factories in the metalworking industry have been occupied by their workers, without much resistance from the owners or the bourgeois State.[129] The trade-union struggle for the new collective contract is proceeding normally, but the basis for it has totally changed: what had hitherto been merely a duel fought through speeches and newspaper articles, between the leaders of the workers' Federation and the leaders of the employers' organization, has today become an action of the broad masses, whose possibilities for initiative are widening and who must govern themselves. The material fact of the occupation of the factories, this act of authority by the working class which violates the sacred principle of private property and destroys the traditional schemas of the social hierarchies, is in itself the origin and cause of new feelings, new passions, both in the consciousness of individuals and in the collective consciousness of the masses. Never have the most advanced worker elements needed cooler heads than at this moment. It is necessary for them to give their comrades a precise understanding of what is taking place, without demagogy; to convince them all of the immense responsibility which rests upon each one of them. It is necessary for them to make every worker aware that he has become a soldier; that he has his orders; that he must be solidly inserted in the proletarian ranks, and that any defection, any weakness, any impulsive gesture must be considered as open treachery and a counter-revolutionary act.

The relative facility with which the occupation of the factories has been carried out should give the workers considerable pause for thought: they must have no illusions on this score. Communists have always praised the seizure of factories by the workers employed in them, but this praise relates not so much to the material fact as to its historic significance. If the working class tends irresistibly to destroy the principle of capitalist ownership, this means that the theses of the Communist International on the characteristics of the present historical period are not simple ideological abstractions, but the precise impression of actual reality: this is the reason why communists have praised and do praise such acts. They demonstrate the inner logic of events, the incapacity of the capitalist order to satisfy the needs of the broad popular masses; they show how powerful and determined the working class has become; they prefigure the imminent transformation of social and historical values. But the pure and simple occupation of the factories by the working class, though it *indicates* the extent of the proletariat's power, does not in or of itself produce any new, definitive position. Power remains in the hands of capital; armed force remains the property of the bourgeois State; public administration, the distribution of basic necessities, the agencies disposing of credit, the still intact commercial apparatus all remain under the control of the bourgeois class. The proletariat has no coercive means to break the sabotage of the technicians and white-collar workers, it cannot secure its own supplies of raw materials, it cannot sell the objects it produces. The occupation of the factories in and of itself – without the proletariat possessing its own armed force, having the means to ration basic necessities according to its own class interests, or having the means to punish physically sabotage by specialists and bureaucrats – cannot be seen as an experience of communist society.

As for the reasons why the occupation of the factories was relatively easy: 1. The metalworkers are the vanguard of the Italian proletariat. The metalworkers' movement is national in scope. If the bourgeois State had attempted to oppose the normal development of the method of struggle adopted by the Federation with armed force, it would have had against it the entire industrial and agricultural proletariat of the nation. The State judged a violent solution inopportune. It preferred the principle of ownership to be trampled upon, *it allowed its own territory to be invaded by the enemy army, while preserving its own army intact, still at full strength.* This tactic adopted by the government, even though in and of itself it constitutes a concrete proof of the State's weakness, cannot be reduced simply to weakness and incapacity. The bourgeois have the deepest contempt for the working class. They deem it incapable of creating anything whatsoever. They see it as a mass of poor devils who are morally and intellectually inferior: a collection of brutes who only worry about filling their bellies, making love and sleeping off their drunken excesses in the most profound torpor. The bourgeois only have admiration and fear for the physical strength of the worker masses, whom they regard as the horse which God the Father has conveniently created for the use of the bourgeois rider. The members of the government have judged it necessary to slacken the reins on the neck of the proletarian horse and let it run freely – until it falls on its knees, gaunt and half-starved, totally dazed, ready, for a handful of hay, to follow its rider back to the stable.

2. The bourgeois State is applying the same method to the proletariat as it is seeking to apply with the Russian workers' State. It would like to be able to convince the working class that communism is a utopia; that it can only aggravate the worker's economic and political situation. It seeks to impart a lesson following the Froebel method; an evening meeting at the Protestant church, with films showing how the simple moral fable can be developed. If the workers were convinced that the occupation of the factories represented an attempt at communist management, the rapid disillusionment would have a terrible effect. The revolutionary cohesion of the class would be broken; the convinced communists would no longer be anything more than a minority; and the majority, humiliated and cast down, like a bare-foot, disarmed army which suddenly finds itself under heavy artillery fire, would bend its back under the capitalist yoke.

Hence it is necessary to tell the mass of workers the truth. It is essential that the workers should not be able to believe for one instant that the communist Revolution is as easy to accomplish as the occupation of an undefended factory. These events, on the contrary, must allow the communists to explain clearly to the masses what the revolution represents in all its complexity: these events show up with blinding clarity the reformist and anarcho-syndicalist utopias. What good is Parliament to the working-class? And what good would the occupation of the factories in the sense given it by the anarchists be, if there is not – or if one does not energetically organize – a political-economic centre (the workers' State) which unites one factory to another; which transforms the banks, to assist working-class management; which breaks, whether by physical sanctions or by rationing, the sabotage of the counter-revolutionaries? And how could the workers at the same time be in the factory and on the streets to defend their conquests, if there is not a State organization to train a loyal and well-positioned armed force, ready in all circumstances and for all eventualities?

The occupation of the factories by the working-class masses is a historical event of the first importance: it is a necessary stage in revolutionary development and the class war. But its significance and potential must be accurately defined, and every element drawn from it that can be of use in raising the political consciousness of the masses and reinforcing their revolutionary spirit.

Unsigned, *Avanti!*, Piedmont edition, 2 September 1920; Milan edition, 5 September 1920.

61. THE COMMUNIST PARTY

I

Since Sorel, it has become commonplace to refer to the primitive Christian communities in assessing the modern proletarian movement. It should be said at once that Sorel is in no way responsible for the intellectual pettiness and crudity of his Italian admirers, just as Karl Marx is not responsible for the absurd ideological pretensions of the "Marxists". In the field of historical research, Sorel is an "inventor". He cannot be imitated; he does not provide his aspiring disciples with a method that can be mechanically applied by anyone at any time to gain useful insights. For Sorel, as for Marxist doctrine, Christianity represents a revolution at the height of its development, i.e. a revolution that has gone as far as it can, as far as the creation of a novel and original system of moral, juridical, philosophical and artistic relations. To assume that this system must form the ideological framework of *every* revolution is a crude and stupid betrayal of Sorel's historical intuition. All this intuition can give rise to is a series of historical researches on the "germs" of proletarian civilization which *must* exist, if it is true (as it is for Sorel) that the proletarian revolution is contained within modern industrial society and if it is true also that from it will arise a new set of rules for living and an absolutely new system of human relations, characteristic of the revolutionary class. So what significance can be attached to the statement that the workers, in contrast to the first Christians, are not chaste, sober or original in their way of life? Leaving to one side the careless generalization that sees all "Turin metal-workers" as a motley crew of brutes who eat roast chicken every day, get drunk each night in the brothels, have no love for their families and seek to satisfy their ideals of beauty and morality in the cinema and in aping bourgeois manners – leaving this careless and puerile generalization to one side, the statement can in no way serve as the premise for an historical judgment. It is equivalent, in historical terms, to the following statement: since modern Christians eat chicken, consort with prostitutes, get drunk, bear false witness, commit adultery, etc., etc., it must be a myth that the ascetics, martyrs and saints ever existed. In a word, every historical phenomenon must be studied in the context of its peculiar characteristics, of its actuality, as a development of the *freedom* that is manifested in ends, institutions and forms which absolutely cannot be confused and compared (other than metaphorically) with the ends, institutions and forms of past historical phenomena.

Every revolution which, like the Christian and the communist revolutions, comes about and can only come about through a stirring within the deepest and broadest depths of the mass of the people, cannot help but smash and destroy the existing system of social organization. Who can imagine and foresee what the immediate consequences will be, when the countless multitudes who today have no will and no power finally make their entry into the arena of historical destruction and creation? Because they have never experienced such "will" or "power", these multitudes will claim to see the will and power they have won manifested in every public and private act. They will find everything that presently exists mysteriously hostile, and will seek to destroy it utterly. But it is the very immensity of the revolution, its quality of being unforeseeable, its boundless freedom, that makes it impossible to hazard so much as a single definitive hypothesis on what feelings, passions, initiatives and virtues are being moulded in such an incandescent furnace. Everything which exists today, everything we see today that lies outside the scope of our own will and force of character – in what way might it all be changed? Would not each day of so intense a life be a revolution? Would not each change in individual consciousness, if it occurred simultaneously throughout the mass of the people, have unimaginable creative results?

On the basis of present observation, nothing in the realm of morality or sentiment can be foreseen. One sentiment alone – a constant feature, such that it has come to characterize the working class – can be proven to exist today: that of solidarity. But the intensity and strength of this sentiment can only be counted on as sustenance of the will to resist and to self-sacrifice for a period of time that even the people's meagre capacity for historical prediction can estimate, more or less correctly. They cannot be counted on, and hence taken for granted, as a sustenance of the historical will during the period of revolutionary creation and the founding of the new society, when it will be impossible to fix any temporal limit to resistance and sacrifice. For then the adversary to be overcome will no longer lie outside the proletariat; will no longer be a physical, external power that is limited and can be controlled. The enemy will lie within the proletariat itself, in its ignorance, its laziness, its ponderous slowness in understanding, when the dialectic of the class struggle has been internalized and within every individual consciousness the new man, in his every act, has to fight the "bourgeois" lying in ambush. Hence the workers' trade union, the body that realizes proletarian solidarity in practice and disciplines it, cannot serve as the model and basis for predictions concerning the future of civilization. It lacks elements to encourage the growth of freedom. It is destined to undergo radical changes as a consequence of general developments. It is determined, not determining.

In its present stage, the proletarian movement is striving to achieve a revolution in the organization of material things and physical forces. Its characteristic features cannot be the sentiments and passions that are general among the masses and responsible for sustaining their will. The characteristic features of the proletarian revolution can only be sought in the party of the working class, the Communist Party, which owes its existence and development to its disciplined organization of the proletariat's will to found a State, systematize the network of existing physical forces and lay the foundations of popular liberty.

In the present period, the Communist Party is the only institution that can seriously be compared with the religious communities of primitive Christianity. To the extent that the Party already exists on an international level, one can hazard a comparison and establish a scale of criteria for judging between the militants for the City of God and those for the City of Man. The communist is certainly not inferior to the Christian in his catacombs. On the contrary! The ineffable end which Christianity held out to its champions is, in its suggestive mystery, ample justification for heroism, a thirst for martyrdom, sanctity: there is no need to draw on the great human reserves of character and determination to elicit a spirit of sacrifice in someone who believes in a heavenly reward and eternal happiness. But the communist worker who puts in eight hours for the Party, trade union or co-operative, after eight hours of work in the factory, week in week out, month in month out, year by year, without looking for any reward – from the point of view of the history of mankind, this communist worker is greater than the slave or artisan who ran all manner of risks to attend his clandestine prayer meeting. In the same way, Rosa Luxemburg and Karl Liebknecht are greater than the greatest saints of Christ. It is just because their cause is concrete, human and restricted that the warriors of the working class are greater than the warriors of God: the moral forces that sustain their will are far greater, by virtue of the fact that this will has a definite goal.

What a force of expansion the worker's sentiments will acquire, bent as he is for eight hours every day over his machine repeating the ritual gestures of his craft, as monotonous as the clicking of a circle of rosary beads, when he becomes the "master" – the measure of all social values? Surely the very fact that the worker still manages to think, even when he is reduced to operating in complete ignorance of the how or why of his practical activity, is a miracle? This miracle of the worker who takes charge each day of his own intellectual autonomy and his own freedom to handle ideas, by struggling against fatigue, against boredom and against the monotony of a job that strives to mechanize and so kill his inner life – this miracle is organized in the Communist Party, in the will to struggle and the revolutionary creativity that are expressed in the Communist Party.

The worker in the factory fulfils merely an executive function. He does not follow the general process of labour and production. He is not a point that moves and so creates a line; he is a pin stuck in a particular place, and the line is made up of a succession of pins that an alien will has arranged in accordance with its own ends. The worker tends to carry this mode of being of his into every aspect of his life. At all times he adjusts easily to the role of material executor, of a "mass" guided by a will that is alien to his own. He is intellectually lazy; he cannot and does not wish to look beyond his immediate horizon, so he lacks criteria in his choice of leaders and allows himself to be easily taken in by promises. He likes to believe he can get what he wants without making a great effort himself or thinking too much. The Communist Party is the instrument and historical form of the process of inner liberation through which the worker is transformed from *executor* to *initiator*, from *mass* to *leader* and *guide*, from brawn to brain and purpose. As the Communist Party is formed, a seed of liberty is planted that will sprout and grow to its full height only after the workers' State has organized the requisite material conditions. The slave or artisan of classical times "knew himself" and achieved his own liberation by taking his place in a Christian community, where he had the concrete experience of being an equal, a brother, because all were sons of the same father. Similarly, the worker takes his place in the Communist Party and there "discovers" and "invents" original ways of living, collaborates "consciously" in the world's activity, thinks, foresees, becomes responsible, becomes an organizer rather than someone who is organized and feels he forms a vanguard that pushes ahead and draws the mass of the people after it.

Even in purely organizational terms, the Communist Party has shown itself to be the particular form of the proletarian revolution. No revolution in the past has involved parties; these arose after the bourgeois revolution and have suffered their decline on the terrain of parliamentary democracy. Even in this field, the Marxist idea that capitalism creates forces it cannot then succeed in controlling has found confirmation. The democratic parties fulfilled the function of selecting political men of merit and securing their success at the polls. Today the men in government are put there by the banks, the great newspapers, the industrial associations. The parties have broken up into a multitude of personal cliques. Arising from the ashes of the socialist parties, the Communist Party repudiates its democratic and parliamentary origins and now reveals its essential features, which have never been seen before in history. The Russian revolution was a revolution carried out by men organized in the Communist Party: in the Party they fashioned for themselves a new personality, acquired new sentiments and brought into being a morality whose goal is to become a universal consciousness striven after by all mankind.

II

Political parties are the reflection and nomenclature of social classes. They arise, develop, decline and renew themselves as the various strata of the social classes locked in struggle undergo shifts in their real historical significance, find their conditions of existence and development radically altered, and acquire a greater and more lucid awareness of themselves and their own vital interests. What has become characteristic of the present historical period, as a consequence of the imperialist war which has profoundly altered the structure of the national and international apparatus of production and exchange, is the rapidity with which the traditional political parties that emerged on the terrain of parliamentary democracy have faded away and been replaced by new political organizations. This general process is subject to an inner, implacable logic of its own, which manifests itself in the peeling away of the old classes and groupings and in vertiginous transitions from one state to another on the part of whole strata of the population, throughout the territory of the State and frequently throughout the territory of capitalist dominion.

Even the social classes which historically have been the laziest and slowest to differentiate themselves, like the peasant class, have not remained untouched by this ferment of reagents dissolving the social body. Indeed, it seems that the lazier and more retarded these classes were in the past, the more swiftly they thrust today towards the dialectically extreme consequences of the class struggle – towards civil war and the liberation of economic relations. In Italy we have seen a powerful party of the rural class, the Popular Party, arise virtually from nothing within the space of two years. At its inception, it claimed to represent the economic interests and political aspirations of all the rural social strata, from the *latifundist* baron to the medium-sized land-holder, from the small land-holder to the tenant farmer, from the share-cropper to the poor peasant. We have witnessed the Popular Party win nearly a hundred seats in Parliament with bloc lists in which the representatives of the *latifundist* barons, the great forest owners, the great and middle land-holders – a tiny minority of the rural population – had an overwhelming predominance. We have seen how internal struggles between tendencies within the Popular Party broke out almost at once and have now become spasmodic – these struggles being a reflection of the party's varied electoral support. The broad masses of the small land-holders and poor peasants could no longer put up with being the passive infantry-mass enabling the medium and large land-holders to secure their interests: under their energetic pressure, the Popular Party split into right and left wings and a centre. Then we have seen the extreme left of the *popolari* adopting a revolutionary stance, under the pressure of the poor peasants, and entering into competition with the Socialist Party, which had also become the representative of vast masses of peasants. We are already witnessing the break-up of the Popular Party, whose parliamentary fraction and Central Committee no longer represent the interests and newly-acquired self-consciousness of their mass electorate or the forces organized in the white unions.[130] These are now represented by the extremists, who do not want to lose control of them, cannot delude them with legal action in Parliament and are therefore led to resort to violent struggle and to invoke new political institutions of government.

We have witnessed the same process of rapid organization and even more rapid dissociation within the other political current that tried to represent the interests of the peasantry – the war veterans' association. It is a reflection of the formidable internal crisis that is racking the Italian countryside and that is manifested in the gigantic strikes in central and northern Italy, in the take-over and distribution of the great estates in Apulia, in the assaults on feudal castles and the appearance of hundreds and thousands of armed peasants in the towns of Sicily.

This profound stirring of the rural classes is shaking the framework of the democratic parliamentary State to its very foundations. As a political force, capitalism has been reduced to corporate associations of factory owners. It no longer possesses a political party whose ideology also embraces the petty-bourgeois strata in the cities and countryside, and so ensures the continued survival of a broadly-based legal State. In fact, capitalism can find political representation today only in the great newspapers (a print-run of 400,000; a thousand voters) and in the Senate, which is immune as a formation from the actions and reactions of the broad masses of the people, but lacks authority and prestige in the country. Hence the political power of capitalism is tending to be identified increasingly with the upper ranks of the military, the Royal Guard and the swarm of adventurers who have cropped up since the Armistice, aspiring each and every one to become the Kornilov or Bonaparte of Italy. Thus the political power of capitalism can only be expressed today in a military *coup d'état* and the attempt to impose an iron nationalist dictatorship which will drive the brutalized Italian masses to revive the economy by sacking neighbouring countries sword in hand.

Since the bourgeoisie is exhausted and worn out as a ruling class, capitalism is exhausted as a mode of production and exchange, and there exists no unified political force within the peasantry capable of creating a State, the working class is ineluctably summoned by history to take upon itself the responsibilities of a ruling class. Only the proletariat is capable of creating a strong and respected State, because it has in communism a programme of economic reconstruction that finds its necessary premises and conditions in the phase of development reached by capitalism in the 1914–18 Imperialist War. Only the proletariat, through its creation of a new organ of public authority, the Soviet system, can give dynamic expression to the fluid and incandescent mass of workers and restore order to the general upheaval of the productive forces. It is entirely natural and historically explicable that in such a period as this the problem should arise of forming a Communist Party, an expression of the proletarian vanguard which has a precise consciousness of its historical mission, which will establish the new social order and which will be both initiator and protagonist of this new and original historical period.

Even the traditional political party of the Italian working class, the Socialist Party, has not escaped the process of decomposition of all forms of association, a process that is characteristic of the period we are passing through. The colossal historical error of the men who have been in charge of the controlling organs of our association from the outbreak of the World War until the present, was their belief that they could preserve the old structure of the party in the face of its inner dissolution. In fact, in terms of its traditions; in terms of the historical origins of the various currents that formed it; in terms of its pact of alliance, whether tacit or explicit, with the General Confederation of Labour (a pact which has the effect of giving an unwarranted power and influence to trade-union bureaucrats at every congress, Council or authoritative assembly); in terms of the unlimited autonomy conceded to the parliamentary group (which gives deputies too a power and influence in congresses, Councils and high-ranking discussions that is similar to that enjoyed by union bureaucrats and just as unwarranted) – in terms of all these things, the Italian Socialist Party is no different from the English Labour Party. It is revolutionary only in terms of the general statements contained in its programme. It is a conglomeration of parties. It moves and cannot help but move slowly and belatedly. It runs the permanent risk of becoming an easy prey for adventurers, careerists and ambitious men without political capacity or seriousness. Because of its heterogeneous character and the numerous sources of friction in its machinery, worn-out and sabotaged as this is by "maids turned mistress",[131] it has never been in a position to take upon itself the burden and responsibility for initiating and carrying out the revolutionary actions that the ceaseless pressure of events demands of it. Here we have the explanation for the historical paradox that, in Italy, it is the masses who drive and "educate" the Party of the working class and not the Party that guides and educates the masses.

The Socialist Party calls itself the champion of Marxist doctrines. One would, therefore, expect the Party to possess in these doctrines a compass to steer it through the confusion of events. One would expect it to possess that capacity for historical foresight that characterizes the intelligent followers of the Marxist dialectic. One would expect it to possess a general plan of action based on this historical foresight, and to be in a position to issue clear and precise orders to the working class engaged in its struggle. But instead the Socialist Party, the champion of Marxism in Italy, is exposed – just like the Popular Party, which represents the most backward classes in the Italian population – to all the pressures of the masses. It shifts and alters its colours as the masses shift and alter their colours. In fact this Socialist Party, which proclaims itself to be the guide and master of the masses, is nothing but a wretched clerk noting down the operations that the masses spontaneously carry out. This poor Socialist Party, which proclaims itself to be the head of the working class, is nothing but the baggage train of the proletarian army.

If this strange behaviour on the part of the Socialist Party, this bizarre state of the political party of the working class, has not yet caused a catastrophe, it is because there exist in the ranks of the working class – in the urban Party sections, the unions, the factories and the villages – energetic groups of communists who are conscious of their historical role, energetic and alert in their activity, capable of guiding and educating the proletarian masses around them. It is also because there exists a potential Communist Party within the Socialist Party – a party that needs only an explicit organization of its own, a centralization and discipline, in order to be able to develop swiftly, take over and renew the membership of the party of the working class, and provide the General Confederation of Labour and the co-operative movement with a new line.

The immediate problem in this period – coming as it does after the metalworkers' struggle but before the congress where the Party will have to adopt a serious and precise attitude to the Communist International – is to organize and centralize the communist forces that are already in existence and functioning. The Socialist Party is visibly breaking up and plunging headlong into chaos. In a very short space of time, its tendencies have taken on a new character. Confronted with the responsibilities of historical action and the obligations accepted through joining the Communist International, individuals and groups have become confused and shifted their positions. Centrist and opportunist equivocation has captured a part of the Party leadership and sown confusion and doubt among the sections. In this general falling away of conscience, faith and will, this tempest of baseness, cowardice and defeatism, the duty of communists is to form tight-knit groups, to rally to each other, to stand ready for the orders that will come. On the basis of the theses approved by the IInd Congress of the IIIrd International, and on the basis of steadfast discipline to the supreme authority of the worldwide workers' movement, sincere and dedicated communists must carry out the necessary preparations for the earliest possible formation of the communist fraction of the Italian Socialist Party. Then, at the Florence Congress, and for the good name of the Italian proletariat, this fraction must become in name and in deed the Communist Party of Italy, a section of the IIIrd Communist

International.[132] The communist fraction must be constructed with an organic and powerfully centralized leading apparatus, its own disciplined forces wherever the working class works, meets and struggles, and a whole range of services and instruments essential to the supervision, activity and propaganda which will enable it to function and develop from today onwards as a real party.

After saving the working class from a disaster in the metalworkers' struggle through their energy and spirit of initiative, the communists must push their attitudes and actions to their logical conclusion. They must (by reconstructing it) save the primordial fabric of the party of the working class. They must provide the Italian proletariat with a Communist Party capable of organizing the workers' State and the conditions needed to bring about a communist society.

Unsigned, *L'Ordine Nuovo*, 4 September 1920, Vol. II, No. 15, and 9 September 1920, Vol. II, No. 17.

62. RED SUNDAY

The bourgeoisie's scribblers are writhing in fury, constrained as they are to acknowledge the activity of the working class in the occupied factories.[133] Working-class activity: initiatives by the working class in production, in internal order and in military defence! Social hierarchies have been smashed and historical values turned upside down. The "executive" classes, the "instrumental" classes, have become the "controlling" classes. They have taken leadership over themselves and found in their own ranks their representatives: men to invest with the power of government; men who will take upon themselves all the functions that turn an elemental and mechanical aggregate into an organic whole, a living creature. All this has set the hacks of the bourgeoisie twisting in rage, believing as they do that the bourgeois class is divinely invested with powers of decision and historical initiative.

What the workers have done has an immense historical importance, and it needs to be understood in all its aspects by the working class. This is a day the workers will devote to thought, discussion and recapitulation of the events that have occurred; for the workers, one day like this is worth ten years of normal activity, normal propaganda and normal absorption of revolutionary notions and concepts.

What has happened in these past few days? The metalworkers' federation had called on the workers to engage in trade-union struggle to win wage improvements. The industrialists refused to acknowledge that there was any real validity in the workers' demands. Then the leaders of the organization, though they are not communists and sign manifestos against Bolshevik methods of emancipating the people, nevertheless, after examining the actual situation, found they had to transfer the struggle to a new domain – a domain where, if violence was not an immediate necessity, the study and organization of violence at once became a necessity. Meanwhile a new fact emerged at once from this new method of struggle. When the workers were fighting to improve their economic situation through strike action, their role in the struggle was limited to having faith in their distant leaders; it was limited to developing the virtues of solidarity and resistance, on the basis precisely of this generic faith. But if, in the course of the struggle, the workers occupy the factories with the intention of continuing production, the moral position of the masses at once takes on a different form and value. The trade-union leaders are no longer able to lead and disappear in the immensity of the membership; the masses are left to solve the problems of the factory on their own, with their own resources and their own men.

Under the capitalists, the factory was a miniature State, ruled over by a despotic lord. The lord had sole right to select the manual workers, clerks, foremen and specialists and distribute them among the workshops, offices and laboratories. The factory was a despotically organized State, with all power resting in the hands of the proprietor or his delegates. The multiplicity of States constituted by all the capitalist factories found united expression in the bourgeois State, which secured the discipline and obedience of the non-property-owning population by giving it a semblance of power and sovereignty; by summoning it every five or seven years to nominate its deputies to Parliament and the municipal councils. Today, after the workers' occupation, this despotic power in the factories has been smashed: the right to choose industrial executives has passed into the hands of the working class. Every factory has become an illegal State, a proletarian republic living from day to day, awaiting the outcome of events. But even if a great uncertainty still hangs over the future of these proletarian republics, given that the enemy forces have not revealed themselves and offer no hint as to their real intentions, the very fact that these republics "live" has an importance and historical value out of all proportion. Life has a logic and inner energy of its own that goes beyond the will and whims of individuals. While these proletarian republics live, they will have to cope with all the problems that face any autonomous and independent power exercising its sovereignty over a delimited territory. The political capacity, the initiative and revolutionary creativity of the working class is now put to the test.

The first problem, the fundamental and unavoidable problem confronting the citizens of the factory-State is that of military defence. This problem arises in a novel form. The bourgeois State builds its army upon three social strata: the bourgeoisie, the petty bourgeoisie and the working people. The people provides the military mass, the big property-owning bourgeoisie and the aristocracy provide the upper ranks of the officers, while the petty bourgeoisie provides the junior commands. The same organization emerges in the capitalist army as in the capitalist factory, where the class of proprietors (or those assimilated to them through financial interests) has despotic command, the proletariat is the passive infantry-mass and the petty bourgeoisie fills the subordinate command posts.

In the factory-republic, there exists one class only, the proletariat: the class which provided the army and industry with a passive infantry-mass. Now the proletariat needs to create its own articulated, organized and disciplined army, an army that is capable of resisting the enemy forces and vanquishing them. The workers tend to see defence as an obligation incumbent upon all, and this conception hits the mark. But then they are led to conclude that everyone, without distinction, should at once fulfil this obligation – and this is a mistake. Military defence needs to be organized in a special corps, with its own commands and roles: the conception of hierarchy can no longer be applied to such a formation, as "there exists one class only". These formations should not be restricted in numbers, since defence may at any moment give way to attack and military initiative.

This problem of military initiative is linked to another: will not this multiplicity of proletarian republics, constituted by the factories occupied and controlled by the workers, be led necessarily – through the inner dialectic of historical development – to confederate themselves, form themselves into a unity and counterpose a central power of their own to the central power of the bourgeois State? Today the working class is confronted by the concrete problem of forming a city-wide Soviet. If such a Soviet is formed, it will need to have an armed force at its disposal. This force can and must be provided by regularly constituted and commanded factory brigades, that can be amalgamated, through a relay of commands, into an urban militia. But conversely, the creation of military nuclei in the factories raises the problem of the Soviet, since defence has no bounds and must proceed according to its own logic.

These problems should be discussed by the workers today in the factory general assemblies, the organs which express the power and sovereignty of the factory proletarian republics. The preparatory and propaganda work for the nomination of workers' deputies needs to be carried out in such a way that, at any given moment, when the march of events brings history to the pitch where the new and unexpected is bound to happen, the forms of the proletariat's power – as it struggles to emancipate itself – will spring from each individual factory or group of factories. And the same remarks apply to this particular revolutionary creation as to that of armed force.

Within the bourgeois State, the functions of supreme command (the government) are in the hands of the capitalists or the social class that is bound by financial interests to the proprietors. The subordinate posts – the role played by the national deputies – are in the hands of the petty bourgeoisie, which allows itself to be dominated economically and morally by the capitalists. The mass of the working people is manipulated politically to satisfy the material interests of the property-owners and the ideological ambitions of the petty bourgeois. To keep this hierarchy of classes intact, the State maintains that it is illegal for deputies to be bound by authoritative mandates. The bourgeoisie counts on the distractions of the surroundings, and on hints concerning the possibility of satisfying personal ambitions, to corrupt deputies – even when these are workers – if they are not bound by an imperative mandate. In the constitution of the proletarian central power, all these conditions are changed. There exists one class only, which elects its deputies from its own ranks, the electoral college being the factory and mandates being authoritative and binding. This means that the old hierarchies are smashed and the workers' power is built on a purely industrial and administrative basis. The anarchists should be the first to welcome this organization of power, since their ideals are given concrete expression.

Today, on the metal-workers' Red Sunday, the workers themselves must construct the first historic cell of the proletarian revolution that the general situation is generating with all the irresistible force of natural phenomena.

Unsigned, Piedmont edition of *Avanti!*, 5 September 1920, Vol. XXIV, No. 224.

63. FIVE MONTHS LATER

April 1920. Harassed by the factory-owners, who base their will to attack on the certainty of a split between the Turin masses and the leaderships of the trade-union organizations, the metalworkers are compelled to descend into the arena. The factory-owners wanted to humble the Turin workers; they wanted to make the latter see that they – the owners – not only held industrial power in their hands, but also the political strength to reduce them to absolute impotence, to break any proletarian attempt to win a measure of freedom of organization and initiative within the factory. The metalworkers moved into struggle and threw all their forces into the battle. Their aim was to win control over production: a control which would be exercised locally by the executive committee of the factory council, and which would be centralized in city, regional and national workers' control committees – committees which would themselves be based, at the various levels, on the factory councils and the craft unions. The struggle of the Turin workers, although it was imposed by the owners and not launched by the workers themselves, at that time appeared as something monstrous, quite outside reality, *deserving to be crushed by the factory-owners.* A climate of mistrust developed with respect to proletarian Turin: the revolutionary leaders of the movement were treated as madmen, fanatics . . . anarchists. People said that the owners were right not to accept control, since workers' control would have meant . . . "*métayage*".[134] The workers were defeated, after a month of struggle – a struggle which was exemplary in the spirit of discipline and self-denial, exemplary in the sacrifices made. They returned to the factory defeated but unbowed; defeated but not humbled; defeated but their hearts swelling with revolutionary passion and the will for revenge. They returned to the factory, the workers of Turin, pursued by howls to which the owners had given the material form of notices: "There is only one power in the factory"; "No discussion during working hours."

September 1920. The trade-union struggle devised by the union leaderships developed in the spirit of the revolutionary period. The go-slow was followed by the occupation of engineering factories throughout the country. The factory councils, which had been presented to the masses in ferment as merely a literary bauble, something quite superfluous, since control is *control . . . over the product* or it is nothing – the factory councils arose naturally everywhere. The workers who are occupying the factories can rely on no one but themselves. They must, therefore, develop their spirit of initiative: from a disciplined, industrial *object* they are becoming a responsible *subject*. They have to create for themselves a collective personality, a collective soul, a collective will. And lo and behold, the Turin experience in self-government, in autonomous initiative, which the workers of that city had begun a whole year earlier and for which they had had to wage a gigantic struggle, has now been realized on a national scale! It has been realized by that category of workers which, in Italy as in all other countries, is in the vanguard of the revolutionary proletariat and draws in all the other industrial categories behind it. Today it is the factory-owners who find themselves driven to the wall; today armed workers are guarding the occupied factories; today, since it is they who led the battle up until the occupation, the union organizations must continue the struggle and prepare all the forces that will be necessary for final victory. Today, the problem of workers' control is posed on a national scale, and posed for all industries; today, five months after the defeat of the Turin proletariat, no one considers control just a mad dream of fanatics – not even the factory-owners. *The Turin workers were right in April 1920*: the Turin workers were truly in tune with history; they were in the furrow of the world revolution. Today, it is acknowledged that there can be two authorities in the factories. Today, it is acknowledged that directly elected workers can discuss even during working hours. Such is the great pedagogic effectiveness of the gun in the worker's hand, the factory in the hands of the working class!

But today, five months after the general strike for workers' control, the latter is no longer enough for the proletarian movement of Turin. Or at least, control is no longer enough in the sense given to the term by the owners and by many workers' leaders. Today, many – too many – even see control as a kind of . . . *métayage*. For the revolutionary working class, it means the path opened towards complete industrial autonomy; towards the definitive expulsion of the owning class as such from the field of production. Control means the creation of popular economic organs, which emanate directly from the factories, which emanate from the factory workers and from the factory workers alone.

No sinecures, no offices for State functionaries or trade-union officials: the Turin workers do not want any. What they want are living bodies, bodies which can be overhauled at any moment, and which always represent the sincere expression of the spirit and will of the masses. Autonomous bodies, independent of the bourgeois State or parliament, which become the historical form of the economic capacity of the revolutionary proletariat ("economic", of course, not in the Italian sense of trade-union or co-operative action, but as the capacity to put into operation and direct the process of production of economic goods). Also, in addition to these workers' control bodies, it is necessary to obtain real guarantees of their political existence. The workers must be able to defend their organizations permanently.

Five months of national and world history have not passed in vain. The step forward taken by the Italian proletariat is gigantic. That which, in the month of April, appeared as a "utopia" has today entered the "public domain". The strength of the Italian proletariat is today multiplied a hundredfold. And that strength has still to realize its full potential.

The outcome of the struggle is still impossible to foresee, for there are a host of unknown factors. But whatever the result, given the development of working-class forces, it cannot fail to satisfy these "minimum" demands of the revolutionary proletariat.

Unsigned, *Avanti!*, Piedmont edition, 14 September 1920.

64. POLITICAL CAPACITY

Today, the metalworkers are to approve or reject, by referendum, the motion voted by the congress of their Federation.[135] The result of this consultation of the work-force in the factories is not difficult to predict. The referendum is an exquisitely democratic and counter-revolutionary form; it serves to valorize the amorphous mass of the population and to crush the vanguards that lead those masses and give them political consciousness.

So the vanguard of the proletariat should not be demoralized or disorganized by this outcome of the revolutionary movement. Its quality as a vanguard will be verified by the strength of mind and political capacity it succeeds in demonstrating. Have the groups of workers which have been at the head of the movement in the last few days taken the exact measure of their powers to act and the forces of passive resistance that exist within the masses? Have they acquired a consciousness of their historical mission? Have they acquired a consciousness of the inner weaknesses which have been revealed in the solidity of the working class, weaknesses which are not individual, that do not modify our assessment of the revolutionary spirit of the proletariat in the present historical phase, but which can be traced to the general relations of a trade organization? Have they transformed their experiences into an active and operative consciousness? Have they become skilled in identifying the deepest hidden feelings that move the popular mind, and the negative feelings, the inhibiting forces that fatigue and immobilize the most generous and daring impulses?

The political capacity of the proletarian vanguard (and hence the real revolutionary capacity of the Italian working class) will be revealed by the attitudes that emerge from today's referendum. Many perils threaten the working class; these perils are not external, they are primarily internal. The greatest danger is the lack of a "spirit of adaptation" to higher circumstances, a spirit of critical, conscious and deliberate adaptation, which cannot and must not be confused with opportunism. Rather, it is the lack of this spirit that leads the working class into opportunism – or, which comes to the same thing, to the triumph of the opportunists among the masses and the maintenance of the hierarchies that have brought the revolutionary movement to its present pass. The revolutionary vanguard needs to consider and analyse the events that have just taken place, not according to its own wishes, passions and will, but objectively, as external data to be subjected to political judgment, and as a historical movement susceptible to conscious extension and development. From a merely objective point of view, the working class can register a great step forward. As a mass guided and disciplined in the factory by its direct representatives, it has proved itself capable of industrial and political self-government. This fact, which should be elementary for revolutionary Communists, has consequences of incalculable social importance. The middle classes of the population have compared the strength of the proletariat with the inadequacy of the entrepreneurial class. Half a century ago, the proletariat was still, as Marx put it, a *sack of potatoes*, a generic imponderable, an amorphous conglomeration of individuals without ideas, without will and without a unitary perspective. Today it is the entrepreneurial class that has become a *sack of potatoes*, an aggregate of the inept and the imbecile, without political capacity, without internal power. The revolutionary events of the past few days have illuminated this position of the two classes contending for the government of production and of society. The prejudices and follies which the capitalist-owned press had disseminated in public opinion have collapsed; the middle classes are lining up with the proletariat, convinced that this young and energetic class holds the key to civilization and human progress. From the test that both classes have had to undergo, the proletariat has emerged higher in public estimation, while capitalism has revealed even further its deficiencies and incapacity. This new political situation has definitively put forward the proletariat as a ruling class; it is a spring that drives it irresistibly towards the conquest of power.

Why then was this result not immediately attained? Or at least, why was no attempt made to attain it? The answer to this question must be sought in the tactics pursued until today, culminating in the referendum. The leaders of the proletarian movement base themselves on the "masses", in other words they ask the prior permission of the masses before acting, consulting them in the forms and at the time they choose. But a revolutionary movement can only be based on the proletarian vanguard, and must be led without prior consultation, without the apparatus of representative assemblies. Revolution is like war; it must be minutely prepared by a working-class general staff, just as a war is by the Army's general staff. Assemblies can only ratify what has already taken place, exalt the successful and implacably punish the unsuccessful. It is the task of the proletarian vanguard to keep the revolutionary spirit constantly awake in the masses, to create the conditions which keep them ready for action, in which the proletariat will respond immediately to the call for revolution. In the same way, the nationalists and imperialists, with their frantic preaching of patriotic vanities and hatred for foreigners, are trying to create the conditions in which the crowd will approve a war that has already been agreed on by the general staff of the Army and by the diplomatic service. No war would ever break out if prior permission had to be obtained from the masses to declare it; parliaments approve wars because they know they have already been inexorably decided, because they know that they will be thrust inexorably aside if they oppose them. Similarly, no revolutionary movement can be decreed by a workers' national assembly. To call such an assembly is to confess in advance one's disbelief in revolution; it amounts, therefore, to exercising a prejudicial pressure against it.

The proletarian vanguard, which today is disillusioned and threatened with dissolution, must ask itself whether it is not itself responsible for this situation. It is a fact that in the General Confederation of Labour there is no organized revolutionary opposition, centralized enough to exercise control over the leading offices and capable not only of replacing one man by another, but one method by another, one aim by another and one will by another. This is the real situation, which lamentations, curses and oaths will not change, only tenacious and patient organization and preparation. It is thus essential that the groups of workers which have been at the head of the masses accept reality as it is, in order to alter it effectively. They must keep the masses firm and united behind their programmes and slogans; they must become capable of producing from among themselves an energetic general staff, which is able to conduct a broad mass action with intelligence and daring. Today, we have the referendum; its result must not be the occasion for dismay and dissolution, but rather a warning of the need for tighter, more disciplined and better organized action. The emancipation of the proletariat is not a labour of small account and of little men; only he who can keep his heart strong and his will as sharp as a sword when the general disillusionment is at its worst can be regarded as a fighter for the working class or called a revolutionary.

Unsigned, *Avanti!*, Piedmont edition, 24 September 1920.

65. EDITORIAL: 9 OCTOBER 1920

In the 3 October issue of *Il Soviet*, Comrade Bordiga reports on how the discussion went between the Italian delegates and the relevant commission of the Moscow Congress, regarding the famous Thesis 17 of Lenin's report on the Tasks of the Second Congress of the Communist International.[136] After giving the text of the Thesis, quoted by us in the Editorial of No. 13 (21 August), Comrade Bordiga reports: "Not one of the Italian delegates accepted this formulation. Serrati and Graziadei observed that at the National Council meeting the Turin section had come out against the party leadership on the question of the Piedmont strike, and that to commend the section amounted to sanctioning not only its accusations, but also its attitude contrary to discipline. Bombacci observed that it was also dangerous to commend the syndicalizing tendencies of *L'Ordine Nuovo* and its interpretation of the factory council movement. Polano maintained that, since the executive committee of the Turin section was formed in large part of abstentionists, approval had in fact been given to our fraction, repudiated on the parliament question. Bordiga too stressed the possibility that the formulation could be misunderstood as implying approval for the entire line of *L'Ordine Nuovo* – which quite apart from being in opposition to the Congress directives on the question of trade unions and the establishment of Soviets, had also been an advocate of party unity until shortly before the Milan Conference.[137]

Lenin and Bukharin formally stated that they had not intended to express a judgment on the general line of *L'Ordine Nuovo*, concerning which they had insufficient documentation, but simply to indicate the precise source of a document to which alone their approval referred.

The grammatical form was then merely modified in the following way: 'proposals drawn up by the section, etc., and published in the number . . . , etc.' Furthermore, at Bordiga's suggestion, the following phrase was added to the end of the second paragraph: 'and also the work to be carried on in the unions'."

It is interesting for comrades and readers to know these judgments on the Turin section and on *L'Ordine Nuovo*. That the Turin section (woe is me!) broke discipline during the April strike has been whispered, but it has never been proved and would be very difficult to prove. The syndicalizing tendencies of *L'Ordine Nuovo* are likewise a myth: we simply made the mistake of believing that only the masses can achieve the communist revolution, and that neither a party secretary nor a president of the republic can achieve it by issuing decrees. Apparently this was also the opinion of Karl Marx and Rosa Luxemburg, and is Lenin's opinion – all of whom are anarcho-syndicalists for Treves and Turati. It is, however, true that *L'Ordine Nuovo*, when it was still a "tribune", published an editorial (by Comrade Tasca) favourable to unity. The theses which we are publishing in this number on the trade unions, on the factory councils and on the formation of Soviets can give readers the means to judge whether the line of *L'Ordine Nuovo* has been in opposition to the directives of the Congress. Are Radek's theses really new to our readers? Are they really in opposition to what *L'Ordine Nuovo* argued on this question even quite recently, in the polemic with Tasca? Was our concern not how to prevent the councils being subordinated to the opportunist trade unions? The truth is that the Italian socialists did not want to take the factory council movement seriously, and therefore they were given a lesson by the Executive Committee of the Communist International.

Unsigned, *L'Ordine Nuovo*, 9 October 1920, Vol. II, No. 17.

66. REACTION

The *Giornale d'Italia*, the *Messaggero*, the *Idea Nazionale*, the *Corriere della Sera* are all frankly calling for *reaction*, for *a man* who will restore order and discipline to the people of Italy, poisoned as they are by the propaganda of the communists and anarchists. The *Corriere della Sera* has even succeeded in identifying the source of this propaganda: command over the subversive and trouble-making forces rests in the hands of – guess who? – "the people around *L'Ordine Nuovo* and *Avanti!* in Turin and *Umanità Nova* in Milan (i.e. Malatesta)". *La Stampa* agrees with the *Corriere* in its identification of the "plague-spreaders";[138] but *La Stampa* does not go so far as to call for reaction – it simply announces it to be inevitable, a calamity that will afflict the Italian people as a result of the activities of the above-mentioned trouble-makers. This outcry in the "bourgeois democratic" newspapers against the Turin communists has been precipitated by the conflicts of the last few days.[139] It should be noted that Turin was the very place where no conflicts occurred, despite the fact that Turin is supposed to be the headquarters of revolutionary delinquency and so should have staged the most prominent displays of "hooliganism, anarchy, and revolutionary cannibalism". It should also be noted that the very newspapers which are branding the Turin communist movement today as the cause of all the evils afflicting Italy and the precipitators of the future reaction, all breathed a sigh of relief when the representative of the Turin working class to the National Council of the General Confederation of Labour quenched the revolutionary ardour of the assembly and the reformist union leaders by ensuring that D'Aragona's resolution won a majority of the votes.[140]

And so this outcry, this demagogic storm of accusations against the Turin movement can be identified with an attempt on the part of reaction to hit Turin, not as a nest of delinquency, but as the seat of clear-headed political thought that threatens to win over the majority of the Italian Socialist Party and transform the Party from an organ prolonging the capitalist death-agony into an organ of struggle and revolutionary reconstruction. Taking advantage of the internal dissensions within the Party, an attempt is clearly being made to reproduce now, in the closing months of this year, the same situation as obtained in August 1917 or April 1920. Once the Turin proletariat is knocked out and this nest of Piedmontese wasps destroyed, they count on the Party being exhausted and the reformists being able to take charge with the agreement of the working masses, starved and brutalized by the white terror.

It is beyond doubt that reaction in Italy is getting stronger and will seek to impose itself through violence at any moment. *The reaction that has always existed*, that obeys its own laws of development and that will culminate in the most atrocious terrorism that history has ever seen. It is no accident that today all eyes are riveted on Fiume and Dalmatia, on D'Annunzio, Millo and Caviglia.[141] Reaction is an outgrowth of the failure of the imperialist war; it is an outgrowth of the disastrous economic conditions to which capitalism has reduced the Italian people; it is an outgrowth of the nationalist illusions and the opportunist delusions of a State that can no longer successfully guarantee food, clothing and housing for the population. Reaction is the attempt to wriggle out of the present situation by means of a new war. It is the attempt to make up the deficit in the State budget by raiding adjoining nations. It is the natural, physiological expression of the régime of national and private property, as it strives by every means to save itself from the abyss.

Reaction has always been present in Italy – it is not through the fault of the communists that it is threatening to arise now. Reaction is the failure of the legal State: it is not just today that the legal State has failed, and it has not exactly failed through the fault of the communists. Was D'Annunzio, who incited soldiers and generals to mutiny against the "legitimate" government, a communist? Was Millo, who refused to obey his "legitimate" superiors, a communist? Were the people who burned the offices of *Avanti!* in Rome and Milan communists? Was Cadorna, when he was making preparations for a military dictatorship in 1917, a communist? Are the arms dealers and speculators who have raked in our national wealth and shipped it overseas – are they communists? These are all manifestations of Italian reaction. No government has sought to stifle it; indeed every government has encouraged it, promoted it and more or less openly abetted it. Every undertaking on the part of reaction has gone unpunished; every excess on the part of reactionary delinquency has been legalized, since no sanctions have been brought against it by punitive justice. Is it a crime to burn down the offices of a socialist newspaper? No, because the guilty parties, who are known and have confessed, not only were not arrested, but on the contrary were allowed to organize other undertakings of a similar nature. Is it a crime to murder a representative of the working class? No, because the murderers and their accomplices, the people behind the murderers, who are well-known and have confessed and boasted of their crime, were not punished or even molested.

For two years now, from the day of the Armistice, the Italian people have lived in a climate of outright terrorism, of outright reaction. The working class no longer enjoys any security of person, and civil guarantees of peace and order have vanished. In the present period, terrorism is striving to move from the private to the public domain. It is no longer content with the impunity granted it by the State – it wants to become the State. This is the significance today of the phrase, the "advent" of reaction: it means that reaction has become so powerful that it no longer considers the mask of a legal State useful to its ends. It means that reaction wishes to make use of all the State's resources for its own ends. It means that Italy is drawing nearer to a new imperialist war whose aim will be the armed plundering of some wealthy neighbouring people.

Reaction is inherent in the economic conditions of the country. And reaction's aim is not to restore order at home, but to prepare for war abroad. Order at home is meaningless under present circumstances – it is utopian. Even if the proletariat were to work sixteen hours a day, the bourgeois government could not make up the deficit in the State budget, nor could it reorganize national production. The government has not been able to prevent the flow of capital abroad. The government cannot bring back to life the 500,000 men killed in the war, and set them to work. The government cannot give back to the 500,000 men wounded in the war their health and productive efficiency. It cannot give back their economic support to the hundreds of thousands of families who have lost it and are forced to live on charity, forced to consume without producing and reduced to obligatory parasitism. The government cannot attract the flow of foreign tourists back to Italy – who before the war used to leave 500 millions in gold in our country. The government cannot reorganize the stream of emigrants, which used to relieve the territory of 250,000 desperate souls a year before the war and represented a remittance of 700 millions in gold for the Italian budget. The government cannot solve the crisis in the steel industry: every year this eats up hundreds and hundreds of millions in gold, undermines the organization of credit and stops the peasants from getting cheap agricultural equipment, thereby preventing a resumption in food production. Italy has been reduced to a running sore by the war, and the blood is still gushing from its mangled body.

Here lies the source of reaction: a wild fear of death through exhaustion, mingled with a frantic desire to hurl ourselves at the body of a neighbouring nation that is still fairly efficient, to devour it, to save ourselves with a blood transfusion. And here too lies the source of communism, which is a consequence of reaction. Communism is the response of the working class to reaction. Only the working class is free of responsibility at home for the state into which the nation has fallen. Only the working class, through its international organization, can hope to obtain abroad the sort of support that will stop the country from sinking any lower, into utter barbarism. Only the working class, which has no privileges whatsoever, can give the majority of the Italian people the surety that the proletarian State will not reinforce privileges and will do all in its power to bring the country out of chaos. This too enrages reaction: for it has to recognize that the working class is the only living force in the country and to recognize in itself nothing but the last, savage spasms of an exhausted organism.

Unsigned, Piedmont edition of *Avanti!*, 17 October 1920, Vol. XXIV, No. 266.

67. PREDICTIONS

There does not exist in our country any broadly organized force, equipped with a clear and precise will, capable of initiating and pursuing a plan of political action which is consonant with the historical process and at the same time an interpretation of real and immediate history – i.e. not a plan coldly predetermined in an abstract fashion. Since such a force does not yet exist (it can only be and will only be, in our view, the Italian Communist Party), the only thing left for the person who wants to carry out a useful job of enlightenment and political education in the present situation is to seek to make predictions – treating the forces in play as elemental forces, driven by obscure, opaque instincts; their movements not carried out in view of a conscious finality, but through a phenomenon of tropism determined by elemental passions and needs: hunger, cold, blind crazed fear of the Incomprehensible. It is above all this last theme (crazed fear, terror of the creature naked as a worm which feels itself being overtaken by a tempest whose laws and precise direction it does not know) which seems to predominate today in Italian society and can provide a fairly satisfactory explanation of current events.

If a powerful class political force does not emerge from this chaos in the near future (and for us that force can only be the Italian Communist Party); if this force does not succeed in convincing the majority of the population that an order is immanent in the existing confusion and that this very confusion has its purpose, since it is impossible to imagine the collapse of a centuries-old civilization and the arrival of a new civilization without an apocalyptic upheaval, a tremendous rupture; and if this force does not succeed in making the working class appear in the consciousness of the masses and in the political reality of the government institutions as a dominant and leading class[142] – then our country will not be able to overcome the present crisis, and for at least two hundred years will no longer be either a nation or a State, but the centre of a *maelström* which will drag all European civilization down into its whirlpools.

The feeling of crazed fear is typical of the petty bourgeoisie and the intellectuals, just as the feeling of nationalist vanity and ambition is characteristic of these same strata of the population. The petty bourgeoisie and the intellectuals, through the position which they occupy in society and through their way of life, are naturally led to deny the class struggle and are thus condemned to understand nothing of the development of either world history or the national history which forms a part of the world system and obeys the pressures of international events. The petty bourgeoisie and the intellectuals, with their blind vanity and their unrestrained nationalist ambition, dominated the Italian war; they disseminated its abstract, bombastic ideology and were carried away or crushed. For the Italian war was in fact only a secondary aspect of the world war, a marginal episode in a gigantic struggle to divide the world, between hegemonic forces which utilized Italy as a simple pawn in their terrible game. Defeated and crushed in the international domain, it was thought that the petty bourgeosie had been defeated on the national level too by the sudden explosion of the proletariat, from the morrow of the Armistice to 16 November.[143]

The class struggle, repressed during the war, once again irresistibly dominated national life and seemed bent on sweeping away all who sought to deny it. But the class struggle, the proletariat, had not managed during the war – repressed and oppressed as it was – to achieve a consciousness of itself and its historic mission. It had not succeeded in expelling from within itself its petty-bourgeois and intellectual slag. For just like capitalism, the proletariat too has its petty bourgeoisie; and the ideology of the petty bourgeois who cling to the working class is not different in form from that of the petty bourgeois who cling to capitalism. One finds the same element of boundless vanity (The proletariat is the greatest force! The proletariat is invincible! Nothing can halt its inexorable forward march!) and the same element of international ambition, without any precise understanding of the historical forces which dominate the life of the world; without the ability to discover one's own place and function in the world system. We see today that the only result of the proletarian class struggle, after the Armistice, was to elevate to the pinnacle of national politics a vain and petulant petty bourgeoisie. We can see today that "maximalism" is no different in form from the petty-bourgeois ideology of the war. The name of Lenin is invoked in place of that of Wilson, the Third International in place of the League of Nations. But the name is only a name, not the symbol of a state of active consciousness. The Third International, just like the League of Nations, is only a crude myth, not an organization of the real wills and actions which can transform the world equilibrium.

The proletariat has only been able to engender a new petty bourgeoisie, incapable and lacking any real historical finality. The class struggle, which should have tended towards its dialectical conclusion in the creation of a workers' State, has become scattered in a multiplicity of petty destructions and [*word missing*] actions. The petty bourgeoisie, which had seemed destroyed, has recovered its breath and regrouped. Having seen that the class struggle was unable to develop and reach a conclusion, it once again denies its very existence; once again it has become convinced that what is involved is simply delinquency, barbarism, bloody greed. Reaction, as a widespread psychology, is a product of this incomprehension: the elements of this psychology are crazed fear and the most profound abjection – the inevitable corollary of the ambition and vanity which characterized the same strata of the population before the economic crisis and the failure of the nationalist programme. But the elemental forces unleashed by the failure of "petty-bourgeois" nationalism and by the despair which invades minds incapable of understanding the laws which govern even this crisis and convinced that the country is a prey to demoniacal spirits, impossible to control or comprehend – these elemental forces cannot fail to produce a political movement; they cannot fail to lead to a political conclusion. Once the conviction that reaction is necessary has become widespread in the employer and petty-bourgeois strata, backing is given to those groups and general programmes which have always supported reaction: the top military hierarchy, fascism, nationalism. The question of the Adriatic again takes on the aspect of a national question; war on Yugoslavia once more becomes a national mission. Reaction once again means war, and not limited war, but a war in the grand style, since the great capitalist States are themselves opposed to the aspirations of the Italian nationalists. Do you not hear the echo close at hand of the slogan: "The proletarian nation must struggle against the capitalist nations! He who has iron has bread!"[144] Do you not have the impression that you can hear once again those political aphorisms on French decadence and the expansionist youth of Italy?

Italy is truly a prey to demoniacal spirits, impossible to control or comprehend: the sole principle of order is to be found in the working class, in the proletarian will to inscribe Italy concretely and actively in the world historical process. This principle of order can only express itself politically in a rigidly organized Communist Party, which sets itself a clear, unambiguous objective. The present problem, the fundamental historical problem of Italian life, is the organization of the Communist Party, in order to provide the living forces which exist in our country, and which can still save it from ruin, with a consciousness and a precise, autonomous movement.

Unsigned, *Avanti!*, Piedmont edition, 19 October 1920.

68. WHAT IS REACTION?

In highly sibylline fashion, *La Stampa* has announced that Giolitti, strengthened by the recent demonstration of confidence (??) the Italian nation has in his policies, is about to put the second part of his government programme into operation: the restoration of the State. In highly sibylline fashion, *La Stampa* foresees (let whomsoever is concerned be warned!) that the second part of Giolitti's government programme – the restoration of the State – will be greeted by anarchists, communists and fascists (!?) with a unanimous and orchestrated howl of protest against reaction.

What then is this "reaction" of which *La Stampa* is giving us a foretaste? What do these phrases like "application of justice", etc. mean? First we must establish the following point: Giolitti has always been a reactionary; indeed Giolitti has been the typical exponent of capitalist reaction in Italy. Capitalism is reactionary when it no longer succeeds in coming to terms with the productive forces of a country. Italian capitalism entered its reactionary phase when the Italian government, having abandoned the free-trade programme of the Count of Cavour and the old Right, became protectionist and "reformist". Incapable of coming to terms with the Italian productive forces within the framework of free competition, capitalism reduced the State to the status of one of its direct commercial agents; capitalism reduced the national army, the bureaucracy, the magistrature, all the branches of executive power, to the status of immediate instruments of its survival and development. Giolitti was the foremost politician representing this shift of policy on the part of capitalism in Italy.

Today Giolitti is continuing with his traditional policies and is bound to do so: he is still the same old reactionary. Today Giolitti is intensifying his reactionary activities because capitalism is revealing itself as less and less capable of coming to terms with the productive forces. The tactic of fostering the "working-class aristocracies" no longer works; the tactic of supporting the co-operators of Reggio Emilia while massacring the poor peasants in the South – this tactic is no longer worth a penny.[145] Neither is the tactic of directly corrupting the Socialist deputies from the South, while filling Parliament with a bellyful of Southern Askaris[146] by means of the police activities of the prefects and the intimidatory activity of De Bellis's cudgel swingers. Today the broad masses of the people are participating in economic and political struggle: and today capitalism is faced with the persistent need to tear the bread out of the mouths of industrial and agricultural workers. Extensive measures are required: the bourgeois State will have to become more and more reactionary, will have to intervene more and more directly and violently in the class struggle, in order to suppress the initiatives taken by the proletariat on its road to emancipation.

This "reaction" is not purely Italian: it is an international phenomenon, because capitalism has become incapable of coming to terms with the productive forces not only in Italy, but all over the world. The phenomenon of "fascism" is not purely Italian, in the same way that the formation of the Communist Party is not purely Italian. "Fascism" is the preparatory phase of the restoration of the State, i.e. of a resurgence of capitalist reaction, an embittering of the capitalist struggle against the most elementary needs of the proletarian class. Fascism is the illegal aspect of capitalist violence: restoration of the State is the legalization of this violence (it is a well-known historical generalization that custom precedes law). Italian fascism has set fire to the offices of *Avanti!* in Milan and Rome, the offices of the *Proletario* in Pula and the *Lavoratore* in Trieste, and no fascist has been punished. The restored State will no longer burn down offices; it will suppress through "legal" means. Fascism has assaulted Chambers of Labour and socialist municipal councils; the restored State will "legally" dissolve Chambers of Labour and municipal councils which insist on remaining socialist. Fascism assassinates working-class militants; the restored State will "legally" send them to prison, and once the death penalty is restored as well, will have them "legally" killed by a new government functionary: the executioner.

This is a universal development. It has already been partially verified and will continue to develop normally in Italy as well. The communists foresaw this development as long ago as the outbreak of the World War, that decisive verification of capitalism's inability to come to terms with the world productive forces without the active and permanent intervention of direct violence. Hence communists will not howl against Giolittian reaction as something new. They will continue to carry on their activity, coldly, methodically, courageously, in their conviction that they represent the future of European and world civilization and in their conviction that they represent the forces which must triumph over all things and all peoples, in order that human civilization may not be submerged forever in the bestiality and barbarity unleashed by imperialism and militarism.

Unsigned, *Avanti!*, Piedmont edition, 24 November 1920, Vol. XXIV, No. 304.

69. SPLIT OR RUIN?

The unitarian social-communists do not want the party to split, as they have no wish to ruin the Italian proletarian revolution.[147] Let us acknowledge at the outset that the unitarian social-communists represent and embody all the "glorious" traditions of the great and glorious Italian Socialist Party (which is to become the Italian Unitarian Social-Communist Party): its glorious ignorance, the glorious and unprejudiced lack of any scruple in polemic and of any sense of responsibility in national politics, the glorious low demagogy, the glorious vanity, the most glorious chicanery – behold the body of glorious and extremely Italian traditions which the unitarian social-communists embody and represent.

The IInd Congress of the Communist International set the PSI the problem of organizing itself on the basis of acceptance of the resolutions adopted by the assembly. The issue is that of splitting away from the reformists, in other words of splitting away from a tiny part of the Party's own membership: a part that plays no vital role in the life of the organism; a part that is estranged from the proletarian masses; a part that can claim to represent the masses only when they have been demoralized by the errors, uncertainties and absenteeism of the revolutionary leaders. The unitarian social-communists were not willing to accept the decisions of the IInd Congress, in order not to split the Party away from the reformists; they claim they do not want to split the Party away from the reformists in order not to split the masses. These people have plunged the masses, both in the Party and in the factories, into the darkest turmoil; they have called into question the correctness of the International Congress; they have repudiated the Party's affiliation to the Congress (Serrati returned to Italy from Moscow in the same way as Orlando returned one fine day from Versailles, to protest, to disclaim responsibility, to uphold the honour and glory of Italians); they have discredited (or have sought to discredit) the highest authority of the workers' International; in an environment as propitious as the Italian, they have spread a putrid stream of gossip, insinuations, cowardly actions and doubts.

What results have they achieved? They have split the Party into three, four, five tendencies. In the big cities, they have split the working masses, whereas once they had been solidly against reformism and reformists. They have sown the seeds of decay and disintegration amongst the rank and file of the Party.

What then is unitarianism? What occult evil influence does this word have, that it can bring about disagreement and division on a vaster scale by claiming that it wishes to avoid a limited and well-defined split? What is, had to be. If it was unitarianism that provoked the current ruin, the truth is to be sought in the fact that the ruin was already there beforehand; unitarianism is to be blamed for nothing but violently pulling down the dam holding back a running sewer. The truth is that the Socialist Party was not a "city" but a "horde".[148] It was not an organism, but a conglomeration of individuals who had sufficient class consciousness to be able to organize themselves into a trade union, but for the most part did not have the political ability or preparation required to organize themselves into the sort of revolutionary party that the present historical period demanded. Italian vanity always forced us to claim that we had a unique Socialist Party, a party that could not and should not suffer the same crises as other Socialist Parties. And so it happened that in Italy the crisis was artificially delayed, is now upon us at the very moment when it would be better to avoid it, and is that much more violent and devastating on account of the determination and stubbornness of those who always denied its existence in words and are still denying it today (we are unitarians, so there!).

It would be ridiculous to whine about what has happened and what is irremediable. Communists are cold and calm reasoners – they have to be. If everything lies in ruins, then everything has to be done again. The Party has to be rebuilt, and henceforth the communist fraction must be considered and esteemed as a party in its own right, as the solid framework of the Italian Communist Party. It must form disciples, organize them on a solid basis, educate them and turn them into the active cells of a new organism, that is developing and will develop until it becomes the whole of the working class, until it becomes the soul and will of the whole of the working people.

The crisis we are passing through today is perhaps the worst revolutionary crisis ever for the Italian people. To see if they comprehend this truth, comrades should ask themselves the following hypothetical question: what would have happened if the Socialist Party had suffered this crisis at the height of a revolution, when it was carrying the full responsibility of a State? What would have happened had the government of a revolutionary State found itself in the hands of men struggling on behalf of tendencies, and who in the passion of this struggle cast doubt on the whole of the most sacred heritage of a worker – his faith in the International and in the ability and loyalty of the men who hold its highest offices? Things would have happened as they did in Hungary: the masses would have fallen back, revolutionary energies would have ebbed and the counter-revolution would have scored a thunderous victory.

Through their bogus mania for unity, the unitarians have today merely succeeded in disbanding a Party; tomorrow, they would have brought about the fall of the revolution.

Although these people have damaged the working class and strengthened reaction, the evil is not decisive: men of good will still have a boundless field to cultivate again and cause to bear fruit handsomely.

Unsigned, *L'Ordine Nuovo*, 11–18 December 1920, Vol. II, No. 22.

70. EDITORIAL: 24 DECEMBER 1920

The new daily which will be published in Turin from 1 January 1921 will have the name *L'Ordine Nuovo*: the executive committee of the Turin section and the general assembly decided this unanimously (less one vote). The questions raised by this decision are numerous and very serious. They cannot be resolved by an act of will. Perhaps it is still difficult today to define accurately the questions themselves, or to discover the best solutions.

Will the daily enjoy the same consent and the same support which the review has succeeded in winning? And let us be clear: will it enjoy the same consent and the same support in the measure that is necessary for a daily, if it wishes to develop its activity usefully and effectively? We have succeeded in creating a type of review of socialist culture which had always been lacking in Italy; but, in fact, to do so was far less difficult than it may have seemed. The problems which arose for the review become a hundred and a thousand times more difficult when they arise for a daily; moreover, to a great extent they change their nature. Will it be possible to create a daily which can aspire to continue the work of the review in a wider field; which can aspire to apply the same spirit which gave birth to the review to all the activities which appertain to a daily? The readers of *L'Ordine Nuovo* understand these preoccupations: they are present to all of us and make us feel the full weight of our new responsibility.

The daily will be called *L'Ordine Nuovo* and will continue the work of the review in its political line and in its guiding spirit. Hence the daily will be Communist, in accordance with the line laid down by the International Congress and by the Conference of Italian Communists,[149] and in accordance with the tradition of the Turin working class and the majority of the Socialist section. It will deal with all the concrete problems which interest the Italian and world working class today: from, on the one hand, the most immediate and pressing problem of the founding of the Italian Communist Party, examined down to the level of its most basic units as the organization of the communist factory and union groups, to, on the other hand, the problem of the relations between party and union, or the constitutional problems of the present historical period characterized by the rise of the workers' States and by the immense, tremendous work of organization and propaganda carried out by international Communism, which seeks to place the revolutionary vanguard, the working class, at the head of the popular masses in struggle. But it is unnecessary to point out to readers of the review the main points of what the daily's programme will be. To the readers of the review, to the comrades who have followed us and helped us up until now, we put the question: will they go on? What we have always said of the review, we repeat with respect to the daily: its life and development would be impossible without an intimate contact with the working-class masses who must themselves concretely work out and realize the forms of the proletarian State. The comrades who have helped and supported the weekly must help us to support the daily. They must distribute it. They must explain and propagate its programme. They must succeed in inspiring the working-class masses with the conviction that a communist paper is the blood and flesh of the working class, and cannot live or struggle or develop without the support of the revolutionary vanguard – in other words of that part of the working-class population which is not discouraged by any defeat, which is not demoralized by any betrayal, which does not lose its faith in itself and in the destiny of its class even if everything seems plunged in the darkest and most atrocious chaos.

Unsigned, *L'Ordine Nuovo*, 24 December 1920, Vol. II, No. 23.

71. THE WORKERS' STATE

An association can be called a "political party" only in so far as it possesses a constitutional doctrine of its own, in so far as it has succeeded in concretizing and promulgating its own notion of the State, and in so far as it has succeeded in concretizing and promulgating among the broad masses a government programme of its own – a programme which would enable it to actually organize a state in practice, i.e. in concrete circumstances, using real men and not abstract phantasies of humanity.

The Italian Socialist Party has always claimed to be the "political party" of the Italian proletariat. This ideological claim imposed certain practical tasks and immediate obligations upon the Socialist Party. The Italian Socialist Party should have been conscious of its highest, its most immediate historical task: the founding of a new state, the workers' state – involving the creation and organization of the "political" conditions needed for the founding of a new state. It should also have had a precise consciousness of the limits and forms of its task, in both national and international terms. The very development of history has provided the critique of this ideological claim on the part of the Socialist Party: the party's current situation provides the setting for this critical and destructive work that is being accomplished not by individual men, but by the whole process of development of the history of a people.

Immediately following the Bologna Congress, the Socialist Party presented itself to the Italian people as a party of revolutionary government. The results in the parliamentary elections of November 1919 revealed a political tendency that should have given the party the energy and enthusiasm it needed to effect a rapid shift from propaganda to action. The November elections created the sort of political situation in Italy that can be summed up in the words: there exist two governments. The whole of the working class and broad sections of the peasantry had declared themselves for the Socialist Party. They had made the explicit declaration that they wholeheartedly supported the party of the dictatorship of the proletariat: the party that was seeking to bring the Italian nation, the working people of Italy, into the system of the Communist International, the system of the world workers' state being tenaciously organized around the first national workers' state – the Russian Soviet Republic – and around the first germ of a world workers' government – the Executive Committee of the Third International. The type of electoral campaign waged by the other mass parties in Italy – the Popular Party and the groups of war veterans – showed how even the most backward sections of the working people were in favour of a radical change of régime; so much so that these petty-bourgeois parties had to hurriedly cloak themselves in red, indulge in demagogy and put forward apparently revolutionary programmes. Bourgeois ideology had failed in its attempts to focus the attention of the masses on the Wilsonian myth; it had failed in its attempt to satisfy, within the limits imposed by the bourgeois state, the demand of the masses for an international solution to the problems raised by the war. The unseemly myth of "Wilson, emperor of the peoples" was replaced by a political passion for "Lenin, head of the Communist International". Through its propaganda and the prestige it had acquired during the war, the Italian Socialist Party had in effect succeeded in creating the general political conditions needed for founding the workers' state; it had succeeded in creating a framework of the broadest possible popular consent to the setting up of a revolutionary government. The merest acquaintance with political psychology would have enabled one to foresee that such a government, after the initial violent take-over of the state machine, would have had a majority of the population on its side and been in effect a majority government.

The party did not succeed in organizing the situation it had created. It did not succeed in consolidating and activating on a permanent basis the government apparatus that had been formed immediately after the Bologna Congress, in the first political consultation with the Italian people staged since the outbreak of the world war. This history of the period from 2–3 December 1919 to the present day is one of continual demonstration of the party's inability to organize the political life of the Italian people, to give it a direction, to guide the vanguard of the popular revolution so as to provide it with a precise awareness of its concrete tasks and specific responsibilities. The Socialist Party has shown that it does not have any ideas of its own concerning the state, that it does not have a programme of its own for revolutionary government. In short, it has shown that it is not a "political party" capable of bearing the responsibility for action, for securing food and shelter for the tens of millions of the Italian people, but is an association of well-meaning men of good-will gathered together to discuss (albeit with little originality and abundant ignorance) what verbal significance they should attach to the new political terminology invented by the restless imagination of the Russian Bolsheviks – dictatorship, Soviet, control, factory council, semi-proletarian, terror, etc., etc.

The Socialist Party has systematically neglected and ignored each and every movement of the mass of the people, whether they were industrial workers or politically backward poor peasants. It did not acquire any notion of the idea of "hierarchy": it allowed the Turin movement in favour of factory councils and workers' control to be crushed in April 1920; in September it allowed the gigantic metal-workers' movement to end pathetically in a Giolittian compromise and in the obvious swindle of trade-union control; in the same way it left the masses of agricultural workers struggling to take over the land in complete isolation. Incapable of forming its own doctrine of a national workers' state or of elaborating a plan of action appropriate for attaining the direct goal of its existence, viz. the founding of such a workers' state, how could the Party be capable of comprehending the doctrine of the world workers' state, of the Communist International? So the clash we see today between the party's majority and its executive committee undoubtedly had to come some time. This turn of events is the latest critical instance of the party's political positions and its ideologies. It has revealed the true nature of the Socialist Party and provides the key to its past attitudes, its past errors. The Italian Socialist Party never understood that it had to base its actions exclusively on the urban working class. It ought to be the party of "all the workers" and instead it turned out to be the party of "no one". It turned out to be merely a parliamentary party, one which could set itself the target of "correcting" or sabotaging the bourgeois state, but could not set itself the target of founding a new state. It has shown itself in practice to be unable to comprehend the hierarchical position which the revolutionary vanguard (the urban proletariat) should occupy in relation to the broader layers of the working people within the national sphere, ever since it confirmed by a majority decision (it would appear to be a majority decision) that it would refuse to obey the supreme power in the world workers' movement, the International Congress and its legitimate expression and governing organ, the Executive Committee. This lack of "public spirit" and "loyalism" to the world workers' state on the part of the Socialist Party shows how it is inherently incapable even of conceiving organically a national workers' state.

In Italy the never-ending parade of "D'Annunzios" ("D'Annunzio" is the traveller who tries to cheat on the railways, the industrialist who conceals his profits, the merchant who draws up false accounts to cheat the tax authorities), this absence on the part of the bourgeoisie of any public spirit or loyalism towards their institutions, has always held back the development of a well-ordered parliamentary state (as, for example, in England). These bourgeois habits have been handed down to the workers' movement to end pathetically in a Giolittian compromise and evident: they have shown themselves capable of splitting the International and successfully paralysing for almost a year the energies of Italy's working class. The communists, through their clear and precise political positions and their unyielding intransigence, seek to protect the frail body of the world workers' state from Italian corruption, from Italian scepticism, from the bad practices of Italian political life – because the communists believe that by defending the Communist International they are effectively defending the future of the proletarian revolution in Italy as well, the future of the Italian working people. Because they have the inner conviction that they have in this way begun the concrete work of political guidance and education which is today the fundamental precondition for the founding of the Italian workers' state.

Unsigned, *L'Ordine Nuovo*, daily edition, 1 January 1921.

72. THE MONKEY-PEOPLE

Fascism has been the latest "performance" offered by the urban petty bourgeoisie on the stage of national political life. The pathetic conclusion to the Fiume adventure was the final scene of the performance.[150] It can be taken as the most important episode in the process of inner dissolution being experienced by this class of the Italian people.

The ruination of the petty bourgeoisie began in the final decade of the last century. With the rise of large-scale industry and finance capital, the petty bourgeoisie lost all importance and was removed from all its vital posts in the field of production: it became a purely political class and specialized in "parliamentary cretinism". This phenomenon, which plays an important role in contemporary Italian history, has been called by various names in its various stages. It was originally called "the coming to power of the left", then it became Giolittianism, then the struggle against the Kaiserist aspirations of Umberto I, and finally it broadened into socialist reformism.[151]

The petty bourgeoisie is encrusted to the institution of Parliament. Parliament has evolved from a controlling organ of the capitalist bourgeoisie over the Crown and Civil Service, to a talk-shop for gossip and scandal, a means of parasitism. Corrupt to the very marrow, enslaved completely to the governing power, Parliament has lost all prestige in the eyes of the mass of the people. The masses are convinced that direct action, external pressure, is the only means of checking and opposing the arbitrary actions of the administrative powers. Red Week in June 1914, in protest at the massacres, was the first, magnificent intervention of the mass of the people in politics, to directly oppose the arbitrary actions of the authorities and to give effective expression to the sovereign will of the people, which no longer found any voice in the Chamber of Representatives.[152] One might say that in June 1914, parliamentarism – and with it the political role of the petty bourgeoisie – set out on the road of its organic dissolution in Italy.

Now that the petty bourgeoisie has lost all hope of regaining a productive role (only today is a hope of this kind re-emerging, with the attempts of the Popular Party to restore the importance of small agricultural holdings and with the attempts of the General Confederation of Labour officials to breathe new life into the corpse of trade-union control), it is desperately seeking to maintain a position of historical initiative. Now it is aping the working class and coming out on to the streets. This new tactic is being tried out in the ways and forms to be expected of a class of chatterboxes, sceptics and corrupt dealers. The succession of events that came to be called the "radiant days of May",[153] with all their journalistic, oratorical, theatrical and vulgar echoes throughout the war, was like the projection into reality of one of the stories in Kipling's *Jungle Book*, the story of the Bandarlog, the Monkey-People. They believed they were better than all the other jungle people, that they had a monopoly on intelligence, historical intuition, revolutionary spirit, governing know-how, etc., etc. What had happened was this: the petty bourgeoisie, which had become enslaved to governmental power as a result of parliamentary corruption, changed its direction, became anti-parliamentarist and sought to corrupt the street.

During the war, Parliament completely collapsed. The petty bourgeoisie sought to consolidate its new position and deluded itself that it had actually accomplished this goal; that it had actually killed the class struggle; that it had taken charge of the working and peasant class and replaced the idea of socialism, inherent in the masses, with a strange ideological mish-mash of nationalist imperialism, "true revolutionism", and "national syndicalism". The direct action of the masses on the 2nd and 3rd of December, after the officials had attacked the socialist deputies in Rome, put a brake on the petty bourgeoisie's political activity.[154] After that, they sought to organize and systematize themselves around bosses who were richer and more reliable than the official State, weakened as it was and exhausted by the war.

The Fiume adventure was the sentimental cause and practical mechanism of this systematic organization; but it immediately became apparent that the latter's solid core was direct defence of industrial and agricultural property from the assaults of the revolutionary class of workers and poor peasants. This activity on the part of the petty bourgeoisie, officially dubbed "fascism", is not without consequences for the framework of the State. *After having corrupted and ruined the institution of Parliament, the petty bourgeoisie is now corrupting and ruining other institutions as well, the pillars of the State: the army, the police, the magistrature.* Aimless corruption and ruin, without any precise goal (the one precise goal would have had to be the creation of a new State – but the "Monkey-People" are characterized precisely by their incapacity to provide themselves with laws and found a State).

To defend himself, the proprietor finances and supports a private organization which, to mask its true nature, must adopt "revolutionary" political attitudes and destroy the most powerful defence of property, namely the State. *Vis-à-vis* the executive power, the property-owning class is repeating the same error it committed in the case of Parliament: it believes it will be better equipped to defend itself from the assaults of the revolutionary class if it abandons the institutions of its State to the hysterical whims of the "Monkey-People", the petty bourgeoisie.

As it develops, fascism rigidifies about its original core and no longer succeeds in hiding its true nature. It conducts a savage campaign against the Right Honourable Nitti, president of the Council: a campaign that extends as far as issuing an open invitation to assassinate the Prime Minister. It leaves the Right Hon. Giolitti alone and allows him to bring the liquidation of the Fiume adventure to a "fortunate" conclusion – the attitude that fascism adopted towards Giolitti signed D'Annunzio's fate and emphasized the true historical goals of this organization of the Italian petty bourgeoisie. The stronger the "*fasci*" grew, the better their supporters were organized and the more audacious and aggressive their demonstrations against the Chambers of Labour and socialist communes became – the more characteristically expressive was their attitude towards D'Annunzio calling for insurrection and barricades. "True revolution"'s pompous declarations were translated into concrete terms by the explosion of a harmless firecracker in an entrance-hall at *La Stampa.*

In this its latest political incarnation of "fascism", the petty bourgeoisie has once again shown its true colours as the servant of capitalism and landed property, as the agent of counter-revolution. But it has also shown itself to be fundamentally incapable of accomplishing any historical task whatsoever. The Monkey-People make news, not history. They leave their mark in newspapers, but provide no material for books. Having ruined Parliament, the petty bourgeoisie is currently ruining the bourgeois State. On an ever increasing scale, it is replacing the "authority" of the law by private violence. It practises this violence in a chaotic and brutal fashion (and cannot help but do so), and in the process it is causing ever broader sections of the population to revolt against the State and against capitalism.

Unsigned, *L'Ordine Nuovo*, daily edition, 2 January 1921.

73. THE LIVORNO CONGRESS

The Livorno Congress is destined to become one of the most important historical events in contemporary Italian life.[155] At Livorno, the question whether the Italian working class has the capacity to form an autonomous class party from its own ranks will finally be resolved. The question whether the experiences of four years of imperialist war, and two years of misery for the productive forces all over the world, will succeed in making the Italian working class conscious of its historical mission will also be resolved.

The working class is both a national and an international class. It must place itself at the head of the working people struggling to emancipate themselves from the yoke of industrial and financial capitalism on both a national and international scale. The national task of the working class is determined by the process of development of Italian capitalism and its official expression, the bourgeois State. Italian capitalism came to power by following this line of development: it subjected the countryside to the industrial cities and central and southern Italy to the North. In the Italian bourgeois State, the question of relations between town and countryside is expressed not only as a question of the relations between the great industrial cities and the countryside immediately surrounding them, but also as a question of the relations between one part of the national territory and another – quite distinct and characteristic – part. Capitalism exercises its predominance and its exploitative practices in the following manner: within the factory, directly over the working class; but within the State, over broader layers of the Italian working people, made up of poor peasants and semi-proletarians. What is indisputable is that only the working class, by seizing political and economic power from the hands of the bankers and capitalists, is in a position to resolve the central problem of national life in Italy – the Southern problem. What is indisputable is that only the working class can bring the painful task of unification that the Risorgimento began to a successful conclusion. The bourgeoisie has unified the Italian people in terms of territory. The working class has the task of concluding this work of the bourgeoisie and unifying the Italian people in economic and spiritual terms. This can happen only by smashing the bourgeois State machine, which is constructed on the hierarchical dominance of industrial and financial capitalism over the nation's other productive forces. Such an event can happen only through the revolutionary efforts of the working class directly subjected to capitalism. It can only happen in Milan, Turin, Bologna, in the great industrial cities that generate those millions of threads which make up the network of industrial and finance capitalism's dominance over the rest of the country's productive forces. In Italy, as a result of the particular configuration of the country's economic and political structure, not only is it true that by emancipating itself the working class will emancipate all the other oppressed and exploited classes, but it is no less a fact that the only way these other classes will ever emancipate themselves is to enter into a close alliance with the working class, and to hold by this alliance through even the harshest sufferings and the cruellest trials.

The break between communists and reformists that will occur at Livorno will have the following special significance. The revolutionary working class will break with those degenerate socialist currents that have decayed into State parasitism. It will break with those currents that sought to exploit the position of superiority enjoyed by the North over the South in order to create proletarian aristocracies; that erected a co-operative protectionist system alongside the bourgeois protectionist system of tariffs (the legal expression of the predominance of industrial and financial capitalism over the other productive forces of the nation), in the belief that they could emancipate the working class behind the backs of the majority of the working people.

The reformists point to the socialism of Reggio Emilia as "exemplary"; they expect us to believe that the whole of Italy and the whole world can become one great Reggio Emilia.[156] The revolutionary working class asserts its repudiation of such spurious forms of socialism. The emancipation of the workers cannot be secured through taking over a few privileges, through a workers' aristocracy or through parliamentary compromise and ministerial blackmail. The workers' emancipation can be secured only through an alliance between the industrial workers of the North and the poor peasants of the South – an alliance designed to smash the bourgeois State; found the workers' and peasants' State; and construct a new apparatus of industrial production that will serve the needs of agriculture, serve to industrialize the backward agriculture of Italy and hence raise the level of the national produce to the benefit of the working masses.

The Italian workers' revolution and the participation of the Italian working people in world affairs can come about only in the context of the world revolution. Already there exist the seeds of a world workers' government in the Executive Committee of the Communist International that emerged at the IInd Congress. At Livorno, the vanguard of the Italian working class, the communist fraction of the Socialist Party, will emphasize that disciplined loyalty to the first world government of the working class is necessary and unavoidable – indeed it will make this the central point of the Congress discussion. The Italian working class accepts a maximum of discipline, because it wants the working classes of all other nations to similarly accept and observe a maximum of discipline.

The Italian working class knows that the condition for its own self-emancipation, and for its ability to emancipate all the other classes exploited and oppressed by capitalism in Italy, is the existence of a system of world revolutionary forces all conspiring to the same end. The Italian working class is willing to help the other working classes in their efforts towards liberation, but it would also like some guarantee that the other classes will help it in its own efforts. This assurance can be given only by a powerfully centralized international authority, which enjoys the full and sincere confidence of all its members and is in a position to launch its forces with the same speed and precision that the world authority of capitalism achieves, on its own account and in the interests of the bourgeoisie.

Thus it should be obvious that the questions which are currently tormenting the Socialist Party, and which will be resolved at the Livorno Congress, are not simply internal party questions or personal conflicts between individuals. At Livorno, the destiny of the working people of Italy will be under discussion. At Livorno, a new era in the history of the Italian nation will begin.

Unsigned, *L'Ordine Nuovo*, daily edition, 13 January 1921.

NOTES

I

1 What's good for you won't do for us.
2 Colours in the political spectrum.
3 After the outbreak of the First World War, the PSI leadership adopted a policy of "absolute neutrality", which they concretized in an appeal, jointly with the Socialist group in parliament, to the government to proclaim this as its official policy. When Italy finally intervened in the war on the side of the Entente (France and Britain), in May 1915, the PSI adopted a centrist policy of "Neither join the war nor sabotage it".
4 Specifying a triple of numbers, as in the Italian state lottery. The point is that the reformists were unwilling to commit themselves to anything, preferring vague generalizations.
5 In his article "The Myth of War" (24 October), A. T. (Angelo Tasca) supported the official PSI line of absolute neutrality. The Mussolini "affair" arose when, as editor of *Avanti!*, he advanced the thesis of "relative neutrality" (18 October). Tasca admonished Mussolini for having ignored the process "by which the proletariat, the best elements of the proletariat, have seen in the war the clearest and most incontestable symbol of the bourgeois system, the purest expression of its own class slavery". Within a few weeks Mussolini performed an about-face, shifting his position from relative neutralism to interventionism. He was then expelled from the Socialist Party and founded, on 15 November, *Il Popolo d'Italia*.
6 When Italy followed up earlier imperialist expansion into Eritrea and Somalia with the invasion of Libya in 1912, Mussolini was prominent in his denunciation of the enterprise, displaying a passion which won him wide support on the left of the PSI, notably among younger members like Gramsci, Tasca and the other future editors of *L'Ordine Nuovo*.
7 Here a line is missing in the text.
8 Enrico Leone, one of the "revolutionary syndicalists" expelled from the Socialist Party in 1908, was among the few who subsequently rejoined it. His leaning was, however, always towards chaotic activism and at times bordered on an apologia for violence. Leone became a sort of precursor of fascism, as a result of the interpretation that Mussolini gave to his writings and to his activities.
9 At the Young Socialists' National Congress, held at Bologna on 20–23

September 1912, in a debate on "the culture and education of youth", Tasca engaged in a polemic with the rapporteur Amadeo Bordiga, who maintained that too much importance could be attached to the necessity for study. ("No one becomes a socialist through education but through real-life necessities imposed by the class they belong to.") Tasca, on the other hand, stressed the urgent need for a cultural renewal, for an intellectual revivifying of Italian socialism. Bordiga called Tasca and his supporters "culturists".

10 A comic character in Rossini's opera *The Barber of Seville*.

11 *Panciafichismo* ("belly full of figs"-ism), a play on words with *pacifismo*, was a term of abuse for the business lobby campaigning to draw Italy out of the war. Similarly *pescecani* ("sharks") were the war-profiteers.

12 As the text soon makes clear, these are the names of cotton industrialists in Turin and the surrounding area.

13 This is the chorus referred to: "En t'iufficine, n't'iufficine ai manca l'aria, – an t'le suffiete, n't le suffiete ai mance l'pan! – Custa l'è la vita prulataria – che l'uvrié, che l'uvrié, a fa tut l'an." ("In the workshops, in the workshops, there is no air; – in the garrets, in the garrets, there is no bread; – This is the proletarian life that the worker, the worker, leads the whole year through.")

14 The *portone* of the typical Italian *palazzo* is a huge wooden door opening onto a paved hallway leading to a courtyard. Access to the building is from this courtyard, not directly from the street.

15 The title *onorevole* means that Poma was a parliamentary deputy.

16 This discussion on the Turin municipal council was just one episode in a wide-ranging debate on education in the first decades of this century, in which the existing Italian system based on the 1859 Casati Act in Piedmont came under fire both from the socialists and from powerful sectors of bourgeois opinion. The most notable critics of the existing system were Benedetto Croce – later Minister of Education under Giolitti in 1921 – and Giovanni Gentile, who as Mussolini's first Minister of Education in 1923 put through a large-scale educational reform. For all this, see Gramsci's writings in prison on the subject, in *Selections from the Prison Notebooks*, pp. 24–43.

17 Consultative assemblies, at the national and regional levels respectively, which were established by the Tsarist autocracy to head off popular demands for representation, but which became a site of agitation against the régime.

18 The Bolsheviks were often referred to in Italy, by assimilation, as maximalists, although the two terms have quite different origins: Bolsheviks meant "those in the majority" (in 1903 at the time of the split in the Russian Social-Democratic Party); the maximalists were so-called

in contradistinction to those who advocated fighting for a minimum programme.

19 Here there is a gap in the text.

20 *Mosche cocchiere*, a reference to La Fontaine's fable *Le Coche et la Mouche*, about a fly who thinks that a coach succeeds in ascending a steep hill due to his efforts.

21 The general election of 1913 was the first to be held in Italy under so-called universal suffrage, which in fact gave the vote to all male citizens over twenty-one.

22 Giovanni Giolitti.

23 Eminent contemporary surgeon.

24 A mythical animal, half-goat, half-stag, sometimes also known as a tragelaphus.

25 A wartime decree of 4 October 1917 which further limited the already curtailed freedom of speech and freedom of the press.

26 In August 1915 the government issued a decree setting up seven "Regional Committees of Industrial Mobilization", with the principal function of settling labour disputes. The question of whether or not to co-operate with them became a subject of controversy between reformists and intransigents within the PSI.

27 In *Le Père Goriot*, Goriot asks Rastignac whether he would still eat oranges if he knew that each time he did so someone would die in China. Rastignac answers that he would, since oranges are a familiar part of his everyday world, while China is far off and unknown.

II

28 This article was published one week after the defeat in parliament of the Orlando government and the formation of a new government led by Francesco Nitti. Orlando's fall was precipitated by his inability to secure Italian interests in the Adriatic at the Paris Peace Conference. Nitti's government included two representatives of the new Popular Party.

29 Vittorio Veneto was the site of the final Italian victory over Austria on 30 October 1918, immediately prior to the latter's collapse and surrender to the Entente.

30 *imposte non proposte*: this is an Italian nuance that does not come across in English. The sense is that the trade unions arose in *response* to hostile historical conditions; they were not an autonomous projection on the part of the workers.

31 The reference is to Minos, legendary King of Crete and constructor of the Labyrinth where the Minotaur dwelt, famous as a pitiless judge.

32 The demonstration in question was an international strike, called for by the IIIrd International.

33 In Roman law, *fidei-commissum* meant a bequest to a third party which was entrusted to the single heir to transmit. Hence in feudalism, it became the juridical formula for the entailment of landed property, which could not be alienated or sub-divided by multiple bequests.
34 This text was appended as a note to an article by Alessandro Cerri.
35 The first Congress of the IIIrd International took place in March 1919.
36 On 21 March 1919, after the Liberal republican Karolyi resigned as Hungarian prime minister, a Socialist-Communist government was formed, to be replaced shortly afterwards by a Soviet government under Bela Kun. On 10 April 1919 Rumanian troops began their counter-revolutionary intervention. On 1 August 1919 the Bela Kun government left Budapest (for Vienna) and the city fell to the Rumanians three days later.
37 See page 79 and note 32 above.
38 Bruno Buozzi, general secretary of the metal-workers' union FIOM; Ludovico D'Aragona, general-secretary of the CGL and a reformist; Armando Borghi, secretary of the anarcho-syndicalist USI.
39 See translator's note.
40 *Sabato Inglese*, literally "English Saturday".

III

41 This article was published on 15 November 1919, the day before the first Italian general election to be held under proportional representation. The election was a massive defeat for the old bourgeois parliamentary groupings, who together only won 252 out of 508 seats. The socialists had a triumphant success, advancing from 52 seats to 156; the remaining 100 seats were won by the Popular Party.
42 After the socialist triumph in the November elections, at the opening of parliament, the socialist deputies walked out as the monarch walked in and were promptly attacked by crowds of nationalists. This attack provoked a spontaneous outburst of strikes and demonstrations by workers in support of the socialists, notably in Northern cities such as Mantua.
43 Character in Italian comic opera, the *serva-padrona*, or maid who is the real mistress of the household, who rules the roost. Title role in one of Mozart's operas.
44 The passage in brackets was censored in *L'Ordine Nuovo*.
45 Monarchist gangs formed by the Tsarist police in the early years of this century to assault revolutionaries and progressive intellectuals and to carry out pogroms.
46 During the strike of 2–3 December, the agricultural labourers of Andria, after being attacked by the police, barricaded the city and defended themselves with arms. They were dispersed after a violent conflict in which about 200 people were wounded.

47 For these committees, see note 26 above.

48 In May 1838 the Milanese rose in the Five Days insurrection and drove the Austrians out of the city. See Gramsci's analysis of the *Risorgimento* in *Selections from the Prison Notebooks*, pp. 44–120.

49 The sentence in brackets was censored in some copies of *L'Ordine Nuovo*.

50 A few days before this article was written, in January 1920, Clemenceau was defeated in the French presidential elections, largely because of dissatisfaction at what was seen in France as the leniency of Versailles towards defeated Germany. A nonentity, Paul Deschanel, succeeded Clemenceau.

51 The strikes in question were the postal and telephone workers' strike (14–20 January 1920) and the railwaymen's strike (20–29 January 1920) both led by the USI. The PSI limited itself to vague gestures of solidarity and the anarchists accused it of being a slave to the Byzantine distinction between economic and political strikes in a revolutionary situation.

52 Pulcinella is the Italian original for the figure of Mr Punch, the buffoon.

53 The "electoral committee" was charged with the task of preparing the elections of the leading bodies of the Turin socialist section.

54 The National Council of the PSI met in Florence on 11–12 January 1920.

55 *Scopone*: a variation on the popular Italian card game *scopa*.

56 Literally "knight of industry", a term which in Italian means a swindler.

57 Tomaso Masaniello (1620–47) was an illiterate fishmonger who rose to sudden prominence as leader of anti-tax riots in Naples in 1647. After releasing all the inmates of the prisons, he became master of the city and was even recognized by the viceroy of Charles V. However, less than six weeks after his rise to power, he apparently went mad and was killed by his friends.

58 The "one big union" was the slogan of the IWW (Wobblies).

59 This refers to the *sciopero delle lancette* of 28 March 1920, a skirmish over the introduction of summer-time which spread from Turin to Bologna and Cremona and which was a prelude to the great April lock-out and general strike in Turin for defence of the factory councils. The *sciopero della lancette* was incidentally hailed by Mussolini as a grand revolutionary gesture of the individual against the State, a victory for ANARCHY.

60 The Royal Guard.

61 The Congress of Bologna was held from 5–8 October 1919. It ended with the defeat of the reformists and the adoption, by an overwhelming majority, of Serrati's motion, which among other things called for the PSI's adhesion to the IIIrd International. A small minority voted for Bordiga's abstentionist position (see "Letter to the IIIrd International", pp. 207–210 below, for an account of the differences at the Congress, the exact votes, etc.).

62 The speech, on 30 March 1920, became famous as the "expiation speech". Its theme was that the bourgeoisie was no longer capable of ruling, but the proletariat was not yet ready to take power – hence the tragedy and "expiation" of the ruling classes.

63 This was a proposal to bring together in an assembly the socialist deputies and representatives from the major political, trade-union and co-operative organizations, to work out proposals for legislation and to put pressure on the government. In such an assembly (in contrast to the Party leadership [*direzione*] or National Council) the reformists would have been in a majority.

IV

64 The Programme of the Communist Fraction was published in *Avanti!* on 17 August 1919. It had first appeared in *Il Soviet* on 13 July 1919, and the text can be found in *Storia della Sinistra Comunista*, Vol. 1, Milan 1964.

65 A. Viglongo, "Towards New Institutions", *L'Ordine Nuovo*, No. 16, 30 August 1919.

66 See note 61 above, for the Bologna congress.

67 See note 3 above.

68 *Il constituente professionale.*

69 The reference is to "Greetings to Italian, French and German Communists", in Lenin, *Collected Works*, Vol. 30, pp. 52–62.

70 The full text of this programme is given in *Storia della Sinistra Comunista*, op. cit., Vol. 2, pp. 69–71.

71 E. Leone and a group of other comrades, while voting for the maximalist leadership's resolution, issued a separate "statement of principles". For the text, see pp. 233–4 below.

72 The relevant passage reads as follows: "Recognizing that the instruments of oppression and exploitation employed under the bourgeois régime (States, municipal councils and organs of public administration) cannot in any way be transformed into organs for the liberation of the proletariat; recognizing that to such organs should be opposed new proletarian organs (workers', peasants' and soldiers' councils; councils of the public economy, etc.) which, functioning initially (under the bourgeois régime) as instruments of the violent struggle for liberation, will subsequently become organs of social and economic transformation and for the reconstruction of the new communist order".

73 For the text of the motion, see appendix to this article (pp. 233–4 below).

74 I.e. leaving out the expression ". . . which, functioning initially (under the bourgeois régime) as instruments of the violent struggle for liberation, will subsequently become . . .".

75 Work-crews, workshops, factories, entire industrial sectors.
76 "The Factory Committees", in *Comunismo*, Vol. I, No. 6, 13–31 December 1919, pp. 402–3.
77 Angelo Tasca, "Impressions of the Socialist Congress", *L'Ordine Nuovo*, Vol. I, No. 22, 18 October 1919.
78 See p. 116 above.
79 The official organ of the USI.
80 As on p. 225 above, this means that the voters elect delegates to the local Soviets, who in turn elect delegates to regional Soviets, who in turn elect delegates to the State Congress of Soviets.
81 "The co-existence of Soviets and bourgeois State power", subsequently reproduced in *Il Soviet*, 28 March 1920.
82 "Electionist maximalism storming local government", in *Il Soviet*, 18 January 1920.
83 Although this sentiment is typical of the documents passed by the First Congress of the Third International, it has not been possible to locate this precise quotation either in the two texts presented to the Congress by Lenin, or in the Manifesto or the Platform of the Comintern, both of which were presented anonymously as collective documents.

V

84 A reference to the "pact of alliance" signed in September 1918 between the CGL and the PSI, whereby each acknowledged the other's authority in their respective "spheres".
85 For this episode, see note 59 above.
86 Ettore Reyna, a reformist socialist member of parliament, presented a draft Bill in 1919 allowing for a degree of worker participation in management.
87 A reference to John H. Whitley's *Works Committees and Industrial Councils, their beginnings and possibilities*, London 1920.
88 See pp. 239–54 above.
89 In the land of the heathen.
90 Bukharin's *The Communist Programme* (1918) was translated into English as *Programme of the World Revolution*, Glasgow 1920.
91 For the Regulations, see pp. 118–24 above.
92 See above, pp. 109–13.
93 It has not been possible to identify this allusion precisely. However, it seems clear from the context that it refers to an episode (perhaps involving the refusal of a porter to carry a load in the rain) which was blown up, distorted and systematically utilized for anti-working class propaganda purposes by the bourgeois press.

94 Chignoli was secretary to the Executive Commission of the Chamber of Labour, a reformist.

95 The reference is to Giordano Bruno's *Lo Spaccio della Bestia Trionfante,* whose first edition appeared in England in 1585, with a dedication to Sir Philip Sidney. Translated recently as *The Exclusion of the Triumphant Beast.*

96 A person employed to bury the dead at times of plague.

97 See above, pp. 109–13.

98 See above, p. 242.

99 The Communist International, No. 1, Moscow, 1 May 1919, pp. 9–10.

100 *Il Capitalismo*, Turin, Bocca, 1910.

101 See "The Factory Council", pp. 260–64 above.

102 Karl Marx, *Selected Works* in one volume, Lawrence & Wishart, 1970, p. 43.

103 See above, p. 263.

104 Note the Sorelian terminology: cf. Gramsci, *Selection from the Prison Notebooks*, London 1971, pp. 126 ff.

105 Karl Marx, op. cit., p. 39.

106 Ibid., p. 40.

107 Here a linc is missing from the original text.

108 J. Sadoul, "Appeal to the French Workers and Peasants", *L'Ordine Nuovo*, Vol. II, No. 4, 5 June 1920.

109 See above, p. 115.

110 See above, p. 106.

111 See above, pp. 101–2.

112 Bela Kun, "Trade Unions and Party", *L'Ordine Nuovo*, 8 November 1919.

113 "The Soviet-type Mechanism of Nationalization", *L'Ordine Nuovo*, Vol. I, No. 14, 16 August 1919.

114 Aron Wizner, militant in the clandestine Polish Revolutionary Socialist Party, who came to Italy as a refugee in 1914 and joined the PSI.

115 See note 20 above.

116 The article in question was "Workers' Democracy", see pp. 65–8 above.

117 See p. 279 above.

118 After the *Risorgimento* and the unification of Italy under the Piedmontese monarchy, the capital of the new state was first Turin (1861–4), then Florence (1864–70) and finally Rome.

119 See pp. 273 and 278 above.

120 This text was apparently never written.

VI

121 In 1919, in the wake of Turkey's defeat in the World War and the

overthrow of the Sultan's rule outside Turkey itself, a mass movement called Khilafat arose in India, initially composed of Moslems embittered by the affront to Islam in the person of the man they regarded as the direct descendant of the Prophet. Directed against the British, the movement took on a more general anti-imperialist character and spread to the Hindu population as well, being backed by Gandhi and other leaders. It issued an appeal to all Indian troops serving with the British Army throughout the world to disobey orders. In Persia, the British negotiated the so-called Anglo-Persian Agreement in August 1919, which sealed their ascendancy in the country. There was widespread opposition within Persia and it was in this context that the Khilafat appeal met with a response from Indian troops stationed in the country. Similarly, in Mesopotamia there was opposition to British occupation of the former Turkish province – an occupation that was shortly to be ratified by the Treaty of Sèvres (August 1920), which established a British mandate over the territory.

122 Albania proclaimed its independence from Turkey in 1912, but was occupied by Italy in May 1915. Albanian insurgents in early 1920 forced the Italian garrisons to retreat to the city of Valona. There were big demonstrations in Italy demanding the withdrawal of troops from Albania. Italy was forced to evacuate in August 1920.

123 I.e. not along the craft lines of traditional union organization.

124 For the events of 2–3 December 1919, see pp. 135–41 above.

125 D.R. "A Letter from Moscow", *L'Ordine Nuovo*, Vol. II, No. 13.

126 Lenin, "Theses on the Fundamental Tasks of the Second Congress of the Communist International", *Collected Works*, Vol. 31, p. 199. Lenin's text refers to the article "Towards a Renewal of the Socialist Party", see pp. 190–6 above.

127 In seventeenth-century Milan, *Untori* were suspected of spreading plague by smearing poisonous substances on walls.

128 The *subbotniki* (Communist Saturday movement) emerged in the summer of 1919. Workers were called on to dedicate their Saturdays (normally holidays) to voluntary unpaid work to meet the demands of the civil war.

129 The occupation of the factories followed protracted negotiations over a new national wage agreement in the engineering industry. When the employers unilaterally broke these off on 13 August 1920, the FIOM leaders decided on a national go-slow. It was the occupation of the Romeo works in Milan by the police, on 30 August, and the proclamation of a lock-out by the employers on 1 September, which sparked off a wave of factory occupations by the workers throughout Northern Italy, most notably in Milan itself, Turin and Genoa. The workers resumed production under workers' control in the occupied factories, while the police and army – although they surrounded the factories – did not intervene. In this situation, the PSI and CGL leaders met in Milan from 9

to 11 September, and decided by 591,245 votes to 409,596, with 93,623 abstentions, to limit the aims of the workers' action to winning recognition by the factory-owners of trade-union control in the plants. Giolitti enacted a decree establishing a paritary committee to study the problem, and promised to introduce a parliamentary bill establishing "workers' control" over industry (see A Note on the Translation, p. xviii above), thus giving the reformists a semblance of satisfaction. The factories were evacuated and work was resumed for the owners on 4 October 1920.

130 The Catholic unions, in contradistinction to the "red" unions.

131 *Serve-padrone*: see note 43 above.

132 Originally fixed for Florence, the Congress was subsequently shifted to Livorno, where greater security could be provided against fascist attacks.

133 Gramsci's article appeared on the first Sunday of the occupation (see note 129 above).

134 *mezzadria*, share-cropping. In other words, "control" would only mean a subordinate participation in capitalist production, analogous to the subordinate participation of the share-cropper in feudal production.

135 The decision by FIOM to end the factory occupations was submitted to the workers' approval by referendum on 24 September 1920. A small majority approved the agreement.

136 "Intorno al Congresso Internazionale Comunista", *Il Soviet*, Vol. III, No. 24. For the text of Lenin's thesis, see p. 321 above.

137 The PSI's National Council meeting held in Milan from 18 to 22 April 1920, for which "Towards a Renewal of the Socialist Party" was written

138 See note 125 above.

139 14 October 1920 was declared a day of demonstrations by the PSI leadership, in agreement with the CGL, in order to force the government to release political prisoners and recognize the USSR. Four deaths resulted.

140 For D'Aragona, see note 38 above.

141 In September 1919, in order to press Italian claims on the eastern shores of the Adriatic, Gabriele D'Annunzio, the nationalist writer, seized Fiume at the head of a band of volunteers, or self-styled "legionaries". In November 1920, shortly after this article was written, Italy and Yugoslavia were to sign the Treaty of Rapallo, whereby Fiume was to become an independent state as envisaged by the peace treaties (Versailles, etc.). On 1 December 1920 D'Annunzio declared war on the Italian government; on 27 December he was forced by General Caviglia's bombardment to evacuate the city. Admiral Millo, governor of Dalmatia, had given tacit support to D'Annunzio's Fiume adventure.

142 *Classe dominate e dirigente*. For this key distinction, here used by Gramsci for the first time, see *Selections from the Prison Notebooks*, pp. 55–9 and n. 5 on p. 55, etc.

143 In other words, from 4 November 1918 up to the elections of 16 November 1919.

144 The theme of the "proletarian nation" was current in Italian nationalist circles from the time of the Libyan war. Blanqui's aphorism "He who has iron, has bread" was printed as a slogan on Mussolini's *Popolo d'Italia* when it first appeared in 1915.

145 Reggio Emilia was a principal bastion of reformist socialism.

146 *Ascari*: native soldiers from the Italian possessions in North and East Africa. Vito De Bellis organized gangs to enforce electoral support for Giolitti in the South, in the elections of 1904 and 1909.

147 The "unitarian communists" led by Serrati, although they accepted in principle the twenty-one conditions for admission to the IIIrd International, refused to either change the name of the Party or expel the reformists. Organized in November 1920, the faction won a big majority at the Livorno Congress in January 1921.

148 Untranslatable pun on the papal pronouncements given "urbi et orbi" to Rome and the world.

149 The Second Congress of the Third International, and the Imola Conference of the Communist Fraction respectively.

150 See note 134 above.

151 The parliamentary "Left" came to power in 1876. (See *Selections from the Prison Notebooks*, pp. 66–8, etc.). Umberto I was king from 1878–1900, when he was assassinated.

152 On 7 June 1914, an anti-militarist demonstration at Ancona was fired on by the police, resulting in three deaths. The PSI called a general strike and there were insurrectionary outbreaks throughout the country. Ancona was held by the insurgents for ten days, and it took 10,000 troops to subdue it.

153 May 1915: agitation in favour of Italy's entry into the war.

154 See pp. 135–41 and note 42 above.

155 This article was written on the eve of the XVIIth Congress of the Socialist Party, which met at Livorno from 15 to 21 January 1921 and consecrated the communist breakaway from the maximalist and reformist currents.

156 See note 135 above.

INDEX

The index does not include entries for 'Italy' or 'Italian Socialist Party (PSI)', given the frequency with which they occur in Gramsci's texts.